The Catholic Biblical Quarterly
Monograph Series
30

_____

Matthew's Parables

Audience-Oriented
Perspectives

Warren Carter
John Paul Heil

The Catholic Biblical Quarterly
Monograph Series
30

Produced in the United States of America

Library of Congress Cataloging-in-Publication Data

Carter, Warren, 1955–
Matthew's parables : audience-oriented perspectives /
Warren Carter, John Paul Heil.
p.   cm. — (Catholic Biblical quarterly. Monograph series ; 30)
Includes bibliographical references and index.
ISBN 0-915170-29-9
1. Jesus Christ–Parables.   2. Bible. N.T.   Matthew–Criticism,
interpretation, etc.   I. Heil, John Paul.   II. Title.   III. Series.
BT375.2.C355   1997
226.2 '.06–dc21
97-44677
CIP

Contents

Abbreviations

Abbreviations used throughout this work are those found in the "Instructions for Contributors," *CBQ* 46 (1984) 393–408, with the following addition:

EDNT   H. Balz and G. Schneider, eds., *Exegetical Dictionary of the New Testament* (Grand Rapids, MI: Eerdmans, 1990–1993).

CHAPTER 1

An Audience-Oriented Approach
to Matthew's Parables

(by Carter)

This book is an experiment in reading the parables within Matthew's gospel.[1] There is a deliberate ambiguity here. Not only is our discussion limited to parables which appear within Matthew's gospel, our central focus concerns what happens as the gospel's audience interacts with the parables in their present form and in their current placement *within* the plot of Matthew's gospel.

This approach is experimental because it is not the way in which most recent parable scholarship has worked with the parables. In recent decades parable scholarship has employed two quite different approaches. It has investigated parables primarily either in relation to the historical Jesus,[2] or in

---

[1] We retain the traditional name for the gospel's author but without advocating a particular view of his identity.

[2] C. H. Dodd, *The Parables of the Kingdom* (London: Collins, 1961); J. Jeremias, *The Parables of Jesus* (New York: Scribner's, 1963); E. Linnemann, *Jesus of the Parables: Introduction and Exposition* (New York: Harper & Row, 1966); R. W. Funk, "The Parable as Metaphor," *Language, Hermeneutic, and Word of God: The Problem of Language in the New Testament and Contemporary Theology* (New York: Harper & Row, 1966) 133–62; J. D. Crossan, *In Parables: The Challenge of the Historical Jesus* (New York: Harper & Row, 1973); J. Breech, *The Silence of Jesus: The Authentic Voice of the Historical Man* (Philadelphia: Fortress, 1983); R. W. Funk, B. B. Scott, and J. R. Butts, *The Parables of Jesus: Red Letter Edition: A Report of the Jesus Seminar* (Sonoma: Polebridge, 1988); B. B. Scott, *Hear Then the Parable: A Commentary on the Parables of Jesus* (Minneapolis: Fortress, 1989). For two recent contributions, see W. R. Herzog, *Parables as Subversive Speech: Jesus as Pedagogue of the Oppressed* (Louisville: Westminster/John Knox, 1994); C. W. Hedrick, *Parables as Poetic Fictions: The Creative Voice of*

relation to the changes that the editor or redactor Matthew makes in transmitting the parables from his sources Mark and Q.[3] Both approaches have provided helpful insights into the parables. But because of the very nature of the questions they ask, both approaches have neglected other aspects such as the ones to be explored in this book.

1. Parables and Jesus

Investigation of the parables as part of the ministry of the historical Jesus has been a growth industry in recent decades. Since the 1950's and 1960's scholars have particularly investigated three aspects of Jesus' use of parables.

First, they have set about reconstructing *the likely version of the parables as Jesus told them*.[4] That is, building on insights from earlier form and tradition criticism, they regarded the present version of the parables as they exist in the gospels to be the result of some forty to fifty years of development in the decades between Jesus and the gospels (30–70/80 C.E.). During that time various groups of followers of Jesus retold Jesus' parables. Influenced by different ecclesial needs (instruction, apologetic, polemic), these transmitters of Jesus' parables reshaped the parables. So did the gospel writers as they incorporated the parables in the gospels. To recover the parables as *parables told by Jesus* meant working back from the present gospel version through this

---

Jesus (Peabody: Hendrickson, 1994). For a review of past research, see N. Perrin, *Jesus and the Language of the Kingdom* (Philadelphia: Fortress, 1976) 89–205; W. S. Kissinger, *The Parables of Jesus: A History of Interpretation and Bibliography* (ATLA Bibliography Series 4; Metuchen: Scarecrow, 1979); D. L. Barr, "Speaking of Parables: A Survey of Recent Research," *TSF Bulletin* 6 (May–June 1983) 8–10; P. Dschulnigg, "Positionen des Gleichnisverständnisses im 20. Jahrhundert: Kurze Darstellung von fünf wichtigen Positionen der Gleichnistheorie (Jülicher, Jeremias, Weder, Arens, Harnisch)," *TZ* 45 (1989) 335–51; C. L. Blomberg, "The Parables of Jesus: Current Trends and Needs in Research," *Studying the Historical Jesus: Evaluations of the State of Current Research* (ed. B. Chilton and C. Evans; Leiden: Brill, 1994) 231–54.

[3] In addition to the commentaries, see J. D. Kingsbury, *The Parables of Jesus in Matthew 13* (Richmond: John Knox, 1969); J. Drury, *The Parables in the Gospels: History and Allegory* (New York: Crossroad, 1985) 70–107; H. Hendrickx, *The Parables of Jesus* (London: Chapman, 1986); J. R. Donahue, *The Gospel in Parable: Metaphor, Narrative, and Theology in the Synoptic Gospels* (Philadelphia: Fortress, 1988) 1–27, 63–125; J. Lambrecht, *Out of the Treasure: The Parables in the Gospel of Matthew* (Louvain Theological and Pastoral Monographs 10; Louvain: Peeters/Eerdmans, 1992).

[4] Note, for instance, the contributions of Jeremias, *Parables of Jesus*; Funk, Scott, and Butts, *Parables of Jesus*; Scott, *Hear Then the Parable*.

process of developing traditions to the time of Jesus. The result of removing layers of tradition was a reconstituted text, the "original" version of the parable. This was the parable to be studied.

Second, these scholars have set about reconstructing *the likely settings in which Jesus told the parables*. Again building on insights from form and tradition criticism, as well as from emerging redaction criticism, these scholars understood the order and context of material as it appears in the gospels not as an accurate historical memory of the order and setting of Jesus' teaching in his ministry. Rather the order and context of material results from the pastoral, theological, and literary concerns of the early communities of disciples and of the gospel writers.

At least three insights point to this conclusion:

1) In 1945 the Gospel of Thomas was discovered at Nag Hammadi in Egypt. This gospel contains 114 sayings of Jesus including parables, some of which are similar to those in the synoptic gospels. The sayings and parables, though, lack any narrative framework and settings. This lack indicates at least that this gospel is not interested in settings. The settings employed in the gospels for parables seem, then, not to be an integral part of the parables or a carefully preserved historical memory.[5]

2) In the time before the synoptic gospels were written, communities of disciples gathered, developed and transmitted collections of Jesus' teachings. Collections were often based on similar forms and content. The gospel writers take over and incorporate these collections in the gospels. For instance there are sequences of conflict stories in Mark 2:1–3:6, of parables in Mark 4, of healing stories in Matthew 8–9, and of events concerning Jesus' passion. The common content or form join these materials together. The gospel writers supply the literary settings.

3) The gospel writers also clearly used transmitted parables to suit their own purposes. One way of doing this was to situate parables in appropriate narrative contexts. The parable of the lost sheep, transmitted in the Q tradition of material common to Matthew and Luke, is used by Luke in 15:3–7 to sustain Jesus' mission to the unlikely outsiders (the lost and sinners) while Matthew employs it in 18:12–14 in the context of teaching about relationships in the community of disciples. It exhorts members of the community of disciples to care actively and watchfully for one another.

Scholars concluded from these and other observations that the settings of

[5] R. Cameron, "Parable and Interpretation in the Gospel of Thomas," *Forum* 2 (1986) 3–39.

parables as found in the gospels reflect the gospel writers' pastoral-theological and literary concerns. These concerns and settings are not necessarily the same as the settings in which Jesus told the parables. Thus in seeking to reconstitute the parable's texts, they also sought to identify settings in the ministry of Jesus for each parable.

Third, scholars have paid particular attention to *the presentation of Jesus' parables, both their style and meaning.*[6] Central to this endeavor has been work on the parables as metaphors and narratives. A metaphor sets two word fields side by side. In so doing meaning is transferred from one to the other enabling the hearer to see or imagine things in a new light. Metaphors do not have just one meaning or point as A. Jülicher's late nineteenth-century work on parables posited. They are capable of yielding multiple insights for hearers.[7] The narrative expands the metaphor in a brief and focussed story of sequential events frequently involving two characters and patterns of three's.[8] It frequently uses a situation from nature or common human experience, yet invariably there is something unusual, reversed or exaggerated in the situation, plot, or characters.[9]

Both metaphor and narrative are especially important in engaging a hearer or reader in the process of making meaning. Both forms grasp the hearers' imagination, drawing them into the parable's situation, causing hearers to reflect on the parable's experience and their own situation. This dynamic interaction between parables and hearers has often been noted. C. H. Dodd, for instance, asserts that parables "arrest," "leave the mind in sufficient doubt," and "tease [it] into active thought."[10] D. O. Via argues that they claim

---

[6] Significant contributors include A. Wilder, *The Language of the Gospel: Early Christian Rhetoric* (New York: Harper & Row, 1964); idem, *Jesus' Parables and the War of Myths* (Philadelphia: Fortress, 1982); Funk, "Parable as Metaphor," 133–62; D. O. Via, *The Parables: Their Literary and Existential Dimensions* (Philadelphia: Fortress, 1967); for a summary, see Funk, Scott, and Butts, *Parables of Jesus*, 16–19.

[7] A. Jülicher, *Die Gleichnisreden Jesu* (2 vols.; Tübingen: Mohr, 1888, 1899); for discussion, see C. Carlston, "Parable and Allegory Revisited: An Interpretive Review," *CBQ* 43 (1981) 228–42; C. L. Blomberg, "Interpreting the Parables of Jesus: Where Are We and Where Do We Go from Here?" *CBQ* 53 (1991) 50–78.

[8] S. Rimmon-Kenan, *Narrative Fiction* (New York: Methuen, 1983) 3, argues that the placing of events in sequence is the basic element of narrative.

[9] See the summary in Funk, Scott, and Butts, *Parables of Jesus*, 16–17.

[10] See Dodd's classic definition, *Parables of the Kingdom*, 16: "At its simplest the parable is a metaphor or simile drawn from nature or common life, arresting the hearer by its vividness or

the interpreter, challenge pre-understanding, create possibility, require decision.[11] R. W. Funk says they lay "bare the structure of human existence that is masked by convention, custom, consensus, [to] expose the 'world' in which man [sic] is enmeshed. . . ."[12] P. Ricoeur avers that they disorient, disclose, reorient.[13] That is, this work has emphasized what the parables as Jesus told them *do* to hearers. Parabolic language is understood as having a dynamic impact, as being more performative than informative.

This work has produced numerous significant insights into the form, settings, content, and style of the parables as Jesus told them. The last aspect named above, the performative impact of the parables on their audiences, has been an especially important emphasis. But while concentrating on particular dimensions of parables, this work has ignored other important features. For instance by seeking to reconstitute the form and relocate the setting of each parable in the life of the historical Jesus, this method has set aside the current canonical form and setting of the parables. It has not valued the present form or current literary setting of the parables as they exist in the gospel. Nor has it paid attention to the interaction between the parables and the larger gospel story. While being concerned with the interaction between the hearer and Jesus' parables, it has not extended this concern to the interaction between the gospel's hearers and its parables.

2. Parables and Matthew

The second approach to parables in recent decades has been informed by redaction criticism.[14] Redaction criticism has focussed its attention not on the historical Jesus but on the gospels. It understands the gospel writer, Matthew, not as an eyewitness recording accurate historical information but as a pastoral theologian retelling the story of Jesus as a "word or address" for his particular community of disciples near the close of the first century. Redaction critics pay particular attention to the way in which Matthew uses

---

strangeness, and leaving the mind in sufficient doubt about its precise application to tease it into active thought."

[11] Via, *Parables,* 26–69.

[12] Funk, "Parable as Metaphor," 155.

[13] P. Ricoeur, *Paul Ricoeur on Biblical Hermeneutics* (*Semeia* 4; ed. J. D. Crossan; Missoula: Scholars, 1975) 27–148, esp. 122–28.

[14] For discussion, see G. Stanton, *A Gospel for a New People: Studies in Matthew* (Edinburgh: T. & T. Clark, 1992) 23–53.

his sources, Mark, Q, and M. Changes to these sources, whether by addition, omission, compression, combination, or rearrangement are usually regarded as being significant for two reasons. Changes are understood to indicate something of the writer's own theological emphases and to reflect the needs of the community situation being addressed.

Work on Matthew's parables, therefore, has concentrated on comparing Matthew's versions with those in Mark and Q (as found in Luke) and in looking for clear signs of Matthean redaction in M material. One classic example is found in the parable of the king who provides a wedding feast for his son but many of the invited guests do not come. The king, in Matthew's version (22:7), then burns their city. This verse seems extreme in the context of the rest of the parable, disrupts the flow from v 6 to v 8, and, significantly, is not in Luke's version (Luke 14:21). Scholars have frequently noted that this Matthean addition to the Q source seems to indicate Matthew's view that the destruction of Jerusalem in 70 C.E. by the Romans was divine punishment. They have interpreted the addition to reflect and address a concern in Matthew's community over the relationship between this community and contemporary Judaism.

Another example of Matthean redaction has been noted above. Matthew uses the parable of the lost sheep in a context that differs from Luke's use of it. Its incorporation into Matthew 18, the community discourse, is understood to reflect Matthew's intent to strengthen internal community relations. A more puzzling example of Matthean redaction concerns the omission in Matthew 13 of the parable of the growing seed (cf. Mark 4:26–29 and Matt 13:23–24). Scholars have suggested possible reasons for this omission: It upsets the pattern of three's evident in the chapter;[15] it gives a misleading sense of the reign's inevitable and uninterrupted progress whereas Matthew wants to emphasize present disappointments and setbacks along with the eventual harvest;[16] its message of a seed growing of its own accord contradicts Matthew's emphasis on the need to bear fruit.[17]

This redaction approach has provided important insights into parables. It has paid attention to the growth of the parables, especially the gospel writer's

[15] W. D. Davies and D. C. Allison, *The Gospel According to Saint Matthew: Volume II: Commentary on Matthew VIII-XVIII* (ICC; Edinburgh: T. & T. Clark, 1991) 407, 370–71.

[16] D. Hill, *The Gospel of Matthew* (NCB; Grand Rapids, MI: Eerdmans, 1972) 230.

[17] E. Schweizer, *The Good News According to Matthew* (Atlanta: John Knox, 1975) 302.

contribution to this process. It has sought to identify central theological and pastoral emphases of the writer. It has found in parables another window through which to look into the life of the early Christian communities for whom the gospels were written.

But while concentrating on these dimensions, this approach has ignored other aspects. In focussing on changes made to the traditions by the gospel writers, it has often given lesser attention to the material that the writers transmit without changes. That is, this approach also has not given the final form of the texts their due. Moreover, in constantly comparing Matthew's text with its sources, Mark, Q, and M, this approach engaged in "sideways" reading. The synopsis, which set out the texts in parallel columns and across which comparisons were made, was a basic tool for this approach.[18] The casualty of such a method was, frequently, the relationship between the parable and the larger gospel context, including the reader's interaction with the parable in the flow and order of the gospel's plot.[19]

Another focus of this approach was the author and his intentions as they could be deduced from the shaping of the gospel material. But identifying such intentions turned out to be very difficult given a variety of readers, the absence of the author, and questions about whether authorial intent can in fact function as the arbiter and controller of meaning. More often interpreters formulated explanations for the changes they observed and then

---

[18] See the reference to the use of the synopsis in the description of a basic redaction approach in G. P. Corrington, "Redaction Criticism," *To Each Its Own Meaning: An Introduction to Biblical Criticisms and Their Application* (ed. S. McKenzie and S. Haynes; Louisville: Westminster/Knox, 1993) 91.

[19] This is supported by observing the order in which the parables are discussed in Lambrecht, *Treasure*. On p. 21 Lambrecht writes: "The present work consists of five major parts. Each of the first four deals with a 'cluster,' a group of Matthean parables. Since in Matthew 13 we are confronted with a parable theory and also with parable explanation, we thought it better not to begin with this group of parables. The sequence is Matthew 18–20; Matthew 21–22; Matthew 13; and Matthew 24–25." It is difficult to follow Lambrecht's reasoning here. Matthew 13, though prior to Matthew 18–20 and 21–22 in the text, is not to be discussed until after them, a decision that also destroys the sequence between Matthew 21–22 and 24–25. Lambrecht seems to suggest that the presence of "a parable theory and . . . parable explanation" somehow supports or requires such a reordering. The audience-oriented approach used in this book reaches the exact opposite conclusion. One of the ways in which the audience uses the "parable theory and . . . parable explanation" of Matthew 13 is to gain strategies for interacting with subsequent parables.

attributed their explanations to the author's intentions. But the fallacy of attributing authorial intent hid an important but ignored dynamic, the role of interpreters in making meaning from texts.

3. An Audience-Oriented Approach

The approach to parables in Matthew with which this book experiments seeks to build on insights from these previous discussions as well as to address areas and issues neglected by them. Several features mark our approach:

1) *Final form:* In contrast to attempts to rediscover and reconstitute the text of the parables as Jesus told them, or to focus on the changes the redactor Matthew makes to the parables, we will be concerned with the final form of the text as it appears in the gospel. How it got to be in this form is not our primary question. Rather we want to examine what happens as the audience interacts with the parables in their present form.

2) *Literary settings:* In contrast to attempts to relocate the telling of the parables in settings particular to the ministry of the historical Jesus, we will be attentive to the literary settings or context in which the parables appear in the gospel.

3) *Gospel context:* In contrast to much recent scholarship which has treated parables as independent units or in relation to their developing form over numerous decades, we will focus on their place within this particular gospel. We will discuss intratextual connections, connections not only between a parable and the section of which it is a part, but also with the larger gospel, its plot, characters, and points of view.

4) *Audience's interaction:* Previous work has often emphasized the parable's origin and transmission. This focus is evident in the quest for the parables as *Jesus* told them and in the attempt to discover *Matthean* intention by attending to redactional changes. We will, however, shift the focus to the interaction between the parables in their final form, literary settings and gospel context, and the gospel's audience. Work on parables and the historical Jesus has been attentive to the dynamic and performative impact of the parables on Jesus' hearers. We will redirect this insight to examine the interaction between the parables and the gospel's audience, attending to the audience's active role in making and living meaning.

a) The Authorial Audience

In narrative or literary criticism the identity of "the reader" has been widely debated. There is no single concept of "the reader" which literary critics employ. Scholars have used diverse constructs including "implied," "virginal," "omniscient," "ideal," "authorial" and "flesh-and-blood" readers. All of these formulations are scholarly constructs, created, as any method is, in order to formulate meaning and to express our understandings of this text.

Our audience-oriented approach is informed by the work of P. J. Rabinowitz and W. Iser.[20] Rabinowitz defines the "authorial audience" as *the hearers or readers that the author has "in mind" in creating the text. The author assumes that this audience possesses the socio-cultural knowledge and interpretive skills necessary to actualize the text's meaning.*[21] That is, authors formulate some impression of the competent, comprehending, informed audience for whom they write, an impression which bears some relation to actual audiences but which is not identical to any audience. In the following discussion we will highlight several important aspects of this construct includ-

[20] P. J. Rabinowitz, "Whirl Without End: Audience-Oriented Criticism," *Contemporary Literary Theory* (ed. G. D. Atkins and L. Morrow; Amherst: University of Massachusetts, 1989) 81–100; idem, *Before Reading: Narrative Conventions and the Politics of Interpretation* (Ithaca: Cornell University, 1987) 15–46, esp. 21–23; idem, "Truth in Fiction: A Reexamination of Audiences," *Critical Inquiry* 4 (1977) 121–42; W. Iser, *The Act of Reading* (Baltimore: Johns Hopkins University, 1978); idem, *Prospecting* (Baltimore: Johns Hopkins University, 1989) 3–69. For further discussion, see J. P. Tompkins, "An Introduction to Reader-Response Criticism," *Reader-Response Criticism: From Formalism to Post-Structuralism* (ed. J. P. Tompkins; Baltimore: Johns Hopkins University, 1980) ix–xxvi; S. R. Suleiman, "Introduction: Varieties of Audience-Oriented Criticism," *The Reader in the Text: Essays on Audience and Interpretation* (ed. S. R. Suleiman and I. Crosman; Princeton: Princeton University, 1980) 3–45. For illustration of narrative or literary approaches in NT studies, see S. Moore, *Literary Criticism and the Gospels: The Theoretical Challenge* (New Haven: Yale University, 1989) and M. A. Powell, *What Is Narrative Criticism?* (Minneapolis: Fortress, 1990). Our approach bears some general compatibility with J. D. Kingsbury, *Matthew as Story* (2d ed.; Philadelphia: Fortress, 1988); D. B. Howell, *Matthew's Inclusive Story: A Study of the Narrative Rhetoric of the First Gospel* (JSNTSup 42; Sheffield: JSOT, 1990); D. J. Weaver, *Matthew's Missionary Discourse: A Literary Critical Analysis* (JSNTSup 38; Sheffield: JSOT, 1990); J. C. Anderson, *Matthew's Narrative Web: Over, and Over, and Over Again* (JSNTSup 91; Sheffield: JSOT, 1994); W. Carter, *Households and Discipleship: A Study of Matthew 19–20* (JSNTSup 103; Sheffield: JSOT, 1994).

[21] Rabinowitz, "Whirl Without End," 85.

ing the use of the term "audience" and the importance of socio-historical location for the authorial audience.

Rabinowitz's definition is akin to, but not the same as, J. D. Kingsbury's explanation of the more common term used in biblical studies, the "implied reader." Kingsbury distinguishes the "implied reader" from the gospel's "real reader" which

denotes any flesh-and-blood person who has actually heard it or read it. . . By contrast, the term "implied reader" denotes no flesh-and-blood person of any century. Instead it refers to an imaginary person who is to be envisaged, in perusing Matthew's story, as responding to the text at every point with whatever emotion, understanding, or knowledge the text ideally calls for. Or to put it differently, the implied reader is that imaginary person in whom the intention of the text is to be thought of as always reaching its fulfillment.[22]

Kingsbury's explanation is helpful particularly in underlining the role which a comprehending reader plays in reading. But other aspects of this formulation are not adequate. We will use the term "audience" or "authorial audience" instead of "implied reader" for two reasons. We prefer the term "authorial audience," firstly, because the term "reader" suggests interaction with the text through the reading of one's own copy. In the ancient world, the world in which the author conceives his audience to exist, interaction with the gospel was by a very different means. In the ancient world texts were generally read aloud. The author's image of his audience did not consist of readers reading their own copies. Rather it consisted of people interacting with the gospel as it was read aloud to them. Though the gospel was written, their interaction took place through hearing not reading, as an oral-aural event.[23] Hearing a text means interacting with it not as a printed object but more as a process and event. S. Moore has commented that Iser's reader-

[22] Kingsbury, *Matthew as Story*, 37–38.
[23] R. M. Fowler, "Who Is 'the Reader' in Reader Response Criticism?" *Reader Response Approaches to Biblical and Secular Texts* (*Semeia* 31; ed. R. Detweiler; Decatur: Scholars, 1985) 5–23; Stanton, *Gospel*, 71–76; W. H. Kelber, *The Oral and the Written Gospel: The Hermeneutics of Speaking and Writing in the Synoptic Tradition, Mark, Paul, and Q* (Philadelphia: Fortress, 1983) chaps. 1–2; P. J. Achtemeier, "*Omne verbum sonat:* The New Testament and the Oral Environment of Late Western Antiquity," *JBL* 109 (1990) 3–27; B. Knox, "Silent Reading in Antiquity," *Greek Roman and Byzantine Studies* 9 (1968) 421–35.

response model offers "clear affinities with the syllable-by-syllable experience of hearing a text read. . . . "[24] The term "audience" will remind us of this dynamic.

This observation in turn points to a second important emphasis conveyed by Rabinowitz's term "authorial audience," the audience's socio-historical context. Rabinowitz explains that this audience is "a contextualized implied reader," more "presupposed" by the text than located in it. That is, unlike some contemporary uses of an "ideal" or "implied" reader, the term "authorial audience" does not refer to an ahistorical audience but seeks to locate the interaction of text and reader in a particular socio-historical context. Unlike Kingsbury's ahistorical "implied reader" constituted by textual features, our construct of the authorial audience has a clear socio-historical setting. Rabinowitz says that the authorial audience "is not reducible to textual features but can be determined only by an examination of the interrelation between the text and the context in which the work was produced."[25] This recognition of a text's circumstances or origin means that though the authorial audience is a convenient scholarly construct, it is located in a particular historical context. It consists of the author's image of the actual, flesh-and-blood audience for whom the author writes. The text provides important clues about this context, as does any extra-textual information about its circumstances of origin. Rabinowitz's concern is to underline that interaction with the text is shaped by the time and circumstances of its production and reception.

In working with Matthew's gospel, we are dependent on the work itself for insight into the assumptions made about the audience. For instance the use of Koiné Greek indicates that the audience is assumed to be familiar with this language. The extensive use of citations from the Jewish scriptures indicates familiarity with this tradition. Source and redaction criticisms indicate some familiarity with traditions about Jesus assumed of the audience. They are not assumed to be hearing the story for the first time, though caution prevents making the claim that the author and audience know exactly the same sources. But the text also indicates assumptions about the audience's literary competency (its ability to recognize genre, for instance) and about its knowledge of various political ("king"), social ("leper") and economic ("householder") realities. The author assumes that the audience for whom the work is written (the audience the writer has "in mind" while writing) knows these

---

[24] Moore, *Literary Criticism and the Gospels,* 84–88, esp. 87.
[25] Rabinowitz, "Whirl Without End," 85.

realities. Because they pervade the cultural context which author and audience share, the author does not explain them. Real readers from another socio-cultural context may find this work difficult to understand or to accept precisely because it does not have this assumed knowledge or share these religious-cultural values.[26] One advantage of joining the authorial audience to engage this text is recognizing the need to make explicit as much of this assumed competency as possible.

The use of the term "authorial audience" therefore moves beyond a focus almost exclusively on the text to incorporate the socio-historical experience and cultural conventions assumed to be familiar to the audience but not elaborated in the text. We seek in this study to join the audience as much as we can, while recognizing the historical and cultural gap. Our approach, then, is a corrective to the often held assumption that narrative, reader-response or audience-oriented work is ahistorical. For Matthew's gospel the authorial audience refers to the author's image or impression of the community or communities of disciples of Jesus for which he writes,[27] as much as we can reconstruct this image.

The reconstruction is of course our work and as twentieth century interpreters we can claim no certainty or objectivity for it. We can, though, sketch some aspects of the authorial audience.

Though somewhat uncertain, this small community of Greek speaking women and men,[28] which lives after the resurrection and before the parousia of Jesus, probably exists as a minority and socially marginal community[29] in the late first century, large cosmopolitan city of Antioch in Syria, though a Galilean location is not impossible.[30] It has either undergone recent separa-

[26] For expanded discussion, see W. Carter, *Matthew: Storyteller, Interpreter, Evangelist* (Peabody: Hendrickson, 1996).

[27] Stanton, *Gospel,* 50–53.

[28] For the possible roles of women, see E. Wainwright, *Towards a Feminist Reading of the Gospel According to Matthew* (BZNW 60; Berlin: de Gruyter, 1991) 325–57; A. C. Wire, "Gender Roles in a Scribal Community," *Social History of the Matthean Community: Cross-Disciplinary Approaches* (ed. D. Balch; Minneapolis: Fortress, 1991) 87–121; J. C. Anderson, "Matthew: Gender and Reading," *The Bible and Feminist Hermeneutics* (*Semeia* 28; ed. M. A. Tolbert; Chico: Scholars, 1983) 3–27; S. Love, "The Household: A Major Social Component for Gender Analysis in the Gospel of Matthew," *BTB* 23 (1993) 21–31.

[29] D. Duling, "Matthew and Marginality," SBLASP 32 (1993) 642–71; Carter, *Households and Discipleship,* 39–55, 204–14; idem, *Matthew,* 77–102.

[30] Traditionally several arguments have been invoked in support of an Antiochene location: the addition of Syria in 4:24; the citations in Ignatius and the *Didache*; the prominence of Peter

tion from or at least been in conflict with the synagogue.[31] It seeks to live its discipleship in the midst of the economic polarities of urbanization, among the economically secure and the poor.[32] R. Stark has outlined the physical hardships and miseries of life in a first-century Greco-Roman city such as Antioch, circumstances which comprise the daily societal experience familiar to the audience: overcrowding from people and animals, poor sanitation, inadequate water supply, filth, disease, high mortality rates, immigration, ethnic divisions, social instability and disorder, vulnerability to natural disasters (fire, earthquake).[33] As a minority and marginal community in this urban context, it is to live faithfully to the teaching of Jesus which, more often than not, conflicts with and provides alternatives to conventional values and structures. The gospel story reminds the audience of its traditions, offers understanding and legitimation for what has happened, and direction for its lifestyle. The "authorial audience" denotes the author's image or impression

(cf. Gal 2:11–14); a sizeable Jewish population. For further discussion, see J. D. Kingsbury, "Reflections on 'the Reader' of Matthew's Gospel," *NTS* 34 (1988) 442–60; D. Senior, *What Are They Saying About Matthew?* (New York: Paulist, 1983) 5–15; U. Luz, *Matthew 1–7: A Commentary* (Minneapolis: Augsburg, 1989) 84–87; W. Carter, *What Are They Saying About Matthew's Sermon on the Mount?* (Mahwah, NJ: Paulist, 1994) 56–77. A Segal, "Matthew's Jewish Voice," *Social History of the Matthean Community: Cross-Disciplinary Approaches* (ed. D. Balch; Minneapolis: Fortress, 1991) 27, suggests "Galilee and Antioch were merely two fixed points in a rather loosely confederated group of congregations. . . ."

[31] The relation of Matthew's community to other Jewish groups and/or synagogue continues to be debated. Stanton, *Gospel,* 146–68, for example, argues for a recent and bitter separation from a synagogue community by which it still feels seriously threatened. Others, for example A. J. Saldarini, *Matthew's Christian-Jewish Community* (Chicago: University of Chicago, 1994) 1–2, accept that while there has been "lengthy conflict" and recent separation from the Jewish assembly (either withdrawal or expulsion), it is still identified with the Jewish community by others, there are still "close relations" with the Jewish community, and that the gospel must be seen in the context of post-70 debates envisioning "Judaism in new circumstances" (p. 5). Also H. C. Kee, "The Transformation of the Synagogue after 70 C.E.: Its Import for Early Christianity," *NTS* 36 (1990) 1–24; S. C. Barton, *Discipleship and Family Ties in Mark and Matthew* (SNTSMS 80; Cambridge: Cambridge University, 1994) 222. The literature is extensive. See the summary of positions in Stanton, *Gospel,* 113–68.

[32] G. D. Kilpatrick, *The Origins of the Gospel According to St. Matthew* (Oxford: Clarendon, 1946) 124–26; Kingsbury, *Matthew as Story,* 152–56; M. Crosby, *House of Disciples: Church, Economics, and Justice in Matthew* (Maryknoll, NY: Orbis, 1988) 39–43; Wire, "Gender Roles," 87–121, esp. 115–18.

[33] R. Stark, "Antioch as the Social Situation for Matthew's Gospel," *Social History of the Matthean Community: Cross-Disciplinary Approaches* (ed. D. Balch; Minneapolis: Fortress, 1991) 189–210.

of the community or communities of disciples of Jesus in these circumstances, at least as we can reconstruct it.

To summarize, we will employ in this study the construct of the "authorial audience" to assist in making meaning of the parables which appear in Matthew's gospel. This term indicates the audience for whom the author writes, the audience which the author has "in mind" in writing. All writers employ such a concept, continually making decisions about the reading/hearing competency and knowledge of their audiences. Such an audience is assumed by the gospel. It has a socio-historical location which it shares with the gospel's author. It is assumed to be able to comprehend the rhetorical strategies and supply the cultural knowledge assumed of it or alluded to in the text. It is assumed to be a consenting, comprehending audience. Actual audiences can, by supplying some of this assumed knowledge, join the authorial audience, at least to some extent, in comprehending the gospel. Joining the authorial audience does not, though, constitute "the definitive reading." It is but one aspect of engaging this text. Whether actual audiences consent to or resist the gospel's and parable's proclamation and demand is another question.

b) Interaction Between the Audience and the Gospel's Parables

Our attention to the interaction between the authorial audience and the parables in Matthew's gospel is also informed by the work of Iser, who focuses on what happens in the "act of reading." He draws attention to the reading process and to the temporal flow which forms an integral part of the process. The audience moves through the sequence of the narrative from its beginning to end. In doing so it is actively involved in formulating meaning through filling in the "gaps" or "blanks" it encounters in the text. It identifies connections between words, clauses, sentences, and larger sections. It orders the events of the narrative into a unity, finding coherent relationships, sequences, hierarchy, and connections of cause and effect among the events.[34] It engages in

---

[34] For discussions of plot, see Aristotle, *The Poetics* (LCL; Cambridge: Harvard University, 1939) 6–14; K. Egan, "What Is a Plot?" *New Literary History* 9 (1978) 455–73; S. Chatman, *Story and Discourse: Narrative Structure in Fiction and Film* (Ithaca: Cornell University, 1978) 43–95; F. Matera, "The Plot of Matthew's Gospel," *CBQ* 49 (1987) 233–53; W. Carter, "Kernels and Narrative Blocks: The Structure of Matthew's Gospel," *CBQ* 54 (1992) 187–204; J. D. Kingsbury, "The Plot of Matthew's Story," *Int* 46 (1992) 347–56; Anderson, *Matthew's Narrative Web*, 133–91; Carter, *Matthew*, 149–75.

building up characters from the numerous pieces of data disclosed in various ways through the narrative.[35] It identifies contrasting points of view which evaluate actions and characters.[36] It supplies knowledge from its general or "universal" knowledge about human experience, or from what has been revealed earlier in the narrative. It also supplies knowledge assumed by the text about spatial, temporal, and social settings, and cultural practices. Moreover it supplies intertextual knowledge, knowledge of other literature cited or alluded to in the gospel.[37]

Through this active process, the audience reviews previous material, poses questions, formulates tentative connections and conclusions to be confirmed or disproved by ongoing engagement with the text. That is, while we recognize that authors use various conventions to communicate with their audience, our assumption is that audiences play an active and vital role in interacting with the text to formulate meaning. As the discussion above of the socio-historical context of the authorial audience recognizes, where an audience lives significantly influences what it sees. The same is true of interpreters.

---

[35] On characters, see Chatman, *Story and Discourse,* 107–38; F. W. Burnett, "Characterization and Reader Construction of Characters in the Gospels," *Characterization in Biblical Literature (Semeia* 63; ed. E. S. Malbon and A. Berlin; Atlanta: Scholars, 1993) 3–28; J. A. Darr, "Narrator as Character: Mapping a Reader-Oriented Approach to Narration in Luke-Acts," *Characterization in Biblical Literature (Semeia* 63; ed. E. S. Malbon and A. Berlin; Atlanta: Scholars, 1993) 43–60; W. Shepherd, *The Narrative Function of the Holy Spirit as a Character in Luke-Acts* (SBLDS 147; Atlanta: Scholars, 1994) 43–90; Carter, *Matthew,* 189–256.

[36] For a discussion of point of view, see B. Uspensky, *A Poetics of Composition* (Berkeley: University of California, 1973); J. M. Lotman, "Point of View in a Text," *New Literary History* 6 (1975) 339–52; Chatman, *Story and Discourse,* 151–58; N. R. Petersen, "'Point of View' in Mark's Narrative," *The Poetics of Faith: Essays Offered to Amos Niven Wilder: Part 1: Rhetoric, Eschatology, and Ethics in the New Testament (Semeia* 12; ed. W. A. Beardslee; Missoula: Scholars, 1978) 97–121; R. A. Culpepper, *Anatomy of the Fourth Gospel: A Study in Literary Design* (Philadelphia: Fortress, 1983) 20–34; Kingsbury, *Matthew as Story,* 33–37; idem, "The Figure of Jesus in Matthew's Story: A Literary-Critical Probe," *JSNT* 21 (1984) 3–36; D. Hill, "The Figure of Jesus in Matthew's Story: A Response to Professor Kingsbury's Literary-Critical Probe," *JSNT* 21 (1984) 37–52; Powell, *What Is Narrative Criticism?,* 23–35; Anderson, *Matthew's Narrative Web,* 53–77; Carter, *Matthew,* 119–48.

[37] These four types of knowledge are discussed by M. A. Powell, "Expected and Unexpected Readings in Matthew: What the Reader Knows," *Asbury Theological Journal* 48 (1993) 31–51; see also U. Eco, *The Role of the Reader* (Bloomington: Indiana University, 1979) 18–23. For further discussion of intertextuality, see W. Carter, "'Solomon in all his glory': Intertextuality and Matthew 6:29," *JSNT* 65 (1997) 3–25.

Two key terms will play important roles in our discussion of the audience's interaction with the parables in Matthew. We will be particularly attentive to *narrative progression*. This term refers to our focus on the process involved in the audience's interaction with the parables. The audience interacts with the parable at the close of the sermon on the mount not as an isolated unit but after engaging the opening seven chapters of the gospel. Likewise it interacts with the parables of "the reign of the heavens"[38] in Matthew 13 after encountering that symbol through the opening twelve chapters. Within Matthew 13 the audience progresses through a sequence of parables about the reign. We will be concerned with what happens through such narrative progressions.

A second key term is *pragmatics*. By this term we mean what emerges in the interaction between the parables and the gospel audience, what the audience thinks and feels, what attitudes and perspectives it gains, what actions and behavior it understands it is to practice in the life of discipleship.[39] We do not understand the audience's interaction with the parables to be restricted to "insight," to cerebral understanding. We understand the audience to interact with parables as rhetorical strategies or "speech acts." From that interaction emerges understanding and activity, insight and a way of life.[40] This

---

[38] Translation of this key phrase is difficult: 1) Translations for βασιλεία reflect an emphasis on space and place (kingdom) or function and action (reign). While "reign" emphasizes function or activity, we recognize the presence of spatial (and temporal) aspects (cf. 5:20; 7:21). J. Louw and E. Nida, *Greek-English Lexicon of the New Testament* (New York: United Bible Societies, 1988, 1989), 1.480, translate: "the fact of ruling." 2) Feminist scholars seek to avoid the patriarchal associations of "kingdom." L. M. Russell, *Household of Freedom: Authority in Feminist Theology* (Philadelphia: Westminster, 1987) 83–85, has proposed "that one way of making it clear that the gospel confronts the old image of kingdom as domination and exclusion and replaces it with a new image of kingdom as love and community is to use an alternative metaphor, that of household." A. M. Isasi-Díaz, "Solidarity: Love of Neighbor in the 1980's," *Lift Every Voice: Constructing Christian Theologies from the Underside* (ed. S. B. Thistlethwaite and M. P. Engels; New York: Harper & Row, 1990) 31–40, 303–5, esp. 304, n. 4, employs "kin-dom" to emphasize the formation of a new community or "kin." 3) W. J. Everett, *God's Federal Republic: Reconstructing our Governing Symbol* (New York: Paulist, 1988); idem, "Sunday Monarchists and Monday Citizens," *Christian Century* 106 (1989) 503–5, proposes "God's Federal Republic" as a means of restating "kingdom of God" for contemporary US churches. We employ "reign of the heavens" as a literal translation of the Matthean phrase recognizing that the context will generate meaning for the symbol.

[39] Moore, *Literary Criticism,* 95–107, complains that much reader-response work has concentrated on cognitive responses at the expense of the affective domain. He characterizes such a reader as the "unfeeling" or emotionally "repressed" reader.

[40] On pragmatics, see H. Frankemölle, "Kommunikatives Handeln in Gleichnissen Jesu:

emphasis reflects a growing concern that scholars attend to the ethical or praxis dimensions of their interpretive work.[41] Actual audiences must decide whether, and if so how, they can actualize in their lives what is required of the authorial audience.

Such an emphasis not only follows from previous work on the dynamic interaction between Jesus' parables and their hearers, but from the gospel itself. The first parable to appear in Matthew, the parable of the wise and foolish builders in 7:24–27, concerns and contrasts "those who hear and do" and "those who hear and do not do" Jesus' teaching. Interaction with this opening parable concerned with moving the audience to the living of Jesus' teaching trains the audience in how to interact with the following parables.

4. Which Parables?

So far we have talked about "the parables in Matthew" but we have not yet indicated which parables we will discuss in the essays which comprise this book. The issue is complicated by the task of defining the flexible literary form "parable," by observing when the gospel does and does not use the term, and by considering its popular associations.[42] For example, the "parable" of the wise and foolish builders to which we have just referred, is not identified by the gospel as a parable yet is commonly identified in popular association as a parable.

Historisch-kritische und pragmatische Exegese: Eine kritische Sichtung," *NTS* 28 (1982) 61–90. For discussion of speech act theory, see J. L. Austin, *How To Do Things with Words* (Oxford: Oxford University, 1962); J. R. Searle, *Speech Acts: An Essay in the Philosophy of Language* (Cambridge: Cambridge University, 1969); idem, *Expression and Meaning: Studies in the Theory of Speech Acts* (Cambridge: Cambridge University, 1979); H. C. White, "Introduction: Speech Act Theory and Literary Criticism," *Speech Act Theory and Biblical Criticism* (Semeia 41; ed. H. C. White; Decatur: Scholars, 1988) 1–24. For application to NT texts, see J. E. Botha, *Jesus and the Samaritan Woman: A Speech Act Reading of John 4:1–42* (NovTSup 65; Leiden: Brill, 1991); D. Neufeld, *Reconceiving Texts as Speech Acts: An Analysis of 1 John* (Biblical Interpretation Series 7; Leiden: Brill, 1994); W. Carter, "Recalling the Lord's Prayer: The Authorial Audience and Matthew's Prayer as Familiar Liturgical Experience," *CBQ* 57 (1995) 514–30.

   [41] E. Schüssler Fiorenza, "The Ethics of Interpretation: De-Centering Biblical Scholarship," *JBL* 107 (1988) 3–17.

   [42] For helpful discussions, see Scott, *Hear Then the Parable*, 7–76; J. L. Bailey and L. D. Vander Broek, *Literary Forms in the New Testament* (Louisville: Westminster/Knox, 1992) 105–14; J. W. Sider, "The Meaning of *Parabole* in the Usage of the Synoptic Evangelists," *Bib* 62 (1981) 453–70; E. Cuvillier, *Le concept de παραβολή dans le second Évangile* (EBib 19; Paris: Gabalda, 1993); G. Haufe, "παραβολή," *EDNT* 3. 15.

The term "parable" appears seventeen times in Matthew, twelve of which are in the collection of parables in Matthew 13 (vv 3, 10, 13, 18, 24, 31, 34 [2x], 35, 36, 53). Three more citations refer to commonly recognized parables, 21:33, 45 ("another parable" referring to the parable of the vineyard and the wicked tenants which follows the parable of the two sons [21:28–43]) and 22:1 (the parable of the wedding feast for the king's son).

The two remaining usages, though, refer to much shorter sayings as "parables":

And if a blind man leads a blind man, both will fall into a pit (15:14–15).

From the fig tree learn the parable: as soon as its branch becomes tender and puts forth its leaves, you know that summer is near (24:32).

These sayings are not often thought of as parables in the sense that while they are comparisons they do not develop the comparison in a narrative form. Yet the gospel is consistent at this point with the Septuagint's practice. The Septuagint translates the Hebrew word *māshāl* with the term "parable." The word *māshāl* derives from the root "to be like" and is used for a number of forms (proverbs, riddles, allegory) which express some degree of comparison (e.g. Ezek 12:22–23; 16:43–45; 17:1–17; 18:1–2; 20:45–49). The word "parable" continues the emphasis on comparison by deriving from the Greek verb "to throw along side."

Yet there are also numerous short comparisons in Matthew that do not use the term "parable" (e.g., 5:13–15; 7:13–27). There are also some longer narrative comparisons, commonly known as parables, which are not introduced as "parables." These include the "parables" of the unforgiving servant (18:23–35), the householder (20:1–16), the faithful or wicked servant (24:45–51), the ten bridesmaids (25:1–13), the talents (25:14–30), and the sheep and the goats (25:31–46).

Several criteria have guided our selection of parables to discuss in this book. Matthew 13 offers the first use of the term "parable" in the gospel as well as its most explicit collection of parables. The term "parable" introduces four of the short comparative narratives (13:3, 24, 31, 33), appears in Jesus' general explanations for the use of parables (13:10, 13, 35) and connects specific parables with their explanations (13:18, 34 [2x], 36). It is also used in the phrase of closure and connection at the end of the parables' collection (13:53).

This use of the term enables the audience to identify some specific features of parables. Three features can be readily observed. First, the parables of Matthew 13 are short narratives. They set actions in a sequence that leads to some resolution. Second, the parables are comparisons. The short narratives are introduced by two forms of comparison, ὡμοιώθη (13:24) and ὁμοία ἐστὶν (13:31, 33, 44, 45, 47, 52).[43] Third, they compare the situation and actions of the parable to some aspect of "the reign of the heavens" (13:3–9 and 18–23, esp. vv 19, 24 [and 38 and 41 and 43], 31, 33, 44, 45, 47, 52). It can be noted that B. B. Scott includes these three features in his definition of a parable as a "*māshāl* that employs a short narrative fiction to reference a transcendent symbol."[44]

These features provide some basis for the audience to identify other parables in the gospel in the absence of the word "parable." The absence of a narrative means we will not discuss 15:14-15 and 24:32 even though the term "parable" is used with them. The phrase ὁμοία ἐστὶν appears three further times in the gospel (11:16; 20:1; 22:39). One of these usages is significant for our purposes (20:1): Ὁμοία γάρ ἐστιν ἡ βασιλεία τῶν οὐρανῶν ἀνθρώπῳ . . . The verse introduces a comparison with the reign of the heavens and is followed by a story about the householder. We will discuss this parable.[45]

Likewise the verb ὁμοιόω appears seven times outside Matthew 13, five seem to indicate parables (7:24, 26; 18:23; 22:2; 25:1).[46] In 7:24, 26, hearing and doing/not doing the words of Jesus are compared to (ὁμοιωθήσεται) two men building houses. The elements of comparison and narrative are present; so too is the reign of the heavens. Entering the reign is the subject of 7:21–23, to which 7:24–27 is connected by the use of the conjunction οὖν ("therefore") in 7:24a. Moreover, the audience knows that the sermon on the mount instructs disciples about life in the reign. In 4:17 Jesus announces its presence and in 4:18–22 calls disciples to encounter it. In Matthew 5–7 he addresses these disciples (5:1–2), blessing them for their present experience of God's reign (5:3, 10), instructing them in and exhorting them to the way of

---

[43] D. A. Carson, "The ΟΜΟΙΟΣ Word-Group as Introduction to Some Matthean Parables," *NTS* 31 (1985) 277–82.

[44] Scott, *Hear Then the Parable,* 8.

[45] Matt 11:16 introduces a comparison for "this generation." The context includes references to the reign of the heavens in 11:11, 12 but is not followed by a narrative. The use in 22:39 connects the two commandments and lacks both explicit references to the reign as well as the comparative story.

[46] The remaining two uses introduce comparisons but not in terms of the reign nor by employing narratives. See Matt 6:8; 11:16.

life that leads to their full participation in the reign (5:19, 20; 6:33) for which they are to pray (6:10). The presence of these features of comparison, narrative, and the reign means we will discuss 7:24–27 as a parable.

The three remaining references (18:23; 22:2; 25:1) introduce stories that are commonly and rightly identified as parables. All three include the verb of comparison, reference to the reign, and narrative. We will discuss all three. This decision draws in several other parables. In 22:1 the narrative begins, "And again Jesus spoke to them in parables," which connects the parable of the wedding feast (22:1–14) to that of the vineyard in 21:33–46. This latter parable is introduced with "Hear another parable," which functions to identify the story of the two sons in 21:28–32 as a parable also. Identifying 25:1–13 (the ten bridesmaids) as a parable means including 25:14–30 (the parable of the talents), even though neither the term "parable" nor a verb of comparison is present in 25:14. The conjunction γάρ ("therefore") and ὥσπερ ("just as") in 25:14 connect this story to the previous one and introduce a comparison thereby extending the comparison of the reign and identifying 25:14–30 as a parable. Because of their narrative and comparative components, as well as their implicit concern with aspects of the reign of the heavens, we will also include as parables the faithful or wicked servant (24:45–51), and the sheep and the goats (25:31–46).

To summarize, we will discuss parables in 7:24–27, 13:1–52, 18:23–35, 20:1–16, 21:28–22:14, and 24:45–25:46. Moreover in discussing these parables in their literary contexts as part of the final version of the gospel we will be attending to the audience's interaction with the material that precedes, and at times, follows, these texts that we have designated parables. This dimension of narrative progression, the audience's movement through the text, means that we will discuss other comparisons that the text employs which are not parables as we have described them above. We will notice that frequently parables are preceded by shorter comparisons which are not developed in a narrative as the parables are. Yet these comparisons such as those found in 7:13–23 or 24:23–44 make significant contributions to the audience's interaction with the parables.[47]

---

[47] Our selection can be compared, for instance, with that of Drury, *Parables in the Gospels*, 70–72. Drury lists sixty-one items under the heading "Parables in Matthew," clearly many more instances than uses of the word "parable" in the gospel. He then sets about discussing Matthew 3–12 under the heading "Figures, Metaphors, and Similes." By parables he seems to mean any comparison or metaphor in the text. See the discussion of Lambrecht, *Treasure*, 19–24. Hendrickx (*Parables of Jesus*) seems to be much more arbitrary in including or excluding parables

To preview the essays of this book, after this introduction Heil will discuss the parable of the wise and foolish builders in 7:24–27 (chapter 2). Two chapters will follow concerned with the parables of Matthew 13. The parables in Matthew 13 focus on the reign of the heavens. Yet by the time the gospel's audience progresses through Matthew 1–12 to Matthew 13, it already knows much about the reign. Accordingly Carter will address the question of the function of Matthew 13 in relation to what the audience already knows about the reign from Matthew 1–12 (chapter 3). Then Heil will discuss the audience's progression through Matthew 13 (chapter 4). In the following chapter Heil will examine the parable of the unforgiving servant in 18:21–35, being attentive to the audience's interaction with this parable after it has moved through a series of comparison from 17:24 (chapter 5). Carter will argue in his treatment of the parable of the householder in 20:1–16 that the audience's interaction with Matthew 19–20 provides a key aspect for its engagement with this parable (chapter 6). Carter will then examine the sequence of three parables located between 21:28 and 22:14 (chapter 7). Heil will look at the gospel's final sequence of parables in 24:45–25:46, being attentive to the series of comparisons through which the audience progresses in 24:23–44 leading up to the parables (chapter 8).

5. Final Comment

In this introduction we have situated our discussion of parables in this book in relation to previous work. We have acknowledged our debt to this work. But we have also indicated areas of neglect from its approaches and have outlined a significantly different approach, that of audience-oriented criticism, to be employed in this study. We have also delineated the parables to be discussed and factors that have shaped this selection.

A final element of the experimental nature of this book should be underlined. It is written by two authors. We focus on a common area (parables in Matthew), employ a similar method (audience-oriented criticism), and have common emphases (the canonical form and location of the text, a concern with narrative progression, the audience's interaction with the text, the prag-

---

for discussion. Donahue (*Gospel in Parable*, 63–125), though offering a very helpful general discussion of parables (pp. 1–27) does not provide an explicit justification for the Matthean parables he chooses to discuss. He starts with Matthew 13 and then moves to the commonly identified, longer narrative parables in 18:23–35, 20:1–16, 21:28–22:14, and 24:45–25:46.

matic result of this interaction). We have chosen to divide up the discussion of the parables according to our particular interests. While we have read and critiqued each other's writing, we have not sought to produce one coherent analysis. This strategy is quite deliberate. It is one way of showing that while an audience shares common texts, methods and emphases, different interpreters hear different things in interacting with a text. Such diversity is to be valued, not eliminated. We see these essays as a contribution to an ongoing conversation about Matthew's parables in which there is room for many diverse voices.

CHAPTER 2

Parable of the Wise and Foolish Builders in Matthew 7:24–27

(by Heil)

The first parable with which the audience interacts is found at the close of the sermon on the mount (Matthew 5–7). The parable exhorts and warns the audience to hear and do Jesus' teaching ("these words of mine"). The audience is not surprised by this emphasis on Jesus' teaching. Two factors in the parable's context have prepared the audience for it. One factor concerns the audience's progress through the sermon. Its engagement with three chapters of Jesus' teaching persuades the audience of the importance of his teaching. But prior to this the audience has interacted with the opening four chapters of the gospel. Through these four chapters the audience has encountered key points of view for the gospel, notably God's controlling point of view.[1] It has learned of the importance of Jesus, the one who does the teaching, in relation to that perspective.

From the beginning of the gospel the audience has seen Jesus presented in relation to God's purposes. The opening verse associates Jesus with Abraham and David, two figures who played central roles in the history of God's dealings with human beings and Israel. The genealogy outlines that history from Abraham, highlighting David's role and the exile in Babylon by the repetition

---

[1] B. B. Scott, "The Birth of the Reader in Matthew," *Faith and History: Essays in Honor of Paul W. Meyer* (ed. J. T. Carroll, C. H. Cosgrove, and E. E. Johnson; Atlanta: Scholars, 1990) 35–54; idem, "The Birth of the Reader," *How Gospels Begin* (*Semeia* 52; ed. D. E. Smith; Atlanta: Scholars, 1991) 83–102.

in 1:6 and in 1:11–12, and by the summary in 1:17. Both the genealogy and the summary end with references to the Messiah, Jesus (1:16, 17).

God's role in the "origin of Jesus the Messiah" (1:18) is made explicit in 1:18–25. The audience learns that Mary, betrothed to Joseph, is pregnant "before they came together" and "from the holy spirit" (1:18).[2] The double reference first rules out human origin for her pregnancy and then explicitly ascribes it to God through the holy spirit. Divine agency is underlined by the account of the appearance of "an angel of the Lord" to Joseph (1:20). The angel, sent from God, discloses that God through the spirit is responsible for Mary's pregnancy.

The angel also reveals the reason for God initiating the pregnancy. God has a double mission for the child, encapsulated in its names. In being called Jesus, he is commissioned "to save his people from their sins" (1:21). In being called Emmanuel, he is "God with us" (1:23). The citation in 1:23 of Isaiah 7:14 confirms for the audience that God is carrying out God's purposes, and the concluding reference to Joseph not "knowing" Mary until the child was born (1:25) confirms the absence of human sexual agency.

The second chapter furthers the audience's understanding. Jesus is identified as "King of the Jews" (2:2) and "Christ" or "anointed one" (2:4) whose birth in Bethlehem is in accord with God's previously disclosed purposes (2:5–6). He is worshipped by Gentiles (2:1–12), opposed by Herod, but protected by God as God's Son in accord with God's purposes (2:13–23).

In the third chapter John the Baptist interprets the significance of Jesus as the one who manifests "the reign of the heavens" (3:2), who makes available to others God's spirit (3:11), and as the one who carries out God's judgment (3:12). Jesus' baptism in 3:13–17 provides the audience with the opportunity to hear God's own voice from heaven declare the special relationship and role that Jesus has as God's beloved Son, the agent of God's saving presence.

In the fourth chapter Jesus seems to confirm this role in the temptations as he remains faithful to God's will by refusing to allow the devil to define his mission as God's Son (4:3, 6). In summary form 4:12–16 repeats Jesus' mission, expressed as bringing light in the darkness and shadow of death. At 4:17 Jesus' public ministry begins with his proclamation of the presence of God's reign, with his calling of disciples (4:18–22), and with extensive teaching, preaching and healing activity (4:23–25).

---

[2] J. P. Heil, "The Narrative Roles of the Women in Matthew's Genealogy," *Bib* 72 (1991) 538–45.

In the context of God's naming and commissioning of Jesus in 1:21, 23, the audience understands Jesus to be carrying out his divinely-given role of manifesting God's saving presence in these actions. Likewise in 5:1–2 when he ascends a mountain, which the audience understands from the biblical tradition to be a place of encounter with and revelation of God, the audience knows that in teaching the disciples he is carrying out his God-given role. His teaching is also a manifestation of God's saving presence and so is to be heard and obeyed as the parable at the end of the sermon emphasizes (7:24–27).

1. Sermon on the Mount

After a prologue containing the beatitudes and the metaphors of salt and light which denote the responsibilities of the community of disciples to continue Jesus' mission as light (5:1–16; cf. 4:12–16), the central section of the sermon commences with Jesus' authoritative proclamation that "I have come" not to destroy but to fulfill the "Law and the Prophets" (5:17) and concludes with the golden rule, the behavior that epitomizes the "Law and the Prophets" (7:12). After each of the four subsections comprising the central section begins with a strong negative command (5:17; 6:1; 6:19; 7:1), the epilogue (7:13–27) commences with the positive command, "Enter through the narrow gate" (7:13). The sermon progresses according to the following structural overview:[3]

Structural Progression of Matthew's Sermon on the Mount

a) 5:1–16: Prologue with beatitudes and metaphors of salt and light
b) 5:17–48: *"Do not* (μὴ) think that I have come to destroy the Law and the Prophets" (5:17)
c) 6:1–18: "Beware *not* (μὴ) to do your righteousness before people (6:1)
d) 6:19–34: *"Do not* (μὴ) treasure for yourselves treasures on earth" (6:19)
e) 7:1–12: *"Do not* (μὴ) judge . . . for this is the Law and the Prophets" (7:1)[4]
f) 7:13–27: Epilogue beginning with the command, "Enter through the narrow gate" (7:13)

---

[3] For recent research on the sermon, see Carter, *Sermon on the Mount*. On the various structures that have been proposed for the sermon, see especially pp. 35–55; see also D. C. Allison, "The Structure of the Sermon on the Mount," *JBL* 106 (1987) 423–45; J. A. Brooks, "The Unity and Structure of the Sermon on the Mount," *Criswell Theological Review* 6 (1992) 15–28.

[4] N. J. McEleney, "The Unity and Theme of Matthew 7:1–12," *CBQ* 56 (1994) 490–500.

The prologue of the sermon (5:1–16) begins with Jesus' ascent up the mountain, the biblical place of divine revelation, and his dramatic sitting down, the position for authoritative teaching (5:1). The elaborate and solemn notice that "he opened his mouth" and taught the disciples and the crowds (5:2) prepares the audience for the divinely authoritative words that will come out of the "opened mouth" of Jesus. In the beatitudes Jesus pronounces authoritative words promising the eschatological blessings of the reign of the heavens, which both challenge and comfort the audience (5:3–12). The prologue concludes with the challenging words of Jesus that directly urge the audience to be the metaphorical "salt" of the earth and "light" of the world (5:13–16).

The next section of the sermon (5:17–48) commences with Jesus' emphatic insistence that he has come not to destroy but to bring to eschatological fulfillment the saving will of God recorded in the Law and the Prophets (5:17). Jesus warns his audience that unless their "righteousness," their doing of God's will, greatly surpasses that of the scribes and Pharisees, they will not even enter into the reign of the heavens (5:20). He then illustrates this greater righteousness in a series of six antitheses (5:21–48). Each of these antitheses contrasts words of the Law and the Prophets spoken to past generations with the new, authoritative words ("But *I* say to you") of Jesus that provoke the audience to perform the greater righteousness.

Jesus initiates the next section of the sermon (6:1–18) by sternly warning his audience not to perform their righteousness simply for show (6:1). His authoritative words in this section teach the audience how to give alms (6:2–5), pray (6:6–15), and fast (6:16–18) in accord with the greater righteousness of the reign of the heavens.

After commanding his audience not to amass for themselves treasures on earth (6:19), Jesus progresses to the next section of the sermon (6:19–34), which centers on how one is to relate to material things and satisfy daily physical needs. Here Jesus' arresting words ("Therefore I say to you," 6:25) comfort the audience not to worry about procuring what they need. If they seek first the reign of God and its righteousness, God will provide all they need (6:33).

Jesus introduces the next section of the sermon (7:1–12) by commanding the audience not to judge others in order not to be judged by God (7:1). His authoritative words in this section teach proper correction of others (7:2–11). The central section of the sermon (5:17–7:12) then concludes with Jesus' commanding word to behave toward others in the way you want others to treat you, for this is the Law and the Prophets (7:12).

The epilogue of the sermon (7:13–27) then progresses through a number of metaphorical contrasts: (1) a comparison of the two gates or ways (vv 13–14); (2) a comparison of good and bad trees to contrast true and false prophets (vv 15–23);[5] and (3) the parable of the wise and foolish builders (vv 24–27). As it climaxes the epilogue, the parable of the wise and foolish builders also climactically concludes the sermon. It calls for hearing and doing "these words of mine" (μου τοὺς λόγους τούτους, v 24), the authoritative words Jesus' dramatically "opened mouth" has spoken (5:2) throughout the entire sermon on the mount.

2. Matthew 7:13–14:
Comparison of the Two Gates or Ways

The opening unit (5:17–20) of the central section of the sermon concluded with Jesus' warning: "For I say to you, unless your righteousness greatly surpasses that of the scribes and Pharisees, you will never enter (εἰσέλθητε) into the reign of the heavens" (5:20). Thus the opening command of the sermon's epilogue (7:13–27), "Enter (Εἰσέλθατε) through the narrow gate" (v 13), warns the audience to enter into the reign of the heavens through the metaphorical narrow gate by doing the greater righteousness Jesus has just elucidated throughout the central section (5:17–7:12) of the sermon.

The opening unit (vv 13–14) of the epilogue involves the audience in a comparison calling them to choose between two contrasting gates or ways. They may choose to be among the many who are entering (εἰσερχόμενοι) through the wide gate and broad way that leads "into the destruction" (εἰς τὴν ἀπώλειαν), the eschatological destruction (v 13).[6] Or they may choose, by doing the greater righteousness outlined in the sermon, to be among the few who find the narrow gate and constricted way that leads "into the life" (εἰς τὴν ζωὴν), the eschatological, eternal life that is equivalent to the reign of the heavens (v 14).[7]

---

[5] On the unity and integrity of 7:15–23, see Allison, "Sermon on the Mount," 430 n. 19.

[6] A. Kretzer, "ἀπόλλυμι," *EDNT* 1. 136; D. A. Hagner, *Matthew 1–13* (WBC 33A; Dallas: Word Books, 1993) 179.

[7] After the rich young man asked what good he must do to have eternal life (ζωὴν αἰώνιον) (19:16), Jesus told him what he must do "to enter into the life" (εἰς τὴν ζωὴν εἰσελθεῖν) (19:17).

With regard to pragmatics, then, the comparison of the two gates or ways (7:13–14) warns the Matthean audience not to be among the many who enter through the wide gate and broad way that ends in final ruin. It urges them to do the greater righteousness Jesus has presented in his sermon on the mount in order to be among the few who find the narrow gate and way by which they may ultimately enter into the eschatological life of the reign of the heavens.

3. Matthew 7:15–23:
Comparison of Good and Bad Trees

Entering into the life of the reign of the heavens through the narrow gate means the audience must beware of false prophets, whose description presents them with another metaphorical contrast, that between ostensibly harmless sheep but actually destructive wolves: The false prophets come (ἔρχονται) to them in the "clothing of sheep," but "inwardly are ravenous wolves" (v 15). These false prophets stand in contrast to Jesus himself, the authoritative teacher (5:1–2; cf. 7:28), who came (ἦλθον) to bring to prophetic fulfillment the Law and the Prophets (5:17; cf. 7:12), thus demonstrating that he is a true prophet (cf. 21:11, 46) who offers true prophecy in the sermon itself.

The audience can recognize the false prophets for what they are, wolves in sheep's clothing, from their "fruits" (καρπῶν) (v 16), a metaphor for the deeds they produce.[8] Jesus then presents a double metaphorical contrast in the form of a question requiring a negative answer: "They do not gather grapes from thorn bushes or figs from thistles, do they?" (v 16). Grapes and figs, edible fruits symbolic of good deeds, are not produced from thorn bushes (ἀκανθῶν) and thistles (τριβόλων), inedible plants with which the audience knows have negative connotations in the biblical tradition.[9] A comparison of sheep and wolves for the false prophets (v 15) progresses to a com-

---

After he was unable to sell his possessions, Jesus declared how difficult it will be for a rich person "to enter into the reign of the heavens" (εἰσελεύσεται εἰς τὴν βασιλείαν τῶν οὐρανῶν) (19:23).

[8] H.-T. Wrege, "καρπός," *EDNT* 2. 251.

[9] In LXX Gen 3:18 the cursed earth will raise up thorns (ἀκάνθας) and thistles (τριβόλους) for human beings as they eat the produce of the field. Thorns (ἄκανθαι) and thistles (τρίβολοι) are also combined with negative connotations in LXX Hos 10:8.

parison between edible fruits and inedible plants (v 16). If prophets do not produce good deeds, edible "fruits" like grapes and figs, it is because they are actually or "inwardly" like thorn bushes and thistles. If the only "fruits" they produce are thorns and thistles, the audience can recognize them as false prophets, outwardly sheep but inwardly wolves.

The sequence of metaphorical contrasts expands to the comparison between good trees that produce only good fruit and bad trees that produce only bad fruit. As thorn bushes and thistles do not produce grapes and figs (v 16) so likewise (οὕτως) every good tree "does" (ποιεῖ) or produces good fruits, but the bad tree "does" (ποιεῖ) or produces evil fruits (v 17). Indeed, a good tree cannot "do" (ποιεῖν) or produce evil fruits, nor can a bad tree "do" (ποιεῖν) or produce good fruits (v 18). In the context of the sermon "doing" good fruits/deeds refers especially to doing the greater righteousness by which the audience can enter into the reign of the heavens (5:20). The third subsection of the sermon began with Jesus' warning: "Beware (Προσέχετε) not to do (ποιεῖν) your righteousness before people in order to be seen by them" (6:1). Now Jesus similarly warns: "Beware (Προσέχετε) of the false prophets" (v 15), portrayed as the bad tree that cannot "do" (ποιεῖν) the good fruits/deeds (v 18) of the greater righteousness. Consequently, every tree (especially false prophets) not "doing" (ποιοῦν) good fruit is cut down and thrown into fire (πῦρ) (v 19), an image of eternal punishment in the last judgment (cf. 3:12; 5:22). The repetition of Jesus' warning, "from their fruits you will recognize them" (ἀπὸ τῶν καρπῶν αὐτῶν ἐπιγνώσεσθε αὐτούς, vv 16, 20), envelops the fruit-producing comparisons in a literary inclusion serving as the criterion for the audience to avoid false prophets.[10]

But the comparisons between the good and bad trees (vv 17–19) also serve as a criterion for the audience's own self-examination. Indeed, the universal formulation, "every tree" (πᾶν δένδρον, vv 17, 19), facilitates an application to every human being, since the audience knows that the tree is a common symbol for human beings in the biblical tradition.[11] The audience must make sure that they are the good tree that "does" (ποιοῦν) good fruit (καρπὸν) (v 19) by doing the greater righteousness by which they will enter into the

---

[10] Anderson, *Narrative Web,* 106.

[11] J. M. Nützel, "δένδρον," *EDNT* 1. 285: "Most frequent in the NT is the usage of the tree as an image for the human being, illustrating the idea that a person's actions determine his or her value before God and thus determine his or her future."

reign of the heavens (5:20). John the Baptist already urged his and Matthew's audience to "do" (ποιήσατε) the fruit (καρπὸν) worthy of repentance (3:8), the repentance necessary to enter into the reign of the heavens that has finally arrived (3:2). Jesus repeated this appeal for repentance in view of the arrival of the reign (4:17). And now, by again repeating the Baptist's words exactly, Jesus emphatically reinforces his warning: "Every tree (person) not doing (ποιοῦν) good fruit (καρπὸν) is cut down and thrown into fire" (3:10; 7:19).

The warning of the previous comparison to be among the few who choose the narrow gate and way that leads "into the life" (εἰς τὴν ζωὴν) (v 14) of the reign rather than among the many who choose the wide gate and way that leads "into the destruction" (εἰς τὴν ἀπώλειαν) (v 13) now progresses to the comparison that warns one to be a good tree that produces good fruit rather than a bad tree that is cut down and thrown "into fire" (εἰς πῦρ) (v 19).[12] The audience is to choose the way that leads into the eternal life rather than into the destruction and fire not only by avoiding false prophets, the wolves, who are bad trees that produce only bad fruit, but by themselves becoming good trees that produce good fruit, the repentance and greater righteousness by which one enters into the reign of the heavens (3:2, 8; 4:17; 5:20).

The metaphorical "every" (πᾶν) tree (vv 17, 19) advances to the literal "every person" as Jesus continues to warn: "Not everyone (πᾶς) who says to me, 'Lord, Lord,' will enter into the reign of the heavens, but the one who does the will of my Father in heaven" (v 21). Jesus' command to enter (εἰσ-έλθατε) through the narrow gate (v 13) means one must do the will of his Father in heaven in order to enter (εἰσελεύσεται) into the reign of the heavens (v 21). Doing the will of Jesus' Father in heaven is thus synonymous with doing the greater righteousness necessary to enter (εἰσέλθητε) into the reign of the heavens (5:20). Every tree "doing" (ποιοῦν) good fruit to avoid the destroying fire (v 19) now becomes every person doing (ποιῶν) the will of the heavenly Father (v 21) that Jesus has revealed throughout the sermon.[13]

The many (πολλοί) who are entering through the wide gate and broad way that the audience knows leads to destruction (v 13) now become the many (πολλοὶ) who will say to Jesus "on that day," the day of final judgment: "Lord,

---

[12] H. Lichtenberger, "πῦρ," *EDNT* 3. 200: "Judgment by fire is frequently contrasted to possession of ζωή (Mark 9:43; Matt 18:8f.) or to entrance into the βασιλεία τοῦ θεοῦ (Mark 9:47; cf. Matt 13:41-43, 50)."

[13] References to the heavenly Father occur throughout all six of the subsections of the sermon: (a) 5:16; (b) 5:45, 48; (c) 6:1, 4, 6, 8, 9, 14, 15, 18; (d) 6:26, 32; (e) 7:11; (f) 7:21.

Lord, did we not in your name prophesy, and in your name expel demons, and in your name do many mighty deeds?" (v 22). But then Jesus will declare to them, "I never knew you; go away from me, you doers of lawlessness" (v 23). Although the many prophesied (ἐπροφητεύσαμεν) in the very name of Jesus (v 22), they are surprisingly the equivalent of "false prophets" (ψευδο-προφητῶν, v 15) since they did not do the will of Jesus' heavenly Father (v 21).[14] Although the many "did" (ἐποιήσαμεν) many mighty deeds in the very name of Jesus (v 22), they are shockingly the equivalent of the tree not "doing" (ποιοῦν) good fruit (v 19) since they neglected "doing" (ποιῶν) the will of Jesus' Father in heaven (v 21).

Despite the apparent closeness evident in the many's address of Jesus twice as "Lord" and in the triple refrain of what they did "in your name" (v 22), Jesus "never knew" them (v 23) as those who did the will of his Father in heaven (v 21). Rather than entering (εἰσελεύσεται) into (εἰς) the reign (v 21), the many are commanded by Jesus to "go away (ἀποχωρεῖτε) from (ἀπ᾽) me" (v 23), the equivalent of entering into the eschatological destruction (v 13), of being cut down and thrown into fire (v 19). Rather than doing (ποιῶν) the will of Jesus' Father in heaven (v 21), as it is revealed in the Law (νόμον) and the Prophets Jesus came to bring to their prophetic fulfillment (5:17; 7:12), the many are "doers (ἐργαζόμενοι) of lawlessness (ἀνομίαν)" (v 23).

Pragmatically, the comparison of good and bad trees (7:15–23) warns the Matthean audience to avoid false prophets as wolves in sheep's clothing, bad trees that produce only bad fruit, who would deter them from doing the will of the heavenly Father revealed in the true prophecy, the authoritative teaching, of Jesus' sermon on the mount. The audience themselves are to be the good tree that produces good fruit by doing the will of Jesus' Father in order to enter into the reign of the heavens. No matter what the audience may accomplish in the name of Jesus, he will not know them at the final judgment unless they do the will of his Father in heaven.

4. Matthew 7:24–27:
Parable of Wise and Foolish Builders

In contrast to his warning that "not everyone" (οὐ πᾶς) who merely says (λέγων) to me (μοι), "Lord, Lord," will enter into the reign of the heavens

---

[14] Allison, "Sermon on the Mount," 430 n. 19: "Those who have prophesied in Christ's name and yet suffer condemnation (7:22–23) surely deserve the label 'false prophets' (7:15)."

(v 21), Jesus begins the parable with a reference to "everyone then" (πᾶς οὖν) who actually hears (ἀκούει) these (τούτους) words,[15] the words of the sermon on the mount, of *mine* (μου) (v 24) rather than of the false prophets (v 15). Everyone then who not only hears but actually "does" (ποιεῖ) Jesus' words, who "does" (ποιῶν) the will of "my" (μου) Father in heaven (v 21) revealed in these words of "mine" (μου), in contrast to merely "doing" (ἐποιήσαμεν) many mighty deeds in the name of Jesus (v 22), will be like (ὁμοιωθήσεται) a wise man in the final judgment (v 24).[16] Everyone then who (ὅστις) hears and does the words of Jesus in the sermon will be metaphorically compared to a wise man, who (ὅστις) built his house, his place of dwelling and shelter, upon the rock, a secure and stable foundation (v 24).

A swift salvo of active verbs, each introduced by καὶ with storm phenomena as subjects,[17] presents the continually accumulating threat of winter weather that hammers the "house," which the audience understands from the biblical wisdom tradition as a metaphor for living: "And (καὶ) the rain descended and (καὶ) the floods came and (καὶ) the winds blew and (καὶ) they fell upon (προσέπεσαν) that house, but (καὶ) it did not fall (ἔπεσεν)" (v 25).[18] The reason the house did not fall is expressed by a pluperfect passive verb that emphasizes the resistant stability of the house: "For it was (and continued to be) founded (τεθεμελίωτο) upon the rock" (v 25).[19]

Hearing and doing the words of Jesus provides permanent protection now and in the final judgment against life's travails and tribulations, symbolized by the onslaught of stormy weather. The wise man who built his house, a symbol for his entire life, upon the rock by hearing and doing the words of Jesus will not only enter through the narrow gate that leads into the life (vv 13–14) of

---

[15] On the parable in 7:24–27 see, in addition to the commentaries, C. L. Blomberg, *Interpreting the Parables* (Downers Grove, IL: InterVarsity, 1990) 258–60.

[16] On ὁμοιωθήσεται here, Carson, "ΟΜΟΙΟΣ Word-Group," 279, remarks: ". . . the verb in the future passive is used exclusively in connection with the kingdom at its consummation. In 7:24, the person who hears and obeys Jesus' words *will be like* (i.e., on the day of judgment) the man who builds on a firm foundation."

[17] J. Gnilka, *Das Matthäusevangelium: Kommentar zu Kap. 1, 1–13, 58* (HTKNT 1/1; Freiburg: Herder, 1986) 280: "In der Darstellung des Unwetters wirken die fünf καὶ wie Hammerschläge."

[18] W. D. Davies and D. C. Allison, *The Gospel According to Saint Matthew: Volume I: Introduction and Commentary on Matthew I-VII* (ICC; Edinburgh: Clark, 1988) 722: "There is a wordplay with προσέπεσαν: 'they fell upon . . . it did not fall.'"

[19] M. Zerwick and M. Grosvenor, *A Grammatical Analysis of the Greek New Testament* (2 vols.; Rome: Biblical Institute, 1974, 1979), 1. 21.

the reign of the heavens (v 21) "on that day" (v 22), the day of final judgment, but will be able to withstand the terrible torments that precede that day.[20] By hearing and doing the words of Jesus (v 24), the audience will build their lives upon a solid foundation of rock (v 25) that will protect them not only on the day of judgment but throughout their lives.

Emphasis falls upon actually doing, rather than merely hearing, the words of Jesus, as he continues the warning with a negative counterpart to the wise man: "Everyone hearing these words of mine and not doing them will be like a foolish man, who built his house upon the sand" (v 26) in contrast to the stability of the rock (v 24). Everyone (πᾶς) not doing (μὴ ποιῶν) the words of Jesus' sermon on the mount (v 26) recalls every (πᾶν) tree not doing (μὴ ποιοῦν) good fruit that will be cut down and thrown into fire at the last judgment (v 19). It stands in contrast to everyone (πᾶς) who will enter into the reign of the heavens for doing (ποιῶν) the will of Jesus' Father in heaven (v 21).

The house of the foolish man experiences exactly the same accumulating assault of stormy weather as the house of the wise man but with a dramatically divergent outcome. Whereas the rain, the floods, and the winds "fell upon" (προσέπεσαν) the wise man's house built upon the rock but it did not fall (οὐκ ἔπεσεν) (v 25), the rain, the floods, and the winds "beat upon" (προσ-έκοψαν) the foolish man's house built upon the sand and it fell (ἔπεσεν)— indeed, its "falling" (πτῶσις) was great! (v 27).[21] The great collapse (πτῶσις μεγάλη) of the foolish man's house numbers him among the many who are entering through the wide gate and broad way that leads into the final destruction (ἀπώλειαν) (v 13), the many who will be excluded from the reign "on that day" of last judgment because they did not do the will of Jesus' Father in heaven (vv 21–23).[22]

The negative example of the foolish man reinforces the warning that the actual doing of Jesus' words is an absolute necessity for entering into the

[20] Gnilka, *Matthäusevangelium*, 1. 282: "Auf was ist das Bild dieser äußersten Bedrohung zu beziehen? Sicherlich auf das bevorstehende endzeitliche Gericht, vermutlich aber sind die Prüfungen der Endzeit miteinzubeziehen (vgl. Mt 24). Das ungewöhnliche Bild legt diese ausweitende Interpretation nahe."

[21] Hagner, *Matthew 1–13*, 191: "This last point receives great emphasis with the deliberate breaking of the symmetrical parallelism of the passage in the brief, ominous concluding words: καὶ ἦν ἡ πτῶσις αὐτῆς μεγάλη, 'and its fall was great,' the last word receiving an additional emphasis. This conclusion is analogous to that of v 23."

[22] Davies and Allison, *Matthew*, 1. 724: "The house, symbolizing a person, has collapsed in condemnation, and its ruin is total."

reign (5:20; 7:21) rather than a mere option. By hearing but not actually practicing the words of Jesus' sermon on the mount, the audience will build their lives upon the instability of sand (v 26) that will not protect them throughout their lives nor on the day of judgment (v 27).

The parable of the wise and foolish builders (7:24–27) has the pragmatic effect of encouraging Matthew's audience to be the wise man who built his house on a foundation of rock by both hearing and doing the words of Jesus in the sermon on the mount. They will thereby not fall when they experience stormy tribulations throughout their lives or on the day of judgment, but will enter into the eternal life of the reign of the heavens. It also warns them not to be the foolish man who built his house on sand by hearing but not actually practicing Jesus' words. It is absolutely necessary that they build their lives upon doing the words of Jesus, otherwise they will suffer the great collapse of final destruction.

5. Conclusion

Our consideration of the parable of the wise and foolish builders (7:24–27) has demonstrated the importance of narrative context and progression for a total interpretation of this first complete parable in Matthew. This parable not only climaxes the previous comparisons in the epilogue of the sermon on the mount (7:13–27), but brings the entire sermon (5:1–7:27) to its climactic conclusion. This parable and the comparisons that precede it work pragmatically on the audience by way of the following progression:

1) The epilogue of the sermon on the mount begins with the comparison of the two gates or ways that warns the Matthean audience not to be among the many who enter through the wide gate and broad way that ends in final ruin, but to do the greater righteousness Jesus has presented in the sermon in order to be among the few who find the narrow gate and way by which they may enter into the eternal life of the reign of the heavens (7:13–14).

2) The comparison of good and bad trees then warns the audience to avoid false prophets as wolves in sheep's clothing, bad trees that produce only bad fruit, who would deter them from doing the will of the heavenly Father revealed in the authoritative teaching of Jesus' sermon on the mount. The audience themselves are to be the good tree that produces good fruit by doing the will of Jesus' Father in order to enter into the reign of the heavens. No matter what the audience may do in the name of Jesus, he will not know

them on the day of judgment unless they do the will of his Father in heaven (7:15–23).

3) Finally, the parable of the wise and foolish builders urges the audience to be the wise man who built his entire life on a foundation of rock by hearing and doing the words of Jesus' sermon on the mount, the revealed will of the heavenly Father, in order not to fall but to enter into the reign whether they experience stormy tribulations throughout their lives or on the day of judgment. They must not become the foolish man who built his house on sand by hearing but not doing Jesus' words, otherwise they will suffer the great collapse of final destruction (7:24–27).

CHAPTER 3

The Parables in Matthew 13:1–52
as Embedded Narratives
(by Carter)

Our focus in this book concerns the audience's interaction with the parables which form an integral part of Matthew's gospel.[1] How do these short parable narratives, with their own plots, characters, settings, and points of view, function embedded within and laid alongside the larger gospel narrative?[2] What functions does the parables' dynamic language "perform" in this context? What does the gospel's authorial audience do with these parables and what do the parables "do" to it?[3]

---

[1] For a discussion of parables in their Matthean contexts, see Carter, *Households and Discipleship*, 146–60; Lambrecht, *Treasure*; B. Gerhardsson, "If We Do Not Cut the Parables Out of Their Frames," *NTS* 37 (1991) 321–35; D. J. Harrington, "The Mixed Reception of the Gospel: Interpreting the Parables in Matt 13:1–52," *Of Scribes and Scrolls: Studies on the Hebrew Bible, Intertestamental Judaism, and Christian Origins* (College Theological Society Resources in Religion 5; ed. H. W. Attridge, J. J. Collins, and T. H. Tobin; Lanham: University Press of America, 1990) 195–201; P. W. Meyer, "Context as a Bearer of Meaning in Matthew," *USQR* 42 (1988) 69–72; Donahue, *Gospel in Parable*, 63–125; J. D. Kingsbury, "The Parable of the Wicked Husbandmen and the Secret of Jesus' Divine Sonship in Matthew," *JBL* 105 (1986) 643–55; idem, *Parables of Jesus*; B. Childs, "Excursus II: Interpretation of the Parables within a Canonical Context," *The New Testament as Canon: An Introduction* (Philadelphia: Fortress, 1985) 531–40; Drury, *Parables in the Gospels*; J. W. Sider, "Rediscovering the Parables: The Logic of the Jeremias Tradition," *JBL* 102 (1983) 61–83. See also the commentaries.

[2] On embedded stories, see M. Bal, "Notes on Narrative Embedding," *Poetics Today* 2 (1981) 41–59; J. Barth, "Tales within Tales within Tales," *Antaeus* 43 (1981) 45–63; M. Berendsen, "Formal Criteria of Narrative Embedding," *Journal of Literary Semantics* 10 (1981) 79–94; R. Shryock, *Tales of Storytelling: Embedded Narrative in Modern French Fiction* (American University Studies 2/206; New York: Lang, 1993).

[3] This formulation reflects the emphasis on the performative or functional (rather than

36

These questions will guide our investigation in this chapter of what happens when the audience encounters the major concentration of parables in Matthew 13. This issue is complicated by at least two factors. In Matthew 13 the audience moves through a sequence of parables. In the next chapter Heil will address the impact of this narrative progression on the audience's interaction with Matthew 13. But prior to that is the observation that by the time the audience hears Matthew 13 it is already familiar with "the reign of the heavens"[4] from various other material in the narrative. A. C. Thiselton focuses this issue of familiarity and the function of the parables in asking: "J. D. Crossan writes, 'Myth establishes world . . . satire attacks world. Parable subverts world.'[5] But if parable *always* subverts world, does this mean that it subverts, on a second reading, the new world of Jesus' world for which it has already made space, or alternatively that the parable can say nothing to one whose world has already been subverted?"[6]

This chapter will address the issue of the function of the parables of the reign of the heavens in Matthew 13 for an audience that is already familiar with this reality from (at least) the previous twelve chapters. My claim is that the audience's interaction with these parables can be helpfully understood as a neglected aspect of the gospel's pervasive redundancy, within which the "reign of the heavens" functions as a "tensive" and "expanding" symbol.[7] The parables in Matthew 13 contribute to the authorial audience's developing

---

propositional or informational) dimensions of language in Austin, *How To Do Things with Words;* Searle, *Speech Acts.* It also reflects our assumption of a dialogical interaction between text and interpreter. See also B. H. Smith, "Narrative Versions, Narrative Theories," *Critical Inquiry* 7 (1980) 213–36.

4 See above, chap. 1 n. 38.

5 J. D. Crossan, *The Dark Interval: Towards a Theology of Story* (Niles, IL: Argus, 1975) 59.

6 A. C. Thiselton, "Reader Response Hermeneutics, Action Models, and the Parables of Jesus," *The Responsibility of Hermeneutics* (ed. R. Lundin, A. C. Thiselton, and C. Walhout; Grand Rapids, MI: Eerdmans, 1985) 79–113, esp. 89. Compare U. Luz, *Matthew in History: Interpretation, Influence and Effects* (Minneapolis: Fortress, 1994) 14: "Many, if not most, of the parables of Jesus are understood only when a change in the life of the reader or listener takes place." How, then, are parables understood after a change has taken place? M. A. Tolbert, *Perspectives on the Parables: An Approach to Multiple Interpretations* (Philadelphia: Fortress, 1979) 41–43, warns about exaggerated claims for the power of parables.

7 E. K. Brown, *Rhythm in the Novel* (Toronto: University of Toronto, 1950) 9, discusses "expanding symbols" (contrasted with "fixed" symbols) as symbols that grow as they "accrete meaning from a succession of contexts." Perrin, *Jesus and the Language,* 29–30, uses the language of "tensive" rather than "steno" symbols in his discussion of the reign of God. See Anderson, *Matthew's Narrative Web,* 197–202.

understanding and pragmatic experience[8] of the "reign of the heavens" not so much by revealing new insights, but by repeating and re-presenting material familiar to the audience from other literary forms in Matthew 1–12 and from pre-gospel traditions about Jesus. This repetition, though, is not to be viewed as unnecessary or as "merely" another attempt to communicate previously conveyed information. Rather, the restatement in embedded metaphoric narratives functions in a performative and dynamic way to confirm and challenge, strengthen and subvert, repeat and renew the authorial audience's experience of the "reign of the heavens."

In developing this argument I will take account of the "knowledge" that the audience learns through the text, as well as that which it brings to the text (as much as this can be reconstructed).[9] The relationship between the parables and the larger narrative will be important.[10]

1. Matthew 1–12 as the Frame
for the Parables in Matthew 13

Six of Matthew 13's seven parables are explicitly connected with "the reign of the heavens" (13:24, 31, 33, 44, 45, 47).[11] The noun βασιλεία ("reign") appears six more times (13:11, 19, 38, 41, 43, 52). The audience is familiar with the symbol "reign of the heavens" from its twelve appearances prior to Matthew 13. Moreover, as disciples of Jesus, the audience is also familiar with this symbol from its cultural-religious context, especially from the scriptures and traditions about Jesus.

It is not easy to identify precisely the contours of this knowledge. N. Perrin's influential 1976 work pointed the way to understand the "reign of the

---

[8] I use "knowledge," "experience," "insight," and "understand" interchangeably in the sense that "understand" (συνιέναι) is used in 13:10–17. It indicates not just insight and intellectual understanding (though that is included) but also active experience of and commitment to living the way of discipleship ("bearing fruit" in 13:8). See G. Barth, "Matthew's Understanding of the Law," *Tradition and Interpretation in Matthew* (ed. G. Bornkamm, G. Barth, and H. Held; London: SCM, 1963) 105–12; for the notion of pragmatics, see chapter 1 n. 37 above.

[9] Powell, "What the Reader Knows," 31–51, identifies four types of knowledge: 1) universal knowledge ("generally assumed for all people everywhere"); 2) what is revealed in the narrative; 3) knowledge presupposed by the spatial, temporal, and social setting of the narrative; 4) knowledge of other literature cited within the narrative.

[10] See, for example, Gerhardsson, "If We Do Not," 325–26; Meyer, "Context," 69–72.

[11] For the central role of the "reign," see Gnilka, *Matthäusevangelium*, 1. 474–75; A. Sand, *Das Evangelium nach Matthäus* (RNT; Regensburg: Pustet, 1986) 276, 296–99.

heavens" not as a stable concept denoting fixed cognitive content but as a "tensive symbol," connotative, experiential, and open-ended, having "a set of meanings that can neither be exhausted nor adequately expressed by any one referent."[12] Perrin's brief study of "Ancient Jewish Literature" demonstrates that the symbol evokes the myth of God's acting on behalf of God's people.[13] But his work, and other studies of OT, Apocrypha, Qumran, Targums, and Pseudepigrapha writings,[14] indicate diverse use of the symbol and varied forms of this myth. If J. J. Collins is right, for instance, Daniel alone employs "kingdom" in three ways, to designate an eternal, Jewish, political, earthly kingdom (Dan 2:44), God's everlasting kingdom or dominion (Dan 3:33 LXX; 4:3 *NRSV*; 4:34–35), and the yet future kingdom of angels to which righteous human beings are exalted after death (Dan 7:18, 27).[15] Psalms of Solomon 17 envisions a national Jewish kingdom. B. Chilton suggests from Targumic literature that "kingdom of the Lord/your God" indicates God's present self-disclosure and action.[16] Recent work on a possible earliest stra-

---

[12] Perrin, *Jesus and the Language,* 29–34, contrasts the pluralistic tensive symbol with the inadequate monolithic steno-symbol (having "a one-to-one relationship to that which it represents"). The language of "idea" or "conception" is inadequate because it denotes "a constant conception," a "consistent well-defined understanding," not recognizing a set of possible meanings. However, a symbol can invoke multiple ideas or conceptions while being connotative, experiential, open-ended. See also D. Duling, "Norman Perrin and the Kingdom of God: Review and Response," *JR* 64 (1984) 468–83; Scott, *Hear Then the Parable,* 56–62.

[13] Perrin, *Jesus and the Language,* 16–32. He defines myth as "a complex of stories . . . which . . . human beings regard as demonstrations of the inner meaning of the universe and of human life" (p. 22).

[14] Perrin, *Jesus and the Language,* 16–32; J. P. Meier, *A Marginal Jew: Rethinking the Historical Jesus: Volume Two: Mentor, Message, and Miracles* (Anchor Bible Reference Library; New York: Doubleday, 1994) 237–88; D. Patrick, "The Kingdom of God in the Old Testament," *The Kingdom of God in 20th-century Interpretation* (ed. W. Willis; Peabody: Hendrickson, 1987) 67–79; J. J. Collins, "The Kingdom of God in the Apocrypha and Pseudepigrapha," *The Kingdom of God in 20th-Century Interpretation* (ed. W. Willis; Peabody: Hendrickson, 1987) 81–95; B. Viviano, "The Kingdom of God in the Qumran Literature," *The Kingdom of God in 20th-Century Interpretation* (ed. W. Willis; Peabody: Hendrickson, 1987) 97–107; M. Lattke, "On the Jewish Background of the Synoptic Concept, 'The Kingdom of God,'" *The Kingdom of God* (Issues in Religion and Theology 5; ed. B. Chilton; London: Fortress/SPCK, 1984) 72–91; B. Chilton, "REGNUM DEI DEUS EST," *SJT* 31 (1978) 261–70; A. Kretzer, *Die Herrschaft der Himmel und die Söhne des Reiches* (SBM 10; Stuttgart: Katholisches Bibelwerk, 1971) 37–49.

[15] Collins, "Kingdom," 81–84; for a dissenting view, see Meier, *Marginal Jew,* 2. 276–79 nn. 34, 53.

[16] Chilton, "REGNUM," 268, 270.

tum of Q has emphasized the socially subversive presence of God's reign in Jesus,[17] while others have observed its present and future dimensions (Q: Matt 8:11–12; Luke 13:28–29; Q: Matt 12:28; Luke 11:20).[18]

The recognition of this diverse usage has important implications for this study. Communication theory has indicated that diverse understandings produce "noise" or interference in the communication between author and audience.[19] On account of such diversity, authors who wish to convey particular, predictable understandings may attempt to proscribe understanding. They may try to "fill" a symbol such as "reign of the heavens" with specific content. A repertoire of strategies is available to an author: redundancy (repetition), varieties of discourse, direct explanation, contextualization, examples, conflicting and contrasting points of view, etc. The audience utilizes such proscribing to overcome the noise, to formulate particular content for the symbol from among various possibilities, and to have its previous knowledge confirmed and/or expanded through the narrative.

Given this diversity, it is not surprising that the author of this gospel begins the audience's literary education about "the reign of the heavens" at the outset of the gospel.[20] The audience hears in the first two chapters a particu-

[17] L. Vaage, *Galilean Upstarts: Jesus' First Followers According to Q* (Valley Forge: Trinity, 1994) 55–65; B. Mack, *The Lost Gospel* (San Francisco: Harper, 1993) 123–27; E. Schüssler Fiorenza, *In Memory of Her: A Feminist Theological Reconstruction of Christian Origins* (New York: Crossroad, 1989) 105–59.

[18] I. Havener, *Q: The Sayings of Jesus* (GNS 19; Wilmington: Glazier, 1987) 50–57; J. R. Michaels, "The Kingdom of God and the Historical Jesus," *The Kingdom of God in 20th-Century Interpretation* (ed. W. Willis; Peabody: Hendrickson, 1987) 109–18; M. E. Boring, "The Kingdom of God in Mark," *The Kingdom of God in 20th-Century Interpretation* (ed. W. Willis; Peabody: Hendrickson, 1987) 131–45.

[19] For summary and bibliography, see Anderson, *Matthew's Narrative Web*, 34–43. C. Cherry, *On Human Communication* (Cambridge: MIT, 1957); N. R. Petersen, *Literary Criticism for New Testament Critics* (Philadelphia: Fortress, 1978) 33–48; S. Wittig, "Formulaic Style and the Problem of Redundancy," *Centrum* 1 (1973) 123–36; S. R. Suleiman, "Redundancy and the 'Readable' Text," *Poetics Today* 1 (1980) 119–42.

[20] Scott, "Birth of the Reader in Matthew," 35–54. For the "reign of the heavens" in Matthew, see J. D. Kingsbury, *Matthew: Structure, Christology, Kingdom* (Philadelphia: Fortress, 1975) 128–60; R. Farmer, "The Kingdom of God in the Gospel of Matthew," *The Kingdom of God in 20th-Century Interpretation* (ed. W. Willis; Peabody: Hendrickson, 1987) 119–30. For (unsuccessful) attempts to distinguish between "Kingdom of Heaven" and "Kingdom of God," see Kretzer, *Herrschaft*, 21–31; M. Pamment, "The Kingdom of Heaven According to the First Gospel," *NTS* 27 (1981) 211–32. See also J. C. Thomas, "The Kingdom of God in the Gospel According to Matthew," *NTS* 39 (1993) 136–46.

lar form of the myth of God acting on behalf of God's people (to use Perrin's terms) before it encounters the symbol "the reign of the heavens" in 3:2.[21]

The opening genealogy provides the audience with a version of the history of God's activity on behalf of God's people (1:1–17). It offers not a record of human "biological productivity but a demonstration of God's providence . . . , the working out of God's plan of creation in a history of salvation."[22] The audience's attention is drawn to three particular moments in that history by 1:1b, by the repetition in 1:1b–2a (Abraham), 1:6 (David), and 1:11–12 (exile), and by the summary of 1:17. Abraham, David, and the exile provide moments in which God's promises and plans for God's people seem thwarted but God faithfully and powerfully acts to save the people.

The audience gains more specific understanding of the myth of God's activity on behalf of God's people in the first kernel or key scene which launches the plot (1:18–25).[23] The scene discloses that Mary's newly conceived child results from God's initiative and action by the holy spirit (1:18d, 20d), not from human intercourse (1:18b–c, 19, 23a, 25). The audience learns of God's purposes for this baby from the explanations of the names. The "angel of the Lord" sent from God to establish God's will instructs Joseph to call the baby "Jesus," which means "to save his people from their sins" (1:21). The author explains that the baby fulfills the promise of one who would be "Emmanuel," "God with us" (1:23). This naming is God's commissioning. It establishes the mission for Jesus' life and death. God's saving activity and presence, previously experienced in the call of Abraham, the kingship of David and the disaster and rescue of exile, are now focussed in and to be manifested by Jesus. Operative in this scene is what M. Perry calls the "primacy effect," the crucial influence of initial placement on an audience's understanding."[24] From this scene, the audience learns the divine point of view by

---

[21] Because of space limitations our discussion of Matthew 1–13 will be largely restricted to the uses of the symbol "reign of the heavens." I readily concede that material in these chapters which does not employ this symbol also contributes to the audience's experience and knowledge of the symbol.

[22] R. E. Brown, *The Birth of the Messiah* (New York: Doubleday, 1977, 1993) 68.

[23] I utilize my previous analysis of the gospel's plot; see Carter, "Kernels," 463–81; idem, *Matthew*, chaps. 10–11. See also Matera, "Plot of Matthew's Gospel," 233–53; M. A. Powell, "The Plot and Subplots of Matthew's Gospel," *NTS* 38 (1992) 187–204. For the language of kernels and satellites, see Chatman, *Story and Discourse*, 53–62.

[24] M. Perry, "Literary Dynamics: How the Order of a Text Creates Its Meanings," *Poetics Today* 1 (1979–80) 35–64, 311–61, esp. 53–58.

which to understand Jesus' subsequent teaching and actions, including his use of the symbol "reign of the heavens."

The rest of the first narrative block or section to 4:16 elaborates this scene. The satellites, or sub-scenes, in Matthew 2 enable the audience to see various responses to God's action in Jesus (2:1): the (gentile) magi joyfully worship (2:2, 10–11); the religious leaders know the scriptures but do not interpret them correctly (in relation to Jesus) and do not act on their knowledge (2:4–6); Herod explodes in murderous rage (2:16–18). God protects the child Jesus, Emmanuel, from the danger of the sinful world, thus guiding and protecting God's initiative and purposes (2:13–23). The audience interprets the four citations of the scriptures (2:6, 15, 18, 23b) as further confirmation that God's purposes are unfolding in these events.

The account in these two opening chapters of God's activity among God's people in Jesus, commissioned to save from sins and manifest God's presence (1:21, 23), provides the context for the audience's first encounter with the symbol "reign of the heavens" in John's preaching (3:2, ἡ βασιλεία τῶν οὐρανῶν). The audience formulates understanding from the symbol's form, the context of Matthew 1–2, and its existing knowledge. It will test, expand or revise these understandings as it continues with the narrative.

The form in which the symbol is expressed (a nominative noun with a genitive of origin)[25] highlights the origin and nature of the reign. The audience knows "the heavens" to be the abode of God (Pss 11:4; 14:2; confirmed by Matt 5:34, 45; 6:1, 9, etc.). The verb ἤγγικεν ("has drawn near") employs a perfect tense[26] to indicate something temporal and spatial that has already happened but which has continuing impact.[27] The "reign of the heavens" which John proclaims has "come near" thus denotes God's "coming near" to rule.[28] In the context of Matthew 1–2, the audience understands this "coming

---

[25] BAGD, 135.

[26] BDF, 318 (4): "A condition or state as the result of a past action."

[27] Louw and Nida, *Lexicon*, 2. 69; BAGD, 213; BDF, #340. For review of the debate about the meaning of ἤγγικεν, see R. Berkey, "ΕΓΓΙΖΕΙΝ, ΦΘΑΝΕΙΝ, and Realized Eschatology," *JBL* 82 (1963) 177–87. Berkey concludes that it is impossible to limit these terms to, or precisely distinguish between, either "nearness" or "arrival." He insists that this abiguity is crucial for understanding the present and future dimensions of the reign of God. "While ἤγγικεν may very well suggest initial arrival, the meaning of the verb is not exhausted at that point" (p. 185).

[28] Compare this construction of a noun with a genitive of origin with the same movement from God to human beings evident in the key scene of 1:18–25, as well as through Matthew 2. The phrase "angel of the Lord" (1:20; 2:13, 19) designates the angel's origin with God as the basis for its role as the emissary of the divine will.

near" not to indicate a general myth of God's kingly activity or an apocalyptic, future-oriented event, but God's presence in Jesus, Emmanuel.[29] If U. Luz is correct in arguing that Matthew's language and theology are generally those of his community, this christological use of βασιλεία τῶν οὐρανῶν reflects knowledge and experience familiar to the audience.[30] The audience fills John's symbol with content from Matthew 1–2 and from its religious experience. It associates the symbol with the myth that God has initiated a further display of God's saving presence in Jesus commissioned to save from sins (1:21, 23). John urges repentance (3:2) as the necessary human response to the proclamation in preparation for encountering Jesus. Repentance means "bearing (good) fruit" in one's living (3:7–10).

This christological locus for God's action is confirmed for the audience by 3:11–12 as John declares further aspects of Jesus' commission, to baptize with the Spirit and determine human destiny in the judgment. Functions typically associated with God are here assigned to Jesus.[31] The audience discerns John to speak reliably on God's behalf because various conventions in the pericope ally him with God's point of view established in Matthew 1–2.[32] John's announcement thus adds to the audience's understanding of the "reign of the heavens" encountered in Jesus. God's action involves God's saving presence, judgment, and gift of the Spirit.

Jesus' baptism also adds to the audience's understanding. Jesus consents

---

[29] Commentators generally overlook the contribution of Matthew 1–2. So Hill, *Matthew*, 90; D. R. A. Hare, *Matthew* (Louisville: John Knox, 1993) 18–19. Given the failure of the linguistic debate to establish one clear meaning for ἤγγικεν, the context and the audience's knowledge established through Matthew 1–2 prior to 3:2 are crucial but frequently neglected indicators of meaning.

[30] Luz, *Matthew 1–7*, 77–78, 167. Redaction and source criticisms may aid in establishing some of this existing knowledge, though it cannot be assumed that the audience knows exactly what the author knows. Unfortunately space does not allow such an investigation here. However, if Luz is right, the audience may already "know" (with reference to "the reign of the heavens") most if not all of what it will hear in the gospel. If this is so, the question of the function/s of the gospel's reuse of the familiar material about the "reign of the heavens" becomes more pressing.

[31] Davies and Allison, *Matthew*, 1. 309–20. They conclude that one, not two functions, are in view.

[32] "In the wilderness" (3:1) invokes God's deliverance in the exodus (Exodus 13); "Judea" recalls Matthew 2's presentation of Judea as a place of danger and divine protection (2:1, 22); his proclaiming confirms Isaiah's word (3:3); his garments link him with the prophets, especially Elijah (3:4; 2 Kgs 1:8); he opposes the religious leaders (3:7–10) whose inadequate response to God's action has been shown in 2:4–6.

to carry out God's commission from 1:21, 23 (3:14-15),[33] John's word about the presence of the Spirit with Jesus is confirmed (3:16), and God expresses approval from heaven (3:17).

In the temptations (4:1–11) Jesus demonstrates loyalty to his commission as God's Son or agent (4:3, 6). Jesus resists the devil's attempt to define his mission and make him the devil's agent, not God's. Ironically the devil parades before him "all the kingdoms (βασιλείας) of the world and their glory" (4:8) but Jesus rejects the devil's claim. He remains faithful to God's commission to manifest God's saving presence or reign (4:8-11; cf. 1:21, 23).

In 4:12–16 the audience encounters a reprise of the myth that informs its understanding of the "reign of the heavens." Jesus' move to Capernaum in "Galilee of the Gentiles" fulfills the scriptures in that light now shines on people in darkness (4:15–16). The audience knows that darkness in the Jewish scriptures denotes death and judgment, while "light" symbolizes God's saving presence.[34] The citation in 4:15 of Isaiah 9:1–2 invokes God acting with salvific intent in a time of "distress and darkness," as well as promises of God's presence (Isa 7:14, "Emmanuel;" 8:8, 10, "God with us"). The addition of ἀνέτειλεν ("has dawned") in 4:16 (λάμψει in Isa 9:2) from Isa 58:8–11 emphasizes divine presence as a key aspect of God's salvation. The audience thus understands this closing scene of the first narrative block to restate the significance of Jesus' presence (cf. 1:18–25). Jesus manifests the saving presence of God which can deliver people from judgment.

Immediately after 4:12–16, the audience encounters the second use of "reign of the heavens" in a scene which initiates new action in the plot. In this second kernel (4:17–25) at the beginning of the second narrative block (4:17–11:1), Jesus begins his public ministry.[35] He demands repentance, proclaims that the "reign of the heavens has come near" (4:17), calls four fishermen to follow (they respond positively, 4:18–22), preaches "the gospel of the reign (βασιλείας[36])," and heals the sick (4:23–25).[37]

---

[33] I understand "fulfill all righteousness" as not primarily indicating moral conduct, but Jesus carrying out the saving activity of God revealed in 1:21, 23. So J. P. Meier, *Law and History in Matthew's Gospel* (AnBib 71; Rome: Biblical Institute, 1976) 75–80. For options, see Davies and Allison, *Matthew*, 1. 325–27.

[34] Exod 10:21–27; Isa 8:22; 13:9–13; Joel 2:2, 10–11; cf. Matt 8:12; 25:30. For "light," see Ps 27:1.

[35] Carter, "Kernels," 474–77.

[36] An objective genitive (see BDF, 162).

[37] See W. Carter, "Matthew 4:18–22 and Matthean Discipleship: An Audience-Oriented Perspective," *CBQ* 59 (1997) 58–75.

The audience makes sense of Jesus' words and actions by using what it knows about Jesus' commission from the first narrative block (1:1–4:16). His proclamation concerning "the reign of the heavens" reminds the audience of John's use of this symbol in 3:2 to refer to Jesus' mission to manifest God's saving presence (1:21, 23). It understands Jesus' proclamation as one means of carrying out his God-given task of manifesting the light of God's saving presence among darkness (4:12–16). In sequence, his actions of calling followers (4:18–22), of preaching and of healing (4:24) also carry out this commission. Jesus' words and actions make this alternative reality, the "reign of the heavens," the saving activity of God, available to people in a new community and in acts of healing and wholeness. Those who respond positively to his words and actions encounter the "reign of the heavens," God's saving activity.[38]

In these actions the audience witnesses the disruptive and transforming presence of the "reign of the heavens." That reign, performed in Jesus' call to the four fishermen (4:18–22), disrupts the brothers' economic and social (household) structures. Their "repentance" means a new focus and priorities, and creates a new community centered on Jesus. The audience engages the continuing story to find out further aspects of their new life. God's saving activity also brings wholeness and new possibilities for those who are healed (4:23–24). The presence of God's saving activity in Jesus is dynamic in its impact, though modest in its scope.

The second narrative block (4:17–11:1) elaborates the kernel's focus on the "reign of the heavens" (4:17–25). In the sermon on the mount (Matthew 5–7), the audience learns more about the life created by the "reign of the heavens," its blessing (5:3–12), responsibilities (5:13–7:12) and future accountability (7:13–27).[39] In Matthew 8–9 the audience's understanding of God's saving presence expands as Jesus manifests God's rule over disease, nature, demons,

---

[38] Such presence does not mean that future manifestations are not possible. See Berkey, "ΕΓΓΙΖΕΙΝ," 181–87. D. A. Hagner, "Matthew's Eschatology," *To Tell the Mystery: Essays on New Testament Eschatology in Honor of Robert H. Gundry* (JSNTSup 100; ed. T. E. Schmidt and M. Silva; Sheffield: JSOT, 1994) 49–71, esp. 51, comments on the use of ἤγγικεν in 3:2 and 4:17: ". . . the kingdom has come in some sense, but short of the expected apocalyptic consummation."

[39] R. Guelich, *The Sermon on the Mount* (Dallas: Word, 1982) 27–33, 97–111; J. D. Kingsbury, "The Place, Structure, and Meaning of the Sermon on the Mount Within Matthew," *Int* 41 (1987) 131–43; Carter, *Sermon on the Mount*, chaps. 4–5.

sin, people, religious, ethnic, and gender barriers, and death.[40] In Matthew 10 the audience sees Jesus commission disciples to proclaim the reign's presence and to perform works of saving power (10:7, 8; cf. 4:17, 19).[41]

Space prevents a consideration of the audience's interaction with all of the second narrative block (4:17–11:1). Discussion of the symbol "reign of the heavens" in this block indicates something of the audience's ongoing "filling in" or expansion of the symbol. "Reign of the heavens" appears eight times after 4:17 (5:3, 10, 19 [2x], 20; 7:21; 8:11; 10:7) along with five variants: "gospel of the reign" (4:23; 9:35); "your reign" (6:10); "reign [of God]"[42] (6:33); "the children of the reign" (8:12). The audience observes the importance of the symbol from the frequent repetition, the variant forms, and the use of different literary forms and contexts (beatitudes, aphorisms, miracle stories, conflict stories). It experiences[43] further dimensions of the symbol and myth of God's activity in Jesus which the symbol invokes from Matthew 1–2.

"Reign of the heavens" appears in the sermon's first and eighth beatitudes.[44] In the first beatitude (5:3) the audience hears Jesus bless not the privileged and powerful but, surprisingly, the poor in spirit, those lacking possessions, power, and hope, who experience God's saving presence.[45] The

---

[40] For discussion, see Davies and Allison, *Matthew*, 2. 1–5.

[41] For discussion and bibliography, see Weaver, *Missionary Discourse*.

[42] The UBS Third and Fourth Editions of the Greek New Testament place τοῦ θεοῦ in square brackets. It is missing from, among others, Sinaiticus and Vaticanus. B. M. Metzger, *A Textual Commentary on the Greek New Testament* (London: United Bible Societies, 1971) 18–19, explains that the square brackets indicate "conflicting interpretations" on the Committee. A minority view saw τοῦ θεοῦ as a "natural supplement, which, if present originally, would not have been deleted." The majority view noted that Matthew "almost never employs βασιλεία without a modifier . . . and explained the absence of a modifier in several witnesses as due to accidental scribal omission."

[43] I continue to use this verb to denote the interaction of the audience with the text. The English words "know" and "understand" are too restrictive and cerebral. For the authorial audience to understand is to live (13:10–17).

[44] For discussion of the beatitudes, see Carter, *Sermon on the Mount*, 82–84; R. Guelich, "The Matthean Beatitudes: 'Entrance-Requirements' or Eschatological Blessings?" *JBL* 95 (1976) 415–34; idem, *Sermon on the Mount*, 109–11; 66–67; M. A. Powell, "Matthew's Beatitudes: Reversals and Rewards of the Kingdom," *CBQ* 58 (1996) 460–79.

[45] I follow Powell, "Matthew's Beatitudes." He argues (pp. 463–65, manuscript) that while the usual association with the *ʿanāwîm*, Israel's dispossessed and abandoned who trust in God, is "surely correct," two considerations indicate a Matthean modification of this link: 1) Matthean universalism (5:13–16), and 2) the addition of "in spirit" which is redundant if the

present tense in 5:3b (ἐστιν) indicates that the reign is theirs already (so also 5:10) while the tenses in 5:4–9 disclose a future dimension to God's purposes.[46] The audience learns from 5:3 that the "reign of the heavens" undermines conventional values and social structures to create a community with different perspectives and social constituencies. The beatitude conceptualizes the experience narrated in 4:24. Jesus' healing of the demoniacs, epileptics, and paralytics, those who frequently lacked material support and social acceptance and whose diseases were widely understood to result from curses and spells, evil powers, sin or divine wrath, manifests God's saving action or reign.[47]

The eighth beatitude (5:10) conveys God's favor on those persecuted ἕνεκεν δικαιοσύνης.[48] To so live means expressing the reality of God's saving presence and reign manifested in Jesus in one's daily life (ἐστιν, 5:10b). The beatitude indicates that the different way of life based on this alternative reality results in conflict with the standards and values of one's society[49] (the world of sin [1:21], death and darkness [4:16]), though some recognize God's activity (5:14–16). The remaining beatitudes depict further aspects of the present blessing, implicit demand, and future completion of the "reign of the heavens."[50]

Three references in 5:19–20 to the "reign of the heavens" shift the audi-

---

ʿānāwîm are in view. Powell concludes that "in spirit" emphasizes "the negative spiritual consequences of poverty," that they lack hope in circumstances of want rather than display piety. This view gains support from 5:8 where the parallel phrase τῇ καρδίᾳ (cf. τῷ πνεύματι) indicates the sphere of the purity, and from Psalm 33:19 (LXX; Eng 34:18), τοὺς ταπεινοὺς τῷ πνεύματι σώσει ("he will save the crushed in spirit"). I appreciate the use of Powell's work.

[46] Guelich, *Sermon on the Mount*, 110–11, 66–67; Hagner, *Matthew 1–13*, 91–92, 96. For a different reading, see G. Strecker, *The Sermon on the Mount* (Abingdon: Nashville, 1988) 30–34; Luz, *Matthew 1–7*, 232–35.

[47] B. J. Malina and R. Rohrbaugh, *Social-Science Commentary on the Synoptic Gospels* (Minneapolis: Fortress, 1992) 70–72, 79–80; H. C. Kee, *Medicine, Miracles and Magic in New Testament Times* (SNTSMS 55; Cambridge: Cambridge University, 1986) 122–24.

[48] B. Przybylski, *Righteousness in Matthew and His World of Thought* (SNTMS 41; Cambridge: Cambridge University, 1980) 1–2, sets out four options for interpreting righteousness: 1) God's demand; 2) God's gift; 3) demand subordinated to gift; 4) varying usage depending on context. I understand 5:10 to indicate human behavior based on and expressive of God's saving presence.

[49] Guelich, *Sermon on the Mount*, 93, 107–9.

[50] Guelich, *Sermon on the Mount*, 62–118; Davies and Allison, *Matthew*, 1. 439–41, 445–47; Luz, *Matthew 1–7*, 235; Powell, "Matthew's Beatitudes."

ence's attention to participation in the future dimension of God's activity.[51] Entry to, and one's place in, the future manifestation of God's purposes depend on living faithfully to one's present experience of God's reign and will be made known by Jesus.[52] Initial response and ongoing accountability to God are basic stances of discipleship. These references highlight God's reign more as a place or realm and goal, than as an action.[53]

In the Lord's prayer (6:9–13) the audience recalls its community prayer[54] for God to manifest God's reign (6:10, ἐλθέτω ἡ βασιλεία σου). In parallel with the other petitions, this petition seeks God's reign to be known in the present through divine and human actions in accord with God's will, as well as in the future completion of God's purposes.[55] The coming of God's reign in the present means familial relationship with God (6:9b), God's redemptive presence (6:9c), doing God's will (6:10b–c), provision of daily necessities (6:11), forgiveness (6:12), and protection from evil (6:13). To pray the prayer challenges pray-ers to do God's will, to show forgiveness and maintain communal unity, to live on the basis of and in the hope of God's reign (6:10, 12b, 14-15; 6:19–7:11).[56] The result is the unity of heaven and earth in the conforming of earth, the realm of humans, to the heavens, the sphere in which God's rule and will are now done.

[51] In advocating the language of symbol rather than concept, Perrin, *Jesus and the Language*, 39–40, does not think it legitimate to use categories of "present" and "future." I agree that the discussion can not be limited to or even focus primarily on the question of the presence or futurity of the reign, but I am not clear that the symbol must be devoid of any temporal dimension. For a similar claim, see Farmer, "Kingdom of God," 123 n. 18; Chilton, "REGNUM," 268.

[52] Schweizer, *Matthew*, 105, suggests that to be "least in the reign" (5:19a) parallels 5:18 and indicates exclusion and punishment. This, though, is unlikely given rabbinic and Matthean recognition of rank in heaven and varying rewards (5:12; 10:41–42; 18:4). So Hagner, *Matthew 1–13*, 109; Davies and Allison, *Matthew*, 1. 497.

[53] Guelich, *Sermon on the Mount*, 149, 160–61, 168–70; Davies and Allison, *Matthew*, 1. 497–501.

[54] Luz, *Matthew 1–7*, 77–78, 369–70, argues that Matthew's version of the prayer derives from Matthew taking over the community's liturgical form. See also Strecker, *Sermon on the Mount*, 110, 210 n. 57, 123; J. Schlosser, *Le Règne de Dieu dans les dits de Jésus* (Ebib; 2 vols.; Paris: Gabalda, 1980), 1. 285–90; Carter, "Recalling the Lord's Prayer."

[55] For the Prayer's future orientation, see R. E. Brown, "The Pater Noster as an Eschatological Prayer," *New Testament Essays* (New York: Paulist, 1965, 1982) 217–53; for various combinations of the present and future, see Luz, *Matthew 1–7*, 376–85; Guelich, *Sermon on the Mount*, 309–16; Schweizer, *Matthew*, 149–59.

[56] G. Bornkamm, "Der Aufbau der Bergpredigt," *NTS* 24 (1977–78) 419–32; Guelich, *Sermon on the Mount*, 322–81.

Jesus' instruction about possessions and anxiety (6:19–34) concludes with an exhortation that the audience, in contrast to the Gentiles' concern with daily material needs, trustingly gives itself to the pursuit of God's reign (6:33). To seek God's reign is to continue to make (ζητεῖτε, present tense) God's saving presence the focus and basis for everyday living as well as to look for the completion of God's purposes.[57] It is to refuse to understand and live in terms circumscribed by the Gentiles' efforts to gain material possessions. It embraces an alternative reality. The saving presence of God is experienced as a life free of anxiety which trusts God to supply what is needed.

The final sermon reference (7:21) recalls the audience to the three references in 5:19–20. Entry to, and one's position in, the future manifestation of the "reign of the heavens" depends on living faithfully to one's present experience of God's reign and will. While the false prophets perform miraculous deeds, they do not do God's will (7:21). By not encountering God's reign in the present they will not participate in its future.[58]

Matthew 8–9 expand the summary account of Jesus' miracles in 4:23–24 to demonstrate the transforming impact of God's reign. In the healing of the gentile centurion's servant (8:5–13), the audience witnesses the importance of human recognition of Jesus' authority and of having faith in his transforming power which effects release from suffering.[59] Jesus' comment on the lack of faith in Israel indicates that response to him, not ethnicity (cf. 3:9) constitutes the community who experience the reign in the present and future (8:11–12). The gentile centurion's faith in Jesus (8:10, 13) is thus a paradigm for present and future participation in (or dismissal from) God's purposes. But the paradigm displays again that the unexpected surprisingly participate while the "rightful" heirs are excluded.[60]

Guelich, *Sermon on the Mount*, 344–45; Luz, *Matthew 1–7*, 463–44; Davies and Allison, *Matthew*, 1. 660–61; Schweizer, *Matthew*, 166. Some see a reference only to the future reign: Luz, *Matthew 1–7*, 407; Strecker, *Sermon on the Mount*, 139–40.

[58] Guelich, *Sermon on the Mount*, 399–400; see also Davies and Allison, *Matthew*, 1. 713, who conclude that it is not possible to identify precisely what the false prophets do wrong.

[59] H. C. Kee, *Miracle in the Early Christian World: A Study in Sociohistorical Method* (New Haven: Yale University, 1983) 187, argues that these two areas—"1) the faith of the beneficiaries and 2) the authority by which Jesus is able to produce results"—are the two primary areas of interest in the Matthean miracle stories.

[60] Who are the "children of the reign"? The usual interpretation understands a contrast between unbelieving Israel (not all Israel since there are believers in Israel [the disciples, the leper, 8:1–4, Peter's mother-in-law, 8:14–15, etc.]) and believing Gentiles represented by the centurion. See Schweizer, *Matthew*, 212–16. However, Davies and Allison, *Matthew*, 2. 27–28,

In 9:35 the audience recognizes a repetition of 4:23. Jesus' speech and deeds, motivated by and expressive of his compassion (9:36), proclaim and perform the "gospel of the reign," the good news of God's saving presence and activity.[61]

The audience recognizes that both elaboration and repetition are at work in 10:7. The disciples are, in continuity with John (3:2) and Jesus (4:17), to proclaim that the "reign of the heavens," God's saving presence and activity in Jesus, is among human beings.[62] This command, part of the instructions about mission throughout Matthew 10, elaborates Jesus' word in 4:19 that disciples will "fish for human beings."[63] Their proclamation is accompanied by the same actions as Jesus performs to manifest God's saving presence (10:8; cf. 4:24).[64] The presence of the reign creates improved bodily, religious, and social well-being through healing. As with Jesus' mission it also effects division through people's responses (9:32–34; 10:16–25).

The third narrative block extends from 11:2–16:20. In the kernel (11:2–6) the audience identifies the block's central issue to be the recognition of Jesus' identity as the one commissioned by God.[65] John poses the key question: Is Jesus the one commissioned by God (11:3)? Jesus responds to John's ques-

---

argue that "the many [who] will come from east and west" does not indicate Gentiles but Jews of the diaspora (cf. 19:28). "In Israel" (8:10) designates a geographical not ethnic reality. The "children of the reign" would then be Jews in Israel who reject Jesus and are rejected, while Jews not privileged to live in the land or to hear his preaching find eschatological salvation. On this reading the Gentile "in Israel" manifests the faith that others "in Israel" should exhibit. R. H. Gundry, *Matthew: A Commentary on His Literary and Theolgical Art* (Grand Rapids, MI: Eerdmans, 1982) 145, is not convinced, arguing that a distinction of Palestinian and diaspora Jews with salvation only for the latter was not possible since no one doubted the salvation of diaspora Jews. Hagner, *Matthew 1–13*, 205, is also not convinced, seeing the "exclusivism" of the tradition (the return of diaspora Jews, so Ps 107:3) "turned on its head in an apparent reversal of salvation-history" with the calling of Gentiles. In either reading, the "children of the reign" are no longer constituted by ethnicity but by response to Jesus.

[61] Davies and Allison, *Matthew*, 1. 414; Kingsbury, *Matthew: Structure*, 136–37.

[62] The verb μετανοεῖτε ("repent") present in 3:2 and 4:17 is missing in 10:7.

[63] J. Manek, "Fishers of Men," *NovT* 2 (1958) 138–41; C. Smith, "Fishers of Men," *HTR* 52 (1959) 187–203; W. Wuellner, *The Meaning of "Fishers of Men"* (Philadelphia: Westminster, 1967) 213–16; Davies and Allison, *Matthew*, 1. 398–99; D. E. Garland, *Reading Matthew* (New York: Crossroad, 1993) 48.

[64] In Matthew 8–9 Jesus has healed the sick (8:5–13, 14–16; 9:1–8, 20–22, 27–31, 35), raised the dead (9:18–19, 23–26), cleansed lepers (8:1–4), and cast out demons (8:16, 28–34; 9:32–34).

[65] Carter, "Kernels," 476–77, 480.

tion by pointing to his actions (narrated in the second kernel and narrative block) as the means by which people can recognize who he is (11:4–5). God's blessing rests on those who discern God's saving presence or reign in him (11:6). The negative phrasing of the beatitude ("not scandalized") suggests the possibility that some will be offended. The audience knows from Matthew 5–10 that this is so.

This third narrative block (11:2–16:20) describes the division that the revelation of "the reign of the heavens" in Jesus' words and actions bring about. Some encounter God's saving presence by these means (11:25–30; 12:46–50; 13:10–17, 58; 14:22–33; 15:21–28; 16:13–20) while others (certain cities, religious leaders, and the crowds[66]) do not "understand" or recognize it. They express hostility and rejection (11:16–24; 12:1–14, 22–45; 13:10–17, 53–58; 14:1–12; 15:1–12; 16:1–12). The parables in Matthew 13 evidence this division and offer some explanation for it.[67]

The symbol "reign of the heavens" appears twice in the third narrative block prior to Matthew 13 (11:11, 12), with a variant in 12:28 ("reign of God").[68] The audience perceives division in response to God's saving presence in Jesus in each instance.

The first satellite scene of the narrative block elaborates John's transitional and double role in relation to the "reign of the heavens" (11:7–19). John is a prophet who bears witness to God's reign in Jesus (3:1–12; 11:9a), yet he is more than a prophet, caught up in the beginning of God's reign (11:12–13), and who like Abraham, Isaac, and Jacob will participate in the completion of God's purposes (8:11). The reference in 11:11b to the "least in the reign" being greater than John highlights the first role. It recalls that previous references to being least in the reign assessed present actions and teaching in the light of the rewards of the future judgment (5:19)[69] and identified disciples among the least (10:42). In this context "the least in the reign" connotes those

---

[66] For the crowds' roles, see W. Carter, "The Crowds in Matthew's Gospel," *CBQ* 55 (1993) 54–68.

[67] Garland, *Matthew,* 145–52; Davies and Allison, *Matthew,* 2. 374–75; Kingsbury, *Parables,* 16, 42–52, 130–32.

[68] For completeness the two other uses of βασιλεία before Matthew 13 appear in 12:25, 26. In 12:25 it refers to political kingdoms and reign; in 12:26 to Satan's reign. The two references provide the context for 12:28 and Jesus' explanation that the "reign of God" is present in his exorcisms.

[69] Matt 5:19 uses ἐλάχιστος while 11:11 uses μικρότερος. Louw and Nida (*Lexicon,* 1. Section 79.125) list them as synonyms.

ples with John who bears witness to Jesus but who is not yet certain of God's actions in Jesus (cf. 11:2–6).[70]

The difficult v 12[71] indicates violence and opposition to God's reign.[72] The audience knows John to be in prison (11:2), an act that bears witness to God's reign. Jesus has warned about opposition to himself and to disciples in the proclamation of God's reign (10:16–18, 22–25). Division and opposition accompany God's saving presence, will, and activity.

Such opposition provides the context for the remaining usage of "reign of the heavens" before Matthew 13. In 12:22–32, the audience hears again the religious leaders' interpretation that Jesus' exorcisms display Beelzebul's activity (12:24; cf. 9:32–34). The audience knows their claim is false. It has seen the leaders' inability to recognize God's activity in Jesus and has heard Jesus' verdict on them as "evil" (9:4; confirmed by 12:34–35, 39, 45).[73] It has seen Jesus express allegiance to God and as God's agent reject Satan's attempt to direct him (3:13–17; 4:1–11). It has also witnessed Jesus' exorcisms which in 4:24 follow his declaration of the presence of God's reign (4:17).

The audience's verdict on the religious leaders' claim is confirmed by Jesus' rejection of the leaders' analysis (12:25–28). Jesus observes that "every kingdom (πᾶσα βασιλεία) divided against itself is laid waste" (12:25). This

[70] Davies and Allison, *Matthew,* 2. 251–52, consider three identifications of "who is least in the reign": 1) Jesus (by humility, by being younger than or a disciple of John); 2) anyone in the reign when it comes in the future; then the least in the reign will be greater than the greatest in the present age who is not in the reign. The comparison is between eras according to Hagner, *Matthew 1–13,* 306. 3) A reference to "anyone now in the reign." This option assumes the reign to be present but John is not included in it. Hence even the least in the reign is greater than John. Davies and Allison consider options 2 and 3 but favor 2 since 11:12 indicates John is included in the reign.

[71] Davies and Allison, *Matthew,* 2. 254–56, offer seven options. They prefer option 3, Perrin's view that the symbol invokes the myth of the war between God and forces of chaos and evil. John the Baptist, disciples, and Jesus are caught up in this conflict.

[72] The verb βιάζεται is best taken as a passive not a middle; attack is made on the reign of the heavens.

[73] In Matthew 13 the audience will understand from Jesus' description of the Devil as the "evil one" (13:39) who has children ("children of the evil one," 13:38) that the religious leaders are agents of the Devil in opposing God's purposes. Hence in 16:1 and 19:3 they "test" or "tempt" (πειράζω) Jesus, just as the Devil did earlier (4:1, πειρασθῆναι). See J. D. Kingsbury, "The Developing Conflict between Jesus and the Jewish Leaders in Matthew's Gospel: A Literary-Critical Study," *CBQ* 49 (1987) 57–73, esp. 60, 64; Carter, *Matthew,* 229–41.

statement provides the basis for saying that it makes no sense to claim that Jesus is Satan's agent who employs his powers to destroy Satan's reign (ἡ βασιλεία αὐτοῦ, 12:26). Rather Jesus is God's agent in whom God's activity to save from Satan's opposing and destructive reign is encountered. His exorcisms display the presence of the Spirit, bringing well-being and new life for those set free (able to speak and see, 12:22). They exemplify God's active and powerful presence, God's reign, which delivers people from Satan's reign (12:28). Jesus' exorcisms perform his God-given commission (1:21, 23).[74]

To summarize, by the time it reaches Matthew 13, the audience understands a great deal about the "reign of the heavens." This symbol represents the myth of God's commission to Jesus to manifest God's saving, transforming presence among human beings (1:21, 23) in his words and deeds (4:17–25; 11:2–5). For those who repent and follow Jesus (4:17–22), who live in desperate circumstances (5:3), who have faith in Jesus (8:5–13), it means the blessing and demand of God's presence in the present and accountability in the future judgment. The presence of God's reign disturbs and reorients human existence (4:18–22). It provides new priorities, possibilities, and focus, an alternative reality out of step with the commitments of the surrounding society (6:19–34). It releases people from the destructive impact of disease and demons, creating wholeness and community (4:23–24; 9:32–34; 12:28). It results in hostility (5:10–12; chaps. 11–12) as well as vindication in the judgment (7:21). To reject Jesus' proclamation is to reject God's reign and to face condemnation in the judgment (10:32–33, 40–42).

2. Matthew 13 and the Parables of the "Reign of the Heavens"

In this framework we can assess the audience's interaction with parables of the "reign of the heavens" in Matthew 13.[75] Matthew 13, a satellite in the third narrative block (11:2–16:20), explains in part the division in Israel evident in the diverse responses to the manifestation of God's saving presence in Jesus'

---

[74] Matt 12:27 indicates that others do exorcisms. Distinctive about Jesus' exorcisms is their display of God's saving presence. See Davies and Allison, *Matthew,* 2. 339; Kee, *Medicine,* 73; J. P. Heil, "Significant Aspects of the Healing Miracles in Matthew," *CBQ* 41 (1979) 274–87.

[75] For discussion of various proposals about the structure of Matthew 13, see Hagner, *Matthew 1–13,* 362–65.

ministry (Matthew 11–12). It also instructs the audience on how disciples live out their positive response until the judgment.[76]

The audience knows from two observations that "the kingdom and its fate in the world"[77] are central to Matthew 13. The opening phrase of 13:1, "that same day," enables the audience to link this chapter with the previous chapter's content about Jesus' "true" family (12:46–50) and his protracted dispute with the religious leaders over the "reign of the heavens" (12:22–45). In addition the audience finds in Matthew 13 the greatest number of uses of the "reign of the heavens" in the gospel. The symbol appears eight times (13:11, 24, 31, 33, 44, 45, 47, 52), with four variant expressions, "the word of the reign" (13:19), "the children of the reign" (13:38; cf. 8:12), "from his [the Son of Man's] reign" (13:41), "in the kingdom of their father" (13:43).[78]

The beginning of Matthew 13 focuses the audience's attention on the present appearance of God's reign. As the chapter progresses, attention moves more to God's future purposes. The opening parable (the sower and the seed, 13:3–9) describes the manifestation of God's reign in Jesus' preaching and its positive and negative reception.[79] The parable provides the disciples with the opportunity to ask why Jesus uses parables to address the crowds. The audience learns that parables confirm the division between understand-

[76] Commentators have emphasized both functions: 1) *An apologetic function:* it depicts the reception of "the reign of the heavens" and explains Israel's reaction to Jesus in contrast to that of the disciples or church; see W. Wilkens, "Die Redaktion des Gleichniskapitels Mark 4 durch Matth.," *TZ* 20 (1964) 305–27, esp. 318, 322, 324–25; Kingsbury, *Parables*, 36–37, 52, 130–37; Drury, *Parables in the Gospels*, 81–85; Davies and Allison, *Matthew*, 2. 370–450, esp. 374–75 (including bibliography); Gnilka, *Matthäusevangelium*, 1. 474–75; Garland, *Matthew*, 144–52; Hagner, *Matthew 1–13*, 361–402, esp. 367, 369, 376 (including bibliography); Lambrecht, *Treasure*, 286–87. Harrington, "Mixed Reception," 195–201, takes a similar approach but emphasizes "an inner-Jewish" context (p. 196). 2) *A paranetic or catechetical function:* it instructs disciples or the church how to live until God completes God's purposes. See Kingsbury, *Parables*, 36–37, 52, 108–10, 134–37; J. Dupont, "Le point de vue de Matthieu dans le chapitre des paraboles," *L'Evangile selon Matthieu: Rédaction et théologie* (BETL 29; ed. M. Didier; Gembloux: Duculot, 1972) 221–59; Sand, *Matthäus*, 276, 283; Donahue, *Gospel in Parable*, 66–70; Lambrecht, *Treasure*, 286–87; Hagner, *Matthew 1–13*, 372.

[77] Davies and Allison, *Matthew*, 2. 449; Gnilka, *Matthäusevangelium*, 1. 474–75.

[78] For a detailed reading through the sequence of the parables in Matthew 13 see the next chapter of this book.

[79] In the context of Jesus' preaching and teaching since 4:17, and the accounts of diverse responses, the audience identifies Jesus as the sower in 13:3, 24, 31 long before the self-referential explanation in 13:37.

ing disciples who have received the divine revelation of God's action in Jesus and non-understanding or hardhearted crowds (13:10–17).

Jesus elaborates the parable of the sower by naming factors which influence negative and positive responses to Jesus' proclamation of God's saving presence ("the word of the reign," 13:18–23). He then tells a further parable emphasizing that the "reign of the heavens" coexists in the world with opposition until the judgment (13:24–30).[80]

The parable of the mustard seed (13:31–32) elaborates the nature of God's present activity. It contrasts the apparently insignificant way in which the reign now appears in Jesus' ministry with its very different future. The audience finds a repetition and extension of the contrast between present appearance and final purpose in the parable of the woman working with leaven. The parable, utilizing the audience's experiences of and religious traditions about leaven, portrays the reign's secretive, corrupting and transforming presence in Jesus and the community of disciples (13:33).[81]

After a statement of the revelatory function of parables (13:34–35), the audience hears Jesus explain the "parable of the weeds in the field" (13:36–43) to the disciples. God's saving presence in Jesus has produced a community of disciples ("children of the reign," 13:38) as well as opposition to God's reign from the devil. God's purposes will, though, prevail in the future judgment.

Two further parables of the man finding treasure (13:44) and of the merchant buying the pearl (13:45–46) highlight for the audience the searching for, intense commitment to, and rejoicing which God's reign requires. The final parable of the net with fish of every kind anticipates the judgment in which all are held accountable (13:47–50).

Two questions can be pressed: What does the audience hear about the "reign of the heavens" in these parables and what is the significance of the means by which it hears, namely stories embedded within a larger story?

---

[80] Carson, "ΟΜΟΙΟΣ Word-Group," 279, argues that the use of the aorist passive in 13:24 (ὡμοιώθη) indicates "the kingdom of heaven *has* (already) *become like* this." This tense contrasts with the use of the future passive (ὁμοιωθήσεται) which points to the "apocalyptic advent of the kingdom" (7:24, 26; 25:1) and with the phrase ὅμοιός ἐστιν (13:31, 33, 44, 45, 47, 52) in which the primary emphasis is not on temporal aspects (pp. 280–81).

[81] For the ambivalent valuing of leaven, see R. W. Funk, "Beyond Criticism in Quest of Literacy: The Parable of the Leaven," *Int* 25 (1971) 149–70; idem, "The Looking-Glass Tree Is for the Birds," *Int* 27 (1973) 3–9; S. Praeder, "The Parable of the Leaven," *The Word in Women's Worlds* (Wilmington: Glazier, 1988) 11–35.

In relation to the first question the audience hears much familiar material about the "reign of the heavens":[82]

1) The parables remind the audience that this reign is present in Jesus' proclamation and actions (13:3 8, 18 23, 24, 31, 33, 37-38, 44, 45–46, 47; cf. 3:2; 4:17–25; 5:3–10; 11:11–12; 12:28). Well-being, new priorities, different values, and new community attest to its disturbing, transforming presence.

2) The parables remind the audience that the presence of the "reign of the heavens" expresses and results from God's action and initiative (cf. 1:18–25). Jesus proclaims its presence because God has commissioned him to do so (13:3, 11, 16-17, 24, 31, 33, 34–35, 37). While humans search for and discover God's reign (13:44–46; cf. 7:7–11), it remains God's creative action and gift of revelation (13:11, 16; cf. 11:25–27).

3) The parables remind the audience of the reign's divisive impact. Some people believe and receive it ("understand"), while others do not (13:3–8, 10–17, 18–23, 44, 45–46; chaps. 5–10, 11–12).

4) The parables remind the audience that participating in the reign requires that they "invest" everything to live on this basis (13:44–45). Receiving the reign (advent) means the undoing of past priorities and commitments (reversal), and opens to new possibilities (actions).[83] The call of the first disciples in 4:18–22 (who abandon the family fishing business) and the subsequent instruction in Matthew 5–7 have established this pattern for the audience.

5) The parables remind the audience that encounter with the "reign of the heavens" means persevering in a new way of life, an alternative reality and community, even in the midst of evil and opposition, until God's purposes are completed (13:5–8, 20–23, 30; chaps. 5–7; 12:46–50). The audience is warned of danger from opposing human beings (13:21; cf. 5:10–12; 10:16–25; 12:1–14) and from commitment to wealth (13:22; cf. 6:19–34). The audience's prior experiences of life in God's reign as being out of step with and in conflict with societal values is confirmed.

---

[82] Parable scholarship, for instance, Ricoeur, *Biblical Hermeneutics*, 80, has highlighted the "untranslatable" nature of metaphors. Ricoeur recognizes, though, that this claim "does not mean they cannot be paraphrased, but the paraphrase is infinite and does not exhaust the innovation in meaning." Rabinowitz, *Before Reading*, 15–20, notes that paraphrase or restating is one of two fundamental ways in which we display understanding. I recognize that the following discussion does not exhaust the meaning of the parables and that it utilizes a different form of discourse than that experienced in the parables. The discourse could be said to be "second-order" statement in that it generalizes the particular experience of the parables.

[83] For this language, see Crossan, *In Parables*, 27–120.

6) The parables remind the audience that the presence of this reign results not only in joy (13:20, 44; cf. 2:10) but also in opposition from Satan and Satan's allies (13:19, 25, 38–39; cf. 4:1–11, 24; 8:28–34; 12:22–32). God's reign and the community constituted by it exist at present alongside, as an alternative to, and in struggle with the reign of Satan (13:26–30, 37–41; cf. 12:25–28).

7) The parables, especially the mustard seed and the leaven (13:31–34), remind the audience of the apparently ordinary mode by which the reign is present. The audience already knows that God's reign, God's saving presence, has not drawn near in an overwhelming, cosmic display of divine power to destroy all evil (cf. 13:24–30) but in Jesus' words and actions (4:17–25; 11:2–6). Some are not able to recognize God's presence in him (8:5–13; 9:3–4, 32–34; 10:14–33; 11:16–24; 12:1–14, 22–32). Nevertheless the audience knows and is reminded by the images of the small mustard seed and of leaven that God's reign, even though many may be incredulous, is disruptive, corrupting, and transformative (the actions of the man and the merchant, 13:44, 45–46; the teaching of Matthew 5–7; the actions of Matthew 8–9, 11:2–6).

8) The parables remind and reassure the audience of the ultimate, yet future completion of God's purposes despite its present, apparently modest manifestation and the prevalence of unbelief and opposition (13:24–30, 31–33, 36–43, 47–50). God's purpose to save from sin will be completed in a universal judgment which vindicates the righteous and condemns the evil, and overcomes Satan's opposition. This action involves Israel, the nations (cf. 1:5–6; 2:1–12; 8:5–13),[84] and the church just as God's present actions in Jesus do. The audience knows of human accountability to God for its response to the presence of God's saving action or reign (3:11–12; 7:21–27). It has also learned previously that the task of judgment belongs not to them in the present but to God/Jesus in the future (7:1–5; cf. 13:24–30).[85]

Along with these restatements of the familiar, two new understandings perhaps emerge for the audience. The first concerns explanations for nega-

---

[84] "The field is the world," 13:38; the reference to the birds nesting in the branches of the mustard tree in 13:32 has been interpreted as representing Gentiles using Ezek 17:23; 31:6; Dan 4:9, 18; Joseph and Asenath 15. See Kingsbury, *Parables*, 82; Gundry, *Matthew*, 267; Davies and Allison, *Matthew*, 2. 420. Funk, "The Looking-Glass Tree," 7, claims the parable is a "light hearted burlesque," a "serious satire," of these traditions.

[85] Kingsbury, *Parables*, 73, notes that the servant in 13:28b proposes the present separation of the weeds and the wheat. This task does not at this point belong to the community of disciples.

tive responses to the "reign of the heavens." While in a sense none of the four explanations is new, their collection into one section is new. People do not embrace God's reign in Jesus because 1) God has not revealed it to them (13:11, 16, 35; cf. 11:25–27), 2) they are hardhearted and other commitments prevent allegiance (13:15, 21–22; cf. 6:19–34; 12:22–45), 3) Satan hinders God's actions (13:18, 25, 39; cf. 4:1–11), and 4) some, such as the "evil" religious leaders, do not recognize God's working in Jesus (13:24–30, 31–34; 9:32–34; 12:16–21, 22–34).

The second aspect concerns the contrast between the apparently insignificant way in which God is presently at work and God's future action. The audience is aware of the future, glorious completion of God's purposes (3:11; 7:21–27; 8:10–12; 10:32–33). Yet it also knows that the gospel has not presented Jesus' present activity as insignificant. Jesus carries out God's purposes (1:18–25). His birth distresses a king and all Jerusalem (2:3). Foreigners come to worship (2:1–12). Opposition, displacement, death result (2:13–23). Crowds from all over Galilee, Judea, and "beyond the Jordan" follow Jesus (4:25). "Great crowds" (8:1) seek healing (8:16; 9:35–36), glorifying God (7:28–29; 9:8) and marveling (9:33). The audience has heard Jesus instruct the disciples to pray for more laborers for the great harvest (9:37–38). He has commissioned them to mission (Matthew 10). His presence is so disruptive that some religious leaders plot his death (12:14).

The parables of the mustard seed and the leaven enable the audience to place this activity and popular excitement in a different perspective. What is happening now is small in contrast to the cosmic goal of God's purposes. The present coexistence of the "reign of the heavens" alongside that of Satan contrasts greatly with the time when God overcomes all evil. The audience gains a sense of this larger context and in this perspective views the present of the narrative. The contrast may also confirm its prior knowledge of the "reign of the heavens." If that knowledge consisted of apocalyptic expectations of God's reign as well as experience of its presence, the parables confirm both aspects.

In sum, the parables of Matthew 13 seem to repeat previous material about the "reign of the heavens" more than they reveal new understanding (cf. 13:34–35). The parables disclose in their plots, characters, settings, and perspectives the "reign of the heavens," yet that disclosure is commensurate with the audience's understandings gained from the first twelve chapters. But several factors indicate that the audience's interaction with parables in Matthew 13 "does" more than repeat largely familiar content.

3. Redundancy, Expanding Symbols, and Performative Language

J. C. Anderson defines redundancy as "the availability of information from more than one source."[86] It functions to "increase predictability by decreasing the number of possible alternatives. This reduces uncertainty, facilitating the communication process." By repeating key points, redundancy enhances cohesiveness in the audience's understanding, overcomes forgetfulness and "noise," persuades the hearer, limits meaning, and solicits assent. Anderson summarizes its functions:

> to highlight or draw attention;
> to establish or fix in the mind of the implied reader;
> to emphasize importance;
> to create expectations, increasing predictability and assent (anticipation);
> to cause review and reassessment (retrospection);
> to unify disparate elements;
> to build patterns of association or draw contrasts.[87]

Along with verbal repetition Anderson notes other examples of redundancy: "symbol, imagery, theme, and setting." In these items, conveying fixed information does not always occupy the central place. Other aspects of language come to the fore, particularly its performative role and polyvalency. These dimensions, evident in our discussion above of the audience's interaction with the "reign of the heavens" in Matthew 1–13, are elaborated in E. K. Brown's work on expanding symbols.[88] For Brown an expanding symbol is one in which the audience's experience of the symbol grows as the symbol appears in a range of contexts through the narrative. It provides glimpses of a reality that is too big to be grasped in one view but aspects of which can be revealed in "sudden flashes."

> The expanding symbol is a device far more appropriate for rendering an emotion, an idea, that by its largeness or its subtlety cannot become wholly explicit . . . the expanding symbol is repetition balanced by variation, and that variation is in progressively deepening disclosure . . . By the use of an expanding symbol, the novelist persuades, and impels his [sic] readers towards two beliefs. First, that beyond the verge of what he [sic] can

---

[86] Anderson, *Matthew's Narrative Web*, 23–25, 34–45, esp. 36.

[87] Ibid., 44.

[88] Brown, *Rhythm in the Novel*, 33–59; Anderson, *Matthew's Narrative Web*, 25, 193–202.

express, there is an area which can be glimpsed, never surveyed. Second, that this area has an order of its own which we should greatly care to know . . . The use of the expanding symbol is an expression of belief in things hoped for, an index if not an evidence of things not seen.[89]

Brown's discussion indicates that repeated symbols require the audience to participate in creating meaning through retrospection and anticipation. The audience reviews previous uses, it carries forward a body of associations and experiences which expands as it connects with and is reshaped by new usages. The symbol both limits options and opens up new areas. It conceals and reveals. It "represents" content as well as performs diverse functions. Our discussion above of the audience's interaction with the symbol "reign of the heavens" has evidenced both aspects.

The importance of the informative and performative dimensions of the audience's interaction with the symbol "reign of the heavens" is further underlined by R. Shryock's work on the relationship between embedded stories and embedding stories.[90] He argues that it is inadequate to see this relationship primarily in terms of a communication model. This model understands the relationship of embedded narrative to embedding narrative referentially, as communicating "information" or a message from author to audience. Shryock invokes the insight of speech act theory that language does not only convey information or represent a world, it also functions to do things to an audience. Without discarding referential dimensions, Shryock emphasizes the perlocutionary functions of embedded narratives.

What happens, then, when the audience interacts with these embedded stories in Matthew 13 after the first twelve chapters of the gospel? If Brown and Shryock are right, the interaction does not merely illustrate an already known referent, the "reign of the heavens." Something more happens for the audience, which enables the audience to experience the referent in a different way.[91]

B. Gerhardsson formulates the audience's interaction with the parables in performative terms, to "understand" ("to take it to their hearts"), "agree" and "bear fruit in action."[92] Using the rhetorical handbook *Ad Herennium* (IV.xlv–xlviii.59–61), he argues that the parables perform these functions in

[89] Brown, *Rhythm in the Novel,* 56–59.
[90] Shryock, *Tales of Storytelling,* 1–15, esp. 12–13.
[91] Scott presses this question, *Hear Then the Parable,* 42–51.
[92] Gerhardsson, "If We Do Not Cut," 325–29.

their gospel frames by illustrating, clarifying, concretizing, and making vivid aspects of the "reign of the heavens."[93] But his analysis is inadequate precisely because he does not take his own argument seriously enough. To "not cut the parables from their frames" means not detaching them not only from the immediately preceding or following verse,[94] but from the document or text of which they are a part. The point of pressing the question of the parables' function in performative terms is not just to recognize that they illustrate or clarify the "reign of the heavens" named in the introductory formula. Rather the question concerns what happens when the audience interacts with parables about the "reign of the heavens" after it has experienced twelve chapters of narrative about that reign and (if Luz is right[95]) when it has experienced this reign in its living and traditions before the gospel is written.

Attention to at least two aspects of parables offers insight into the impact of the redundancy at work in them as narratives embedded in the larger gospel narrative. One aspect concerns the nature of the interaction between an audience and a narrative. Some critics emphasize that an audience's perceptions and values are challenged and overturned through its participation in the narrative. Narratives re-present reality. Reality is redrawn. W. Iser, for instance, argues that the interaction enables the audience to absorb "the unfamiliar into [its] range of experience . . . [and] . . . discover what had previously seemed to elude our consciousness."[96] Others, though, criticize Iser for a one-sided focus. P. J. Rabinowitz and T. Eagleton point to his neglect of the possibility that a text may legitimate and provide insight into what is already experienced. It may order the known rather than reveal the unknown.[97]

---

[93] Gerhardsson, "If We Do Not Cut," 326–27. The author of *Ad Herennium* identifies four possible functions for a *similitudo* (parable); Gerhardsson finds the last two applicable to Matthew 13. For *Rhetorica ad Herennium* see H. Caplan's Loeb edition, *[Cicero] Ad C. Herennium De Ratione Dicendi (Rhetorica ad Herennium)* (LCL 403; Cambridge: Harvard University, 1954); M. H. McCall, *Ancient Rhetorical Theories of Simile and Comparison* (Cambridge: Harvard University, 1969) 57–86, esp. 65–74.

[94] Gerhardsson, "If We Do Not Cut," 325 n. 4.

[95] Luz, *Matthew 1–7*, 167, argues that "the usage of his community has guided the evangelist."

[96] W. Iser, "The Reading Process: A Phenomenological Approach," *Reader-Response Criticism: From Formalism to Post-Structuralism* (ed. J. P. Tompkins; Baltimore: Johns Hopkins University, 1980) 65–68; idem, *Act of Reading*, 152–59. P. Ricoeur, "Appropriation," *Hermeneutics and the Human Sciences* (ed. J. B. Thompson; Cambridge: Cambridge University, 1981) 182–93, esp. 185, 189–90, speaks of the "metamorphosis" of the reader.

[97] Rabinowitz, "Whirl Without End," 93–94; T. Eagleton, *Literary Theory: An Introduction* (Minneapolis: University of Minnesota, 1983) 78–80; J. Fetterly, *The Resisting Reader* (Bloomington: Indiana University, 1978).

Given the Matthean authorial audience's experience of discipleship and familiarity with traditions about Jesus, as well as with Matthew 1–12, the latter view of Rabinowitz and Eagleton seems more likely. The parables in Matthew 13 seem more to confirm what is already known about the "reign of the heavens" than to reveal new insights. But that is not to say they are "merely" illustrative. Paradoxically, the familiar includes the knowledge or experience that the presence of God's reign in Jesus is disruptive and dynamic, as yet incomplete, surprisingly transformative given its modest means of being present, requiring a commensurate lifestyle accountable in the yet-future judgment. The latter piece of knowledge does not permit the audience's familiarity to breed contempt or even indifference. By interacting with the re-presentation of the parables, by participating in their plots, characters, settings, and points of view, the audience confronts again the reality of God's active and transforming presence. As familiar as that reality may be, interaction with the parable narratives offers the audience the opportunity to re-encounter the reign, to have its expectations and experiences shaped anew, and its commitment strengthened. The parables enable the audience to experience the reign with fresh and refreshed, "understanding" eyes, aware anew of its gift, claim and power for living. The redundancy confirms, repeats, strengthens, and thereby challenges, renews, and subverts the familiar.

The second dimension involves the metaphoric nature of parables. It has been customary, rightly, to emphasize the vibrant impact of metaphor on the audience. Metaphor is "a bearer of the reality to which it refers. The hearer not only learns about that reality but participates in it."[98] Metaphors bring together the familiar and unfamiliar, the similar (epiphor) and the different (diaphor), the everyday and the extravagant, realism and hyperbole. By bringing into proximity two entities that were previously distant, they redescribe, disclose, create. They say something "new about reality," they create a new vision, they provide the properties of one entity as the lens for seeing the other. They disrupt "normal" seeing.[99]

Has the authorial audience's familiarity with the parables as part of the traditions about Jesus tamed the metaphors? Does interaction with parables of Matthew 13 "merely" repeat and confirm their previous experience and information?

[98] Wilder, *Language of the Gospel*, 92.
[99] So, for instance, Ricoeur, *Biblical Hermeneutics*, 75–106, 114–18; Funk, "Parable as Metaphor," 133–62; Scott, *Hear Then the Parable.* 42–51.

Such claims would be reductionist unless the performative nature of "confirming" is underlined. Such claims overlook what happens in the act of hearing a metaphoric narrative. The familiar is relived. The audience participates in the reality to which the metaphor refers. It encounters again the destabilizing and disturbing presence of the "reign of the heavens" in the metaphoric transfer accomplished through the narrative. The redundancy functions to represent the familiar, but the "familiar" reality of the parables, the "reign of the heavens," is subversive, dynamic, surprising, transformative.

4. Conclusion

By participating in the reality narrated by Matt 1:1–13:52, the audience has been discipled for the "reign of the heavens" (13:52), and more discipling awaits it in Matthew 14–28. Disciples understand the mysteries of God's reign, the action of God's saving presence in Jesus' actions and teaching. To them it has been given to know (13:11). To them Jesus has revealed "what has been hidden since the foundation of the world" (13:35). Interaction with the parables of Matthew 13 confirms the audience's social and literary experiences of God's reign. But such confirmation and repetition challenges the audience to renew its commitment and experience. Being discipled for the "reign of the heavens" remains a continuing dynamic, transformative, disturbing, communal experience because it requires disciples to live this reality in its ongoing daily (Antiochene?) existence, in the time "in-between" their call and the yet future completion of God's purposes.[100]

[100] I wish to thank Professors J. P. Heil, M. A. Powell, and J. D. Kingsbury for their responses to earlier drafts of this chapter. An earlier form appeared as "Challenging by Confirming, Renewing by Repenting: The Parables of the 'Reign of the Heavens' in Matthew 13 as Embedded Narratives," *Society of Biblical Literature 1995 Seminar Papers* (ed. E. H. Lovering, Jr.; SBLSP 34; Atlanta: Scholars, 1995) 399–424.

CHAPTER 4

Narrative Progression of the Parables Discourse in Matthew 13:1–52

(by Heil)

A consideration of the various progressions involved in Gospel narratives provides a basis for a new reading of the parables discourse in Matt 13:1–52.[1] Our new reading takes account of the following three narrative progressions:

1) Each unit of the parables discourse has its own narrative progression. This is clearly evident for the parables, which have their own narrative integrity and can stand alone as narratives. But it is also true for the non-parabolic sections (such as 13:10–17, 34–35) which function as narrative units with their own integrity. Each of these parabolic and non-parabolic units takes the authorial audience through an experiential process by way of a par-

---

[1] On the Matthean parables discourse, see, in addition to the commentaries, Kingsbury, *Parables*; L. Marin, "Essai d'analyse structurale d'un récit-parabole: Matthieu 13,1–23," *ETR* 46 (1971) 35–74; Dupont, "Le point," 221–59; B. Gerhardsson, "The Seven Parables in Matthew XIII," *NTS* 19 (1972–73) 16–37; O. L. Cope, *Matthew: A Scribe Trained for the Kingdom of Heaven* (CBQMS 5; Washington: The Catholic Biblical Association, 1976) 13–29; L. Sabourin, "The Parables of the Kingdom," *BTB* 6 (1976) 137–60; W. S. Vorster, "The Structure of Matthew 13," *Neot* 11 (1977) 130–38; D. Wenham, "The Structure of Matthew XIII," *NTS* 25 (1978–79) 516–22; G. A. Phillips, "History and Text: The Reader in Context in Matthew's Parables Discourse," *Reader Response Approaches to Biblical and Secular Texts* (Semeia 31; ed. R. Detweiler; Decatur: Scholars, 1985) 111–38; J. G. du Plessis, "Pragmatic Meaning in Matthew 13:1–23," *Neot* 21 (1987) 33–56; C. Burchard, "Senfkorn, Sauerteig, Schatz und Perle in Matthäus 13," SNTSU 13 (1988) 5–35; Donahue, *Gospel in Parable,* 64–70; F. Martin, "Parler: Matthieu 13," *Sémiotique et Bible* 52 (1988) 17–33; Howell, *Matthew's Inclusive Story,* 193–98; Harrington, "The Mixed Reception of the Gospel," 195–201; Lambrecht, *Treasure,* 149–79; idem, "Parables in Mt 13," *TvT* 17 (1977) 25–47; F. Genuyt, "Matthieu 13: L'enseignement en paraboles," *Sémiotique et Bible* 73 (1994) 30–44.

ticular narrative sequence. This realization avoids reducing the parables to making distinct "points," without a consideration of how these points evolve, are related to, and may modify one another in the narrative sequence. The Matthean audience experiences the point(s) in a particular order that forms a narrative whole, a story, that progresses to a climax.[2]

2) The parables discourse as a whole has its own narrative progression. Its parabolic and non-parabolic units are arranged in a particular structure that the audience experiences in sequence. Where a unit occurs in the sequential structure, the narrative context created by the discourse contributes to the meaning of that unit and the response it evokes from the audience. Although the parables may stand on their own as integral narratives, the audience experiences them sequentially embedded in the context of the discourse.[3]

3) The parables discourse itself occurs within the overall narrative progression of Matthew's gospel. By the time the audience hears the parables discourse it has already heard the first twelve chapters of Matthew, including two previous major discourses—the sermon on the mount (5:1–7:29) and the missionary discourse (9:35–11:1). We are concerned not only with how the parables discourse as a whole but with how its individual elements relate to and advance the preceding narrative context.[4]

Based on an alternation in the audiences addressed by Jesus, the parables discourse progresses according to the following narrative structure:

    I. Matt 13:1–9: Audience of Crowds (with Disciples)
        A. Introduction to Speaking in Parables (13:1–3a)
        B. Parable of the Sower (13:3b–9)
    II. Matt 13:10–23: Audience of Disciples (without Crowds)
        A. Purpose of Speaking in Parables (13:10–17)
        B. Allegorical Explanation of the Parable of the Sower (13:18–23)
    III. Matt 13:24–35: Audience of Crowds (with Disciples)
        A. Parable of the Weeds (13:24–30)

[2] Blomberg, "Interpreting the Parables of Jesus," 50–78; idem, *Interpreting the Parables,* rightly insists that parables may have more than one point, but seems to treat the parables more as mechanisms that produce distinct points than as organic narratives in which the points work together in the overall experience of the story.

[3] Gerhardsson, "If We Do Not Cut," 321–35.

[4] For a similar approach to the parables discourse in Mark, see J. P. Heil, "Reader-Response and the Narrative Context of the Parables about Growing Seed in Mark 4:1–34," *CBQ* 54 (1992) 271–86.

In the first movement of the discourse (13:1–9) Jesus utters the parable of the sower (13:3b–9) as one example of the parables in which he spoke many things to "them" (αὐτοῖς) (v 3a), that is, to "the whole crowd" (πᾶς ὁ ὄχλος) standing on the shore (v 2c), the "many crowds" (ὄχλοι πολλοί) who gathered before him (v 2a). Although only the crowds are explicitly mentioned as the audience of Jesus (13:1–3a), the disciples are implicitly present.[5]

That the disciples have also heard the parable of the sower becomes clear as the second movement of the discourse (13:10–17) begins. The disciples (μαθηταί) approach Jesus and ask why he speaks to "them" (αὐτοῖς), the crowds, in parables (v 10). After Jesus tells his disciples why he speaks in parables to "them" (αὐτοῖς), the crowds (v 13), he utters an allegorical explanation of the parable of the sower (13:18–23) only to his disciples.[6] Although the crowds are implicitly present in this second movement, Jesus addresses only his disciples.

The third movement of the discourse (13:24–35) begins as Jesus resumes speaking explicitly to the crowds while his disciples are implicitly present. Jesus addresses each of the three parables in this section to "them" (αὐτοῖς in vv 24, 31, 33), that is, the same "them" that earlier referred to the crowds

---

[5] Immediately before the discourse Jesus pointed out his disciples (μαθητάς) as his true mother and brothers (12:49) because they do the will of his Father in heaven (12:50).

[6] In contrast to the unseeing eyes and unhearing ears of the crowds (vv 13–15), Jesus declared to his disciples: "Your (ὑμῶν) eyes, however, are blessed because they see and your (ὑμῶν) ears because they hear (ἀκούουσιν)" (v 16). Indeed, many prophets and righteous ones longed to see what "you," the disciples, see and did not see it, and "to hear (ἀκοῦσαι) what you hear (ἀκούετε) and did not hear (ἤκουσαν) it" (v 17). Thus, the "you" (ὑμεῖς) whom Jesus then tells to "hear" (ἀκούσατε) the explanation of the sower parable (v 18) refers to the disciples only.

(αὐτοῖς in vv 3, 10, 13, 14). The parallel between "the crowds" and "them" at the end of this section confirms this: "All these things Jesus spoke in parables to the crowds (τοῖς ὄχλοις) and without a parable he spoke nothing to them (αὐτοῖς)" (v 34).

That the disciples have heard the parables in the third movement of the discourse becomes evident as the fourth movement (13:36–52) begins. After Jesus leaves the crowds (ὄχλους) and returns to the house (see 13:1), his disciples (μαθηταὶ) approach him again (see 13:10) with a request: "Explain to us the parable of the weeds of the field" (v 36).[7] The disciples have heard not only the first parable of the third section, the parable of the weeds (13:24–30), but also the other two, the parables of the mustard seed (13:31–32) and of the leaven (13:33), since there is no indication of a change in scene or audience until the beginning of the fourth movement. Since Jesus has left the crowds, he addresses the parables of the fourth section only to the disciples. Whereas the three parables of the third section are all introduced with a reference to "them" (αὐτοῖς), the crowds (vv 24, 31, 33), the three parables following Jesus' allegorical explanation of the parable of the weeds (13:36–43) to his disciples all lack this introduction and begin simply, "The reign of the heavens is like . . ." (vv 44, 45, 47). Only the disciples hear the parables of the treasure (13:44), the pearl (13:45–46), and the fish net (13:47–50). Only they understand "all these things" and are thus likened to a scribe "discipled" (μαθητευθεὶς) for the reign of the heavens (13:51–52).[8]

---

[7] That the second and fourth movements, addressed exclusively to the disciples, similarly begin with a request of the disciples to Jesus further confirms the four-part structure of the discourse. Just as the second movement begins, "And approaching the disciples said to him" (καὶ προσελθόντες οἱ μαθηταὶ εἶπαν αὐτῷ, v 10), so the fourth movement begins, "And his disciples approached him saying" (καὶ προσῆλθον αὐτῷ οἱ μαθηταὶ αὐτοῦ λέγοντες, v 36)

[8] This four-part structure of the discourse based on the alternation of audiences addressed has generally been neglected. It is recognized, however, by D. Patte, *The Gospel According to Matthew: A Structural Commentary on Matthew's Faith* (Philadelphia: Fortress, 1987) 185. Many point to only a two-part structure based on the change of scene and audience in 13:36 and ignore the similar introduction and change of audience in 13:10. On the structure of the discourse, see Kingsbury, *Parables,* 12–15; Dupont, "Le point," 231–32; Gerhardsson, "Seven Parables," 16–37; Vorster, "Structure," 130–38; Wenham, "Structure," 516–22; Burchard, "Senfkorn," 5–19; Lambrecht, *Treasure,* 174–77; Gnilka, *Matthäusevangelium,* 1. 473–75; U. Luz, *Das Evangelium nach Matthäus* (EKKNT 1/2; Zürich: Benziger, 1990) 292–95; Davies and Allison, *Matthew,* 2. 370–72; Hagner, *Matthew 1–13,* 362–64.

1. Matthew 13:1–9:
Audience of Crowds (with Disciples)

A. Introduction to Speaking in Parables (13:1–3a)

The introduction to the parables discourse progresses according to the following alternation of actions by Jesus and the crowds:

a¹   On that day, Jesus, going out of the house, sat beside the sea. (v 1)
b¹   And many crowds gathered before him, (v 2a)
a²   so that he got into a boat and sat down, (v 2b)
b²   and the whole crowd was standing on the shore. (v 2c)
a³   And he spoke to them many things in parables, saying, (v 3a)

This opening unit continues the separation between Jesus and the crowds that began in the previous unit (12:46–50).[9] Jesus goes out of the house, in which "on that day" (v 1) he had been speaking to the crowds (ὄχλοις, 12:46). Inside the house Jesus distinguished his disciples (and by implication himself) from not only his mother and brothers outside of the house but also from the crowds inside (12:46). As those who do the will of his Father in heaven, the disciples are the real members of Jesus' family (12:49–50).[10] After he sat beside the sea (v 1) and many crowds (ὄχλοι) gathered before him (v 2a), Jesus further separates himself from them as he got into a boat and again sat down (v 2b). As the mother and brothers of Jesus were standing (εἰστήκεισαν) outside in separation from Jesus inside the house (12:46), so now the whole crowd (ὄχλος) was standing (εἰστήκει) on the shore (v 2c) in separation from Jesus sitting inside the boat (v 2b). From his position of "sitting" inside the boat in contrast to the many crowds "standing" outside on the shore Jesus spoke to them many things in parables (v 3a).

In the first discourse, the sermon on the mount, Jesus sat down (καθίσαντος) on the mountain and taught his disciples who came to him (5:1–2) the will of his Father in heaven (5:16, 43–48; 6:1–18; 7:21), while the crowds Jesus taught, preached to, and healed (4:23–25) were also present

---

[9] For a recent treatment of 12:46–50, see Barton, *Discipleship*, 178–84.

[10] On the role of the crowds as outsiders here in contrast to the disciples, see M. J. Wilkins, *The Concept of Disciple in Matthew's Gospel* (NovTSup 59; Leiden: Brill, 1988) 139–40; Carter, "Crowds," 61–62.

(4:25; 5:1) and heard the sermon (7:28).[11] In the second, the missionary, discourse Jesus authorized his disciples to share in his ministry to the crowds (4:23–25; 9:35) by likewise healing and preaching (10:1, 7–8).[12] He thus commissioned his disciples, whom he invited to join him in becoming "fishers of people" (4:19), to join him now as fellow "workers" in the "great harvest" represented by the crowds of people (9:36–38; 10:10) and as fellow shepherds (10:6) of the crowds for whom Jesus feels compassion because they are "tormented and oppressed, like sheep without a shepherd" (9:36).[13]

In the third discourse Jesus again sat down (ἐκάθητο) not on the mountain as in the first discourse (5:1) but beside the sea (13:1). The crowds who gathered before him, however, were so many (πολλοί, 13:2), the "harvest" of people so great (πολύς, 9:37), that Jesus, the "fisher" of people (4:19) appropriately sat (καθῆσθαι) in a boat on the sea, while the whole crowd, the "fish" he has collected before him, appropriately stand on the seashore (13:2; cf. 13:48). Although Jesus speaks many things in parables directly to the crowds (13:3a), he indirectly addresses the implicitly present disciples (cf. 12:49; 13:10), those he has empowered to join him in his ministry to the many crowds as shepherds (10:6), harvesters (9:37; 10:10), and fishers of people (4:19).

With regard to pragmatics, the introduction to the parables discourse (13:1–3a) calls for the authorial audience, by identifying with the disciples, to do the following: 1) As those urged to become members of the true family of Jesus by doing the will of his Father in heaven (12:49–50) in order to enter the reign of the heavens (7:21), they are to hear what Jesus, *the* revealer of the Father (11:27), reveals in the parables discourse, as he did in the sermon on the mount, about the will of his Father. 2) As those invited to share in Jesus' ministry to the crowds as shepherds, harvesters, and fishers of people, they are to hear what Jesus reveals in the parables discourse, as he did in the missionary discourse, about how they are to perform their ministry to people.

---

[11] Carter, *Sermon on the Mount,* 80–81.

[12] Jesus does not authorize his disciples to teach until the climactic conclusion of the narrative in 28:20.

[13] Weaver, *Missionary Discourse,* 75–84; M. Grilli, *Comunità e Missione: Le direttive di Matteo: Indagine esegetica su Mt 9,35–11,1* (Frankfurt: Lang, 1992) 89–95; J. P. Heil, "Ezekiel 34 and the Narrative Strategy of the Shepherd and Sheep Metaphor in Matthew," *CBQ* 55 (1993) 700–702.

B. Parable of the Sower (13:3b–9)

The parable of the sower, a narrative in itself, tells an agricultural story about what happens to the seed a sower sows (v 3b). As the parable focuses upon the seed that is sown, it imparts to its listeners the sower's experience of a threefold progressive failure of the seed to produce. The seed that falls along the way and is devoured by birds (v 4) presents the first stage of failure. Here the seed disappears before it even has a chance to grow. The second stage of failure is the seed that falls on rocky ground and actually begins to sprout. But it grows prematurely with no depth of soil and is scorched by the sun because it has no root (vv 5–6). The third stage of failure is the seed that falls among thorns. Although this seed grows, so do the thorns, which outgrow it and choke it (v 7). This final failure to produce serves as a climactic point summing up a threefold progressive failure of the seed sown by the sower.[14]

After first bringing its audience through an experience of the protracted failure of seed to grow and produce, the parable confers a contrasting experience of surprising and extraordinary success. Some seed does fall upon the good soil and "produces fruit." Indeed, this seed produces an abundant yield of "a hundredfold, or sixtyfold, or thirtyfold" (v 8), which stands in stark contrast to and far exceeds the previous threefold failure.[15] As a vivid agricultural story this parable enables its audience to share the sower's experience of the inevitable and overwhelming success of the seed that falls on good soil despite and along with the repeated failures of the seed that does not fall on good soil.[16]

After concluding the story, Jesus adds: "Let whoever has ears hear!" (v 9). This impassioned appeal points to a deeper meaning and reference for this parabolic story that requires an attentive and penetrating "hearing." It challenges not only the crowds and the disciples but also the authorial audience to "hear," in the sense of "understand," all that Jesus is communicating by this

---

[14] Donahue, *Parable,* 34: "The parable achieves a dramatic effect, not by simply listing the three failures in contrast to the one great harvest but by depicting a progression in the growth of the seed. . . . This rhythmic and ascending progression involves the hearer in the unfolding mystery of growth."

[15] On the miraculous nature of the yield, see R. K. McIver, "One Hundred-Fold Yield—Miraculous or Mundane? Matthew 13.8, 23; Mark 4.8, 20; Luke 8.8," *NTS* 40 (1994) 606–8.

[16] Heil, "Mark 4:1–34," 273–74.

parable.[17] The previous context heard by the audience gives it the ears to hear and understand the parable.

The sower who went out (ἐξῆλθεν) to sow (v 3b) portrays Jesus who just went out (ἐξελθὼν) of the house (v 1) and addressed the crowds in parables (v 3a). Just as the sower sowed the seed, a symbol which the audience knows indicates the effective word of God (Isa 55:10–11),[18] upon the soil, so Jesus spoke (sowed) the word of God included in "the many things he spoke in parables" (seed) (v 3a) to the crowds standing upon the soil of the seashore (v 2c). The crowds epitomize the continued failure of repentance on the part of both the crowds and the Jewish leaders that Jesus as the sower of the word of God's reign (4:17) has already experienced (9:3–4, 11, 33–34; 11:1–24; 12:14, 23–24, 38–45) and can expect to experience in the future (vv 4–7).[19] But the implicitly present disciples, as those who, in contrast to the crowds, form the true family of Jesus by doing God's will (12:49–50), represent the surprising success of the seed that falls on good soil and produces fruit (καρπόν) (v 8a). They produce the fruit (καρπὸν) worthy of the repentance (3:8) required to enter the reign of the heavens (3:2). Their success points to an even greater success ("hundred, sixty, or thirtyfold") in the future that will far surpass previous failures (v 8b).

But the sower who went out (ἐξῆλθεν) to sow (v 3b) also portrays the disciples. Jesus commissioned them to preach (sow) the same word of God (seed) that he and John the Baptist preach: "Repent for the reign of the heavens has arrived!" (3:2; 4:17; 10:7).[20] As Jesus went out (ἐξελθὼν) of the house (τῆς οἰκίας) (v 1), away from the crowds who have not heard his appeal to do the will of God and become his true family (12:46–50), so his disciples may find themselves coming out (ἐξερχόμενοι ἔξω) of the house (τῆς οἰκίας) that does not receive them and hear their words (10:14). Like Jesus the disciples can expect to experience the threefold failure of the sower (vv 4–7) in

---

[17] Earlier Jesus exclaimed to the crowds (11:7) this same appeal, "Let whoever has ears hear!" (11:15), in reference to John the Baptist as Elijah (11:13–14). But later only the disciples "understood" (συνῆκαν, 17:13) that Elijah had already come in the person of John the Baptist (17:10–13). See also Anderson, *Matthew's Narrative Web*, 86.

[18] C. A. Evans, "On the Isaianic Background of the Sower Parable," *CBQ* 47 (1985) 464–68.

[19] D. J. Verseput, *The Rejection of the Humble Messianic King: A Study of the Composition of Matthew 11–12* (Frankfurt: Lang, 1986); Kingsbury, "Developing Conflict," 57–73.

[20] Weaver, *Missionary Discourse*, 84; Grilli, *Comunità*, 109; Anderson, *Narrative Web*, 87: "The message of John, Jesus, and the disciples is of one piece."

their ministry (10:16–23). But they can take courage in the far greater success (v 8) they will also experience (10:40–42).

The parable of the sower (13:3b–9) works pragmatically on Matthew's audience in a double way: (1) It encourages them to "produce fruit" (3:8; 13:8) and be part of the great success that will far exceed failures to hear God's word, by repenting and doing God's will in order to become the true family of Jesus (12:49–50) and enter the reign of the heavens (7:21). (2) It encourages them to preach the word of God's reign despite the many failures they will experience, because the success will eventually and inevitably far outstrip the failure.

2. Matthew 13:10–23: Audience of Disciples (without Crowds)

A. Purpose of Speaking in Parables (13:10–17)

That the disciples have been present and heard the sower parable becomes evident as they approach Jesus and ask why he speaks in parables to "them" (αὐτοῖς), the crowds (v 10). Since Jesus' ministry to the crowds is paradigmatic for their own share in that ministry (9:35–10:8), the disciples have a special concern for his use of parables. But with an emphatic "to you" (ὑμῖν) Jesus first explains why he speaks in parables to "them" (αὐτοῖς), the disciples (v 11a): "*To you* it has been given (δέδοται) (definitively by God, divine perfect passive) to know the mysteries of the reign of the heavens, but to them (the crowds) it has not been given (οὐ δέδοται)" (v 11b). In further contrast to the crowds, the disciples not only do the will of God and form Jesus' true family (12:49–50), but God has granted them to know the mysteries (τὰ μυστήρια) of the reign of the heavens (v 11b), the many things (πολλὰ) Jesus speaks in parables (v 3a). Furthermore, this contrast will become even starker in the future: "For whoever has, it will be given to him and he will have an abundance; but whoever does not have, even what he has will be taken from him" (v 12). God will give the disciples an abundant knowledge of the reign's mysteries, while he will take away whatever knowledge the crowds may have.

The reason (διὰ τοῦτο, v 13) why (διὰ τί, v 10) Jesus speaks in parables to "them" (αὐτοῖς), the crowds, is because "seeing they do not see and hearing (ἀκούντες) they do not hear (ἀκούουσιν) nor understand (συνίουσιν)" (v 13). Despite Jesus' appeal after the sower parable, "Let whoever has ears hear (ἀκουέτω)!" (v 9), the crowds have not heard nor understood how the failures of the seed to produce fruit (vv 4–7) refer to their failures to repent at seeing and hearing the arrival of the reign of the heavens (3:2, 8; 4:17; 11:20–21; 12:41).

The failures of the crowds to repent are embraced not only by the failures that precede inevitable success in the sower parable but by God's scriptural plan. The prophecy of Isaiah (6:9–10) that the people of Israel fulfilled in the past is again, in a complete way, fulfilled (ἀναπληροῦται) for "them" (αὐτοῖς), the crowds (v 14a).[21] God himself speaks through Isaiah as now quoted by Jesus: "You shall indeed hear (ἀκοῇ ἀκούσετε) but not at all (οὐ μὴ, emphatic negative) understand (συνῆτε), you shall indeed see but not at all (οὐ μὴ) perceive (ἴδητε)" (v 14b). The crowds fail to understand because they have willfully closed their "hearts," their minds and inner selves, to what they see and hear: "For (γὰρ) the heart (καρδία) of this people has become dull."[22] Their ears have become hard of hearing (ἤκουσαν), and they have closed their eyes, lest (μήποτε) they see with their eyes and hear (ἀκούσωσιν) with their ears and understand (συνῶσιν) with their heart (καρδίᾳ) and "turn" or repent (ἐπιστρέψωσιν) and "I" (God) will heal (ἰάσομαι) them (v 15). Although the crowds have willfully failed, there is still hope for them. All they have to do is open their hearts and repent and God will heal them.[23]

With an emphatic "your" (ὑμῶν) Jesus continues the contrast between the crowds and his disciples: "*Your* eyes, however, are blessed because they see and your ears because they hear" (v 16). In contrast to the crowds, who do not hear and understand (vv 13–15), and in accord with Jesus' appeal, "Let whoever has ears (ὦτα) hear (ἀκουέτω)!" (v 9), the disciples' ears (ὦτα) hear (ἀκούουσιν) and understand the sower parable and the mysteries of the reign of the heavens (v 11) that it and the other parables Jesus speaks (v 3a) contains. Jesus solemnly assures his disciples: "For amen I say to you, many

---

[21] On the quotation in 13:14–15 as an interpolation, see Davies and Allison, *Matthew*, 2. 393–94. But on its genuineness, see R. H. Gundry, *The Use of the Old Testament in St. Matthew's Gospel* (NovTSup 18; Leiden: Brill, 1967) 116–18. On ἀναπληροῦται he remarks: "The prefixing of ἀνά, the vivid present tense in Mt, and the first position show a deliberate emphasis on the word; i.e., the quotation, partially fulfilled in Isaiah's generation, now receives a full measure of fulfilment" (p. 117).

[22] A. Sand, "καρδία," *EDNT* 2. 250: "Καρδία refers thus to the *inner person*, the seat of understanding, knowledge, and will . . . ."

[23] C. A. Evans, *To See and Not Perceive: Isaiah 6.9–10 in Early Jewish and Christian Interpretation* (JSOTSup 64; Sheffield: JSOT, 1989) 64: "Although the Lord would be willing, he is not able to heal the people, since it will not repent."

prophets and righteous ones longed to see what you see and did not see it, and to hear (ἀκοῦσαι) what you hear (ἀκούετε) and did not hear (ἤκουσαν) it" (v 17). The privilege of the disciples to see and hear contrasts not only with the unwillingness of the crowds to see and hear but also with the prophets and righteous ones of the past who longed (ἐπεθύμησαν) to see and hear what the disciples now see and hear. Their privilege to see, hear, and understand the mysteries of the reign of the heavens in the parables further equips them to fulfill their ministry as the "prophets" and "righteous ones" (10:40–42; cf. 5:12; 7:22) now sent to the unrepenting crowds.[24]

Pragmatically, this unit on the purpose of speaking in parables (13:10–17) calls for the audience to accept and appreciate their privilege of understanding the mysteries of the reign of the heavens in the parables they hear from Jesus. This privilege empowers them to fulfill their responsibility to proclaim the reign even to those unwilling to repent in order to enter it, with the hope that they will open their hearts to see, hear, and understand.

B. Allegorical Explanation of the Parable of the Sower (13:18–23)

With another emphatic "you" (ὑμεῖς) Jesus advances the contrast between the crowds who do not hear and understand (vv 13–15), the prophets and righteous ones who have not heard (v 17), and the disciples whose ears are blessed because they hear (ἀκούουσιν, v 16): "You then hear (ἀκούσατε) the parable of the sower" (v 18). That Jesus enables his disciples (you) to "hear" in the sense of understand the parable of the sower demonstrates not only how their (your) ears are blessed because they hear (v 17) but how they (to you) have been given to know the mysteries of God's reign (v 11a). That he gives the disciples, who have already heard the parable of the sower (vv 3b–9), an additional allegorical explanation of it begins to illustrate how to those who have "it will be given" and they will have an abundance (v 12a).

In his allegory of the sower parable Jesus further explains why the crowds, although they hear (ἀκούοντες, v 13; ἀκοῇ ἀκούσετε, v 14), do not really hear (οὐκ ἀκούουσιν, v 13) nor understand (οὐδὲ συνίουσιν, v 13; οὐ μὴ συνῆτε, v 14): "When anyone hears (ἀκούοντος) the word of the reign and

---

[24] On the role of the disciples as "prophets," proclaimers of the reign of the heavens (10:7), and "righteous ones," those identified with the "righteousness" Jesus put forth as distinctive of the reign of the heavens (3:15; 5:6, 10, 20; 6:33), in their mission to the crowds, see Weaver, *Missionary Discourse*, 119–23; Grilli, *Comunità*, 167–74.

does not understand (μὴ συνιέντος), the evil one comes and snatches what was sown in his heart; this one is what was sown along the way" (v 19; cf. v 4). The crowds do not understand because not only have they allowed their heart (καρδία) to become dull lest they understand (συνῶσιν) with their heart (καρδία) (v 15), but the devil snatches away the word of the reign sown in their heart (καρδία) (v 19). The seed sown (ἐσπαρμένον) by the sower represents not only the word (λόγον) of the reign but the person who hears the word: "This one" (οὗτος), the person who hears the word (cf. vv 20–23) but does not understand, is sown (σπαρείς) along the way (v 19).²⁵ Both the crowds themselves and the devil, symbol of the mystery of evil, but not the sower, either Jesus or his disciples who share in his ministry of proclaiming the word of the reign, are responsible for the failure of the crowds to understand, repent and enter the reign of the heavens.

The allegory progresses to a different type of failure. The person sown upon the rocky ground is the one who hears the word and immediately receives it with joy (v 20). This person has no root in himself but endures only for a time; when tribulation or persecution (διωγμοῦ) arises on account of the word, he immediately falls away (σκανδαλίζεται) (v 21; cf. vv 5–6). Not only can Jesus and the disciples expect this kind of failure in those to whom they preach, but the disciples themselves are susceptible to it. In the first discourse Jesus advised the disciples of persecution: "Blessed are those persecuted (δεδιωγμένοι) for the sake of righteousness, for theirs is the reign of the heavens" (5:10). Blessed are the disciples whenever others persecute (διώξωσιν) them for the sake of Jesus, for thus did they persecute (ἐδίωξαν) the prophets before them (5:11–12). Whereas the person sown on rocky ground (πετρώδη, v 20) has no root in himself (v 21), Jesus assured his disciples that whoever hears his words and does them is like a wise man who built his house on rock (πέτραν). When the winds came, the house did not fall for it was founded upon the rock (πέτραν) (7:24–25). In the second discourse Jesus alerted the disciples he sent to preach the word of the reign (10:7) about persecution (10:16–25). He exhorted them that "whoever perseveres to the end," rather than endures for only a time (v 21), "will be saved" (10:22). Whenever they persecute (διώκωσιν) the disciples in one city, they are to persevere

²⁵ On the seed as a double-duty metaphor representing not only the word but the people who hear the word, see Heil, "Mark 4:1-34," 278; G. Lohfink, "Das Gleichnis vom Sämann (Mk 4,3–9)," *BZ* 30 (1986) 36–69; L. Ramaroson, "'Parole-semence' ou 'Peuple-semence' dans la parabole du Semeur?" *ScEs* 40 (1988) 91–101. Background for the seed as people metaphor is provided by Hos 2:25; Jer 31:27; 4 *Ezra* 8:41.

by going to others (10:23).²⁶ And warning of the rejection that accompanies his ministry (11:5), Jesus declared blessed anyone who does not fall away (σκανδαλισθῇ, cf. v 21) because of him (11:6).²⁷

Progressing to yet another type of discipleship failure, the person sown among the thorns is the one who hears the word, but the worries (μέριμνα) of the world and the lure of wealth choke the word and it becomes unfruitful (v 22; cf. v 7). The audience recalls that in the sermon on the mount Jesus cautioned the disciples against storing up treasures on earth rather than in heaven, for where their treasure is there will their heart be. They cannot serve both God and wealth (6:19–21, 24). He encouraged them: "Do not worry (μεριμνᾶτε) about your life (6:25) . . . Can any of you by worrying (μεριμνῶν) add a single moment to your life? (6:27) . . . Why do you worry (μεριμνᾶτε) about clothing? (6:28) . . . So do not worry (μεριμνήσητε), saying, 'What will we eat?' or 'What will we drink?' or 'What will we wear?' (6:31) . . . Seek first the reign of God and its righteousness, and all these things will be given you as well. Do not worry (μεριμνήσητε) about tomorrow, for tomorrow will bring worries (μεριμνήσει) of its own" (6:33–34).²⁸ In the missionary discourse Jesus directed his disciples not to be concerned about their physical needs or payment for their ministry, but to trust that God will provide what they need: "You have received without payment, give without payment. Do not acquire gold or silver or copper for your belts, or a traveler's bag for the road, or two tunics, or sandals, or a staff; for the worker deserves his keep" (10:8–10).²⁹

In climactic contrast to the previous failures the person sown upon good soil is the one who hears the word and understands, who indeed bears fruit and produces a hundredfold, or sixtyfold, or thirtyfold (v 23; cf. v 8). In contrast to the crowds who hear but do not understand (μὴ συνιέντος, v 19; οὐ μὴ συνῆτε, v 14; οὐδε συνίουσιν, v 13), the disciples hear and understand (συνιείς, v 23); they have been given to know the mysteries of the reign of the heavens (v 11). In contrast to the disciples who fail by falling away in persecution (vv 20–21) or because of worries and the lure of wealth become unfruitful (ἄκαρπος) (v 22), the disciples who succeed by hearing and under-

²⁶ Weaver, *Missionary Discourse*, 90–102; Grilli, *Comunità*, 123–39.

²⁷ Verseput, *Rejection*, 72–75; Weaver, *Missionary Discourse*, 131.

²⁸ R. J. Dillon, "Ravens, Lilies, and the Kingdom of God (Matthew 6:25–33/Luke 12:22–31)," *CBQ* 53 (1991) 605–27; O. Wischmeyer, "Matthäus 6,25–34 par: Die Spruchreihe vom Sorgen," *ZNW* 85 (1994) 1–22.

²⁹ Weaver, *Missionary Discourse*, 85–86; Grilli, *Comunità*, 113–14.

standing bear fruit (καρποφορεῖ). They not only produce the fruit of repentance needed for them to enter the reign of the heavens (3:8; 3:2; 4:17), but they bring others into the reign by proclaiming the word of the reign that produces the fruit, the harvest (cf. 9:37–38), of people to populate the reign in an abundance ("hundred, sixty, or thirtyfold") that far surpasses the failure of those who hear the word but do not understand (v 19).

Jesus' allegorical explanation of the parable of the sower (13:18–23) involves Matthew's audience in the following pragmatics: 1) They are to continue to proclaim the word of the reign even to people who hear but do not understand; their failure is due not to any deficiency on the part of the word or its proclaimers but to willfully closed hearts and ultimately to the mystery of evil (v 19). 2) Bolstered by Jesus' promise that whoever endures to the end will be saved (10:22), they are to persevere through the persecution they will encounter in preaching the word of the reign (vv 20–21). 3) With trust that God will provide all they need, they are to avoid the lure of wealth and not worry about their physical needs in proclaiming the word of the reign (v 22). 4) They are to hear and understand the word of the reign not only by producing the fruit of personal repentance necessary to enter the reign but by producing the fruit of people needed to populate the reign through their preaching of the word that will inevitably yield a successful harvest of people far in abundance to all failures (v 23).

3. Matthew 13:24–35: Audience of Crowds (with Disciples)

A. Parable of the Weeds (13:24–30)

Another parable Jesus put before "them" (αὐτοῖς), the crowds (cf. vv 3, 10, 13, 14), with the disciples still implicitly present (v 24a). Although the crowds will hear but not understand the parable (vv 11, 13–15, 19), the disciples (and audience) will hear and understand the mysteries of the reign it reveals (vv 11–12, 16–17, 23). According to the parable the reign of the heavens has already become like (ὡμοιώθη) the story of a man who sowed good seed in his field (v 24b).[30]

---

[30] Carson, "ΟΜΟΙΟΣ Word-Group," 279: "The aorist passive introduces the parable of the tares (13.24), in which, even though there is mention of the eschatological 'harvest', the focus remains on the mixture of wheat and tares at present. The kingdom of heaven *has* (already) *become like* this."

That the parable tells the story of a man who sowed (σπείραντι) seed links it closely with the parable of the sower (σπείραντος, v 18) (vv 3b–9) and its explanation (vv 18–23), upon which it builds. The evil one (ὁ πονηρὸς) who comes (ἔρχεται) and snatches away what was sown (ἐσπαρμένον) in the heart of the one who hears the word of the reign but does not understand (v 19) progresses to the enemy (ὁ ἐχθρὸς) who came (ἦλθεν) and sowed (ἐπέσπειρεν) weeds among the wheat and went away (v 25). When the crop from the good (καλὸν) seed (v 24) sprouted and bore fruit (καρπὸν ἐποίη-σεν), as the seed sown on good (καλὴν) soil, the one who hears and under-stands, bears fruit and produces (καρποφορεῖ καὶ ποιεῖ, v 23; cf. v 8) in the sower parable, then the weeds (ζιζάνια) appeared as well (v 26).[31] The weeds represent the non-understanding crowds, while the wheat from the good seed represents those who hear and understand.

The disciples approaching (προσελθόντες) Jesus and asking why he speaks to the crowds in parables (v 10) progresses to the servants (δοῦλοι) of the householder (οἰκοδεσπότου) approaching (προσελθόντες) and asking, "Lord (Κύριε), did you not sow good seed (those who understand) in your field? Where then have the weeds (non-understanding crowds) come from?" (v 27). In the missionary discourse Jesus related himself closely to his disci-ples as a lord to his servants and as a householder to the members of his household: "A disciple is not above the teacher, nor a servant (δοῦλος) above his lord (κύριον). It is sufficient for the disciple that he be like his teacher, and the servant (δοῦλος) like his lord (κύριος). If they have called the house-holder (οἰκοδεσπότην) Beelzebul, how much more so the members of his household (οἰκιακοὺς)" (10:24–25).[32] As those who do God's will, the disci-ples who were with Jesus in the house (οἰκίας, 13:1) are members of his household (οἰκιακοὶ), his true family (12:49–50; cf. 10:35–36).

After the householder (Jesus) explains that an enemy has done this, the ser-vants (disciples) offer to go and collect the weeds (v 28). The householder declines lest in collecting they uproot together with the weeds (non-understanding crowds) the wheat (those who understand) (v 29). For the sake of the wheat, then, they must allow both to grow together until the har-vest; then at harvest time he will tell the harvesters, "Collect first the weeds and bind them into bundles to be burned (κατακαῦσαι), but the wheat

---

[31] "ζιζάνιον," *EDNT* 2. 103: "The word . . . refers most probably to darnel, which looks like wheat during the early stages of its growth."

[32] Weaver, *Missionary Discourse,* 105–7; Grilli, *Comunità,* 140–42.

(σῖτον) gather (συναγάγετε) into my barn (ἀποθήκην)" (v 30). The audience recalls that after John the Baptist exhorted the Pharisees and Sadducees who came to be baptized by him to produce the fruit of repentance (3:7–8) in order to enter the reign of the heavens (3:2), he warned that the "coming stronger one" (Jesus) will baptize with the holy spirit and fire (3:11). As the eschatological judge, he "will gather (συνάξει) his wheat (σῖτον) into his barn (ἀποθήκην), but the chaff he will burn (κατακαύσει) with unquenchable fire" (3:12).[33] Whereas John used eschatological harvest imagery with climactic emphasis on the burning to sternly warn, Jesus employs the same imagery with climactic emphasis on the gathering of the wheat to comfort and encourage. The weeds will not harm the wheat and the enemy will not prevail; the householder will gather his wheat and ultimately triumph over the power of evil.

The parable of the weeds (13:24–30) communicates the following pragmatic message to Matthew's audience: As understanding disciples sent to preach the word of the reign that will lead others who understand (wheat) into the reign, they must be patient that some, because of the mystery of evil, will not understand (weeds), knowing that they (weeds) will not prevent those who do understand and repent (wheat) from being gathered into the reign of the heavens. Such an attitude of patience gives them knowledge of another one of the mysteries of the reign (13:11). They experience even now what it means to live in the reign of the heavens they confidently look forward to entering at the final harvest.

B. Parable of the Mustard Seed (13:31–32)

As Jesus put the parable of the weeds before them, so he put another parable before "them" (αὐτοῖς), the crowds, with the disciples present (v 31a; cf v 24a). Progressing from the parable of the weeds in which the reign of the heavens has become like (ὡμοιώθη) the story of a man who sowed (ἀνθρώπῳ σπείραντι) good seed in his field (ἐν τῷ ἀγρῷ αὐτοῦ) (v 24b), in this parable the reign of the heavens is like (ὁμοία ἐστὶν) the story of a grain of mustard, which a man (ἄνθρωπος) took and sowed (ἔσπειρεν) in his field (ἐν τῷ ἀγρῷ αὐτοῦ) (v 31b). Against the background of what the reign has already become like (ὡμοιώθη) because the mystery of evil (weeds) has already become a reality that must be tolerated (vv 24–30), the reign is now like

---

[33] Anderson, *Narrative Web*, 88.

(ὁμοία ἐστὶν) a grain of mustard that a man sowed in his field. Just as the man who sowed good seed in his field represented first of all Jesus but also his disciples whom he sent to likewise preach the word (v 24b), so now the man who sowed the grain of mustard represents both Jesus and his disciples (v 31b). The good seed (καλὸν σπέρμα, v 24b) that represented those who hear and understand, inclusive first of all of the disciples themselves but also of those who will hear and understand the word of the reign they preach, progresses to a grain of mustard (κόκκῳ σινάπεως, v 31b).

Although the grain of mustard, a seed symbolic not only of the word of God's reign but of those who hear and understand it (cf. vv 19–23), is, on the one hand (μέν), the smallest of all the seeds, when, on the other hand (δὲ), it has grown (αὐξηθῇ), as the wheat must be allowed to grow together (συναυξάνεσθαι) with the weeds until the harvest (v 30), it is the greatest of the shrubs and becomes a tree (v 32a).[34] So great has this tree become that the birds of the sky come and dwell in its branches (v 32b). From the OT the audience knows that this great tree that "has grown" (αὐξηθῇ) by the creative activity of God (divine passive) (Gen 1:11–12; Isa 55:10–11) from the smallest of all seeds symbolizes a worldwide kingdom that provides a safe and secure dwelling place for the birds of the sky, symbolic of all the peoples of the world (LXX Ezek 17:23; 31:5–6; Dan 4:10–12, 20–21).[35] Although those who hear and understand the word of the reign, the disciples and those to whom they preach, may be small (grain of mustard), they will inevitably, "when grown" by God (v 32a), become a great "tree," the reign of the heavens, providing a dwelling place for all peoples of the world.

Pragmatically, the parable of the mustard seed (13:31–32) encourages the Matthean audience to live with the present small number of those who hear and understand the word of the reign with the sure hope of the inevitable greatness of the reign of the heavens that God will populate with all those who will ultimately hear, understand, and repent. Such an attitude of hope gives them knowledge of another one of the mysteries of the reign of the heavens (13:11). They experience even now, while it is still relatively small, the incomparable greatness of the reign of the heavens that will ultimately embrace all peoples of the world.

---

[34] On the proverbial smallness of the mustard seed, see C.-H. Hunzinger, "σίναπι," *TDNT* 7. 287–91.

[35] J. P. Heil, *The Gospel of Mark as a Model for Action: A Reader-Response Commentary* (New York: Paulist, 1992) 111.

C. Parable of the Leaven (13:33)

As Jesus spoke (ἐλάλησεν) many things in parables to them (αὐτοῖς) (v 3a), so he spoke (ἐλάλησεν) yet another parable to them (αὐτοῖς), the crowds, in the presence of the disciples (v 33a). Building upon the previous parable, the audience's focus on the reign of the heavens that is like (ὁμοία ἐστὶν) a grain of mustard (v 31) now moves to the reign being also like (ὁμοία ἐστὶν) leaven (v 33). As a man who took (λαβὼν) a grain of mustard and sowed (ἔσπειρεν) it in his field (v 31) represented both Jesus and his disciples, so now a woman who took (λαβοῦσα) leaven and hid (ἐνέκρυψεν) it in three measures of flour (v 33) likewise represents both Jesus and his disciples in their shared ministry of preaching the word of the reign. The grain of mustard (κόκκῳ σινάπεως, v 31b) that represented both the word and those who hear and understand it, the disciples themselves as well as those who will hear and understand the word of the reign they preach, progresses to leaven (ζύμῃ, v 33b).

Whereas the grain of mustard, when it has grown (αὐξηθῇ) by the creative activity of God, becomes a kingdom (tree) great enough to embrace the people of the world (birds) (v 32), from the leaven (ζύμη) that a woman hides in three measures of flour, an enormous quantity, the "whole" (ὅλον) is leavened (ἐζυμώθη) by God (divine passive) (v 33).[36] Although those who hear and understand the word of the reign, the disciples and those to whom they preach, may now be imperceptibly hidden (leaven) among the people of the world, they will inevitably, when the "whole" is "leavened" by God and his reign, effect a total and penetrating influence upon the whole world.

Pragmatically, the parable of the leaven (13:33) encourages Matthew's audience to live with the present hiddenness of those who hear and understand the word of the reign with the sure hope that the reign in which they will dwell (13:31–32) will inevitably, through the hidden, "leavening" activity of God, totally transform the whole world. Such an attitude of hope gives them knowledge of yet another one of the mysteries of the reign of the heavens (13:11). They realize even now, while it is still hidden, the pervasive effect they, with God working through them as members and agents of the reign of the heavens, will exert upon the whole world.

---

[36] On the three measures as an exceptionally large amount, which constitutes the "whole" here, see Hagner, *Matthew 1–13*, 390; L. Morris, *The Gospel According to Matthew* (Grand Rapids, MI: Eerdmans, 1992) 353; Gundry, *Matthew*, 268–69; Burchard, "Senfkorn," 34; Luz, *Matthäus*, 2. 333; Davies and Allison, *Matthew*, 2. 423.

D. Purpose of Speaking in Parables (13:34–35)

The many things (πολλὰ), the mysteries (τὰ μυστήρια) of the reign of the heavens (v 11) Jesus spoke (ἐλάλησεν) in parables to the crowds (v 3a), climactically progresses to "all these things" (ταῦτα πάντα) Jesus spoke (ἐλάλησεν) in parables to the crowds (v 34a), even though they do not understand (vv 12–15). Although Jesus spoke to his disciples without parables (vv 10–17), he was speaking to the crowds exclusively in parables: "without a parable he was speaking (ἐλάλει) nothing to them" (v 34b). That the prophecy (προφητεία) of Isa 6:9–10 is fulfilled (ἀναπληροῦται) for the non-understanding crowds by Jesus speaking to them in parables (vv 13–15) progresses to Jesus' speaking to the crowds in parables (v 34) in order that what was said through the prophet (προφήτου)[37] might be fulfilled (πληρωθῇ) (v 35a): "I will open my mouth in parables, I will utter things hidden from the foundation of the world"[38] (Ps 78:2 in v 35b).[39]

The audience recalls that in the sermon on the mount Jesus opened (ἀνοίξας) his mouth (στόμα) and taught his disciples (5:1–2) about the reign of the heavens (5:3, 10, 19, 20; 6:33; 7:21) with the crowds also present (5:1; 7:28). Now he opens (ἀνοίξω) his mouth (στόμα) in parables to the crowds with the disciples also present. Although the crowds will not understand, the disciples will understand (vv 11–12, 16–17) the things hidden (κεκρυμμένα) from the foundation of the world, the mysteries (τὰ μυστήρια) of the reign of the heavens (v 11), that Jesus reveals in the parables (v 35). In the missionary discourse Jesus already encouraged his disciples to proclaim the hidden

---

[37] F. Van Segbroeck, "Le scandale de l'incroyance: La signification de Mt. XIII, 35," *ETL* 41 (1965) 360–65, and Lambrecht, *Treasure*, 167–68, accept the variant reading "through Isaiah the prophet." For the reasons to accept the shorter reading without "Isaiah," see Metzger, *Textual Commentary*, 33; Gundry, *Use*, 119 n. 2.

[38] The longer variant "from the foundation of the world" enjoys the preponderance of external evidence; see Metzger, *Textual Commentary*, 33–34. According to Gundry, *Matthew*, 271: "Inclusion (of κόσμου) is also favored by the full form of the expression in 25:34. In fact, the parallel between these two distinctive occurrences of the expression again suggests an identification between the kingdom and the parables."

[39] Gundry, *Matthew*, 270: "Matthew puts down his usual 'through the prophet' either out of sheer habit or out of a view that the whole OT is prophetic in a large sense. Or perhaps he had in mind the designation of Asaph, the author of Psalm 78(77) according to its traditional title, as a prophet in 1 Chr 25:2; 2 Chr 29:30. Asaph is not named by the evangelist, however, because the psalm does not appear in the prophetic section of the Hebrew OT." On the text of the psalm quote, see Gundry, *Use*, 118–19, 211.

things God has empowered Jesus to reveal: "Do not fear them, for nothing is hidden (κεκαλυμμένον) that will not be revealed (by God, divine passive), and secret (κρυπτὸν) that will not be made known (by God, divine passive). What I tell you in the darkness say in the light, and what you hear in your ear proclaim upon the housetops" (10:26–27; cf. 11:25–27).[40]

In this unit on the purpose of speaking in parables (13:34–35), which climaxes the third movement of the parables discourse (13:24–35), Jesus provides a pragmatic model. He fulfills God's written prophetic plan by revealing the long-hidden mysteries of the reign of the heavens in the parables he speaks to the crowds, even though they will not understand, because his disciples will understand. So also the Matthean audience is to play its role in God's plan by revealing the mysteries of the reign it has heard and understood from Jesus in its own ministry of preaching. Those who do not understand will not prevent those who do understand from entering the reign of the heavens (13:24–30) that will embrace all peoples (13:31–32) and penetrate the whole world (13:33).

4. Matthew 13:36–52: Audience of Disciples (without Crowds)

A. Allegorical Explanation of the Parable of the Weeds (13:36-43)

Then, leaving the crowds, Jesus went into the house (οἰκίαν, v 36a), returning to the more private domain of the house (οἰκίας, v 1) he left before speaking to the crowds publicly beside the sea. He returns to the house in which he distinguished his disciples, as his true family who does the will of his Father, from the crowds (12:46–50). At the beginning of the second movement of the parables discourse (vv 10–23) the disciples, approaching (προσελθόντες) Jesus, asked a question focusing on the crowds: "Why do you speak in parables to them (αὐτοῖς)?" (v 10). Now, at the beginning of the fourth movement of the discourse (vv 36–52), inside the house and away from the crowds, the disciples approached (προσῆλθον) Jesus with a request focusing on them-

---

[40] Weaver, *Missionary Discourse,* 108: "That which is to be revealed is nothing other than that which Jesus himself has communicated orally to his disciples. God's revelation has to do with the message of Jesus. . . . That revelation which is first described in terms of the action of God is now described as the task of the disciples. . . . Thus it is Jesus' disciples through whom God's revelation is going to take place." See also Patte, *Matthew,* 196; Grilli, *Comunità,* 142–44.

selves: "Explain to us (ἡμῖν) the parable of the weeds of the field" (v 36b). This prepares for a primary focus on discipleship in the fourth movement of the parables discourse. As a further illustration that the disciples have been given to know the mysteries of the reign of the heavens (v 11), after he explained to them the parable of the sower (vv 18–23), Jesus now explains to them the parable of the weeds.

In his allegory Jesus places the following identifications upon elements of the weeds parable: The sower of the good seed (v 24) is the Son of Man (v 37), Jesus himself (8:20; 9:6; 10:23; 11:19; 12:8, 32, 40);[41] the field (v 24) is the world; the good seed are those who belong (υἱοὶ) to the reign; the weeds are those who belong (υἱοὶ) to the evil one (v 38);[42] the enemy who sowed them (v 25) is the devil; the harvest (v 30) is the end of the age; the harvesters (v 30) are angels (v 39). Just as the weeds are collected and burned up with fire (v 30), so will it be at the end of the age (v 40). The Son of Man will send his angels, and they will do the collecting (v 41a). The allegory to this point is precisely what is expected based on the parable of the weeds (vv 24–30) in its narrative progression. But then comes the surprise. The Son of Man will send his angels and they will collect (συλλέξουσιν) not from the weeds, those who belong to the evil one (v 38), as expected from the parable of the weeds (vv 28–30; cf. v 40),[43] but rather from his reign (βασιλείας, v 41), from the good seed as those who belong to the reign (βασιλείας, v 38),[44] all causes of sin (Zeph 1:3) and those who do lawlessness (Ps 37:1) (v 41)![45]

---

[41] On the Son of Man (υἱὸς τοῦ ἀνθρώπου) as an apocalyptic messianic title that Jesus applies to himself, based on the transcendent figure that functions as an agent of God's reign in Daniel 7, see C. C. Caragounis, *The Son of Man: Vision and Interpretation* (WUNT 38; Tübingen: Mohr-Siebeck, 1986) 232–50. See also my review of Caragounis in *CBQ* 49 (1987) 665–66.

[42] On the figurative meaning of υἱοὶ (sons) as expressing "nongenealogical membership," see F. Hahn, "υἱός," *EDNT* 3. 383; BAGD, 833.

[43] The three occurrences of the verb "collect," συλλέξωμεν in v 28, συλλέγοντες in v 29, and συλλέξατε in v 30, in the parable of the weeds all have the weeds (ζιζάνια) as their object, whereas the verb "gather" (συναγάγετε) is used for the wheat (σῖτον) in v 30. And in the allegory the weeds, not the wheat from the good seed, are "collected" (συλλέγεται) and burned (v 40).

[44] The reign of the Son of Man corresponds not to the field that represents the world (v 38) but to the good seed, the wheat, that represents those who belong to the reign (v 38). The good seed as well as the weeds are sown and grow together "in the field," the world (vv 24–25). *Contra* Luz, *Matthäus*, 2. 341: "Das 'Reich des Menschensohns' entspricht dem 'Acker', ist also die Welt."

[45] Gundry, *Matthew*, 273; idem, *Use*, 137–38. According to D. Marguerat, "L'Église et le monde en Matthieu 13,36–43," *RTP* 110 (1978) 119, the καὶ ("and") is explicative: "all causes of sin, that is, those who do lawlessness." See also Hagner, *Matthew 1–13*, 394.

Like the weeds that are collected and burned with fire (πυρὶ), so at the end of the age (v 40) the angels of the Son of Man will collect all "causes of sin" (σκάνδαλα) and those who do lawlessness within his reign (v 41) and "throw them into the furnace of fire (πυρός), where there will be the weeping and gnashing of teeth" (Ps 112:10) (v 42). The audience remembers that in the sermon on the mount Jesus warned his disciples that although they may prophesy, expel demons, and perform many mighty deeds in his name (7:22; cf. 10:1, 7–8), if they work lawlessness (ἀνομίαν) rather than do the will of his Father they will be separated from him and not enter the reign (7:21, 23). Now he warns his disciples that although they may belong to the reign (v 38), if they do (ποιοῦντας) lawlessness (ἀνομίαν) rather than do (ποιήσῃ) the will of his Father as members of his true family (12:49–50) they will be excluded from the reign (v 42).[46] As the audience recalls, Jesus shockingly warned that although Israelites may be those who belong (υἱοὶ) to the reign (βασιλείας) of the heavens (8:12a), if they lack faith (8:10, 13), "they will be thrown into the outer darkness, where there will be the weeping and gnashing of teeth (ἐκεῖ ἔσται ὁ κλαυθμὸς καὶ ὁ βρυγμὸς τῶν ὀδόντων)" (8:12b). Now he shockingly warns that although disciples may be those who belong (υἱοὶ) to the reign (βασιλείας) (v 38), if they do lawlessness (v 41) they will likewise experience the extreme anguish of exclusion from the reign, as they will be thrown into the fire, "where there will be the weeping and gnashing of teeth" (ἐκεῖ ἔσται ὁ κλαυθμὸς καὶ ὁ βρυγμὸς τῶν ὀδόντων) (v 42).[47]

The allegory climaxes not with warning but with encouragement for the disciples and Matthew's audience: "Then the righteous will shine like the sun (Dan 12:3)[48] in the reign of their Father" (v 43a). In contrast to those disciples who do lawlessness (ἀνομίαν) (v 41) and are excluded from the reign (v 42) (cf. 7:23), the righteous (δίκαιοι), those who do the righteousness (δικαιο-σύνην) (5:20; 6:1, 33), the will of Jesus' Father, that enables them to enter the reign of the heavens (5:20; 7:21), will shine like the sun in the reign of their Father (v 43a).[49] The disciples' being in "his reign" (βασιλείας αὐτοῦ), that

---

[46] On the parenetic nature of 13:40-43, see M. de Goedt, "L'explication de la parabole de l'ivraie (Mt. XIII, 36–43)," *RB* 66 (1959) 41–44.

[47] Gundry, *Matthew*, 145–46; Morris, *Matthew*, 195–96; Davies and Allison, *Matthew*, 2. 31; B. Schwank, "Dort wird Heulen und Zähneknirschen sein," *BZ* 16 (1972) 121–22; B. Charette, *The Theme of Recompense in Matthew's Gospel* (JSNTSup 79; Sheffield: JSOT, 1992) 140–41.

[48] Gundry, *Matthew*, 274; idem, *Use*, 138.

[49] Marguerat, "L'Église," 119: ". . . l'ἀνομία représente chez Mt le concept antithétique de la 'justice' (δικαιοσύνη); l'iniquité est stigmatisée comme une non-pratique (7,21; 13,41) de la Loi,

is, the reign of the Son of Man (v 41; cf. vv 37-38), Jesus, progresses to their being in "the reign of their Father" (βασιλείᾳ τοῦ πατρὸς αὐτῶν) (v 43a). This corresponds to their being members of the true family of Jesus by doing the will, the righteousness, of his Father, the Father Jesus reveals (11:27), who is also "their Father," that qualifies them to enter the reign of the heavens (5:20; 7:21; 12:49–50).[50]

With the same impassioned appeal that he concluded the sower parable (v 9) Jesus now concludes his explanation of the weeds parable: "Let whoever has ears hear!" (v 43b). In the case of the sower parable this appeal urged the disciples and the Matthean audience to hear, in the sense of "understand," how the sower parable applied to the crowds (failure) and to themselves (success). But in accord with the primary focus on discipleship in this fourth movement of the discourse, the appeal now progresses to urging the disciples and the audience to hear and understand how the warning and encouragement of the explanation of the weeds parable applies especially to themselves as disciples.

The allegorical explanation of the parable of the weeds (13:36–43) works pragmatically on the Matthean audience in a double way: 1) It warns them to avoid causing others to sin by doing the lawlessness that will disqualify them from the reign of the heavens, even though they belong to the reign as "good seed," as disciples who hear and understand the reign's mysteries. 2) It encourages them to be "the righteous," those who do the will of the Father Jesus reveals to them (11:27), in order to enter the reign of "their Father" as members of the true family of Jesus (12:49–50).

B. Parable of the Treasure (13:44)

Having left the crowds (v 36), Jesus utters the first parable that he addresses exclusively to his disciples.[51] As the reign of the heavens is like (ὁμοία ἐστὶν)

---

telle qu'elle a été interprétée par le Christ matthéen à l'aide du principe herméneutique du primat du commandement d'amour (24,12)." The antithetical parallelism between ἀνομία (lawlessness) and δίκαιοι (righteous) is confirmed in 23:28.

50 Gundry, *Matthew,* 274: "The kingdom of the Son of man becomes the Father's kingdom not because of any essential or temporal difference between the kingdoms, but solely for a warning emphasis on the Son of man's judgmental authority and an assuring emphasis on the Father's care of the righteous."

51 Jesus addressed the parables of the sower (vv 3–9), the weeds (vv 24–30), the mustard seed (vv 31–32), and the leaven (v 33) to both the crowds and the disciples. That he now speaks para-

the story of mustard seed (v 31) and is like (ὁμοία ἐστὶν) the story of leaven (v 33), so now it is like (ὁμοία ἐστὶν) the story of treasure hidden in the field (v 44a).[52] That the treasure is hidden (κεκρυμμένῳ) likens it to the things hidden (κεκρυμμένα) from the foundation of the world (v 35), the mysteries (τὰ μυστήρια) of the reign of the heavens (v 11), that Jesus reveals in the parables (v 35).[53] As the parable of the mustard seed took place in the field (ἐν τῷ ἀγρῷ, v 31), and the parable of the weeds took place in the field (ἐν τῷ ἀγρῷ, v 24), which Jesus identified as the world in his allegory (v 38a), so now the treasure is hidden in the field (ἐν τῷ ἀγρῷ) (v 44a).

As a man (ἀνθρώπῳ) sowed good seed in his field (v 24), and a man (ἄνθρωπος) sowed a grain of mustard in his field (v 31), both of whom represent Jesus as well as his disciples in their shared ministry of preaching the word of the reign, so now a man (ἄνθρωπος) who found the treasure hid (ἔκρυψεν) it (v 44b), similar to the woman who hid (ἐνέκρυψεν) the leaven (v 33). "Out of his joy he goes and sells all that he has and buys that field" (v 44c). Those who discover the reign of the heavens joyfully commit themselves and all that they have at their disposal to it.

Jesus' calling of the first disciples, who left their nets (4:20), their boat, and their father (4:22), everything (cf. 19:27), to follow him indicates the kind of total commitment appropriate for disciples who discover the reign. Jesus indicated not only his own complete commitment to the reign but the urgent and total commitment required of a disciple when he warned a scribe who wanted to follow him (8:19): "Foxes have holes and the birds of the sky nests, but the Son of Man has nowhere to lay his head" (8:20). To another one of his disciples (μαθητῶν), who wanted to bury his father first (8:21), Jesus urged: "Follow me and let the dead bury their own dead!" (8:22).[54] In contrast to those who hear the word of the reign and immediately receive it with joy (μετὰ χαρᾶς) (v 20), but have no root in themselves and endure only for a time (v 21), disciples, out of joy (ἀπὸ τῆς χαρᾶς),[55] commit themselves completely to the reign (v 44c). That disciples joyfully set their heart on the reign

---

bles only to his disciples accords with the emphasis upon discipleship in the fourth movement of the parables discourse (vv 36–52).

[52] For possible OT background in Prov 2:1-9, see Gundry, *Matthew*, 275.

[53] Hedrick, *Parables*, 119.

[54] B. R. McCane, "'Let the Dead Bury Their Own Dead': Secondary Burial and Matt 8:21–22," *HTR* 83 (1990) 31–43; J. Kiilunen, "Der nachfolgewillige Schriftgelehrte: Matthäus 8.19–20 im Verständnis des Evangelisten," *NTS* 37 (1991) 268–79.

[55] Gundry, *Matthew*, 276: "ἀπὸ τῆς χαρᾶς has an emphatic position."

of the heavens as their heavenly treasure (θησαυρῷ) accords with what the audience heard Jesus advise in the sermon on the mount: "Do not treasure (θησαυρίζετε) for yourselves treasures (θησαυροὺς) on earth . . . treasure (θησαυρίζετε) for yourselves treasures (θησαυροὺς) in heaven . . . for where your treasure (θησαυρός) is, there your heart will be also" (6:19–21).

Pragmatically, the parable of the treasure (13:44) provides the Matthean audience with a criterion for judging whether they are the righteous who will shine in the reign of their Father, rather than the doers of lawlessness who will be excluded (vv 41–43): Do they experience the reign of the heavens as a hidden treasure to which they joyfully give their hearts and all they have in a complete commitment?

C. Parable of the Pearl (13:45–46)

Progressing to the next parable Jesus addresses exclusively to his disciples, as the reign of the heavens is like (ὁμοία ἐστὶν) a treasure hidden in the field (v 44), so now it is like (ὁμοία ἐστὶν) a man who is a merchant seeking good pearls (v 45).[56] Whereas in the parable of the weeds a man (ἀνθρώπῳ) sowed good (καλὸν) seed (vv 24, 27, 37–38), now a man (ἀνθρώπῳ) seeks good (καλοὺς) pearls (v 45). The man (ἄνθρωπος) who unexpectedly found (εὑρὼν) a treasure hidden in the field (v 44) becomes a man (ἀνθρώπῳ) who is a merchant seeking good pearls and who finally found (εὑρὼν) one (ἕνα) not merely good but very valuable pearl (vv 45–46).[57] The parable of the treasure describes the kind of activity any man who found a treasure he was not looking for would do with verbs in the present tense: He goes (ὑπάγει), sells (πωλεῖ) all he has (ἔχει), and buys (ἀγοράζει) (v 44). But the parable of the pearl progresses to describing what a particular man, a merchant seeking good pearls,

[56] Although in both parables the reign of the heavens is compared to the whole stories of the treasure and of the pearl respectively, the different narrative progressions within these two parables are noteworthy. The parable of the treasure begins with a focus on the hidden treasure and progresses to a man who finds and buys it. But the parable of the pearl begins with a focus on a man who is a merchant seeking good pearls and progresses to his having found one very valuable pearl which he bought. Whereas the parable of the treasure puts the emphasis on the hidden treasure that anyone who unexpectedly finds will buy, the parable of the pearl puts the emphasis on the merchant who finally found and bought what he has been seeking.

[57] Gundry, Matthew, 278: "δέ, a favorite of Matthew, contrasts the finding of the one very valuable pearl with the search for merely good pearls. . . . ἕνα . . . does not reflect the indefinite meaning 'a' of the corresponding Aramaic numeral, but carries an emphatic meaning, 'one, a single.'"

who finally found one very valuable pearl, actually did with verbs in the past tense: Going away (ἀπελθὼν), he sold (πέπρακεν) all he had (εἶχεν), and bought (ἠγόρασεν) it (v 46).[58] Those who seek the reign of the heavens find it to be so extremely valuable that they give it their total devotion.[59]

That the disciples are to experience the reign as one who seeks (ζητοῦντι) and finds (εὑρὼν) what is a priority worth a complete commitment (vv 45–46) corresponds to what, as the audience recalls, Jesus commanded in the sermon on the mount: "Seek (Ζητεῖτε) first the reign (of God)[60] and its righteousness, and all these things will be added to you" (6:33). Again in the sermon on the mount Jesus assured that what disciples prayerfully seek God will enable them to find: "Ask and it will be given (divine passive) to you, seek (ζητεῖτε) and you will find (εὑρήσετε), knock and it will be opened (divine passive) to you. For everyone who asks receives, and the one who seeks (ζητῶν) finds (εὑρίσκει), and for the one who knocks, it will be opened (divine passive)" (7:7–8).

Pragmatically, the parable of the pearl (13:45–46) provides the Matthean audience with yet another criterion for determining whether they are the righteous who will shine in the reign of their Father, rather than the doers of lawlessness who will be excluded (vv 41–43): Do they experience the reign of the heavens as those who have found and committed themselves completely to what is the most valuable thing they can seek in their lives?

D. Parable of the Fish Net (13:47–50)

Moving to the third parable Jesus addresses exclusively to his disciples, as the reign of the heavens is like (ὁμοία ἐστὶν) a treasure (v 44) and is like (ὁμοία

[58] For the different aspects of Greek verb tenses, see M. Zerwick, *Biblical Greek* (Rome: Biblical Institute, 1963) 77–78. On the verb forms involved in 13:44–46, see K. L. McKay, "On the Perfect and Other Aspects in New Testament Greek," *NovT* 23 (1981) 320; idem, "Time and Aspect in New Testament Greek," *NovT* 34 (1992) 223; idem, *A New Syntax of the Verb in New Testament Greek: An Aspectual Approach* (Studies in Biblical Greek 5; New York: Lang, 1994) 47–48, 50. On πέπρακεν ("he sold") in 13:46 S. E. Porter, *Verbal Aspect in the Greek of the New Testament, with Reference to Tense and Mood* (Studies in Biblical Greek 1; New York: Lang, 1989) 268, states: "In the immediate context of narrative progression but the larger context of a parable, the reference is timeless, with the Perfect drawing attention to the significance of the reaction."

[59] Gundry, *Matthew,* 278–79: "Matthew emphasizes the desirability of whole-hearted devotion to the kingdom not only with a description of the pearl as very valuable, but also by using asyndeton ('finding . . . going away,' without a connective) and putting 'sold' in the perfect tense."

[60] For a text-critical discussion, see Metzger, *Textual Commentary,* 18–19.

ἐστὶν) a merchant seeking good pearls (v 45), so now it is like (ὁμοία ἐστὶν) a dragnet (σαγήνη) that was thrown into the sea and gathered (fish) of every kind (v 47).[61] Whereas in the parable of the weeds the harvesters were directed to gather (συναγάγετε) the wheat (v 30), now a dragnet gathered (συναγαγούσῃ) fish of every kind (v 47). "When it was full, hauling it upon the seashore and sitting down, they collected the good into containers, but the rotten they threw out" (v 48).[62]

This advances the imagery of Jesus and his disciples as "fishers" of people (4:19) in their shared ministry of proclaiming the word of the reign.[63] As the many crowds at the beginning of the parables discourse were gathered (συν-ήχθησαν) before Jesus (v 2), the "fisher" of people, so now a dragnet gathered (συναγαγούσῃ) fish, representative of people, of every kind (v 47). As Jesus, the "fisher" of people, sat down (ἐκάθητο) first beside the sea (v 1) and then sat down (καθῆσθαι) in the boat while the whole crowd, the "fish," stood upon the seashore (ἐπὶ τὸν αἰγιαλὸν) (v 2), so now hauling the net full of fish upon the seashore (ἐπὶ τὸν αἰγιαλὸν), the fishermen sat down (καθίσαντες) (v 48). Whereas in the allegory of the weeds parable the angels will collect (συλλέξουσιν) from the reign of the Son of Man all scandals and those who do lawlessness and will throw (βαλοῦσιν) them into the furnace of fire (vv 41–42), the fishermen collected (συνέλεξαν) the good fish/people into containers but the rotten fish/people they threw (ἔβαλον) out (v 48).

In the allegory of the weeds parable, that the weeds are collected (συλλέγεται) and burned by fire leads to the comparison with the final judgment: "Thus it will be at the end of the age" (οὕτως ἔσται ἐν τῇ συντελείᾳ τοῦ αἰῶνος) (v 40). That the fishermen collected (συνέλεξαν) the good fish/people into containers but the rotten fish/people they threw out (v 48) similarly proceeds to a comparison with the final judgment: "Thus it will be at the end of the age" (οὕτως ἔσται ἐν τῇ συντελείᾳ τοῦ αἰῶνος) (v 49a). The angels (ἀγγέλους) collecting from the reign those disciples who do lawlessness (v 41) progresses to the angels (ἄγγελοι) separating the evil ones, the

---

[61] "σαγήνη," EDNT 3. 222: "A dragnet is larger and more complex than a casting net (ἀμφίβληστρον) . . . so that many and various fish can be caught in it."

[62] For possible OT background in Ezekiel 47 to the parable of the fish net, see J. D. M. Derrett, "Ἦσαν γὰρ ἁλιεῖς (Mk I 16): Jesus's Fishermen and the Parable of the Net," NovT 22 (1980) 125–31.

[63] Gundry, Matthew, 279: "The metaphor of fishing may come immediately from Jesus' taking to a boat at the start of chap. 13, and ultimately from fishing for men as a figure of evangelism (4:19)."

rotten fish/people (v 48) that Jesus and his disciples will collect as "fishers" of people, from the midst of the righteous (δικαίων) (v 49), the disciples themselves, the righteous (δίκαιοι) who will shine like the sun in the reign of their Father (v 43), as well as the righteous people, the good "fish" (v 48), they will gather in their ministry (4:19). In contrast to the enemy, the devil (v 39), who sowed weeds (evil people) in the midst (ἀνὰ μέσον) of the wheat (righteous people) (v 25), the angels will separate the evil ones from the midst (ἐκ μέσου) of the righteous (v 49).[64]

The statement that the angels will throw (βαλοῦσιν) them (αὐτοὺς), the disciples who do lawlessness (v 41), "into the furnace of fire, where there will be the weeping and gnashing of teeth" (v 42) functioned as a shocking, salutary warning for disciples to avoid doing lawlessness and become the righteous who enter the reign of the heavens (v 43). But now the statement that the angels will throw (βαλοῦσιν) them (αὐτοὺς), the evil ones, from the midst of the righteous (v 49), "into the furnace of fire, where there will be the weeping and gnashing of teeth" (v 50) functions as a soothing encouragement for patience. In their mission to be "fishers" of people (4:19) the disciples can be patient with the evil people, the rotten "fish," they will gather along with the righteous people, the good "fish," encouraged that the angels of God will separate the evil from the good at the end of the age.[65]

The parable of the fish net (13:47–50) works pragmatically on the Matthean audience by encouraging them to persevere in their ministry of being "fishers" of people for the reign of the heavens. Their complete commitment to the reign (vv 44–46) as those who are righteous (v 43) enables them to live patiently with the undesirable, evil people they may gather along with the righteous people, leaving the separation of the bad from the good to God's final judgment. By so living they understand and experience another of the mysteries of the reign of the heavens (v 11).

---

[64] Gundry, *Matthew*, 280: "'From the midst' forms an antithetic parallel with the sowing of the tares 'in the midst' of the wheat (v 25). Like the phrase to which it corresponds, it also shows that the wicked are to be understood as false professors of discipleship *within the kingdom* rather than as the wicked in general. For if the latter, the righteous would have been located among the wicked and separated from them (rather than vice versa), or the wicked would have been separated from the world (rather than from the midst of the righteous)."

[65] The parable of the weeds (vv 24–30) calls for patience with the weeds as those who do not understand, because they will not prevent those who do understand from entering the reign. But the parable of the fish net (vv 47–50) calls for patience with the bad fish as those who, although gathered along with the good for the reign, prove to be wicked.

*E. Concluding Simile of the Disciple
as Scribe of the Reign (13:51–52)*

In climactic contrast to the crowds, who do not understand (οὐδὲ συνίουσιν, v 13; μὴ συνῆτε, v 14; μὴ συνιέντος, v 19), Jesus asks his disciples,
"Have you understood (Συνήκατε) all these things?" (v 51a). "All these
things" (ταῦτα πάντα) echoes "all these things" (ταῦτα πάντα) Jesus spoke in
parables to the crowds (v 34), that is, the mysteries (τὰ μυστήρια) of the reign
of the heavens (v 11), the things hidden (κεκρυμμένα) from the foundation
of the world (v 35).[66] That the disciples answer with a resounding "Yes!"
(v 51b) climactically confirms that they have been given to know the mysteries
of the reign of the heavens revealed by Jesus in the previous parables (v 11).

In response Jesus pronounces the climactic conclusion of the entire parables discourse: "Therefore (Διὰ τοῦτο) every scribe discipled with respect to
the reign of the heavens is like a man who is a householder, who brings out of
his treasure new and old" (v 52).[67] "Every scribe (γραμματεὺς) discipled
(μαθητευθεὶς) with respect to the reign of the heavens" refers to the disciples
(μαθηταὶ, vv 10, 36) who have understood the mysteries of the reign Jesus has
just revealed to them in the parables. They stand in contrast to the scribes
(γραμματεῖς) whose teaching authority Jesus surpassed in the sermon on the
mount (7:28–29). As a climactic conclusion to the previous parables in which
the reign of the heavens is like (ὁμοία ἐστὶν) a hidden treasure (v 44), a man
who is a merchant seeking good pearls (v 45), and a dragnet thrown into the
sea (v 47), every discipled scribe is like (ὅμοιός ἐστιν) a man who is a householder (οἰκοδεσπότῃ) (v 52), that is, like Jesus, the householder (οἰκοδεσπότην, 10:25; οἰκοδεσπότου, 13:27).[68]

Every discipled scribe, like the householder Jesus, brings out of his treasure
(θησαυροῦ, v 52), the hidden treasure (θησαυρῷ, v 44) that contains the mysteries of the reign of the heavens, which disciples understand (v 51) and to
which they completely commit themselves (vv 44–46), "new (καινὰ) and old
(παλαιά)" (v 52). The householder Jesus brought out "the old," the mysteries
(τὰ μυστήρια) of the reign of the heavens (v 11), hidden (κεκρυμμένα) in the

---

[66] D. E. Orton, *The Understanding Scribe: Matthew and the Apocalyptic Ideal* (JSNTSup
25; Sheffield: JSOT, 1989) 146–47.

[67] After surveying the occurrences of διὰ τοῦτο ("therefore") in Matthew, Orton, *Scribe*,
141, concludes: ". . . the phrase διὰ τοῦτο in Matthew is used most frequently *in a position of
climax*, when, with some intensification of emphasis, Jesus makes a portentous statement. . . ."

[68] Crosby, *House*, 69.

hidden (κεκρυμμένῳ) treasure (v 44) from the foundation of the world (v 35), and "the new," the parables he used to reveal the mysteries of the reign. This accords with the metaphor the householder Jesus pronounced with household imagery about combining and preserving what is new and what is old to meet the needs of a new situation: "No one sews a patch of unshrunken cloth on an old (παλαιῷ) cloak, for its fullness pulls away from the cloak and the tear becomes worse. Neither do they put fresh wine into old (παλαιούς) wineskins; otherwise, the skins burst and the wine is poured out and the skins are ruined. Rather they put fresh wine into new (καινούς) wineskins, and both are preserved" (9:16–17).[69] The disciples, who have understood the old mysteries revealed in the new parables (v 51), and as scribes discipled with respect to the reign of the heavens (v 52), are now empowered and equipped to bring out of the treasure new expressions of the old mysteries to meet new situations in their ministry of proclaiming and bringing about the reign of the heavens.[70]

With regard to pragmatics, the parabolic climax and conclusion of the parables discourse (13:51-52) enables Matthew's audience to realize that their understanding and experience of the mysteries of the reign of the heavens communicated by the parables of Jesus makes them scribes discipled for the reign of the heavens. The treasure of the hidden mysteries of old that Jesus communicates anew in his parables of the reign empowers and equips them to likewise communicate the old mysteries of the reign of the heavens in new ways for new situations.

Conclusion

The first movement of the parables discourse, addressed explicitly to the crowds and implicitly to the disciples (13:1–9), first alerts the Matthean audience to hear a further revelation of God's will in the parables Jesus speaks (13:1–3a). They are to hear what Jesus will further reveal about the reign of the heavens they themselves are to enter and experience, as well as bring others to enter and experience in the ministry they share with Jesus. The para-

---

[69] H.-J. Klauck, *Allegorie und Allegorese in synoptischen Gleichnistexten* (NTAbh 13; Münster: Aschendorff, 1978) 173. Although the sequence ends with a statement that both the new wine and the new wineskins are preserved, the sequence as a whole expresses concern that both the old (cloak, v 16; wineskins, v 17a) and the new (wine and wineskins, v 17b) be preserved.

[70] On "bringing out of the treasure" as an image for communicating, see 12:34–35.

ble of the sower (13:3b–9) encourages the audience not only to be part of the great success that will far exceed failures to hear God's word, by repenting and doing God's will in order to become the true family of Jesus (12:49–50) and enter the reign (7:21), but to preach the word of God's reign despite the many failures they will experience, because the success will inevitably far surpass the failure.

The second movement of the discourse, addressed only to the disciples (13:10–23), invites the audience to accept and appreciate their privilege of understanding the mysteries of the reign that they hear in the parables. This privilege enables them to proclaim the reign even to those unwilling to repent in order to enter it, with the hope that they will eventually open their hearts to see, hear, and understand (13:10–17). Jesus' allegorical explanation of the parable of the sower (13:18–23) assures the audience that failures to hear and understand the word of the reign are due to willfully closed hearts and ultimately to the mystery of evil (v 19). They are to persevere through the persecution they will encounter in preaching the word of the reign (vv 20–21), and they are to avoid the lure of wealth and not worry about their physical needs in proclaiming the word of the reign (v 22). They are to hear and understand the word of the reign not only by personally repenting to enter the reign, but by leading others to populate the reign through their preaching of the word that will inevitably yield a successful harvest of people far in abundance to all failures (v 23).

In the third movement of the discourse, addressed to both the crowds and the disciples (13:24–35), the parable of the weeds (13:24–30) calls for the audience to be patient that some will not understand, knowing that they will not prevent those who do understand and repent from being gathered into the reign of the heavens. Such patience gives them knowledge of another of the reign's mysteries, as they experience even now what it means to live in the reign they confidently look forward to entering fully in the future. The parable of the mustard seed (13:31–32) encourages the audience to live with the present small number of those who understand with the sure hope of the inevitable greatness of the reign that God will populate with all those who will ultimately hear, understand, and repent. Such hope gives them knowledge of another of the reign's mysteries, as they experience even now, while it is still small, the incomparable greatness of the reign that will embrace all peoples. The parable of the leaven (13:33) encourages the audience to live with the present hiddenness of those who understand with the sure hope that the reign will inevitably, through the hidden activity of God, totally transform the

world. Such hope gives them knowledge of yet another of the reign's mysteries, as they realize even now, while it is still hidden, the pervasive effect they,
with God working through them as agents of the reign, will exert upon the
whole world. The purpose of speaking in parables (13:34–35) calls the audience to play their role in God's plan by revealing the reign's mysteries in their
own ministry of preaching.

In the fourth movement of the discourse, addressed only to the disciples
(13:36–52), the allegory of the weeds parable (13:36–43) not only warns the
audience to avoid doing the lawlessness that will disqualify them from the
reign, but encourages them to be the righteous who enter the reign of their
Father as members of the true family of Jesus (12:49–50). The parable of the
treasure (13:44) provides the audience with a criterion for judging whether
they are the righteous who will shine in the reign of their Father: Do they
experience the reign as a hidden treasure to which they joyfully commit themselves completely? The parable of the pearl (13:45–46) provides yet another
criterion for determining whether they are the righteous: Do they experience
the reign as those who have found and committed themselves completely to
what is the most valuable thing they can seek in their lives? The parable of the
fish net (13:47–50) encourages the audience to persevere as "fishers" of
people for the reign. Their commitment enables them to experience another
of the reign's mysteries, as they live patiently with the evil people they gather
along with the righteous, leaving the separation of the bad from the good to
God. The conclusion of the discourse (13:51–52) enables the audience to
realize that their understanding of the mysteries communicated by the parables makes them scribes discipled for the reign. The treasure of the hidden
mysteries of old that Jesus communicates anew in his parables equips them to
likewise communicate the old mysteries of the reign of the heavens in new
ways for new situations.

CHAPTER 5

Parable of the Unforgiving Forgiven Servant in Matthew 18:21–35
(by Heil)

A progression of comparisons also characterizes the fourth major discourse in Matthew, the so-called community discourse in 17:22–18:35.[1] After an introductory superscription (17:22–23) this discourse moves the audience through a sequence of five shorter comparisons (17:24–18:20) before climaxing with a clear-cut parable of the reign of the heavens (18:21–35). After the introduction each unit of the discourse exhibits a key comparison:

1. Matt 17:22–23: Sadness in Galilee when Jesus predicts his death and resurrection
2. Matt 17:24–27: Comparison with the free sons of a king and avoiding scandal
3. Matt 18:1–5: Comparison of becoming like children to enter the reign of the heavens
4. Matt 18:6–9: Entering Life compared to Gehenna by avoiding scandal of little ones
5. Matt 18:10–14: Not losing a little one compared to a man who did not lose one sheep
6. Matt 18:15–20: Comparison of an incorrigible brother with pagans and tax collectors
7. Matt 18:21–35: Parable of the unforgiving forgiven servant

---

[1] On the Matthean community discourse, see, in addition to the commentaries, W. G. Thompson, *Matthew's Advice to a Divided Community: Mt. 17,22–18,35* (AnBib 44; Rome: Biblical Institute, 1970); T. L. Brodie, "Fish, Temple Tithe, and Remission: God-based Generosity of Deuteronomy 14-15 as One Component of Matt 17:22–18:35," *RB* 99 (1992) 697–718. We follow those who begin the discourse at 17:22 rather than 18:1.

96

As for the rationale of the above structure, the gathering together of the disciples in Galilee, Jesus' prediction to them of his death and resurrection, and their response of great sadness establish the integrity of the opening unit of the discourse (17:22–23). The question of the collectors of the double drachma to Peter in Capernaum (v 24) and Jesus' response to Peter inside the house about not scandalizing (σκανδαλίσωμεν, v 27) them secure the unity of the second unit (17:24–27). The disciples' question to Jesus "at that hour" (ἐν ἐκείνῃ τῇ ὥρᾳ, 18:1) closely connects the third unit (18:1–5), in which the disciples approached (προσῆλθον) Jesus (18:1), with the second, in which those who take the double drachma approached (προσῆλθον) Peter (17:24)[2] and the theme of the "child" (παιδίον, vv 2, 4, 5; παιδία, v 3) constitutes its unity.[3] The theme of scandal (σκανδαλίσῃ, v 6; σκανδάλων, σκάνδαλα, and σκάνδαλον, v 7; σκανδαλίζει, vv 8, 9) not only links the fourth unit (18:6–9) to the second (17:27) but establishes it as a distinct unit. The theme of "one of these little ones" (ἑνὸς τῶν μικρῶν τούτων, v 10; ἐν τῶν μικρῶν τούτων, v 14) forms an inclusion that defines the fifth unit (18:10–14). References to gatherings of "two or three" members of the community (vv 15, 16, 19, 20) delineate and unify the sixth unit (18:15–20). Finally, the theme of forgiving (ἀφήσω, v 21; ἀφῆτε, v 35) a brother (ἀδελφός, v 21; ἀδελφῷ, v 35) forms an inclusion that embraces the seventh unit (18:21–35).[4]

1. Matthew 17:22–23: Sadness in Galilee When Jesus Predicts His Death and Resurrection

The disciples were previously separated into two groups. Jesus took three of them, Peter, James, and John, up the mountain to witness his transfiguration

---

[2] Christian S. Léguisse, "Jésus et l'impôt du Temple (Matthieu 17,24 27)," *Sabu* 24 (1974) 361–62, who sees the phrase, "at that hour," as indicative of a new beginning, so that 17:24–27 is a transition that does not belong to the community discourse.

[3] Some include v 5 with the fourth rather than the third unit: Thompson, *Matthew's Advice*, 100–103; J. Gnilka, *Das Matthäusevangelium: Kommentar zu Kap. 14, 1–28, 20 und Einleitungsfragen* (HTKNT 1/2; Freiburg: Herder, 1988) 124–26. But the occurrence of "child" (παιδίον) in v 5 indicates that it belongs with 18:1–4, along with the other references to "child" in those verses. Those who treat 18:1–5 as a unit include: Schweizer, *Matthew*, 360–63; J. P. Meier, *The Vision of Matthew: Christ, Church and Morality in the First Gospel* (New York: Paulist, 1979) 128–29; idem, *Matthew* (NTM 3; Wilmington: Glazier, 1980) 200–201; Sand, *Matthäus*, 365–67.

[4] *Contra* Davies and Allison, *Matthew*, 2. 750–51, who divide 18:21–35 into two units, 18:21–22 and 18:23–35.

(17:1–2). But the other disciples were left behind and were unable to heal the son brought to them by his father (17:14–16). A new narrative sequence begins as the previously separated disciples "gathered together" (συστρε-φομένων, 17:22).⁵ That they gathered together again "in Galilee" (ἐν τῇ Γαλιλαίᾳ, v 22) after the events in the region of Caesarea Philippi (16:13–17:21) further indicates the beginning of a new narrative section, which extends until Jesus finished the words of the community discourse, "left Galilee" (μετῆρεν ἀπὸ τῆς Γαλιλαίας), and went to the district of Judea across the Jordan (19:1). The audience knows that Galilee represents the primary locale of Jesus' ministry (4:23; 9:35; 11:20–23) where he called the first disciples (4:18–22) and stands in sharp contrast to the dangerous region of Judea Jesus left after his birth (2:1, 22) and baptism by John there (3:13; 4:12). The community discourse (17:22–18:35) serves as the last narrative section before Jesus goes to Jerusalem in Judea to suffer, be killed, and be raised (16:21; 19:1).

Jesus' prediction of his death in 17:22–23 is his second statement about his destiny. The audience recalls that the first prediction of his death and resurrection to his disciples emphasized the necessity of God's plan: "It is necessary (δεῖ) that he go to Jerusalem and suffer much from the elders, chief priests, and scribes, and be killed, but on the third day be raised" (16:21). When Jesus commanded the disciples who witnessed his transfiguration to tell the vision to no one until the Son of Man has been raised from the dead, they asked why the scribes say, "It is necessary (δεῖ) that Elijah come first" (17:9–10). Jesus' reply moved from the divine necessity of Elijah's coming first to the human response that they did not recognize him when he came but did to him whatever they wished (17:11–12). The disciples understood him to be speaking about John the Baptist (17:13). As the scribes did not recognize John's role in God's plan, so Jesus predicts the same fate for himself: "So also the Son of Man is going to suffer under them" (17:12).

To his disciples gathered together in Galilee Jesus repeats the prediction of his death and resurrection but in a new and different way. The prediction that

⁵ On the meaning of συστρεφομένων as "gathered together" ("sie versammelten sich"), see Gnilka, *Matthäusevangelium*, 2. 112; Luz, *Matthäus*, 526. A recognition that the disciples were previously separated into two different sub-groups, the one that "saw the vision" (17:9) of the transfiguration (17:1–8), designated as "the disciples" (οἱ μαθηταὶ) in 17:10, 13, and the other that could not heal the boy while Jesus was away with the first sub-group, designated as "the disciples" (οἱ μαθηταὶ) in 17:16, 19, would answer Luz's question (p. 526 and n. 3) of why the disciples gathered together in 17:22, when they were just with Jesus in 17:19.

expressed primarily human agency, that Jesus as Son of Man (ὁ υἱὸς τοῦ ἀνθρώπου) is going (μέλλει) to suffer under those who did not recognize John the Baptist as Elijah (17:12), progresses to a prediction expressing both divine and human agency: "The Son of Man (ὁ υἱὸς τοῦ ἀνθρώπου) is going (μέλλει) to be delivered into the hands of men" (17:22). That Jesus as the Son of Man is going to be delivered (παραδίδοσθαι) into the hands of men expresses human agency because, as the audience knows, Judas has already been introduced as the one who delivered (παραδοὺς) him (10:4). It also expresses divine agency because Jesus' suffering and death has already been assigned to divine necessity (16:21) and "delivered" (παραδίδοσθαι) can be understood as a divine passive.[6] The divine necessity, expressed in the passive voice and aorist tense, that Jesus "be killed" (ἀποκτανθῆναι, 16:21) progresses to the human agency embraced by that divine necessity, expressed in the active voice and more imminent future tense. The men (ἀνθρώπων) into whose hands the Son of Man (ἀνθρώπου) is going to be delivered "will kill" (ἀποκτενοῦσιν) him (17:23). That Jesus "be raised" (ἐγερθῆναι, 16:21; ἐγερθῇ, 17:9) on the third day as part of God's plan progresses to "he will be raised" (ἐγερθήσεται) on the third day by God in triumphant vindication over the men who "will kill" him (17:23), as they fail to recognize his role in God's plan (17:12).

The gathered disciples' response to this prediction, "and they were greatly saddened" (17:23), indicates more acceptance of the divine necessity and inevitability of Jesus' death than Peter's vehement protest after the first prediction (16:22–23). Whereas the disciples who saw the transfiguration did not react to Jesus' prediction of his own suffering (17:12), but only understood that he was speaking to them about John the Baptist (17:13), now the whole group of disciples was greatly saddened. Their great sadness has a double reason: 1) The divine necessity that the Jesus whose glorious transfiguration Peter wanted to preserve and prolong (17:4), the Jesus who lamented, "How much longer will I be with you?" (17:17), will not be with them much longer but will suffer and die. 2) The human failure of the "men" who will kill Jesus (17:23) despite his identity as God's beloved Son and Christ (16:16; 17:5), who preached the nearness of the reign of the heavens (4:17). He will be killed just as John was killed despite his status as Elijah (17:12–13), who also preached the nearness of the reign of the heavens (3:2).

---

[6] Gnilka, *Matthäusevangelium*, 2. 112.

That the disciples "were greatly saddened" indicates that Jesus' prediction that he "will be raised on the third day" has not properly registered with them.[7] In contrast to Jesus' strong conviction that he will be raised by God after being killed by people, the disciples' great sadness advances the theme of their "little faith." In response to the disciples' inability to heal the boy brought to them by his father (17:16), Jesus lamented, "O faithless (ἄπιστος) and perverse generation, how much longer will I be with you?" (17:17). When the disciples asked Jesus why they could not expel the demon from the boy, he replied that it was because of their "little faith" (ὀλιγοπιστίαν, 17:20) in the wonder-working power of God.[8] If they have faith (πίστιν) the size of a grain of mustard (cf. 13:31–32), they will be able to command a mountain to move and "it will be moved" (by God, divine passive), and nothing will be impossible for them (17:19–20). Their great sadness at Jesus' prediction of his death and resurrection (17:23) further confirms their "little faith," their failure to share the firm faith of Jesus himself in God's power to raise him from the dead.

The great sadness at Jesus' prediction of his death and resurrection by the entire community of disciples gathered together in Galilee (17:22–23) introduces a new narrative section, the community discourse (17:22–18:35), with the following pragmatic effects upon the Matthean audience: On the one hand, the audience shares the disciples' great sadness that human beings will kill the Jesus God sent them as his beloved Son and Christ to bring about the reign of the heavens. But, on the other hand, they are called to surpass the little faith in God's plan and power demonstrated by the disciples' great sadness, as they share the strong faith of Jesus himself in God's power to raise him from the dead in triumph over human failure.[9]

---

[7] Luz, *Matthäus*, 2. 527.

[8] This is the final, climactic reference to the "little faith" of the disciples; the previous references are in 6:30; 8:26; 14:31; 16:8. On the Matthean theme of "little faith," see J. P. Heil, *Jesus Walking on the Sea: Meaning and Gospel Functions of Matt 14:22–33, Mark 6:45–52 and John 6:15b–21* (AnBib 87; Rome: Biblical Institute, 1981) 63.

[9] On the passion prediction in 17:22–23 as an introduction to the community discourse, Brodie, "Matt 17:22–18:35," 703, states: "It has the effect, before the discourse develops, of setting the hearers together in the shadow of Jesus' death and resurrection. The rule which follows, therefore, may be a Rule for the Congregation, a *Gemeindeordnung*, but is not some detached code. It is an extension of God's presence working in the human fate of Jesus, and it involves people to the core ('they were greatly saddened')."

2. Matthew 17:24–27: Comparison with the Free Sons of a King and Avoiding Scandal

As Jesus and the community of his disciples which gathered in Galilee (συστρεφομένων δὲ αὐτῶν ἐν τῇ Γαλιλαίᾳ, 17:22) came to Capernaum (ἐλθόντων δὲ αὐτῶν εἰς Καφαρναοὺμ, 17:24),[10] the setting narrows to the city where Jesus dwelt in fulfillment of God's prophetic plan for his ministry in Galilee (4:13–16). But Capernaum (11:23; cf. 8:5) also numbers among those cities that failed to repent (11:20) in preparation for entering the reign of the heavens (3:2; 4:17; 7:21) when Jesus performed his mighty deeds in them (11:20–24). In Capernaum those who take the double drachma (δίδραχμα), the amount of the temple tax (Exod 30:11–16),[11] approached Peter, the first-called, leader, and representative spokesman of the community of disciples (4:18; 10:2; 14:28–31; 15:15; 16:16–19, 22–24; 17:1, 4). To their question, "Does your teacher not pay the double drachma?" (17:24), Peter answered, "Yes" (17:25a).[12]

As Peter came into the house (ἐλθόντα εἰς τὴν οἰκίαν) in Capernaum (cf. 8:5, 14), the setting has progressed from the region of Galilee (v 22) to the city of Capernaum (v 24) to the house in Capernaum (v 25). Jesus anticipated Peter with his own question, "What do you think (Τί σοι δοκεῖ), Simon?"

---

[10] The close continuity between 17:22–23 and 17:24 further confirms that the community discourse begins at 17:22 rather than at 17:24, as proposed by Crosby, *House*, 70. Recent treatments of 17:24–27 include: J. D. M. Derrett, "Peter's Penny," *Law in the New Testament* (London: Darton, Longman & Todd, 1970) 247–65; Légasse, "Jésus et l'impôt," 361–77; N. J. McEleney, "Mt 17:24–27—Who Paid the Temple Tax?: A Lesson in Avoidance of Scandal," *CBQ* 38 (1976) 178–92; R. J. Cassidy, "Matthew 17:24–27—A Word on Civil Taxes," *CBQ* 41 (1979) 571–80; W. Horbury, "The Temple Tax," *Jesus and the Politics of His Day* (ed. E. Bammel and C. F. D. Moule; Cambridge: Cambridge University, 1984) 265–86; R. Bauckham, "The Coin in the Fish's Mouth," *Gospel Perspectives: Volume 6: The Miracles of Jesus* (ed. D. Wenham and C. Blomberg; Sheffield: JSOT, 1986) 219–52; D. E. Garland, "Matthew's Understanding of the Temple Tax (Matt 17:24–27)," *SBLASP* 26 (1987) 190–209; A. G. van Aarde, "Resonance and Reception: Interpreting Mt 17:24–27 in Context," *Scriptura* 29 (1989) 1–12; idem, "A Silver Coin in the Mouth of a Fish (Matthew 17:24–27)—A Miracle of Nature, Ecology, Economy and the Politics of Holiness," *Neot* 27 (1993) 1–25.

[11] W. Pesch, "δραχμή, δίδραχμον," *EDNT* 1. 353–54; BAGD, 192. Cassidy, "Matthew 17:24–27," 571–80, argues that the double drachma refers to a civil rather than temple tax.

[12] That the collectors of the double drachma use the plural pronoun in referring to Jesus as your (ὑμῶν) teacher confirms Peter as the representative spokesman for the community of disciples.

(v 25), that begins a comparison between those who take (λαμβάνοντες, v 24) the double drachma temple tax and the kings of the earth who take (λαμβάνουσιν, v 25) revenues or tribute.[13] To his question of whether kings take taxes "from their sons or from others" (v 25), Peter's answer, "from others," leads Jesus to draw for him the inference: "So then the sons are free" (v 26). Since Peter admitted that Jesus pays the double drachma (v 24–25), this extends the comparison. Jesus compares himself and those who pay the temple tax to either the others from whom kings take taxes or the sons who are free of taxes.

The formulation "the kings (βασιλεῖς) of the earth (γῆς)" (v 25) implies a comparison with God as the King of Jerusalem and of heaven. In the sermon on the mount Jesus directed his audience not to swear "by heaven, for it is the throne of God; nor by the earth (γῆ), for it is his footstool; nor by Jerusalem, for it is the city of the great King (βασιλέως)" (5:34–35). Those who take the temple tax collect it for the God who is King and Lord of the temple in Jerusalem. In Exod 30:11–16 (LXX) it is repeatedly emphasized that the temple tax is "for the Lord" (κυρίῳ, vv 12, 13, 14, 15; κυρίου, v 16). The "sons" (υἱοί), who are free of the taxes of earthly kings (v 26), invite a comparison both with Jesus, *the* "Son" (υἱός) of God (2:15; 3:17; 4:3, 6; 8:29; 11:27; 14:33; 16:16; 17:5), the heavenly King, and with the other "sons" (υἱοί) of God, the heavenly Father (5:9, 45), as well as with the "sons" (υἱοί) of the reign (βασιλείας) of the heavens (8:12; 13:38). Jesus' comparison thus proceeds as follows: If even the "sons" of earthly kings are free of taxes, then surely Jesus and his disciples, *the* Son and "sons" of God and of the reign of the heavens, are free of paying the temple tax to their heavenly Father.[14]

Although Jesus and his disciples as sons of the reign of the heavens are free of the temple tax, Jesus nevertheless directs Peter to pay it, so that "we," Jesus and Peter as representative of the community of disciples, "not scandalize" (μὴ σκανδαλίσωμεν) them (v 27). Since "being scandalized" obstructs one's entrance into the reign of the heavens (5:20, 29–30; 11:6, 11–12; 13:11, 21, 41,

---

[13] Légasse, "Jésus et l'impôt," 369, recognizes both the involvement of the reader and the parabolic nature of Jesus' question: ". . . la formule d'introduction 'Que t'en semble' (τί σοι δοκεῖ) nous situe en plein dialogue scolaire: à travers l'apôtre c'est le lecteur qui est interpellé et éveillé au problème. Celui-ci prend la forme d'une courte parabole."

[14] On the comparison involved here, see Meier, *Matthew*, 196–97; Bauckham, "Coin," 221; C. L. Blomberg, *Matthew* (NAC 22; Nashville: Broadman, 1992) 270.

52, 57; 15:12), not scandalizing those who take the temple tax (v 24) means not hindering them from entering the reign of the heavens. Jesus' divinely authoritative empowerment of Peter to find in the mouth of the first fish he catches a "stater" (στατῆρα), a coin worth double the temple tax,[15] and give it to them for both Jesus and himself (v 27) climaxes with a subtle irony. Peter, one of the "sons" of the reign of the heavens, is to take (λαβὼν) the stater (v 27) provided by God through Jesus' power as *the* Son of God[16] and give it to those who take (λαμβάνοντες) the temple tax for God (v 24) in contrast to the kings of the earth, who take (λαμβάνουσιν) taxes from others rather than from their own sons (vv 25–26).

Jesus' miraculous empowerment of Peter illustrates how "nothing is impossible" for those who have faith in the power of God (17:20). Jesus and Peter, the representative of the community of disciples, are not to scandalize, not to hinder from entering the reign of the heavens, even those who take the temple tax from the "sons" of the reign, even those associated with the temple establishment, which includes the "men" (17:22–23), the elders, chief priests, and scribes, who will kill Jesus in Jerusalem (16:21).

With regard to the pragmatics of the comparison of this second unit of the community discourse (17:24–27), their faith in the power of Jesus as *the* Son of God to provide what they need empowers Matthew's audience, although they like Jesus and Peter are "free sons" of the reign of the heavens, not to exercise their freedom, if it means they will hinder anyone, even apparent enemies, from entering the reign of the heavens.

3. Matthew 18:1–5: Comparison of Becoming Like Children To Enter the Reign of the Heavens

"At that hour" (ἐν ἐκείνῃ τῇ ὥρᾳ, 18:1) in which those who take the double drachma approached (προσῆλθον) Peter in Capernaum (17:24) the disciples likewise approached (προσῆλθον) Jesus (v 1) in the house (17:25) at Capernaum. Their question, "Who then (ἄρα) is greatest in the reign of the heavens?" (v 1), flows from Jesus' statement, "So then (ἄρα) the sons are free" (17:26), with its implicit comparison between the sons of earthly kings and the sons of the reign of the heavens. After Jesus called a child and stood it in their midst (v 2), he presents another comparison. Unless the disciples turn

[15] BAGD, 764; "στατήρ," *EDNT*, 3. 267.
[16] Bauckham, "Coin," 225; Garland, "Temple Tax," 207.

and become "like" (ὡς) children, they will not even enter into the reign of the heavens (v 3).[17]

That the disciples must turn or be converted (στραφῆτε, v 3) continues the call for repentance or conversion at the arrival of the reign of the heavens (3:2; 4:17).[18] The audience remembers that in the sermon on the mount Jesus told his disciples ("For I say to you") that unless (ἐὰν μὴ) their righteousness far surpasses that of the scribes and Pharisees, "you will not enter into the reign of the heavens" (5:20). At the sermon's conclusion he further warned that not everyone who calls him Lord "will enter into the reign of the heavens," but the one who does the will of his Father in heaven (7:21). Adding to these entrance requirements, he now warns, "Amen I say to you," that unless (ἐὰν μὴ) the disciples are converted and become like children, "you will not enter into the reign of the heavens" (v 3). This follows closely upon Jesus' previous plea for the disciples introduced with the same formula, "For amen I say to you" (ἀμὴν γὰρ λέγω ὑμῖν, 17:20; cf. 18:3), to increase their faith. If (ἐὰν) they have faith like (ὡς) a grain of mustard, nothing will be impossible for them (17:20).

Jesus' further appeal, whoever humbles oneself "like" (ὡς) this child, extends the comparison and answers the disciples' question (v 1) with a provocative paradox: "This one" (οὗτός), the one with child-like humility and lowliness, is paradoxically the greatest in the reign of the heavens (v 4). That "whoever" (ὅστις), each disciple in the community, will humble (ταπεινώσει) oneself "like this child" (ὡς τὸ παιδίον τοῦτο) (v 4) explains to the audience what it means for the disciples to be converted (στραφῆτε) and "become like children" (γένησθε ὡς τὰ παιδία) (v 3).[19] Jesus has already presented to the audience his own child-like humility as *the* Son of the heavenly Father for imitation: "Learn from me, for I am meek and humble (ταπεινὸς) of heart" (11:29).[20]

Jesus confirms his own child-like humility with his additional appeal: "And

[17] On the low social status of children in antiquity and their role in Matthew, see Carter, *Households and Discipleship*, 95–114.

[18] W. Schenk, "στρέφω," *EDNT* 3. 281; BAGD, 771.

[19] Schenk, "στρέφω," 3. 281: "Στρέφω is used of *conversion* in . . . Matt 18:3 (v. 4 uses ταπεινόω synonymously)." See also H. Giesen, "ταπεινόω," *EDNT* 3. 335.

[20] H. Giesen, "ταπεινός," *EDNT* 3. 333: "In the cry of rejoicing in Matt 11:29 the qualification τῇ καρδίᾳ is not intended as an intensification of the humble condition; rather, it delimits the area in which Jesus is lowly and gives to ταπεινός in combination with πραΰς the sense of humble."

whoever receives one such child in my name, receives me" (v 5). The exhortations to convert and become metaphorically "like" children (v 3) and to humble oneself "like" a child (v 4) progress to literally receiving any real child (ἐν παιδίον τοιοῦτο) into the household community of Jesus' ("in my name") disciples (v 5).[21] Whoever receives (δέξηται) one such child in the name of Jesus, "receives me" (ἐμὲ δέχεται), Jesus himself (v 5). And, as Jesus stated in the missionary discourse, whoever "receives me" (ἐμὲ δεχόμενος) "receives (δέχεται) the one who sent me" (10:40), God the Father himself.[22] The audience recalls that the magi's worship of the child (παιδίον, 2:8–11) Jesus prefigured this reception of Jesus in receiving a child. Acquiring a child-like humility (vv 3–4) and actually receiving children into the community (v 5) will thus enable the disciples to better accept and participate in Jesus' own humble submission to God the Father's will that he be killed (17:22–23) as well as his humble refusal to exercise his freedom in order to avoid scandalizing anyone from entering the reign of the heavens (17:24–27). By welcoming into their household community marginal children with whom Jesus identified himself, the disciples can assure Jesus' humble presence among them after he has been killed and raised.

Pragmatically, the comparison of the third unit (18:1–5) provokes the audience to shun the usual concept of greatness by humbling themselves like children in imitation of Jesus himself in order to experience entrance into and the paradoxical greatness of the reign of the heavens. They are to enable Jesus himself to be present among them by welcoming into their familial and household community the children who represent Jesus in his humility of submitting himself to the will of God his Father.

4. Matthew 18:6–9: Entering Life Compared to Gehenna by Avoiding Scandal of Little Ones

The fourth unit (18:6–9) continues the second unit's theme of avoiding scandal (17:24–27) and the third unit's theme of child-like humility for entrance into the reign of the heavens (18:1–5). Jesus and Peter not scandalizing (μὴ

---

[21] Nearly the entire community discourse takes place in "the house" (τὴν οἰκίαν, 17:25), underscoring that the community of disciples is a familial, household community. It was in "the house" (τῆς οἰκίας, 13:1) that Jesus pointed to the disciples as his true family (12:49–50). According to W. Egger, "παιδίον," EDNT 3. 4, Matt 18:4 places "the whole discourse on the household of God under the banner of the child." See also Crosby, House, 71.

[22] Weaver, Missionary Discourse, 117–18; Grilli, Comunità, 168–70.

σκανδαλίσωμεν) those who collect the temple tax (17:27) progresses to anyone, especially anyone among the community of disciples, who scandalizes (σκανδαλίσῃ) a disciple, "one of these little ones" who believe in Jesus (v 6). "Whoever (ὅστις) will humble oneself like this (τοῦτο) child" (v 4) and "whoever (ὃς ἐὰν) welcomes one (ἕν) such (τοιοῦτο) child" (v 5) progress to "whoever (ὃς δ' ἂν) scandalizes one (ἕνα) of these (τούτων) little ones" (v 6). Appropriate to the paradox that the one who humbles oneself like a "little child" (παιδίον, diminutive of παῖς)[23] is "greatest" (μείζων, vv 1, 4) in the reign of the heavens, the disciples are now described as a community of "little ones" (μικρῶν) (v 6). Since they believe (πιστευόντων) in "me" (ἐμέ), Jesus (v 6), they have the child-like faith (πίστιν) Jesus urged his disciples to have (17:20), as they believe they receive "me" (ἐμέ), Jesus, when they receive a little child in his name (v 5).

That it would be preferable for anyone who scandalizes a fellow disciple to have an ass's millstone (μύλος ὀνικὸς)[24] hung around his neck and be drowned in the depth of the sea (v 6) introduces the comparison of this unit. The exaggerated and unrealistic image is a characteristic that this comparison shares with the parables.[25] Since it would be extraordinary if not impossible for human beings to hang such a heavy millstone around someone's neck and then toss both the millstone and the person into the depth of the sea, the verbs "be hung" (κρεμασθῇ) and "be drowned" (καταποντισθῇ) can be taken as divine passives. That "it would be preferable" (συμφέρει) implies a comparison with something that is worse than such an inescapable and definitive death. But what could be worse that being drowned in the depth of the sea?

As the audience remembers, in the sermon on the mount Jesus stated that it would be preferable (συμφέρει, 5:29, 30) for one whose right eye or right hand scandalizes (σκανδαλίζει, 5:29, 30) him to lose those parts of his body rather than be thrown into fiery Gehenna (5:29, 30; cf. 5:22), the place of eternal punishment.[26] In accord with what Jesus advised in the missionary

---

[23] BAGD, 604.

[24] "μύλος," *EDNT* 2. 445: "The image here is that of an especially heavy (bored) millstone." "ὀνικός," *EDNT* 2. 519: "A donkey-driven millstone was significantly heavier than that of a hand mill." See also BAGD, 529.

[25] Donahue, *Gospel in Parable*, 15–17; Scott, *Hear Then the Parable*, 35–42; Blomberg, *Interpreting the Parables*, 45–47.

[26] On the origin and significance of "Gehenna" as the "place of eternal punishing fire" and the "place of eternal torment for the godless after the final judgment," see O. Böcher, "γέεννα," *EDNT* 1. 239 and also BAGD, 153.

discourse, it would be preferable to have one's body drowned in the sea than to have the God who can destroy both body and soul throw one into Gehenna (10:28).[27] And in accord with the parables discourse it would be preferable to be drowned in the depth of the sea than to have the Son of Man, who will collect from his reign all scandals (σκάνδαλα) and those who do lawlessness, throw one into the furnace (κάμινον) of fire, that is, Gehenna,[28] where there will be the extreme and everlasting torment of the despairing "weeping and gnashing (βρυγμὸς) of teeth" (13:41–42).[29] The implicit comparison between being drowned in the sea and being thrown into the place of eternal punishment thus shocks the community of disciples into avoiding the extremely serious offense of scandalizing, that is, doing anything to hinder from entering the reign of the heavens "one of these little ones," a fellow disciple who believes in Jesus (v 6).[30]

Jesus then places scandal within the community of disciples into a global context: "Woe to the world because of the scandals (τῶν σκανδάλων), for the scandals (τὰ σκάνδαλα) must come, but woe to the person through whom the scandal (τὸ σκάνδαλον) comes" (v 7). Although "the scandals" in general "must" (ἀνάγκη) inevitably come into the world according to the necessity of God's plan,[31] the person through whom "the scandal" comes individually experiences the "woe" (οὐαὶ) that contributes to the "woe" (οὐαὶ) of the world, that is, the "threat of judgment and exclusion from eschatological salvation."[32] In the context the person through whom "the scandal" comes refers to whomever in the community of disciples scandalizes (σκανδαλίσῃ) one of the little ones, a fellow disciple, who believes in Jesus (v 6). The "woe" of such a disciple refers to being thrown into fiery Gehenna, an eternal punishment worse than being drowned in the depth of the sea (v 6). The progression from the general "scandals" of the world to "the" specific "scandal" of an individual (v 7), which parallels the previous progression from the general exhortation of the community of disciples (v 3) to the specific exhortation of the individual (vv 4–6), sharpens the warning for each individual disciple to avoid scandalizing a fellow disciple.

---

[27] Weaver, *Missionary Discourse*, 109; Grilli, *Comunità*, 145–48.

[28] Böcher, "γέεννα," *EDNT* 1. 240: "In other places in the NT where the eternal punishment of fire is considered, the idea of γέεννα is always in the background, even when the word is not actually present. This is true especially for the use of κάμινος (Matt 13:42, 50)."

[29] V. Hasler, "βρυγμός," *EDNT* 1. 227–28.

[30] Patte, *Matthew*, 250.

[31] A. Strobel, "ἀνάγκη," *EDNT* 1. 78.

[32] H. Balz, "οὐαί," *EDNT* 2. 540.

Moving from scandalizing to being scandalized and from third-person address to the more personal and individual second-person singular address, Jesus develops the comparison of this unit. If "your" (σου) hand or "your" (σου) foot scandalizes "you" (σε), cut it off and throw it away from "you" (σοῦ); it is better for "you" (σοί) to enter into life maimed or lame than to have two hands or two feet and be thrown (by God, divine passive) into the eternal fire (v 8). Similarly, if "your" (σου) eye scandalizes "you" (σε), take it out and throw it away from "you" (σοῦ); it is better for "you" (σοί) to enter into life with one eye than to have two eyes and be thrown (by God) into the Gehenna of fire (v 9). The implicit comparison that it is preferable (συμφέρει) for one who scandalizes a disciple to be drowned in the depth of the sea than to be thrown into fiery Gehenna (v 6) progresses to the explicit comparison that it is better (καλόν) for a disciple to enter into eternal life without a self-scandalizing hand, foot, or eye than to be thrown into the eternal fire of Gehenna (vv 8–9).[33]

The child-like humility required for the disciples to enter into (εἰσέλθητε εἰς) the reign of the heavens (v 3) progresses to the humility of eliminating a scandalizing part of one's body in order to enter into (εἰσελθεῖν εἰς) eternal life (vv 8–9). The comparison in the sermon on the mount that it is preferable (συμφέρει) to lose a scandalizing part of one's body than to be thrown with one's whole body into Gehenna (5:29–30) now moves the audience forward to the comparison that it is better (καλόν) to enter into the eternal life without a scandalizing part of one's body than to be thrown with those parts into the eternal fire of Gehenna (vv 8–9). The extreme importance of doing whatever is necessary to avoid Gehenna compared with entering "into the life" (εἰς τὴν ζωὴν, vv 8–9) accords with Jesus' previous comparative exhortation in the sermon on the mount: "Enter (Εἰσέλθατε) through the narrow gate, for the gate is wide and the way is broad that leads into the destruction (εἰς τὴν ἀπώλειαν),[34] and those who enter through it are many. How narrow the

---

[33] The parallel between "the Gehenna of fire" (τὴν γέενναν τοῦ πυρός, v 9; cf. 5:22) and "the eternal fire" (τὸ πῦρ τὸ αἰώνιον, v 8) confirms that "the life" (τὴν ζωὴν, vv 8–9) means eternal or eschatological life. L. Schottroff, "ζῶ," *EDNT* 2. 106: "Matthew . . . uses the noun ζωή, along with βασιλεία τῶν οὐρανῶν or χαρά, etc., as an expression for eschatological salvation, which in his Gospel is vividly and emphatically set over against eternal punishment."

[34] Hagner, *Matthew 1–13*, 179: "εἰς τὴν ἀπώλειαν, 'to destruction,' refers, as elsewhere in the NT, to the final ruin brought by eschatological judgment. The counterpart in v 14 is ζωήν, 'life.' Surprisingly, in Matthew this is the only occurrence of the word ἀπώλεια with this meaning, despite Matthew's frequent reference to final, apocalyptic judgment."

gate and confined the way that leads into the life (εἰς τὴν ζωὴν), and those who find it are few!" (7:13–14). The comparison between entering eternal life and being thrown into the place of eternal punishment thus shocks each individual disciple into avoiding being scandalized by any part of his body (vv 8–9), especially since such scandal can in turn cause a disciple to scandalize a fellow disciple (vv 6–7).

The fourth unit's (18:6–9) comparisons with being thrown into the eternal fire of Gehenna have the following pragmatic effects: They shock each member of the audience to avoid not only scandalizing a fellow disciple (vv 6–7) but also being scandalized by any part of one's body (vv 8–9), which could cause the scandal of a fellow disciple, in order to enter eternal life.

5. Matthew 18:10–14: Not Losing a Little One Compared to a Man Who Did Not Lose One Sheep

Returning to the second-person plural address of the entire community of disciples (cf. v 3), the fifth unit (18:10–14) continues the fourth unit's focus on the disciples as child-like "little ones" who believe in Jesus (v 6). The individual warning for anyone who scandalizes (σκανδαλίσῃ) one of these little ones (v 6) progresses to Jesus' communal warning: "See that you do not treat contemptuously (καταφρονήσητε) one of these little ones" (v 10). As Jesus tells the community, "for I say to you" (cf. v 3), these little ones enjoy a special heavenly protection.[35] In accord with their entrance and greatness in the reign of the heavens (οὐρανῶν, v 3, 4) "their angels in the heavens (οὐρανοῖς) constantly look upon the face of my Father in the heavens (οὐρανοῖς)" (v 10).[36] That their angels constantly look upon the face (πρόσωπον) of "my

---

[35] On the use of γὰρ, "for," here R. A. Edwards, "Narrative Implications of *Gar* in Matthew," *CBQ* 52 (1990) 648, notes: "The disciples are informed about the status of certain angels in the heavenly realm, which is once again the kind of privileged information that often is present in this Gospel. Acceptance depends on the reader's acknowledgment of the authority of the speaker."

[36] On the heavenly protection of "guardian angels" here, see Gnilka, *Matthäusevangelium*, 2. 131–32; Sand, *Matthäus*, 370; Davies and Allison, *Matthew*, 2. 770–72; Gundry, *Matthew*, 364; A. Stock, *The Method and Message of Matthew* (Collegeville: Liturgical Press, 1994) 289–90; I. Broer, "ἄγγελος," *EDNT* 1. 14: "The idea of the guardian angel, frequent already in the OT and in the rabbis, but less common in the apocryphal writings, occurs in Matt 18:10 (cf. also Acts 12:15)."

Father" (v 10) underscores the special relation each little one has not only with the Jesus in whom they believe (v 6) but with God his Father.[37]

Jesus' question addressed to the whole community of disciples, "What do you think?" (Τί ὑμῖν δοκεῖ, v 12),[38] introduces the comparison of this unit, as it develops Jesus' previous question addressed only to Peter, "What do you think (Τί σοι δοκεῖ, Simon?" (17:25).[39] The disciples (and the audience) are expected to affirm Jesus' question that opens the parable of the lost sheep:[40] Will not (οὐχὶ) a man who has a hundred sheep leave the ninety-nine on the mountains and go and search for the one that went astray? (v 12).[41] Indeed, if he finds it, as Jesus solemnly assures the community, "Amen I say to you," he rejoices over it more than over the ninety-nine that did not go astray (v 13).

The one sheep, the "one of them" that strayed (πλανηθῇ) (v 12), represents "one of these little ones" that the disciples are not to treat contemptuously (v 10). The man who seeks (ζητεῖ) the one strayed (πλανώμενον) sheep (v 12) represents God, Jesus, and his disciples. As the audience knows, in Ezek 34:16 (LXX) God says that, in contrast to the shepherds (kings) of Israel, "I myself will seek" (ζητήσω) the lost (ἀπολωλός) and bring back the strayed (πλανώμενον) sheep.[42] To the Canaanite woman who pleaded for him to heal her daughter (15:22) Jesus replied: "I was not sent (by God, divine passive) except to the lost (ἀπολωλότα) sheep of the house of Israel" (15:24).

---

[37] K. Berger, "πρόσωπον," *EDNT* 3. 181: "To 'see' someone's face means to have contact with that person. The decisive poles of relationship (countenance and seeing) thus metaphorically represent the entire relationship. This also refers to contact with God either through the cult or by eschatological fellowship with God: The cultic sense . . . is seen . . . probably also in Matt 18:10 (the contact the 'little ones" angels have with God is probably to be understood as intercession)."

[38] On the omission of 18:11, see Metzger, *Textual Commentary,* 44–45.

[39] The parallel progression between these two questions further confirms that 17:24–27 belongs to the community discourse.

[40] On the parable of the lost sheep in 18:12–14, see, in addition to the commentaries, Thompson, *Matthew's Advice,* 156–63; J. Dupont, "Les implications christologiques de la parabole de la brebis perdue," *Jésus aux origines de la christologie* (BETL 40; ed. J. Dupont; Gembloux: Duculot, 1975) 331–50; H. Weder, *Die Gleichnisse Jesu als Metaphern: Traditions- und redaktionsgeschichtliche Analysen und Interpretationen* (FRLANT 120; 2d ed.; Göttingen: Vandenhoeck & Ruprecht, 1980) 168–77; Scott, *Hear Then the Parable,* 405–17; Blomberg, *Interpreting the Parables,* 179–84; Lambrecht, *Treasure,* 37–52.

[41] The interrogative word οὐχὶ, "not," expects the answer "Yes"; see Zerwick and Grosvenor, *Grammatical Analysis,* 1. 58; BAGD, 598.

[42] Heil, "Ezekiel 34," 704.

Jesus had already included his disciples in his ministry to the lost sheep when he told them not to go to the Gentiles or the Samaritans (10:5) but to "go rather to the lost (ἀπολωλότα) sheep of the house of Israel" (10:6).[43]

Drawing out the comparison between the one lost sheep and God's will, Jesus concludes: "Thus (οὕτως) it is not the will before your Father in heaven that one of these little ones be lost" (v 14). That not one (ἕν) of these little ones be lost (ἀπόληται) corresponds to the man seeking the one (ἕν) sheep that strayed (πλανώμενον) (v 12) and finding (εὑρεῖν) the sheep that was thus lost (v 13). The little ones' angels looking upon the face of my (μου) Father in heaven (v 10) progresses to what is the will (θέλημα) before your (ὑμῶν) Father in heaven (v 14).[44] Jesus' heavenly Father is the heavenly Father of his disciples. The audience recalls that in the sermon on the mount he exhorted them to be perfect as your (ὑμῶν) heavenly Father is perfect (5:48), and to do the will (θέλημα) of my (μου) Father in heaven in order to enter the reign of the heavens (7:21). He pointed to his disciples (12:49) as his true family who does the will (θέλημα) of my (μου) Father in heaven (12:50). Now they are to do the will of Jesus' Father, who is also their Father, by not allowing even one of the little ones, even one of their fellow disciples, to stray and be lost from the community (v 14). And since "lost" (ἀπόληται) also connotes "perish" in the sense of being destined for eternal destruction and death,[45] the community of disciples is not to allow even one of their little ones to be thrown into the eternal fire of Gehenna (cf. 18:6–9).[46]

With regard to pragmatics, the comparison of the fifth unit (18:10–14) calls for the Matthean audience to do the will of their heavenly Father by exercising a special care and concern for each one of their fellow believers. They are not to look down upon or treat contemptuously any member of their community, but rather to go out of their way to bring back any straying member and thus experience the joy of finding and accompanying one who is lost into the eternal life of the reign of the heavens.

---

[43] Weaver, *Missionary Discourse,* 84; Grilli, *Comunità,* 101–7; Heil, "Ezekiel 34," 702.

[44] We opt for the reading "your Father" here rather than the variants, "my Father" or "our Father"; see Metzger, *Textual Commentary,* 45; Davies and Allison, *Matthew,* 2. 776 n. 109.

[45] Kretzer, "ἀπόλλυμι," 1. 135–36; BAGD, 95; Morris, *Matthew,* 466 n. 39.

[46] Davies and Allison, *Matthew,* 2. 776: "The will of God concerning the little ones, that they should not perish, becomes an imperative for the believer." See also Patte, *Matthew,* 252.

6. Matthew 18:15–20: Comparison of an Incorrigible Brother with Pagans and Tax Collectors

Returning to the second-person singular address of an individual within the community of disciples, the sixth unit (18:15–20) continues the fifth unit's focus on a straying member of the community, as Jesus proceeds: "If your (σου) brother sins against you (σὲ), go and correct him between you (σοῦ) and him alone. If he heeds you (σου), you have gained your (σου) brother" (v 15; cf. LXX Lev 19:17).[47] The previous unit's one sheep (v 12), representative of "one of these little ones" (vv 10, 14) who believe in Jesus (v 6), now becomes "your brother," a fellow member of the familial household of disciples (12:46–50), who sins (ἁμαρτήσῃ) "against you" (v 15) as a concrete example of the one sheep who strays (πλανηθῇ) from the community (v 12). Just as the man left the ninety-nine sheep and went (πορευθεὶς) and sought out the one that strayed (v 12), so a disciple is to go (ὕπαγε) and correct a brother disciple who sins against him, but to do so privately, "between you and him alone" (v 15). If he heeds the correction, the disciple has restored his brother to the community (v 15) in correspondence to the man who found and rejoiced over the one lost sheep (v 13).[48] By thus "gaining" (ἐκέρδησας) his brother (v 15) for the community and the reign of the heavens, the disciple has done the will of his heavenly Father that not one of the little ones be "lost" (ἀπόληται) (v 14).[49]

---

[47] On the inclusion of the textual variant εἰς σὲ, "against you," Gundry, *Matthew,* 367: ". . . Matthew's inserting 'between you and him alone' in the next clause and expanding the section about forgiving a brother who has sinned against a brother (vv 21–35) favor the originality of 'against you.'" See also Davies and Allison, *Matthew,* 2. 782 n. 3.

[48] Thompson, *Matthew's Advice,* 187–88: "Matthew has emphasized the shepherd's concern for the one sheep going astray as background for the zeal which a disciple is to show toward a brother who has sinned (p. 187). . . . the parable is central to the discourse. It explains the prohibition addressed to all the disciples (v. 10a), establishes the doctrinal statement about the will of the Father (v. 14) and provides concrete imagery for the application to the individual disciple (vv. 15-17). The shepherd's natural response to the sheep going astray is a common human experience which helps the disciples understand the will of the Father that not 'one of these little ones' be lost, and the Father's will determines that a disciple should react to his brother who has sinned by imitating the shepherd in his spontaneous zeal to prevent his brother from being lost" (p. 188).

[49] On the correspondence between "not losing" and "gaining" here, see BAGD, 429; Matt 16:25–26; Luke 9:25. Gundry, *Matthew,* 367: "'Have gained' contrasts with the distinctive 'be lost' in v 14."

Jesus' command for the disciple to go (ὕπαγε) and correct "your brother" (ἀδελφόν σου), "your brother" (ἀδελφός σου) who sins against you (v 15), develops his previous plea for reconciliation in the sermon on the mount: "If you bring your gift to the altar and there remember that your brother (ἀδελφός σου) has something against you, leave your gift there at the altar and go (ὕπαγε) first and be reconciled with your brother (ἀδελφῷ σου), and then come and offer your gift" (5:23-24).[50] And such correction presupposes what Jesus previously advised in the sermon on the mount: "Why do you notice the splinter in the eye of your brother (ἀδελφοῦ σου), but neglect the beam in your own eye? How can you say to your brother (ἀδελφῷ σου), 'Let me take the splinter out of your eye,' while the beam is in your own eye? Hypocrite, first take the beam out of your own eye, and then you will see clearly to take the splinter out of the eye of your brother (ἀδελφοῦ σου)" (7:3–5).

If the sinning brother does not heed the correction, the disciple is to persist by taking with him one or two others, so that, in accord with Deuteronomy 19:15, "Every matter may be established upon the evidence of two or three witnesses" (v 16). If he refuses to heed them, the disciple is to tell the church, the assembled community (ἐκκλησία, cf. 16:18), and if he refuses to heed even the entire assembly of disciples, then is introduced the comparison of this unit: "Let him be to you like (ὥσπερ) a pagan and a tax collector" (v 17).[51]

Although being treated like a pagan (ἐθνικὸς) and a tax collector (τελώνης) implies exclusion from the community (v 17),[52] it does not mean that the community is to treat the sinning member contemptuously (v 10) or as irretrievably "lost" (v 14). The audience recalls from the sermon on the mount that the disciple is to love the sinning brother even if he is an enemy (5:43–45). If the disciple continues to love and greet the sinning brother, he

---

[50] Gundry, *Matthew*, 368: "The gaining of one's brother includes far more than personal reconciliation, then; it means winning back to the church a professing disciple who stands in danger of forfeiting salvation through sin against a fellow disciple."

[51] On the problem of communal correction in 18:15–17, see G. Segalla, "Perdono 'cristiano' e correzione fraterna nella comunità di 'Matteo' (Mt 18,15–17.21–35)," *Studia Patavina* 38 (1991) 503–5; S. Tellan, "La Chiesa di Matteo e la correzione fraterna: Analisi di Mt 18,15–17," *Laurentianum* 35 (1994) 91–137.

[52] Gundry, *Matthew*, 368: "The command to ostracize him takes a singular address, σοι, because of the parallel with the preceding instructions. The involvement of the church in the final plea and the switch to the second-person plural in v 18 show, however, that all the disciples are to join in the ostracism." See also Davies and Allison, *Matthew*, 2. 785; D. C. Sim, "The Gospel of Matthew and the Gentiles," *JSNT* 57 (1995) 27–28.

will be loved and greeted in return, for even tax collectors (τελῶναι) love those who love them (5:46), and even pagans (ἐθνικοὶ) greet those who greet them (5:47). For a brother who sins (ἁμαρτήσῃ, v 15) to be treated like a tax collector (τελώνης, v 17) means extending to him the same compassion and mercy that Jesus, the friend of tax collectors (τελωνῶν) and sinners (ἁμαρτωλῶν) (11:19), demonstrated when he and his disciples shared table fellowship with the tax collectors (τελωνῶν) and sinners (ἁμαρτωλῶν) (9:10–11). He exhorted his opponents to go and learn the meaning of Hosea 6:6, "I desire mercy and not sacrifice," for Jesus did not come to call the righteous but sinners (ἁμαρτωλούς) (9:13).

The authority to "bind and loose" on earth what will then be considered "bound and loosed" by God in heaven that Jesus gave Peter along with the "keys" to open and close the reign of the heavens for those on earth (16:19; cf. 23:13) he now extends to the whole community of disciples: "Amen I say to you (ἀμὴν λέγω ὑμῖν), whatever you bind (δήσητε) on earth will be bound (δεδεμένα) in heaven, and whatever you loose (λύσητε) on earth will be loosed (λελυμένα) in heaven" (v 18). Jesus thus gives the community the power to "bind and loose," that is, to make whatever authoritative decisions, especially about the forgiveness of sins (cf. John 20:23), that are necessary "on earth" to restore to the community and guide into the reign "of the heavens" a sinning member (vv 15–17) who strays from the community (vv 10–14).[53]

Continuing to address the community, "Again I say to you," Jesus adds that "if two of you agree on earth about any matter for which they ask, it will be done for them by my Father in heaven" (v 19). That every matter (πᾶν ῥῆμα) concerning the correction of a sinning member be established on the evidence of two (δύο) or three witnesses (v 16) progresses to every matter (παντὸς πράγματος) for which two (δύο) agreeing disciples ask about in prayer (v 19). Again the audience recalls that in the sermon on the mount Jesus similarly assured his disciples of God's answer to their prayers in a con-

---

[53] On the meaning of the technical terms "bind" and "loose," see F. Staudinger, "δέω," EDNT 1. 293–94; K. Kertelge, "λύω," EDNT 2. 368–69; Luz, Matthäus, 2. 465–66; Sand, Matthäus, 372–73; Davies and Allison, Matthew, 2. 635–41. Gnilka, Matthäusevangelium, 2. 139: "Mit der Vollmacht zu lösen ist im konkreten Fall die Möglichkeit gegeben, den Sünder, der die Zurechtweisung annimmt, wieder in die Gemeinschaft zurückzuholen, und zwar nicht nur bei der Verhandlung seines Falles, sondern auch zu jedem Zeitpunkt in der Zukunft." Gundry, Matthew, 369: "Here, association with the problem of a sinning disciple points to disciplinary retention of sins by means of ostracism, and to forgiveness of sins by means of restoration to fellowship."

text of communal correction (7:1–5): "Ask (Αἰτεῖτε) and it will be given you.
. . . For all who ask (αἰτῶν) receive. . . . What man among you, whose son
will ask (αἰτήσει) him for bread, will give him a stone? Or if he will ask (αἰτήσει) for a fish, will give him a snake? If you then who are cheap know how to
give generous gifts to your children, how much more will your Father in
heaven give generous things to those who ask (αἰτοῦσιν) him?" (7:7–11).[54]
So also when two disciples agree "on earth" about any matter involving a sinning brother for which they ask (αἰτήσωνται), it will be done for them by "my
Father in heaven," the same "Father in heaven" whose face the angels of the
little ones constantly look upon (v 10), and the same "Father in heaven"
whose will it is that not even one little one be lost (v 14).[55] As whatever the
community binds and looses "on earth" will be bound and loosed "in heaven"
(v 18), so whatever two agreeing disciples ask for in prayer "on earth" will be
done for them by God "in heaven" (v 19).

"For" (γάρ), as Jesus concludes this unit on communal correction, "wherever two or three are gathered in my name, there am I in their midst" (v 20).[56]
The gathering (συνηγμένοι) of two or three disciples in the name of Jesus
(v 20) climaxes the references to the two or three witnesses needed for the
matter of correcting a sinning member (v 16) and to the two disciples who
agree (συμφωνήσωσιν) on any matter (v 19). As the reception of one child "in
my name" is the reception of "me," Jesus himself (v 5), so in the gathering of
two or three disciples "in my name" Jesus himself is present in their midst
(v 20). Indeed, just as Jesus placed a child "in their midst" (v 2), so he himself
is "in their midst" (v 20; cf. 1:23). Jesus thus reinforces that his Father will
answer the prayer of two disciples agreeing about a matter of communal correction (v 19) by assuring his own presence in any gathering of disciples concerned with restoring a sinning member to the community (v 20).[57] In
addition to welcoming a child in Jesus' name (v 5) such a gathering of disci-

---

[54] On the coherence between 7:1–5 and 7:7–11, see McEleney, "Matthew 7:1–12," 490–500,
who on the translation of 7:11 notes: "In Matt 7:11, the listeners are not really called 'wicked,' as
the *NAB* has it. They are indeed πονηροί, but πονηρός in this verse has the same connotation
of 'ungenerous, cheap, begrudging,' which it has in Matt 6:23; 18:32; 20:15."

[55] On the use of αἰτέω, "ask," to refer to prayer, see W. Radl, "αἰτέω," *EDNT* 1. 43.

[56] Edwards, "*Gar* in Matthew," 648: "The present intimacy of Jesus and the Father are
assumed: if you gather in my name, I am there and my presence will lead to the Father's support
of your requests. This is another example of the privileged information that is typical of Jesus'
use of *gar* clauses."

[57] Gundry, *Matthew*, 370; Gnilka, *Matthäusevangelium*, 2. 140.

ples (v 20) assures Jesus' presence with the community even after he has been killed and raised (17:22–23).

The sixth unit (18:15–20) with its comparison works pragmatically by calling each member of the audience to privately correct a fellow believer who sins, but to seek the help of others and of the whole believing community if necessary. If this fails, the community is still to extend to the sinner the same mercy, fellowship, and love Jesus demonstrated to pagans and tax collectors. The audience is assured of divine ratification of their decisions, of divine answer to their prayers, and of Jesus' presence among them as they strive to restore a sinner to the community.

7. Matthew 18:21–35:
Parable of the Unforgiving Forgiven Servant

As those collecting the didrachma approached (προσῆλθον) Peter and questioned him (17:24), and as the disciples at that same hour approached (προσῆλθον) Jesus and questioned him (18:1), so now the Peter whom Jesus empowered to pay the temple tax for both of them in order to avoid scandal (17:27) approaches (προσελθὼν) Jesus and questions him (18:21). Peter's question about forgiveness advances Jesus' previous instruction about correction. Whereas Jesus directed any individual disciple whose fellow disciple, "your brother" (ἀδελφός σου), sins (ἁμαρτήσῃ) "against you" (εἰς σὲ) to go and correct and thus gain "your brother" (ἀδελφόν σου) for the community (v 15), an actual, named disciple, Peter, now asks Jesus how many times "should I forgive" (ἀφήσω) if "my brother" (ἀδελφός μου) will sin (ἁμαρτήσει) "against me" (εἰς ἐμὲ) (v 21). To Peter's offer to forgive a generous but limited as many as "seven times" (ἑπτάκις) (v 21) Jesus counters with a surprising increase in the generosity to an unlimited number of as many as "seventy times seven" (ἑβδομηκοντάκις ἑπτά) (v 22).[58]

With a "therefore" (Διὰ τοῦτο) oriented to explaining why Peter should forgive in an unlimited way,[59] Jesus introduces the comparison of this unit

---

[58] This represents a dramatic reversal of Lamech's unrestrained vengeance in Gen 4:24 (LXX): "If Cain is avenged seven times (ἑπτάκις), then Lamech seventy times seven (ἑβδομηκοντάκις ἑπτά)." See also "ἑπτάκις," *EDNT* 2. 48; "ἑβδομηκοντάκις," *EDNT* 1. 369.

[59] *Contra* D. Patte, "Bringing Out of the Gospel-Treasure What Is New and What Is Old: Two Parables in Matthew 18–23," *Quarterly Review* 10 (1990) 83–84, who denies the continuity between the parable (18:23–35) and Peter's question about forgiveness (18:21–22), which he

with another parable of the reign:[60] The reign of the heavens "has become like" (ὡμοιώθη) a man (cf. 13:24, 31, 44, 45), a king, who wanted to settle accounts with his servants (v 23).[61] One servant who was a debtor of an incredibly huge and obviously exaggerated amount of "ten thousand talents" (μυρίων ταλάντων) was brought to the king (v 24).[62] As the servant had no way of paying back such a huge amount, the lord ordered him to be sold, along with his wife and children and all his possessions, in payment of the debt (v 25). That the king (v 23) is now referred to as the lord (ὁ κύριος, v 25) facilitates an association with Jesus, whom Peter has just addressed as "Lord" (Κύριε, v 21).

Then falling down the servant worshipped him saying, "Have patience with me, and I will pay you back everything" (v 26). That the servant "worshipped" (προσεκύνει) him associates this king (v 23) who is "the lord" (v 25)

---

sees as an interruption, as he fails to recognize that 18:15-20 focusses upon fraternal correction rather than forgiveness.

[60] On the parable in 18:23–35, see, in addition to the commentaries, J. D. M. Derrett, "The Parable of the Unmerciful Servant," *Law in the New Testament* (London: Darton, Longman & Todd, 1970) 32–47; Thompson, *Matthew's Advice,* 202–37; T. Deidun, "The Parable of the Unmerciful Servant (Mt 18:23–35)," *BTB* 6 (1976) 203–24; B. B. Scott, "The King's Accounting: Matthew 18:23-34," *JBL* 104 (1985) 429–42; idem, *Hear Then the Parable,* 267–80; M. C. de Boer, "Ten Thousand Talents? Matthew's Interpretation and Redaction of the Parable of the Unforgiving Servant (Matt 18:23–35)," *CBQ* 50 (1988) 214–32; Donahue, *Gospel in Parable,* 72–79; Blomberg, *Interpreting the Parables,* 240–43; Patte, "Bringing Out," 82–93; Segalla, "Perdono," 506–18; Lambrecht, *Treasure,* 53–68; B. Weber, "Alltagswelt und Gottesreich: Überlegungen zum Verstehenshintergrund des Gleichnisses vom 'Schalksknecht' (Matthäus 18,21–35) auf dem Hintergrund des 'Erlassjahres'," *TZ* 50 (1994) 124–51; Herzog, *Parables as Subversive Speech,* 131–49.

[61] On ὡμοιώθη, "has become like," as the introduction to the parable, Carson, "ΟΜΟΙΟΣ Word Group," 479, remarks: ". . . the kingdom *has become like* the situation in which a servant may be forgiven much and yet not be forgiven: such a person will be called to account."

[62] Such exaggeration is a common characteristic of the fictional nature of parables. Jeremias, *Parables of Jesus,* 210–11: ". . . the sum exceeds any actual situation; it can only be explained if we realize that both μύρια and τάλαντα are the highest magnitudes in use (10,000 is the highest number used in reckoning, and the talent is the largest currency unit in the whole of the Near East). The magnitude of a debt beyond conception was intended to heighten the impression made upon the audience by its contrast with the trifling debt of 100 denarii (v. 28)." B. Schwank, "τάλαντον," *EDNT* 3. 332: "Roughly speaking, we might compare one talent with the modern 'million.'" See also BAGD, 803. On Matthew's use of monetary concepts in conjunction with forgiveness, see B. Weber, "Schulden erstatten–Schulden erlassen: Zum matthäischen Gebrauch einiger juristischer und monetärer Begriffe," *ZNW* 83 (1992) 253–56.

with both Jesus and his Father, the only ones worthy of such "worship" in Matthew.[63] However much the servant's pleading worship may indicate his good intentions, the enormous amount of his debt renders his promise to pay back "everything" (πάντα, v 26) a virtual impossibility. That the lord (ὁ κύριος) has compassion (σπλαγχνισθεὶς) on that servant (v 27) further enables the audience to link "the lord" with Jesus, who in his ministry as "shepherd" has previously had compassion (ἐσπλαγχνίσθη, 9:36; 14:14; σπλαγχνίζομαι, 15:32) on the crowds (see also 20:34).[64] Exemplifying the kind of unlimited forgiveness Jesus called for (v 22) when Peter asked how many times "should I forgive" (ἀφήσω) (v 21), the lord released the servant and forgave (ἀφῆκεν) him the loan (v 27), the enormous debt of ten thousand talents (v 24).[65] The forgiveness of an enormous debt representative of an egregious sin complements the forgiveness of the same fault an unlimited number of times.

The dual dimension of "the lord," representative of both Jesus and God his Father, who forgave (ἀφῆκεν) the servant an exceedingly large debt (v 27) advances the theme of the divine forgiveness of sins now available to human beings through Jesus. The audience recalls that when Jesus saw the faith of those who brought the paralytic to him, he announced, "Courage, child, your sins are forgiven (ἀφίενταί)" (9:2). The response of some of the scribes that this man "blasphemes" (βλασφημεῖ), that is, exercises a prerogative reserved for God (9:3; cf. Mark 2:7), underlines the divine nature of the forgiveness.[66] Jesus explained that the words, "your sins are forgiven (ἀφίενταί)," are equivalent to and complement the divine power of the words of healing, "rise and walk" (9:5). To demonstrate that as the Son of Man, a heavenly figure, he has the divine authority "on earth" to forgive (ἀφιέναι) sins, Jesus pronounced

---

[63] Note the use of προσκυνέω for "homage" or "worship" either of Jesus as King (2:2, 8, 11), Lord (8:2; 15:25), and Son of God (14:33) (see also 9:18; 20:20; 28:9, 17) or of his Father as the Lord God (4:9–10). According to BAGD, 716, when human beings are the object of προσκυνέω, they "are to be recognized by this act as belonging to a superhuman realm." See also M. A. Powell, "A Typology of Worship in the Gospel of Matthew," *JSNT* 57 (1995) 8.

[64] Heil, "Ezekiel 34," 700–701, 703–4.

[65] The technical monetary term commonly translated as "loan" (δάνειον) complements the other monetary terms, "debtor" (ὀφειλέτης, v 24) and "to pay back" (ἀποδοῦναι and ἀποδοθῆναι, v 25; ἀποδώσω, v 26); see Weber, "Schulden," 254. It is therefore not an "embarrassing" word nor need it mean that the king transformed the "debt" into a "loan," as Derrett, "Unmerciful Servant," 37–40, proposes.

[66] O. Hofius, "βλασφημία," *EDNT* 1. 220: "Blasphemy against God can be referred to explicitly. But βλασφημέω used absolutely also means *blaspheme God.*"

the words of healing (9:6).[67] The crowds then glorified God who gave such authority, the divine authority to forgive sins, to human beings (9:8).

That the servant went out and found one of his fellow servants who owed him a hundred denarii (v 28) exemplifies Peter's case of a disciple whose fellow disciple, a brother, sins against him (v 21). In stark contrast to the servant's debt of ten thousand talents (μυρίων ταλάντων, v 24) his fellow servant owes a significant but much less amount of one hundred denarii (ἑκατὸν δηνάρια, v 28), one hundred days' wages.[68] Whereas the lord ordered the servant who could not possibly pay back (ἀποδοῦναι) his enormous debt to be sold with his family and possessions in order to be at least partially paid back (ἀποδοθῆναι) (v 25), the servant resorts to violence by seizing and choking his fellow servant, demanding, "Pay back (ἀπόδος) what you owe!" (v 28). As the servant himself fell down and worshipped the lord saying, "Have patience with me, and I will pay you back everything" (v 26), so his fellow servant fell down and begged the servant saying, "Have patience with me, and I will pay you back" (v 29). Whereas the servant made the impossible promise of repaying everything (πάντα), the fellow servant made the quite possible promise of simply repaying the much lesser amount of his debt. In sharp contrast to the lord, who had compassion on the servant, releasing him and forgiving him his debt (v 27), the servant refuses the much more reasonable request of his fellow servant as he went and threw him into prison until he should pay back what was owed (v 30).

That the fellow servants explained to their lord everything that happened because they were greatly saddened (ἐλυπήθησαν σφόδρα) by it (v 31) enables the audience to liken them to the disciples, who were likewise greatly saddened (ἐλυπήθησαν σφόδρα) when Jesus predicted his death and resurrection at the beginning of the community discourse (17:23). As the disciples were greatly saddened that Jesus would be killed by people who failed to appreciate him as God's agent for bringing about the reign of the heavens, so the fellow servants are greatly saddened that the servant failed to appreciate the divine forgiveness he received from the lord since he did not extend it to his fellow servant.

When the lord calls in his servant, he appropriately addresses him as

---

[67] On the "Son of Man" as an apocalyptic messianic title that Jesus applies to himself, based on the transcendent figure that functions as an agent of God's reign in Daniel 7, see Caragounis, *Son of Man*, 232–50. See also my review of Caragounis in *CBQ* 49 (1987) 665–66.

[68] B. Schwank, "δηνάριον," *EDNT* 1. 296; BAGD, 179.

"ungenerous" (πονηρέ) servant,[69] since he failed to extend any generosity to his fellow servant, although "I," the lord, generously forgave (ἀφῆκα) "you," the servant, "all" (πᾶσαν) this debt (v 32), the enormous debt of ten thousand talents (v 24), "all" (πάντα) that the servant vainly promised to pay back (v 26). Although the lord forgave the servant since "you begged (παρεκάλεσάς) me" (v 32), the servant himself did not extend even the slightest patience much less forgiveness to his fellow servant who begged (παρεκάλει) for patience in order to repay his debt (v 29).

The lord then forces his servant to realize his failure to appreciate the forgiveness he received by extending it to his fellow servant: "Was it not necessary for you to have mercy (ἐλεῆσαι) on your fellow servant, as I also had mercy (ἠλέησα) on you?" (v 33). With the "as" (ὡς), the lord compares his generous and compassionate divine mercy with the servant's human mercy that must flow from it. The audience knows the servant to be condemned. The servant has failed to actualize Jesus' beatitude, "Blessed are the merciful (ἐλεήμονες), for they shall receive mercy (ἐλεηθήσονται)" (5:7). The lord (κύριος, vv 25, 27, 31, 32) of the parable's mercy advances the theme of the mercy the Lord Jesus demonstrated throughout his ministry to those who cried out to him, "Lord have mercy" (Κύριε ἐλέησον) (15:22; 17:15; cf. 9:27). Indeed Jesus exhibited the mercy God his Father called for in Hosea 6:6: "It is mercy (ἔλεος) I desire and not sacrifice" (9:13; 12:7).

As the servant himself seized, choked (v 28), and threw his fellow servant in prison "until he should pay what was owed" (v 30), so now his angry lord delivered him to the torturers (βασανισταῖς) for an eternal punishment, quite appropriately "until he should pay back all that was owed" (v 34).[70] Since the servant, who vainly promised to repay "all" (πάντα) of his enormous debt (v 26), failed to appreciate that his lord forgave him "all" (πᾶσαν) of this debt (v 32), he will now be forced to repay "all" (πᾶν) that was owed (v 34). The servant who begged his lord for patience (v 26) but denied patience to his fellow servant (vv 29–30) will now have all the time he needs in eternity to repay all of his debt (v 34). The servant's eternal loss of the lord's forgiveness (v 32) because he did not extend the mercy he received from the lord to his fellow servant (v 33) underscores Jesus' previous teaching about the eternal

[69] On the meaning of πονηρέ here as "ungenerous, cheap, begrudging" rather than "wicked," see McEleney, "Matthew 7:1–12," 499.
[70] W. Stenger, "βασανίζω," *EDNT* 1. 200: "The *torturers* to whom a master spoken of in a parable consigns his unmerciful servant (Matt 18:34) point to the eschatological punishment."

loss of God's forgiveness: Every sin and blasphemy will be forgiven people, but blasphemy against the Spirit will not be forgiven. Whoever speaks against Jesus as the Son of Man will be forgiven, but whoever speaks against the holy Spirit will not be forgiven neither in this age nor in the age to come (12:31–32).

In answer to Peter's question of how many times "I should forgive" (ἀφήσω) when "my brother" (ἀδελφός μου) sins against me (v 21) Jesus draws out the consequence of the parable as an explanation (διὰ τοῦτο) of his call for unlimited forgiveness (v 22): Thus also my Father will do to "you" (ὑμῖν), not just Peter but the whole community of disciples he represents with his question, unless "you forgive" (ἀφῆτε) each one "his brother" (ἀδελφῷ αὐτοῦ) from your hearts (v 35). To forgive from "your hearts" (καρδιῶν ὑμῶν), from the intellectual and emotional center of your beings,[71] means to forgive like the lord of the parable, who generously forgave from his compassion (v 27) and mercy (v 33). The unforgiving servant of the parable did not take the forgiveness he received to heart, so that he was not able to forgive from his heart (vv 32–33). Each disciple in the community risks the loss of God's forgiveness in eternal punishment, if he does not forgive a fellow disciple as a heartfelt response to the same generous, merciful, compassionate, and unlimited forgiveness he has received from God.

The audience's interaction with this parable extends the knowledge it gained earlier in the discourse. The comparison that "thus (οὕτως) it is not the will before your Father in heaven that one of these little ones be lost" (v 14) now progresses in the parable to "thus (οὕτως) also my heavenly Father will do to you, unless you forgive, each one his brother, from your hearts" (v 35). Just as the disciples were compared with the shepherd who sought the one lost sheep so that they should not allow even one straying disciple to be lost from the community (vv 12–14), so now the disciples are compared to the unforgiving forgiven servant so that they should each extend to one another the same forgiveness they have received from God, their Father (vv 23–35).

With a comparison between human and divine forgiveness Jesus taught the disciples to pray: "Forgive us our debts (cf. 18:28, 30, 32, 34), as (ὡς) we also have forgiven our debtors (cf. 18:24)" (6:12). He then taught that divine forgiveness depends upon human forgiveness: "For if you forgive people their transgressions, your heavenly Father will also forgive you. But if you do not

---

[71] Sand, "καρδία," *EDNT* 2. 250: "Καρδία refers thus to the *inner person*, the seat of understanding, knowledge, and will . . . ."

forgive people, neither will your Father forgive your transgressions"
(6:14–15). This unit's comparison about forgiveness reinforces and complements this teaching. Not only does divine forgiveness *depend* upon human
forgiveness, but divine forgiveness, once it is received, *demands* human forgiveness from the heart.

With regard to pragmatics, the comparison of the seventh and final unit
(18:21–35) of the community discourse urges each member of the audience
to forgive a fellow believer in an unlimited way because this is the way God
forgives. The audience's experience of God's generous, compassionate, and
merciful forgiveness available to them through Jesus should be taken to heart
and move them to forgive one another in the same way that Jesus and his
Father forgives, from their hearts.

Conclusion

The community discourse (17:22–18:35) functions as Jesus' final gathering
together with his disciples in Galilee before he goes on to his suffering, death
and resurrection in Judea (17:22–23; cf. 19:1; 16:21). As such it climaxes the
previous major discourses Jesus addressed to his disciples in Galilee—the
sermon on the mount (5:1–7:29), the missionary discourse (9:35–11:1), and
the parables discourse (13:1–53). It involves the Matthean audience in a
sequential series of comparisons that indicate how Jesus will be present with
them as a community of disciples and how they are to relate to one another as
members of the community after the death and resurrection of Jesus.

1) After the audience identifies with the disciples' great sadness at Jesus'
prediction of his death and resurrection (17:22–23), the first comparison is
between the kings of the earth and the reign of the heavens. It calls the audience, who like Jesus and Peter are "free sons" of the reign of the heavens, to
believe in the power of Jesus as *the* Son of God to provide what they need not
to exercise their freedom, if it means they will hinder anyone, even apparent
enemies, from entering the reign of the heavens (17:24–27).

2) The comparison between children and the disciples provokes the audience to shun the usual concept of greatness by humbling themselves like marginal children in imitation of Jesus himself in order to experience entrance
into and the paradoxical greatness of the reign of the heavens. They are to
enable Jesus himself to be present among them after his death and resurrection by welcoming into their familial and household community the children
who represent Jesus in his humility (18:1–5).

3) The comparisons with being thrown into the eternal fire of Gehenna shock and provoke each member of the audience to avoid scandalizing, that is, hindering from entering the reign of the heavens, a "little one," a fellow disciple who believes in Jesus. Each member must also avoid being scandalized by any part of one's body, which could in turn cause the scandal of a fellow disciple, in order to assure one's entry into the eternal life of the reign of the heavens (18:6–9).

4) The comparison between the shepherd seeking a single lost sheep and the disciples calls for the audience to do the will of their heavenly Father by exercising a special care and concern for each one of their fellow believers. They are not to look down upon or treat contemptuously any member of their community, but rather to go out of their way to bring back any straying member and thus experience the joy of finding and accompanying one who is lost into the eternal life of the reign of the heavens (18:10–14).

5) The comparison between an incorrigible disciple and the pagans and tax collectors invites each member of the audience to privately correct a fellow believer who sins, but to seek the help of others and of the whole believing community if necessary. If this fails, the community is still to extend to the sinner the same mercy, fellowship, and love Jesus demonstrated to pagans and tax collectors. The audience is assured of divine ratification of their decisions, of divine answer to their prayers, and of Jesus' presence among them, even after his death and resurrection (17:22–23), as they strive to restore a sinner to the community (18:15–20).

6) The comparison between the parable of the unforgiving forgiven servant and the disciples urges each member of the audience to forgive a fellow believer in an unlimited way because it is the way God himself forgives. The audience's experience of God's generous, compassionate, and merciful forgiveness through the Jesus who is present in the community (18:5, 20) even after his death and resurrection (17:22–23) demands that they forgive one another "from their hearts," the same way that Jesus and his Father forgives (18:21–35).

CHAPTER 6

Parable of the Householder
in Matthew 20:1–16

(by Carter)

1. The Parable in the Context of Matthew 19–20

Matt 19:1 concludes Jesus' community discourse (17:22–18:35) with the formulaic clause "When Jesus had finished these sayings." The audience knows from the clause's three previous uses (7:28; 11:1; 13:53), two of which have been associated with parables, that it functions to close a discourse of Jesus and connect it with the ongoing story. Matt 19:1 also moves the story ahead as Jesus leaves Galilee, the setting for his ministry since 4:17, and enters Judea on his way to Jerusalem (21:1). In 19:2, his addressees and his activity also change. The disciples (cf. 18:1, 21) give way briefly in 19:2 to the crowds, while works of healing replace his teaching. In 19:3, new characters appear (the Pharisees) while the instruction of the community discourse and healings of 19:2 give way to a dispute (19:3–12).

After the four exchanges in Matthew 19 between Jesus and the religious leaders (19:3–9), disciples (19:10–15), the "rich man" (19:16–22), and the disciples (19:23–30), the opening words of Matthew 20, "For the reign of the heavens is like . . . ," signal for the audience a change of form.[1] The formula

---

[1] In addition to the discussions cited below and the commentaries, see T. Manson, *The Sayings of Jesus* (London: SCM, 1949) 218–21; C. L. Mitton, "Expounding the Parables VII: The Workers in the Vineyard (Matthew 20:1–16)," *ExpTim* 77 (1966) 301–11; G. de Ru, "The Conception of Reward in the Teaching of Jesus," *NovT* 8 (1966) 202–22, esp. 202–12 for previous research; Via, *Parables*, 147–55; Crossan, *In Parables*, 111–15; J. D. M. Derrett, "Workers in the Vineyard: A Parable of Jesus," *JJS* 25 (1974) 64–91; J. Riches, "Parables and the Search for a New Community," *The Social World of Formative Christianity and Judaism* (ed. J. Neusner et al.;

ὁμοία with a dative ("like") recalls the audience not only to the sequence of parables in Matthew 13 (13:31, 33, 44, 45, 47, 52) and to the individual parable beginning at 18:23, but also to the pervasive previous concern with the reign of the heavens. The presence of a solitary parable in 20:1–16 requires the audience to find a good continuance in the narrative's sequence.[2]

Several details have been noted, though, which may pose problems for the audience's attempt to integrate the parable with its context. T. W. Manson argues that there is a contradiction between the elevated role prophesied for the twelve in 19:28 and the equal treatment of all the workers portrayed in the parable.[3] M. A. Tolbert[4] argues that the apparent links of the parable with 19:16–30 provided by 19:30 and 20:16[5] are in fact non-existent because the parable does not use the reversal theme in a significant way. In addition, the use of a parable with a wealthy householder as its hero seems to contradict the previous pericope's hostility to wealth (cf. 19:21, 23, 24).

None of these factors, however, poses a major difficulty for the audience. Manson's claimed inconsistency between 19:28 and the equality of the workers arises because he reads 19:28–29 as a reference to the twelve alone, rather than understanding them as representative of all disciples who have "left everything" and "followed" Jesus (19:27). In affirming the equal treatment for

---

Philadelphia: Fortress, 1988) 235–63, esp. 245–52, 254–57; L. Schenke, "Die Interpretation der Parabel von den 'Arbeitern im Weinberg' (Mt 20:1–15) durch Matthäus," *Studien zum Matthäusevangelium: Festschrift für Wilhelm Pesch* (ed. L. Schenke; Stuttgart: Katholisches Bibelwerk, 1989) 245–68. For discussion of the parable's interpretation from the second to the sixth centuries, see J. M. Tevel, "The Labourers in the Vineyard: The Exegesis of Matthew 20:1–17 in the Early Church," *VC* 46 (1992) 356–80.

[2] As redaction critics have noted, Mark 10:31–32 lacks a parable at this point. Matthew has inserted this parable from "M" material. Gundry, *Matthew*, 395–99, notes that the parable has numerous Mattheanisms in it, indicating considerable shaping of the material.

[3] Manson, *Sayings of Jesus*, 218.

[4] Tolbert, *Perspectives*, 60.

[5] In tradition and redaction discussions, 20:16 is widely recognized as an addition to an original parable; so Via, *Parables*, 148–49; Breech, *Silence of Jesus*, 142–43. Schweizer, *Matthew*, 391, notes in 18:14, 35 a similar technique; Matthew "has taken a saying, introduced a parable with it, then restated the saying another way at the end." Crossan, *In Parables*, 112, argues that Matthew has added 20:14–15 as well as 20:16 to a parable of Jesus. The importance of the good/evil contrast in the gospel suggests v 15 is redactional (cf. Matt 5:45; 7:11, 17-18; 12:34; 22:10), but v 14 (both 20:14a and b) is necessary to complete the story. For further discussion on the original form and redactional changes, see Scott, *Hear Then the Parable*, 285–87.

all workers in the payment (20:9–12), the parable coheres with the promise of 19:28–29 that all disciples will share equally in the final vindication of Jesus.[6]

Tolbert's objection that the parable is not related to the reversal motif of 19:30 and 20:16 lacks force because the parable is not as devoid of the "first/last" motif as she insists. In addition to the explicit reversal of the first and last in 20:8b and 20:10a, the very important formulation of the parable's ending (20:13–16, see below) means that 20:16b functions as a warning of a reversal that will take place in the judgment if a wrong evaluation of the householder's present action continues.

Nor is the use of the wealthy landowner a major difficulty. The audience knows by Matthew 19 that not all disciples are required to sell everything in order to follow Jesus. Both Jesus and Peter, for instance, have houses (8:14; 9:10, 28; 13:1, 36). The instruction to sell all is given in 19:21 to one whose heart is set on, and whose identity is defined by, wealth (a "rich man," πλού-σιος; 19:23, 24). Such a drastic measure is necessary when wealth prevents commitment to the reign of God (cf. warnings of 6:19–34; 13:22).

The audience finds, moreover, several points of connection between the parable and its context. The parable concerns the "reign of the heavens" (20:1) which has been at the heart of Jesus' proclamation and actions since 4:17. As we observed in chapter 3 above, this tensive symbol has also been given content not only in Jesus' words and actions but also in previous parables (13:31, 33, 44, 45, 47; also 18:23). Since Matthew 13, the audience has encountered the symbol ten times. In 16:19 Peter is given the "keys of the kingdom,"[7] and 16:29 repeats the familiar emphasis on the future manifestation of God's reign in Jesus' return. In the opening four verses of Matthew 18, the symbol appears three times as the disciples inquire about being the greatest in the "reign of the heavens." Jesus' response points to the humbleness and marginality of children as the way of entry to and style of life in God's reign (18:1, 3, 4).[8] The parable of the king in 18:23-35 likens, or better, contrasts, God's merciful actions and their shaping of appropriate human behavior to

---

[6] See the discussion of 19:28–29 in Carter, *Households and Discipleship*, 125–27.

[7] For discussion of the wide range of possible interpretations, see Davies and Allison, *Matthew*, 2. 634–41. They argue that Peter's key provides access to "the royal dominion of God in the last time," and understand this role to be particularly expressed in Peter's teaching authority (pp. 638–39). See also Garland, *Matthew*, 172–73.

[8] Davies and Allison, *Matthew*, 2. 757–58; Carter, *Households and Discipleship*, 90–114.

the actions of the unmerciful, forgiven but unforgiving servant.[9] In Matthew 19 the different and marginal quality of the way of life created by the presence of God's reign is imaged by outsiders such as "eunuchs" (19:12) and children (19:14), and by the impossibility of the rich man's entry to the reign (19:23–24).[10] The use of the phrase "reign of the heavens" in 20:1 enables the audience to draw this material together. The parable of 20:1–16 continues the gospel's ongoing definition and description of life in relation to God's saving presence, and present and future action.

In addition to the symbol "reign of the heavens," other linguistic items assist the audience to connect this parable with its context. The connective γάρ ("for") in 20:1 secures the link with 19:16–30 by indicating to the audience that an example follows.[11] The repetition from 19:30 of the πρῶτος ("first") and ἔσχατος ("last") pairing in 20:8 and 20:16 (cf. also πρῶτος in 20:10, and ἔσχατος in 20:12, 14) reinforces the connection. Πρῶτος appears again in 20:27 (redefined by διάκονος in 20:26 and δοῦλος in 20:27) thereby linking 20:1–16 with the following pericope, 20:17–28. Further, the householder's self-designation as "good" (ἐγὼ ἀγαθός εἰμι, 20:15b) builds on Jesus' comment to the young man in 19:17 that "there is one who is good" (ἀγαθός).[12]

Along with these links the audience hears a third and vital connection between the parable and the rest of Matthew 19–20. The parable's main character is identified in 20:1 as a householder (οἰκοδεσπότης).[13] This designa-

---

[9] See Heil's discussion in the previous chapter.

[10] Carter, *Households and Discipleship*, 56–145.

[11] Edwards, *"Gar* in Matthew," 636–55, esp. 654.

[12] Patte, *Matthew*, 275–78, develops this linguistic link at a thematic level arguing unconvincingly that the two chapters are concerned with "good things." The householder's hiring of workers is a good thing for them since it supplies their means of living. In 19:3–9 Jesus proclaimed marriage to be a good thing which God has gifted from the beginning. The Pharisees, though, are like the rich young man and the workers hired for the vineyard; they cannot accept the goodness of God and so cling to their previous understandings and/or wealth.

[13] The noun οἰκοδεσπότης is first used in the fourth century by Alexis, though Plato, *Laws*, 954B, uses a similar form οἰκίας δεσπότης ("master of the house") and Xenophon, *Memorabilia* II.i.32, has φύλαξ οἴκων δεσπόταις ("for masters a guardian of houses"). Josephus, *Against Apion*, 2.128, uses the noun of "domestic masters," as does an inscription cited in *Papers of the American School of Classical Studies at Athens*, vol. III (Boston: Damrell and Upham, 1888) Inscription No. 150, p. 90. It is also used for God in Epictetus, *Dis* III.xxii.4, as the "Lord of the Mansion who assigns all its place," and in Philo, *Somn*. I.149, for God as

tion is important because it assumes and builds on the audience's cultural knowledge and experience of conventional patterns of household management. This knowledge has been employed through Matthew 19, and continues to be used in 20:17–29.[14]

This assumed knowledge and experience can be briefly elaborated. At least since the time of Aristotle the structure, members, and roles of the household had been a topic of frequent discussion in philosophical literature.[15] At its

---

"Master of the whole world's household." Matthew employs it in 10:25 as self-designation for Jesus, and in parables in 13:27, 52; 21:33; 24:43 (as well as in 20:1, 11).

[14] Attempts to identify the coherence of Matthew 19–20 usually employ one of three approaches. Two lines of interpretation emphasize either that instruction about discipleship draws the chapters together, so J. C. Fenton, *Saint Matthew* (Harmondsworth: Penguin, 1963) 311; Gundry, *Matthew*, 375; Kingsbury, *Matthew as Story*, 80–81; Patte, *Matthew*, 262–63; Garland, *Matthew*, 197–98; Stock, *Matthew*, 298, 300, 302–5, or that the journey motif provides the unifying strand, so Hare, *Matthew*, 219, 224. But while these approaches identify general thematic concerns, they fail to explain the choice of the particular material.

A third line of interpretation accounts for the selection and organization of Matthew 19–20 on the basis of Matthew's dependence on Mark 10, so Hill, *Matthew*, 278–79; Schweizer, *Matthew*, 379–400; F. W. Beare, *The Gospel According to Matthew* (San Francisco: Harper & Row, 1982) 384; D. J. Harrington, *The Gospel of Matthew* (SP 1; Collegeville: Liturgical Press, 1991) 274, 279. At best, however, this observation, assuming Marcan priority, transfers the problem to Mark, fails to explain Matthew's significant redaction of the material, and does not clarify the use of this unit as a part of Matthew's gospel.

[15] In discussions of NT passages concerning household structure (Col 3:18–4:1; Eph 5:21–6:9; 1 Pet 2:18–3:7; also 1 Tim 2:1–15; 5:1–2; 6:1–2; Titus 2:1–10), the question of the origin of household codes has received much attention. Prior to the 1970's the dominant view was that they derived from Stoicism and Hellenistic Judaism. So M. Dibelius, *An die Kolosser, and die Epheser, an Philemon* (HNT; Tübingen: Mohr, 1913). K. Weidinger, *Die Haustafeln, ein Stück urchristlicher Paranese* (UNT 14; Leipzig: Heinrich, 1928), extended Dibelius's emphasis on the Stoics (especially Hierocles) to include Hellenistic Judaism (Pseudo-Phocylides, Tobit, Philo, Josephus). D. Schroeder, *Die Haustafeln des neuen Testaments* (Ph.D. Diss. Hamburg, 1959), sees some Stoic influence (especially Epictetus) but emphasizes Philo and the OT Decalogue, as well as ethical material from Jesus. Like Schroeder, J. Crouch, *The Origin and Intention of the Colossian Haustafel* (FRLANT 109; Göttingen: Vandenhoeck & Ruprecht, 1972), acknowledges Stoic influence but wants to elevate the influence of Oriental Judaism, especially Pseudo-Phocylides, Philo, and Josephus (but rejects Schroeder's emphasis on the Decalogue). K. H. Rengstorff, *Mann und Frau im Urchristentum* (Cologne: Westdeutscher, 1954) 7–52, emphasizes the difference between NT and the Hellenistic and Jewish material to argue that the content derives from Christian interest in the house. Since the mid 1970's the work of D. Lührmann, K. Thraede, and D. Balch has established some consensus that the primary tradition is an Aristotelian one which has influenced the thought of Stoicism, Hellenistic Judaism, and the NT. D. Lührmann, "Wo man nicht mehr Sklave oder Freier ist:

heart this debate concerned the organization of society, the duties of citizens, and the pursuit of the good life.

In his discussion of household management,[16] Aristotle regards the household as the basic unit of the state or city. It consists of four dimensions: three relationships (husband-wife; father-children; master-slave) and the task of earning wealth. Moreover, the structure is hierarchical in that in each of the three pairs the former rules over the latter, and patriarchal[17] in that the husband/father/master controls and provides for the household.

And now that it is clear what are the component parts of the state, we have first of all to discuss household management; for every state is composed of households. Household management falls into departments corresponding to the parts of which the household in its turn is composed; and the household in its perfect form consists of slaves and free men. The investiga-

---

Überlegungen zur Struktur frühchristlicher Gemeinden," *WD* 13 (1975) 53–83, esp. 71–79; idem, "Neutestamentliche Haustafeln und Antike Ökonomie," *NTS* 27 (1980–81) 83–97; K. Thraede, "Ärger mit der Freiheit: Die Bedeutung von Frauen in Theorie und Praxis der alten Kirche," *"Freunde in Christus werden . . .": Die Beziehung von Mann und Frau als Frage an Theologie und Kirche* (ed. G. Scharffenorth and K. Thraede; Berlin: Burckhandthaus, 1977) 35–182, esp. 49–69; idem, "Zum historischen Hintergrund der 'Haustafeln' des NT," *Pietas: Festschrift für Bernhard Kötting* (ed. E. Dassman and K. S. Frank; Münster: Aschendorff, 1980); D. Balch, "Household Ethical Codes in Peripatetic Neopythagorean and Early Christian Moralists," *SBLASP* 16 (1977) 397–404; idem, *Let Wives Be Submissive: The Domestic Code of 1 Peter* (SBLMS 26; Chico, CA: Scholars, 1981); idem, "Household Codes," *Greco-Roman Literature and the New Testament* (ed. D. Aune; Atlanta: Scholars, 1988) 25–50; idem, "Neopythagorean Moralists and the New Testament Household Codes," *ANRW* II.26.1 (1992) 380–411, esp. 393. See also D. Verner, *The Household of God* (SBLDS 71; Chico, CA: Scholars, 1983); E. Schüssler Fiorenza, "Discipleship and Patriarchy: Early Christian Ethos and Christian Ethics in a Feminist Perspective," *The Annual of the Society of Christian Ethics* (1982) 131–72; eadem, *In Memory of Her,* chaps. 5–8. Previous scholarship has established that the topics of marriage, children, wealth, and slavery are standard elements of discussions of household management and structure in antiquity. Yet this insight has not been extended to the discussion of Matthew 19–20. See Carter, *Households and Discipleship.*

[16] Plato, *Laws,* 690A–D, offers a less specific precursor. All citations and references derive from the Loeb Classical Library editions unless otherwise stated.

[17] G. Lerner, *The Creation of Patriarchy* (New York: Oxford University, 1986) 239, defines patriarchy as "the manifestation and institutionalization of male dominance over women and children in the family and the extension of male dominance over women in society in general. It implies that men hold power in all the important institutions of society and that women are deprived of access to such power. It does *not* imply that women are either totally powerless or totally deprived of rights, influence and resources."

tion of everything should begin with its smallest parts, and the primary and smallest parts of the household are master and slave, husband and wife, father and children; we ought therefore to examine the proper constitution and character of each of these three relationships, I mean that of mastership, that of marriage . . . and thirdly the progenitive relationship . . . There is also a department which some people consider the same as household management and others the most important part of it, and the true position of which we shall have to consider: I mean what is called the art of getting wealth (*Politics*, I.ii.1–2).

The Aristotelian tradition consisting of these four elements and the patriarchal structure of power relationships continues into the first century in the *Oeconomica*,[18] the *Magna Moralia* (second century B.C.E.),[19] Philodemus' Περὶ οἰκονομίας (first century B.C.E.),[20] Arius Didymus' *Epitome* (first century B.C.E.), and Hierocles' "On Duties" (early second century C.E.)[21] as well as in the Neopythagorean works of Kallicratidas, Okkelos, Perictyone, and Phintys (first centuries B.C.E.–C.E.).[22] This household management tradition

[18] The *Oeconomica* is a three volume work deriving, in all likelihood, from different authors and periods. The first part is attributed by the Epicurean Philodemus (ca.110–35 B.C.E.) to Theophrastus who succeeded Aristotle as head of the Peripatetic school in 322 B.C.E. The second book which is not concerned with the ordering of households but focusses on the ordering of public affairs, probably derives from the latter half of the third century B.C.E., while the third part may be Aristotle's treatise "Rules for Married Life" translated into Latin. For discussion and text, see G. C. Armstrong, *Aristotle: The Metaphysics* (LCL; vol. XVIII; Cambridge, MA: Harvard University, 1935) 321–424.

[19] F. Dirlmeier, "Die Zeit der 'Grossen Ethik'," *Rheinisches Museum für Philologie* 88 (1939) 214–43, suggests the *Magna Moralia* originated in the second half of the second century B.C.E. Armstrong, *Aristotle: The Metaphysics*, 428, depicts it as a "standard or comprehensive" statement of the Peripatetic school's thinking.

[20] For text, see C. Jensen, *Philodemi Peri Oikonomias* (Leipzig: Teubner, 1906). Philodemus disputes parts of the tradition, especially whether the marriage relationship should be included, and emphasizes the gaining of wealth.

[21] The source of Hierocles' writing is Stobaeus. An English translation appears in A. Malherbe, *Moral Exhortation: A Greco-Roman Sourcebook* (Philadelphia: Westminster, 1986) 85–104. See also K. Guthrie and D. R. Fideler, *The Pythagorean Sourcebook and Library* (Grand Rapids, MI: Phanes, 1987) 275–86.

[22] The dating of these texts is disputed but a consensus supports the first centuries B.C.E.–C.E. So E. Zeller, *Die Philosophie der Griechen in ihrer geschichtlichen Entwicklung dargestellt* (Leipzig: Niestlé, 1919, 1923); K. Praechter, "Metapos, Theages und Archytas bei Stobaeus," *Philologus* 50 (1891) 29–57; F. Willhelm, "Die Oeconomic der Neupythagoreer Bryson,

also appears in Dionysius of Halicarnassus (*Roman Antiquities*, 2.24–28), in the Stoics Seneca (*De Beneficiis*, 2.18.1–2–3.18–38; *Ep.* 89:10–11; 94:1–2), Epictetus (*Dis.* 3.2.4), and Dio Chrysostom (*Concerning Household Management*, fragments), and in the Hellenistic Jews Sirach (7.19–28), Philo (*Decalogue*, 165–67, *Posterity and Exile of Cain*, 181); Pseudo-Phocylides (153–227), and Josephus (*Against Apion*, 2.199–216). Within NT literature it is explicitly evident in Col 3:18–4:1, Eph 5:21–6:9, 1 Peter 2:18–3:7, 1 Tim 2:1–15; 5:1–2; 6:1–2, and Titus 2:1–10. Other data—marriage contracts, funerary inscriptions, discussions of education, child rearing, and slavery practices—attest the widespread impact of this understanding of household structures.[23]

L. Hartman notes that the writings which evidence this household tradition differ from one another and from the NT texts in style and genre. The tradition includes imperatives, dialogue, exposition, and narrative. Because of this diversity of style, Hartman argues that "*what* is said (rather) than *how* it is said" (Hartman's emphasis) identifies the tradition of household management.[24]

The audience utilizes its knowledge of this structure to connect the parable about "the householder" (20:1) with Matthew 19. First, through the sequence of pericopes in Matthew 19 the audience recognizes three of the four conventional topics of the household management tradition. The opening pericope concerns the relationship of a husband and wife (19:3–12). The second pericope centers on children (19:13–15). The third pericope involves a "rich man" and his wealth (19:16–30). The fourth, utilizing the image of masters and slaves, will appear in 20:17–28. Matthew 19–20, then, progresses as follows:

Matt 19:3–12:	Marriage and Divorce
Matt 19:13–15:	Children
Matt 19:16–30:	The Acquisition of Wealth

Kallikratidas, Periktione, Phintys," *Rheinisches Museum für Philologie* 70 (1915) 161–223; W. Burkett, "Hellenistische Pseudopythagorica," *Philologus* 105 (1961) 16–43, 226–46; Balch, "Neopythagorean Moralists," 381–92. H. Thesleff, *An Introduction to the Pythagorean Writings of the Hellenistic Period* (Abo: Abo Akademi, 1961) 30–116, argues that these texts probably derive from the middle of the third to second centuries B.C.E.

[23] Carter, *Households and Discipleship*, 56–192.

[24] L. Hartman, "Some Unorthodox Thoughts on the 'Household-Code Form'," *The Social World of Formative Christianity and Judaism* (ed. J. Neusner et al.; Philadelphia: Fortress, 1988) 219–32, esp. 229.

Matt 20:1–16:   The Story of the Householder
Matt 20:17–28:   Being a Slave Contrasted with "Ruling Over"
Matt 20:29–34:   Conclusion: The Two Blind Men[25]

Second, the audience recognizes the presence of the patriarchal power structure exhibited in "ruling over." In 19:3, for instance, the audience perceives this dimension in the Pharisees' question about a man divorcing his wife "for every cause" (κατὰ πᾶσαν αἰτίαν, 19:3). Their question assumes the husband's power over his wife and concerns only the extent of its use. In 19:13 the disciples reflect and reinforce the inferior and marginal status of children by seeking to exclude them from Jesus. The rich person in 19:16–30 is a man who, outside the household, maintains his social position by exercising economic power over others. In 20:17–28, the motif of "power over others" pervades the pericope in the references to the power of the religious leaders and Gentiles over Jesus (20:17–19), the ambition of the disciples' mother (20:20–23), the rule of the Gentiles (20:25), and the contrast of the ruler-servant/slave (20:26–28).

The audience observes, though, a third dimension to the use of the household management tradition through these sections. Matthew's Jesus is critical of it, and instructs disciples (and the audience) in what could be called, somewhat anachronistically, a more egalitarian household order. For example, he rejects the assumption that a man has unlimited power over his wife. Rather husband and wife become one flesh (19:5–6). Divorce can take place only when there is unfaithfulness but remarriage is not permitted (cf. 5:31–32).[26] If such a mutual relationship with its curtailment of male power is not possible for a man, it is better not to marry (19:10–12). Such a way of life is symbolized as being a "eunuch because of the reign" (19:12). The audience knows that Jesus is employing and affirming an identity which was usually excluded from households because of the inability to procreate and which was viewed as socially marginal.

Likewise, in 19:13–15, Jesus rejects the marginalization of children and rebukes the disciples for excluding them. He instructs them that children provide a metaphor for belonging to the reign of God. The image embraces all disciples, thereby creating a community or household of equals in which all

[25] Space prevents a discussion of the role of this closing pericope. See Carter, *Households and Discipleship*, 193–203.

[26] Carter, *Households and Discipleship*, 56–89.

members relate to each other, not in the hierarchy of parent and child, but as children or brothers and sisters (cf. 12:46–50). Subsequently the audience will learn that the role of "father" is forbidden to members of this community (23:9).

The two subsequent pericopes continue to subvert the household tradition. The next pericope (19:16–30) involves a character who is identified not by his name but by his age, gender ("a young man," νεανίσκος, 19:20, 22), and wealth as a "rich man" (πλούσιος, 19:23, 24). But his encounter with Jesus indicates to the audience that defining identity and social position in terms of age, gender, and wealth is inadequate. Jesus offers him a new identity and social role defined by "following Jesus" (disciple), and "giving to the poor" (19:21). To follow Jesus involves participating in a new social structure, the community or family of disciples (12:46–50). This family is constituted by "doing the will of your Father in heaven" (12:50) and not by birth relationships, hierarchy, conventional roles, gender and "ruling over" others. To follow Jesus and thereby belong to the community of disciples also means to give to the poor thereby lessening social hierarchy and identifying with the marginalized among whom God's presence is particularly encountered (5:3; 25:31–46).

In 20:17–28 Jesus opposes the use of power to "rule over" others (20:25) and recasts the discussion of master-slave relationships. His own death will display the destructiveness of such power (20:17–19). It will also display a different understanding of power, that which "ransoms" or liberates others from tyranny rather than rules over them. Moreover, contrary to the tradition's focus on the power of masters, Jesus instructs the disciples to live as servants and slaves (20:26–28). As with the pericope on children (19:13–15), the image is applied to all disciples. Absent is any instruction for masters. Subsequently the audience will hear Jesus instruct his disciples that the role of masters, like that of fathers, is prohibited to them (23:10).

To summarize, in Matthew 19–20 the audience recognizes the use of the four traditional elements of discussions of household management, the relationship of husband and wife, children, slaves, and wealth. It also encounters the tradition's hierarchical and patriarchal power relationship of "ruling over." But this tradition is employed only to be subverted in Jesus' teaching as Jesus proposes a pragmatic of a more egalitarian, alternative lifestyle for the community of disciples.

Given that the rest of the pericopes in Matthew 19–20 is built on key motifs derived from discussions of household management, a parable at 20:1 about a householder conducting household business is appropriate. Further, given the egalitarian thrust of the three pericopes in Matthew 19 and of 20:17–28, it is not surprising that the motif of equality should be explicitly stated in this parable (ἴσους, "equal," 20:12). Previous discussions have overlooked the significance of these household aspects for the parable's integration with its context. But given the context and subject matter, it is difficult to conclude other than that the parable continues the concern of Matthew 19–20 with household management, a significant reason for its placement here.[27]

Taking these links as our guide, we will address the question of how the parable functions in this literary context to instruct the authorial audience about life in the transformative, present, and future reign of the heavens,[28] rather than how it functioned in the context of the ministry of Jesus[29] or of Jewish understandings of reward.[30]

---

[27] For a discussion of the use of the literary context of a parable as an interpretative clue, see Tolbert, *Perspectives*, 52–54.

[28] The parable is frequently understood as depicting the judgment scene. G. Bornkamm, "End-Expectation and Church in Matthew," *Tradition and Interpretation in Matthew* (ed. G. Bornkamm, G. Barth, and H. J. Held; Philadelphia: Westminster, 1963) 29, argues that it promises disciples of Jesus, not Israel, reward in the coming new age. Barth, "Matthew's Understanding," 120, sees it as warning disciples against the desire for reward. Breech, *Silence of Jesus*, 142, claims in passing that Matthew presents the idea that "those Christians who joined the movement late will receive the same heavenly reward as those who were working from the beginning." Lambrecht, *Treasure*, 81–84, argues that it warns Christians about not resenting God's merciful goodness displayed in the judgment. See also Hare, *Matthew*, 230–31. In the reading below, I recognize future judgment as an element of the parable but I emphasize the impact of the presence of the reign of God on the present lives of disciples. See also Donahue, *Gospel in Parable*, 83–85; Schenke, "Interpretation der Parabel," 267–68.

[29] For example, Mitton, "Expounding the Parables," 309–10; P. Bonnard, *L'évangile selon saint Matthieu* (CNT; Neuchâtel: Delachaux & Niestlé, 1963, 1970) 291–93. Dodd, *Parables of the Kingdom*, 92, emphasizes Jesus' display of God's love for sinners in contrast to the complaining "legally minded." Jeremias, *Parables of Jesus*, 37–38, takes a similar approach, but makes explicit polemic against the Pharisees. Crossan, *In Parables*, 114, argues the parable shatters understandings of graciousness. Scott, *Hear Then the Parable*, 297 n. 51, also sees Jesus' association with outsiders and grace as central to the parable, but in relation not to the amount of payment but in terms of the call of the householder to all the workers.

[30] H. Heinemann, "The Conception of Reward," *JJS* 1 (1948) 85–89; de Ru, "Conception of Reward," 202–22.

2. Structure of the Parable

The parable divides into two scenes; 20:1–7 deal with the hiring of the workers and 20:8–16 with their payment.[31] Within 20:1–7, the passing of time introduces four divisions:

1) 20:1–2:   he went out (ἐξῆλθεν) early in the morning
2) 20:3–5a: going out (ἐξελθών) about the third hour
3) 20:5b: going out (ἐξελθών) about the sixth hour and the ninth hour
4) 20:6–7:   about the eleventh hour, going out (ἐξελθών)

The four divisions include essentially the same elements though with some small differences in stylistic presentation. The "going out" of the householder, a constant feature of each scene, is followed in 20:1–2 by indirect discourse with the workers and their being sent away (ἀπέστειλεν) into the vineyard. In the second division, his "going out" is followed by direct discourse (20:4) in which he is more directive but less precise about the payment and the length of time for working. The third division summarizes very briefly two further occurrences of the same action, while the fourth division receives emphasis from the length of its presentation and from the presence of dialogue. The placing of the reference to the hour first highlights the time element for the audience by disrupting the pattern of the three previous divisions.

The second scene (20:8–16) consists of five divisions:

1) 20:8:   when evening comes, the workers are called
2) 20:9:   the arrival (καὶ ἐλθόντες) of those hired at the eleventh hour and their payment
3) 20:10:   the arrival (καὶ ἐλθόντες) of those hired first, their expectations and payment
4) 20:11-15: the discussion between these workers and the householder
   a) 20:11-12: the workers' reaction: direct discourse
   b) 20:13-15: the householder's response: direct discourse
5) 20:16:   conclusion

As with the first section the element of time and the order of hiring are important (20:9–10). But the five hirings of 20:1–7 are now combined into

---

[31] Gnilka, *Matthäusevangelium*, 2. 175; Scott, *Hear Then the Parable*, 288. Donahue, *Gospel in Parable*, 79, subdivides the second scene into vv 8–11 (the payments) and vv 12–15 (dialogue); cf. Sand, *Matthäus*, 403. I will suggest below that there are five divisions.

two groups, the eleventh-hour workers (the last) and the rest (the first, 20:10), with the last being paid first (20:8–10; cf. 20:16). This reversal is crucial for the narrative. Also important is movement; in contrast to the first section, the householder is stationary and the workers are summoned to him (20:9–10) and ordered from him (20:14). The dialogue between the first-hired workers and the householder (20:12–15) marks the climax of the scene. D. Crossan notes inclusio between 20:13 and 20:2 with the reference to the denarius as the wage, and a chiastic balancing of the sequence of references to the first and the last—the first (20:2), the last (20:6–7), the last (20:9), the first (20:10–13).[32]

The structure draws the audience's attention to several significant dimensions of the story. The householder emerges as the focus of the story, initiating and controlling the action. Response to his actions is a significant aspect of hearing the parable. Further, the action is predicated on temporal markers which emphasize the sequential nature of the narrative structure. The clear progression of time as the basis for the hiring of the workers creates in the workers (20:10) and in the audience expectations about payment for labor. Third, apart from the householder and his steward, the characters are divided into two groups, the first and the last. The contrast between the two groups (especially the reversal in the order of payment, 20:8), their treatment and responses, plays an essential role in the conclusion of the story. Fourth, the division of the story into two main sections (20:1–7 and 20:8–16) highlights a basic issue in the parable, the relationship between hiring (20:1–7) and payment (20:8–16). The "first" expect one particular relationship between labor and payment to be operative, while the householder enacts another which he claims is both right and good.

Accordingly our interpretation will highlight the way in which the parable redefines for the audience "what is right" (ὃ ἐὰν ἦ δίκαιον, 20:4) in terms of equal treatment, upsetting the expectations and assumptions of the "first" who look for justice to uphold hierarchy.[33] In the emphasis on the redefinition of "what is right" in terms of equal treatment, this interpretation will differ somewhat from those readings which emphasize the generosity of the householder as the key to the passage.[34] There is no denying the presence of

---

[32] Crossan, *In Parables*, 113–14; Scott, *Hear Then the Parable*, 288–89.

[33] Riches, "Parables," 244–46.

[34] Jülicher, *Gleichnisreden Jesu*, 1. 459–71; Heinemann, "Conception of Reward," 86–87; Jeremias, *Parables of Jesus*, 39; Linnemann, *Jesus of the Parables*, 83; J. Dupont, "Les Ouvriers

both generosity and graciousness in the parable, but the inadequacy of an interpretation which concentrates on the householder's generosity is seen in that he is not consistently generous. While generous to those hired at the eleventh hour, he is not generous to those hired early in the morning; he merely keeps a contract to pay them a minimal wage. If his generosity were the focus, we might expect an equally inflated payment to those who had worked all day.

3. The Parable's Redefinition of "What Is Right"

The opening verse creates a comparison between "the reign of the heavens" and the householder. The use of the householder as the main character builds on the audience's awareness of the use of household management material through Matthew 19, but the audience must continue to listen to clarify the nature of the comparison. The verse introduces the householder as a man of wealth (his vineyard, hiring workers), fulfilling the socio-economic role stipulated in the discussions of household management.[35] He is active outside his household on their behalf, taking responsibility for securing their support by attention to the public aspects of household management. Why he needs workers is not stipulated precisely, nor does this piece of information appear necessary for the stereotypical scene being created. Whether this gap in information will be supplied later is a question that remains open for the audience. The parable's strategy to reorient the audience to another order of reality begins by first orienting it to a realistic, everyday scene. The audience's expectations for this scene will subsequently either be shattered[36] or confirmed, depending on its reading of Matthew 19.

The householder's going out early in the morning presents him as pur-

---

de la Vigne," *NRT* 79 (1957) 785–97; Dodd, *Parables of the Kingdom,* 91–95; de Ru, "Conception of Reward," 206–8; Via, *Parables,* 149–54; Patte, *Matthew,* 274–75; Garland, *Matthew,* 204–6; Stock, *Matthew,* 308–11.

[35] The context of understandings about household management indicates the significance of the vineyard. That is, I do not agree with the reading of, for instance, Drury, *Parables in the Gospels,* 92–95, who understands the reference to the vineyard to indicate an allegory of salvation history in which "the last" portray the arrival, late in the day, of (gentile?) Christians. For discussion of the variant forms of this reading of the parable in the early church, see Tevel, "Labourers in the Vineyard," 362–72.

[36] Donahue, *Gospel in Parable,* 13–17; Ricoeur, *Biblical Hermeneutics,* 125–26; Riches, "Parables," 241–42, 250–57.

poseful in his household management. From 20:1 the audience learns of his goal to hire laborers for his vineyard. The repetition of "workers" and "into his vineyard" in 20:2, as well as the verb "he sent them," underlines that he is a man who achieves what he sets out to do. The participle "agreeing with" (συμφωνήσας) may indicate fairness of practice as he negotiates with the workers for the payment of a denarius for a day's work.

This agreement has stimulated investigation of the knowledge that the audience might employ at this point. For instance, Scott argues that patron-client relationships are evident here.[37] But while some aspects of this relationship are present, the model cannot be pressed. For example, in the wealth of the householder and in the need for workers, there is evidence of the hierarchical social structure on which a patron-client relationship depends, and true to that relationship, the workers are employed to render services in return for a livelihood. But there is no indication of two crucial aspects of the patron-client relationship. First, the workers are not retained on any long-term basis but are hired on a daily basis. Further, the parable alludes only to an economic contract between the householder and the workers. The second level of patron-client relationships in which the patron extends general protection and benefit to the client in an ongoing association, and the client promotes the honor of the patron, is absent.[38] The relationship seems, rather, to be that of a householder hiring day laborers to perform a certain task.

Attracting more attention has been the question of how the audience might understand the value of the denarius as payment for a day's work. Although the evidence for Syria (a possible location for Matthew's community) is not clear, the wage seems to have been about sufficient for the support of a day laborer and his family at a minimal level.[39] Interest in this question has been particularly motivated by those who argue that the parable is con-

[37] Scott, Hear Then the Parable, 295–96, also 205–8.

[38] S. Einstadt and L. Roniger, "Patron-Client Relations as a Model of Structuring Social Exchange," Comparative Studies in Society and History 22 (1980) 42–77, esp. 49–51, 70–71; F. Danker, Benefactor: Epigraphic Study of a Graeco-Roman and New Testament Semantic Field (St. Louis: Clayton, 1982); P. Garnsey and R. Saller, The Roman Empire (Berkeley: University of California, 1987) chap. 8.

[39] F. Heichelheim, "Syria," An Economic Survey of Ancient Rome (ed. T. Frank; Baltimore: Johns Hopkins University, 1938), 4. 121–258, esp. 179–80; Scott, Hear Then the Parable, 290–92; F. Gryglewicz, "The Gospel of the Overworked Workers," CBQ 19 (1957) 190–98, collects information on length of day, output of work and rest periods.

cerned with the generosity of the householder for the poor. But if the conclusion is right that a denarius was a minimal level of payment there is little support for a claim of generosity. What is significant about the denarius is that it is part of the verisimilitude of the scene, the everyday world, to which the audience is initially oriented.

The direction the story is to take is not clearly presented by this opening stereotypical situation. Whether it is to proceed on the basis of action by the workers, by the householder, or by a third party, is not indicated. The second hiring (20:3–5a), though, with several important similarities to and differences from the first, supplies the audience with a key aspect of the forward movement of the rest of the parable. The householder hires more workers and sends them to his vineyard. Again the need for the laborers and the nature of their task is not explained. But the time has changed, it is now the third hour, and the householder has become more directive in ordering the workers to the vineyard. Most importantly, there is no discussion of or agreement over the level of the wage and the length of time for employment. Instead of the very explicit agreement in 20:2 (a denarius for a day's work), the householder informs the workers that he will pay them (δώσω ὑμῖν, "I will give you") "whatever is right" (ὃ ἐὰν ᾖ δίκαιον, 20:4).[40]

The audience knows that the concept of rightness involves the doing of one's duty, the fulfilling of expectations and obligations (cf. Joseph, 1:19).[41] The householder's zealousness and careful agreement with the first workers suggest he can be trusted to do "what is right." But precisely what is meant here is not articulated. The blankness of the expression invites the audience

---

[40] I am following at this point the traditional reading that the workers of 20:5a and those approached in 20:5b do go to the vineyard to work. F. C. Glover, "Workers for the Vineyard," *ExpTim* 86 (1975) 310–11, challenges this reading, arguing that 20:5 (οἱ δὲ ἀπῆλθον, "and they went away") should be interpreted not as their going away to the vineyard to work, but as their refusal to work without a negotiated wage contract. He notes similar uses of ἀπέρχομαι and the adversative δέ in 19:22 and 22:5 for the refusal of an invitation. Those who go at the eleventh hour are so desperate that they will work without a stipulated wage. Hence, on Glover's reading, the reason that there are only two groups at the payment, the first and the last, is that only two groups were hired. Glover's observations are interesting; 21:29 is, though, a significant problem for his thesis because ἀπέρχομαι and δέ indicate the acceptance of an invitation. Second, in 20:8 ἀπὸ τῶν ἐσχάτων ἕως τῶν πρώτων ("from the last ones until the first ones"), the terms ἀπὸ . . . ἕως ("from . . . until") suggest several different groups and a graduated series of payments rather than only two groups. Third, the repeated instruction "go also" (ὑπάγετε καί, 20:4, 7) counts against his reading.

[41] G. Schrenk, "δίκαιος," *TDNT* 3. 182–91.

to supply some definition or content and to listen to find out if their definition is confirmed or overturned. The indefiniteness of the term invites the supplying of content that is coherent with the rest of the story and, since 20:1–16 is an integral part of Matthew 19–20, coherent with the rest of this larger unit. Those of the audience who have understood through Matthew 19 that so much of what is conventionally expected of a householder regarding marriage, children, and wealth has been opposed, and that a new set of requirements has been indicated, may guess that some unexpected or equalizing action will be taken. Others may define "what is right" on the basis of 20:2 in terms of paying them for a day's work less three hours, a denarius less perhaps three-twelfths.[42] They will find themselves at the end of the story on the side of the first-hired workers, surprised or protesting at the householder's action.

The uncertainty is maintained by 20:5. The householder carries out the same action on two further occasions and hires two more groups of workers, but again the text does not supply any information on how much they will be paid. The question remains urgent, though, as two more time periods are marked off and another hiring follows in 20:6–7. The repetition in these verses of vocabulary used in the previous five verses summarizes the first scene by emphasizing the householder's initiative and act of hiring.[43]

Matt 20:8 begins the second scene. The initial marker is, as with the first scene, a temporal one, but instead of morning it is now evening, the time when, as the audience knows, payment should be made (cf. Deut 24:14–15; Lev 19:13).[44] The householder (now the "master," κύριος) shows himself to know and to do "what is right" by having the steward summon the workers to be paid (20:8). Somewhat surprisingly, those who were hired last "at the eleventh hour" (20:6–7) are paid first (ἔσχατος, πρῶτος, 20:8b–9). The reversal of order is a literary device so that the first-hired workers witness the payment to the last-hired, enabling the subsequent conflict between the

---

[42] Manson, *Sayings of Jesus,* 220, indicates that a πονδίον was one-twelfth of a denarius, so such an amount is a possible payment.

[43] Note "day" (τὴν ἡμέραν, ὅλην τὴν ἡμέραν, 20:2, 6), "standing" (ἑστῶτας, ἑστήκατε, 20:3, 6 [2x]) "idle" (ἀργούς, ἀργοί, 20:3,6), "hire" (μισθώσασθαι, ἐμισθώσατο, 20:1, 7), "into the vineyard" (εἰς τὸν ἀμπελῶνα, 20:1, 4, 7, cf. 2), "others" (ἄλλους, 20:3, 6), the imperative "go" (ὑπάγετε, 20:4, 7), "going out" (ἐξῆλθεν, ἐξελθών, 20:1, 3, 5, 6). The indication of hours should also be noted (20:1, 3, 5 [2x], 6).

[44] Sand, *Matthäus,* 402.

first-hired workers and the householder to take place.[45] The open question of how much the workers will be paid, of how much "what is right" signifies, is answered as the householder pays the workers the same wage as that negotiated with the workers who have worked all day.

The amount is generous for an hour's work, but in the subsequent statement of the first-hired workers' expectations (20:10a) and of their grumbling (20:11–12), the issue is not generosity, but "what is right." On seeing what the last were paid, the first think they will receive more (20:10). Perhaps they calculate that if one hour's work is worth one denarius, twelve hours' work must be worth twelve denarii, not to mention compensation for the heat of the day (20:12). But whatever their exact calculation, the passing of the hours, which has been so strictly marked in the narrative, underlines the expectation that they would receive greater payment for more work. Instead their expectations are upset as they too are paid a denarius (20:10b).

Their complaint (20:11) against the householder is that he has made the later-hired workers "equal to us" (20:12). In their eyes (cf. 20:15), justice should have maintained the differentiation among the workers by ensuring payment according to achievement.[46] Instead the householder's understanding of "what is right" and payment of the same amount to the last-hired workers has evened out the distinctions and treated all in solidarity.[47] As a reflection of the solidarity with which the householder views the workers, he addresses them with the singular "friend" (ἑταῖρε, 20:13).[48] Instead of using the payment to reinforce distinctions of value, the wage is used to express their equality and solidarity which derives from the fact that all were sent by the householder to work in the vineyard (20:2, 4, 5, 7).

In response to the first-hired workers' protests against the "equal" treatment, the householder justifies his action by using a series of declarations and questions which invite the protesting workers (and audience) to understand a different reality. The use of the singular vocative ἑταῖρε ("friend,"

---

[45] Via, *Parables*, 148–49.

[46] Via, *Parables*, 152.

[47] L. Schottroff, "Human Solidarity and the Goodness of God: The Parable of the Workers in the Vineyard," *God of the Lowly* (ed. W. Schottroff and W. Stegemann; New York: Orbis, 1984) 138.

[48] With Linnemann, *Jesus of the Parables*, 154, and Scott, *Hear Then the Parable*, 295, and *contra* Jeremias, *Parables of Jesus*, 137, who thinks only the leader is addressed. The same term will be used again in 22:12 (a parable) and 26:50 (Judas' betrayal) to indicate people in the wrong.

20:13) individualizes the questions and prevents any evasion of the demand for re-evaluation by a "flight into collective anonymity."[49] The householder seeks their acknowledgment that he has kept the agreement of a denarius as the wage and that he has the right to choose (20:14, 15) to do as he wishes with his own wealth (20:15). In fact, the householder claims that what he has done is not only "right" but "good" (ἀγαθός, 20:15), and their grumbling and accusations of injustice indicate their refusal to recognize his goodness.[50] The claim of goodness recalls and builds on the exchange in 19:16–17 between the rich man and Jesus. The rich man questions Jesus in 19:16 about what good thing he must do to have eternal life. Jesus' response asserts that only one is good, namely God (19:17). In claiming that what he has done is good, the householder invokes God's perspective as sanction for his action. In turn this perspective reveals the workers' refusal to see not only as a wrong perspective, but exposes them as people who are evil (πονηρός), opposed to God's purposes (20:15b; cf. 13:19, 38, 49; 16:4; 18:32).

W. Harnisch[51] notes a significant change in the pattern of the householder's assertions and questions in 20:13–15, a change that throws the emphasis onto the final question about the householder's goodness and the workers' wickedness. Matt 20:13 commences with a declaration ("I do you no wrong"), is followed by a rhetorical question ("Did you not agree . . . ?"), and an imperative ("Take . . . go"). The same pattern is repeated in 20:14 with the declaration ("I choose . . .") and rhetorical question ("Am I not allowed . . . ?"), but instead of an imperative, the final open question is used ("Is your eye evil because I am good?"), provoking the audience to provide an answer and inviting agreement. The audience knows that the image of the "evil eye" has nothing to do with generosity (so the NRSV and RSV translations, for example). Rather, as J. H. Elliott has demonstrated, their evil consists of their jealousy or envy resulting from the actions of the householder toward the last-hired.[52] Such a response destroys the community of equality that the householder enacts.

The workers' refusal to accept the householder's redefinition of "what is

---

[49] W. Harnisch, "The Metaphorical Process in Matthew 20:1–15," SBLASP 16 (1977) 231–50, esp. 241.

[50] Linnemann, *Jesus of the Parables*, 84, 86–88.

[51] Harnisch, "Metaphorical Process," 241–42; Gnilka, *Matthäusevangelium*, 2. 176.

[52] J. H. Elliott, "Matthew 20:1–15: A Parable of Invidious Comparison and Evil Eye Accusation," *BTB* 22 (1992) 52–65.

right" as an action of goodness means that they cannot accept the householder's equality of treatment of the last who are now made first (20:16). They wish to retain their understandings and hierarchy of value based on the amount of work and they continue to expect that justice will reinforce those distinctions. The householder's questions invite them and any protesting members of the audience who defined "what is right" in 20:4 as indicating a payment proportional to work to re-examine their understanding of "what is right" in the light of the householder's actions, to abandon their understanding, to gain a new perspective, and to participate in a new reality.[53]

4. The Parable and the Reign of the Heavens

The reign of the heavens is thus compared with the householder's actions and the experience of the story. The householder upsets the expectations of the workers that they will be treated according to the hierarchical structures and values of the status quo. The householder redefines "what is right" so that it is equated not with length of work but with acceptance of his instruction to work. The householder's actions transcend their expectations and system of measurement with different priorities and values.

The reign of the heavens, the powerful and active presence of God manifested in the person of Jesus (4:17; 12:28), is "like this." It upsets expectations about how life "ought" to be ordered and measured.[54] It disorientates and reorientates existence[55] away from human merit and to divine presence and summons. It surprisingly redefines "what is right" in terms of response rather than achievement. It re-presents reality, resisting hierarchical structures, placing all equally before the summons and demand of God, offering a different basis and orientation for ethical living[56] in the time before the eschatological judgment (19:28–29).[57] One aspect of the different values has been set out in the alternative household structure of Matthew 19–20. Against the hierarchical, patriarchal structure that dominated the Jewish and Greco-Roman worlds of Antioch, disciples and the audience are called to an egalitarian way of life in which human beings have an equal value. This human solidarity is

[53] Gnilka, *Matthäusevangelium*, 2. 179.
[54] Via, *Parables*, 154–55; Crossan, *In Parables*, 114; Riches, "Parables," 241–42, 251–52.
[55] Ricoeur, *Biblical Hermeneutics*, 125–26.
[56] Donahue, *Gospel in Parable*, 17.
[57] Gnilka, *Matthäusevangelium*, 2. 181–82.

based on the call of Jesus which treats all human beings as needing to encounter the gift and demand of God. Such an action, creative of a new social world, is declared to be "good" (20:15b; cf. 19:4).

The placement of this parable of the reign of the heavens at this point in 19:1–20:34 has significant pragmatic implications for the audience in several ways. The change to a parable form after the three pericopes of Matthew 19 creates a further opportunity for the audience to absorb the instruction of Matthew 19–20 and to be absorbed by the way of life and identity set forth in it. The anti-structure nature of the alternative household structure created by the presence of God's reign is so fundamentally contrary to the pervasive hierarchy of the surrounding society that the audience is given another opportunity to see and comprehend the radical alternative being proposed.

The parable does not repeat the specific content about marriage, children, and wealth from Matthew 19. It moves, rather, to a more general and fundamental level, underlining the basis for the specific teaching about household organization outlined in the three pericopes of Matthew 19. The audience is made aware that the alternative household organization is an expression of the presence of God's reign in the time "in-between" the call of Jesus and the vindication in the judgment. The reordering of relationships, values and priorities explicated in Matthew 19–20 results from and manifests the reign of God which has drawn near in the person of Jesus. Thus while the parable seems to indicate a change of focus from Jesus in Matthew 19 to the reign (20:1), in effect the parable maintains and even sharpens the focus of Matthew 19 by reminding the audience that the teaching and actions of Jesus manifest God's reign. By means of a different form, the parable re-expresses and re-presents the reign's reality as the basis for Jesus' teaching and for a disciple's identity and way of life.

The gospel is again employing "redundancy,"[58] making available in a different form the basic and general assertion that the reign of the heavens manifested in Jesus upsets the expectations and priorities of the status quo. Redundancy seeks an effective communication, overcoming "noise" or misunderstandings which would hinder the communication. But redundancy also serves to gain the hearers' assent. In being able to predict the probable outcome or the content of a "blank" phrase such as "what is right," the audi-

---

[58] Wittig, "Formulaic Style," 123–36, esp. 125–31; Suleiman, "Redundancy," 119–42; Anderson, *Matthew's Narrative Web*.

ence participates in the world created by the text. Such participation is a significant step toward assent.[59]

In creating the possibility of eliciting assent, the parable takes on an ambiguous function. For those who predict and assent to the householder's action, there is affirmation and strengthening. They encounter the gift and demand of God and are already seeking to live their lives accordingly in the time of transition between the call of Jesus and the final judgment.

But for those who grumble against the redefinition of "what is right" that God's reign initiates, who question the goodness of God's rule, and who reject its household organization as outlined in Matthew 19–20, there is a warning. The question is asked (20:15) whether such ones have an evil eye, an eye of darkness (6:23), which indicates an evil heart. Their response is not consistent with a commitment to God's reign. The possibility is thus raised that they have not welcomed or have not stayed true to the light God has sent (4:16) and have not repented so as to enter God's reign (4:17). The concluding unanswered question (20:15) expresses these possibilities and leaves the workers and the audience (particularly those who have shared the workers' cries of protest) to reassess their response, to formulate a different answer, and to encounter God's reign anew. The failure to recognize a different concept of "what is right," the attempt to limit divine goodness to notions of merit, and to exclude equal dealing with all human beings, will have disastrous consequences if it continues. The audience already knows from the parable of the wise and foolish builders at the close of the sermon on the mount (7:24–27) and from the parable of the unforgiving servant (18:23–35) that condemnation in the judgment awaits the person who persists in having an evil eye and will not pluck it out (cf. 5:29; 18:9). Instead of being first such a one will be last (20:16b); instead of sharing Jesus' destiny and vindication in the judgment (19:28–30), such a "disciple" will be condemned.[60]

The parable is thus positioned in the middle of the two chapters con-

---

[59] Wittig, "Formulaic Style," 130–31, expresses more strongly the likelihood of assent.

[60] In this reading the reversal motif of 20:16 functions as a warning. So also Donahue, *Gospel in Parable*, 83–85; F. Schnider, "Von der Gerechtigkeit Gottes: Beobachtungen zum Gleichnis von den Arbeitern im Weinberg (Mt 20, 1–16)," *Kairos* 23 (1981) 88–95, esp. 94–95; Schweizer, *Matthew*, 395. Tolbert's claim noted earlier, *Perspectives*, 60, that the parable lacks a reversal motif and so is not well related to 19:30 and 20:16 overlooks the function of the questions in 20:15. If a negative answer is given by those who have received the denarius, then the reversal will occur in the judgment. Hence 20:16 is a warning. To use Iser's terms again, there is a blank in the text but the notion of warning supplies an adequate connection.

cerned with the organization of the households of those who have encountered the reign of God and are in transition to their vindication. It recalls for the audience the basis of the anti-structure household and re-presents the transforming reality of God's reign which these households manifest. In this context and with its change of form the parable is inserted to state again for the audience the basis of the distinctive liminal identity and way of life being created as the audience interacts with the pericopes of Matthew 19–20. The alternative household derives from and embodies the reign of God. In this context the parable seeks the audience's assent and pragmatic response.[61]

[61] For an earlier version of this chapter, see Carter, *Households and Discipleship*, 146–60.

CHAPTER 7

The Parables in Matthew 21:28–22:14
(by Carter)

Between Matt 21:28–22:14 the audience hears three parables:

1. Matt 21:28–32: Parable of a man who had two sons
2. Matt 21:33–46: Parable of the householder, the vineyard, and the tenants
3. Matt 22:1–14: Parable of the wedding feast[1]

A number of common elements enables the audience to hold these three parables together as an elaboration of the action of the first part of Matthew 21, especially the conflict scene of 21:23–27. The latter scene introduces the audience for the parables within the plot, the religious leaders in 21:23, 28 ("you"), 45; 22:1 ("them"), as well as a key issue, Jesus' authority. The first parable borrows the phrase "you did not believe him" (21:32) from 21:23–27 (21:25). The uncommon phrase "reign of God" (rather than "reign of the heavens") appears in the first two parables at 21:31 and 21:43, and both para-

---

[1] For bibliography, in addition to the literature cited below, see the commentaries and R. Hummel, *Die Auseinandersetzung zwischen Kirche und Judentum im Matthäusevangelium* (BEvT 33; Munich: Kaiser, 1963, 1966) 146–53; W. Trilling, *Das Wahre Israel: Studien zur Theologie des Matthäus-evangelium* (SANT 10; 3d ed.; Munich: Kösel, 1964) 55–65; R. Walker, *Die Heilsgeschichte im ersten Evangelium* (FRLANT 91; Göttingen: Vandenhoeck & Ruprecht, 1967) 79–83, 91–97; D. R. A. Hare, *The Theme of Jewish Persecution of Christians in the Gospel According to Matthew* (SNTSMS 6; Cambridge: Cambridge University, 1967) 121–22, 146–66, esp. 153–56; S. van Tilborg, *The Jewish Leaders in Matthew* (Leiden: Brill, 1972) 47–63, 70–72; H. Frankemölle, *Jahwe-Bund und Kirche Christi: Studien zur Form- und Traditionsgeschichte des "Evangeliums" nach Matthäus* (NTAbh 10; 2d ed.; Münster: Aschendorff, 1974) 247–56.

bles share the same setting of the vineyard. The second and third parables include the repeated sending of servants (21:34, 36; 22:3, 4) and the repeated resistance to their missions (21:35–36, 39; 22:3, 5–6; cf. 21:29, 23–27). The third parable seems to carry out the punishment threatened in the second parable (21:41, 43; 22:7).[2] The three parables draw on important symbols familiar to the audience from Israel's religious history and the second and third parables in particular encourage the audience to read them as allegories of that history.

In discussing the audience's interaction with this material, two issues in particular will be to the fore: the placement of these parables in this part of the gospel's narrative, and the pragmatic effect of the audience's progression through a sequence of three parables. I will argue that the parables function primarily to provide affirmation and insight for the audience in its way of life faithful to God's purposes. In relation to this overarching function, the parables 1) enable the audience to formulate further explanation for the religious leaders' rejection of John and Jesus' authority as God's Son,[3] 2) gain further understanding of the role of the community of disciples (ἐκκλησία) in God's purposes, and 3) hear an exhortation to a faithful way of living along with a warning about its failure to carry out that role.[4] That is, the audience's interaction with the parables is identity-forming and lifestyle-shaping.

1. The Parables in Narrative Context

In Matthew 21, the audience recognizes a significant development in the gospel's plot.[5] In 21:1-11 Jesus enters Jerusalem. The audience has known of Jerusalem's power, paranoia and resistance to God's purposes since the

---

[2] Van Tilborg, *Jewish Leaders*, 47–49 n. 3, lists among other common material twenty-eight words and expressions that appear at least twice in the parables.

[3] I will argue throughout that the parables do not present the rejection of Judaism but they do present the rejection of the religious leaders; so also Saldarini, *Matthew's Christian-Jewish Community*, 58–64; A. J. Levine, *The Social and Ethnic Dimensions of Matthean Social History* (Lewiston: Mellen, 1988) 206–15. Hill, *Matthew*, 298, 301, seems to suggest a focus on the leaders, but his comments on 21:43 (p. 301) and his introduction to 22:1–14 (p. 302) suggest a rejection of Israel.

[4] For example, Donahue, *Gospel in Parable*, 87–96, argues that the parables function primarily to instruct and warn the Christian community about its discipleship responsibilities; see also Sand, *Matthäus*, 430–31, 435–36.

[5] Carter, "Kernels," 478–79.

account of Herod's desperate and murderous actions (cf. 2:1, 3), and its religious leaders' inability to understand the scriptures in relation to Jesus (2:4–6). Their refusal to join the magi in worshiping him contrasts with the more positive responses of some in Jerusalem who are baptized by John the Baptist (3:5) and who "follow" Jesus (4:25).[6] The reference in 4:5 to Jerusalem as the "holy city" identifies it as a place "set apart" for divine service (cf. 27:53) while the description in 5:35 of Jerusalem as "the city of the great King" invokes the audience's knowledge of Zion traditions about Jerusalem as God's chosen dwelling place (Ps 48:2–3). Yet Jesus' conflict with the religious leaders "from Jerusalem" (15:1) continues the negative impression showing it to be a city that does not live out its divine calling. Jesus' declaration to his disciples that he *must* (δεῖ) go to Jerusalem to be put to death by the religious leaders (16:21; 17:12) contributes to this negative presentation as well as to the understanding that Jerusalem is important for God's purposes (δεῖ, 16:21). In 19:1 Jesus leaves Galilee for Jerusalem. The destination is underlined with a subsequent double reference to Jerusalem by the narrator (20:17) and by Jesus as he warns yet again that he will be put to death there by the religious leaders and the Gentiles (20:18–19).

But what is not yet clear to the audience is *exactly* how Jesus' death will come about in Jerusalem. In his passion predictions Jesus has identified that he will be killed and who will carry it out. Since almost the beginning of the gospel the religious leaders have found themselves on the wrong side of what God is doing and in conflict with Jesus' actions and interpretation of God's will.[7] But it is not clear to the audience how *precisely* their threat to kill Jesus (12:14), and Jesus' teaching in 16:21 that they will do so, will come about. Jesus' entry into Jerusalem in Matthew 21 returns him to the center of their power (cf. 2:1–12; 15:1) and into direct conflict with their understanding of God's will as expressed in the temple worship. In this conflict emerges the central issue of Jesus' authority (21:23–27). His return to and actions in Jerusalem and in the temple provide both the motive and opportunity to kill him (cf. the temple charge in 26:61).

---

[6] While their "following" is a more positive response than that of the religious leaders, I understand the verb "follow" in the sense of accompaniment rather than discipleship. Absent are the two aspects of commitment and cost; so J. D. Kingsbury, "The Verb AKOLOUTHEIN ("To Follow") as an index of Matthew's View of his Community," *JBL* 97 (1978) 56–73, esp. 61, 56–62.

[7] Van Tilborg, *Jewish Leaders*; Kingsbury, "Developing Conflict," 57–73; Anderson, *Matthew's Narrative Web*, 97–126; Carter, *Matthew*, 229–41.

In 21:23, "the chief priests and elders of the people"[8] approach[9] Jesus while he is teaching in the temple and ask a double question, "By what authority do you do these things and who gave you this authority?" The audience recalls that Jesus' authority has been noticed previously by the crowds in relation to his teaching (7:28–29) and healing/forgiving (9:8).[10] It understands the "these things" (ταῦτα) of their question to refer in its immediate context to Jesus' entry to Jerusalem acclaimed as "Son of David" and "prophet" (21:8–11), his disruptive actions in the temple (21:12–13), his healing of the blind and lame in the temple (21:14), his acceptance of the children's praise as consonant with God's will revealed in scripture (21:15–16), and his teaching (21:23). Yet since most of these actions, though not the temple setting, have been typical of Jesus' ministry since 4:17, the religious leaders' inquiry functions to probe the basis for his whole ministry.

The audience knows the answers to their questions. The angel's announcement to Joseph of Mary's conception of Jesus indicated that God through the holy spirit had initiated this action (1:18–25; cf. 11:25–30). In naming the baby "Jesus," God was commissioning him to save from sins and manifest God's presence (1:21, 23). The religious leaders have also, on several previous occasions, confronted the issue of Jesus' identity and authority but have refused to recognize God's presence at work through him (9:3–8, 32–34; 12:1–14, 22–37, 38–45; 15:1–20; 16:1–12).

Distinctive about the "these things" named by the leaders is their temple location and Jesus' unprecedented attack on the buyers and sellers, the money changers, and those selling pigeons in the temple (21:12). At heart this event is not an attack on abuses or dishonesty or inappropriate commercial activity, nor is it designed to restore, purify, and perfect the temple worship.[11]

---

[8] As many have noted, various designations for the religious leaders appear in the gospel in different combinations. For example in 21:15 "the chief priests" appear with "the scribes" while in 21:23 "the chief priests" appear with "the elders of the people" and in 21:45 the chief priests appear with the Pharisees. These combinations function to create one group consisting of various parties but unified in their common opposition to Jesus.

[9] J. R. Edwards, "The Use of ΠΡΟΣΕΡΧΕΣΘΑΙ in the Gospel of Matthew," *JBL* 106 (1987) 65–74, esp. 67–68.

[10] For the role of the crowds, see Carter, "Crowds," 54–67.

[11] With W. Watty, "Jesus and the Temple—Cleansing or Cursing?" *ExpTim* 93 (1982) 235–39; Harrington, *Matthew*, 295; Garland, *Matthew*, 212; *contra* R. Biers, "Purification of the Temple: Preparation for the Kingdom of God," *JBL* 90 (1971) 82–90; Stock, *Matthew*, 322–23. See also E. P. Sanders, *Jesus and Judaism* (Philadelphia: Fortress, 1985) 61–90.

Rather Jesus' actions attack the very reason for the temple's existence, the offering of sacrifices to God.

The scene assumes the audience's knowledge of the (now destroyed) temple's function. The buyers and sellers provided sacrificial victims for pilgrims visiting the city for its festivals. The money changers exchanged money for Jewish coins necessary to pay the temple tax which financed the provision of sacrificial victims (cf. 17:24–27; Exod 30:11–16).[12] Those selling doves provided sacrifices for outsiders such as women (Lev 12:6–8) and poor lepers (Lev 14:1–2, 21–22) as well as for men and women regarded as being unclean (Lev 15:1–2, 13–14, 25–30). In driving them out and overturning their tables Jesus prevents the temple carrying out its role of providing sacrifices for the atonement of sins. His action is a direct challenge to and critique of its sacrificial system.

This challenge is consistent with knowledge that the audience has gained from the narrative. In 1:21 God has commissioned Jesus to save from sins and in 9:1–8 Jesus has declared the sins of a paralyzed person forgiven without recourse to the temple system. Twice, in 9:13 and 12:7, Jesus has stated God's preference for mercy, not for sacrifice. In 12:6 he declares himself to be greater than the temple. In 17:24–27, though it is not the main point, Jesus declares the community of disciples free from the temple worship and from participation in its sacrifices of atonement through payment of the tax.[13] Subsequently at the close of this three chapter controversy with the religious leaders (Matthew 21–23), he will declare the temple to be "forsaken and desolate" (23:38) and himself to be the means whereby sins are forgiven (26:28). By overturning the means of procuring sacrifices, Jesus' actions prefigure the end of this system which (as the audience knows) took place in 70 C.E. His actions and words set this event in divine perspective.[14]

Jesus interprets his actions with words which the audience recognizes originate in Israel's prophetic traditions (21:13). This interpretation functions for the audience in two ways. First it provides a vision of an alternative worshipping community. "My house," God's house as manifested by Jesus, requires not sacrifice but prayer (cf. 18:18–20). Second, it provides some explanation for Jesus' attack on the sacrificial system.

Jesus' words combine Isa 56:7 ("my house shall be called a house of

---

[12] Garland, "Matthew's Understanding," 190–209.

[13] Ibid., 208–9.

[14] Harrington, *Matthew*, 10–16.

prayer") with Jer 7:11 ("Has this house which is called by my name, become a den of robbers in your sight?") to contrast God's intent with the practice of the temple authorities. Instead of a house of prayer, the temple has become a "den of robbers." The context of the Jeremiah passage indicates that the phrase "den of robbers" refers to the presumption of some who participate in the temple worship. They think they can indulge in numerous immoral and unfaithful actions ("... steal, murder, commit adultery, swear falsely, make offerings to Baal, and go after other gods ... ," Jer 7:9) yet appear in the temple saying "we are safe" from God's imminent judgment (Jer 7:10). The citation from Jeremiah creates an analogy with Jesus' hearers in the story. Like Jeremiah Jesus charges his hearers with thinking that participation in the temple's ritual is sufficient without faithful living shaped by God's will ("But you make it ... ," 21:13b). From earlier material in the gospel the audience is familiar with similar condemnations of presumption, lack of openness to Jesus' teaching about God's will, and the neglect of doing God's will, most of which have been explicitly directed against the religious leaders (cf. 3:8–9; 7:24–27; 12:22–37, 46–50; 15:1–9).

Having challenged the effectiveness of the sacrificial system and the temple leadership, Jesus issues a further challenge to its excluding nature. In 21:14 he heals "the blind and lame" in the temple. People with imperfections were excluded from the temple lest they make it impure (Lev 21:16–24; 2 Sam 5:8) though some traditions also looked for the time when God would gather and restore such people (Mic 4:6–7; Ezek 34:15–16). Jesus' healing of such signifies that he effects something which the sacrificial system could not do. As Jesus Emmanuel (1:21, 23), he overcomes their sin as exhibited in their sickness, extends to them God's saving power and presence, and includes them in God's purposes.[15]

In addition to his healing action with these marginalized people, Jesus receives the acclamation of the children, "Hosanna to the Son of David" (21:15; cf. 21:9). The audience knows that in the first-century society children also are among the marginalized and outcasts.[16] In the gospel narrative children have experienced danger (2:13–23), have been recognized as the humble (18:3), and have been treated as being of no significance (19:13). Yet in the midst of these circumstances they have also been the objects of God's

---

[15] Sickness was widely understood to result from curses and spells, evil powers, sin, or divine wrath; see Kee, *Medicine,* 122–24; Heil, "Healing Miracles," 274–87.

[16] Carter, *Households and Discipleship,* 90–114.

mercy and care, as well as examples of what is required to experience God's saving presence or reign (18:1–6, 10–14; 19:14–15). The marginalized have throughout the narrative been especially perceptive about and receptive to Jesus as Son of David (9:27; 15:22; 20:30–31).

Jesus' actions and the children's acclaim bring an indignant response and question from the religious leaders (21:15–16). As he has done on two previous occasions, Jesus challenges their disapproving words by questioning them, "Have you never read . . ." (ἀνέγνωτε, 12:3, 5; 19:4; see subsequently 21:42; 22:31). His question and citation of Ps 8:3 (LXX) highlight their ignorance of God's purposes revealed in the scriptures. By exposing their ignorance, he shows their response to the children to be one that does not perceive God's merciful power and presence in Jesus. Psalm 8 appropriately celebrates the vocal and laudatory recognition of God's majesty manifested in the creation order in human beings by "babes and infants" and by the psalmist.

After Jesus' challenge to the temple sacrificial system and its leadership, the audience witnesses Jesus curse the fig tree and its instant demise (21:18–22). By this point in the gospel the audience is well familiar with fruit as an image for a faithful way of life (7:15–20; 13:8, 26). It is also familiar with the gospel's use of the image in scenes of conflict with religious leaders. John has demanded from the religious leaders "fruit worthy of repentance" and has warned them that the tree not producing good fruit will be destroyed (3:8, 10b). Jesus informs the religious leaders that their evil hearts are revealed by their "fruits," their evil words (12:33–37). The now-withered, fruitless fig tree demonstrates the truth of these warnings. In the context of Jesus' actions against the temple and its leadership the tree displays the fate of both. Moreover Jesus' words in 21:21–22 about faith and prayer use the tree to demonstrate for the disciples (cf. 21:20) the powerful effect of the believing prayer that marks his house (cf. 21:13).

Jesus re-enters the temple in 21:23 to teach. His house for prayer is also a house for revealing God's will (11:25–27). The religious leaders, absent from 21:18–22, return with their double question, "By what authority do you do these things and who gave you this authority?" The questioners become the questioned as Jesus again responds with a question, making their successful answer the prerequisite for his answering their question. Jesus' question concerns the origin of John's baptism, "From heaven or of human origin?" The audience listens to the leaders debate among themselves (21:25b–26). It discovers that their debate is not concerned with the truth of God's perspective as identified in the story but with finding words that will save face and their own authority.

To take the first option ("From heaven") means "believing John." From the context of the gospel's reference to John, believing him involves several dimensions. First, it involves acknowledging him as carrying out God's will (3:7–10). To believe John would mean accepting his testimony that "God's reign is at hand" (3:2). It would mean being prepared for God's action through repentance (3:2–3), through a baptism in which sin is confessed, and through a life of appropriate actions (3:2–6, 8). It would mean recognizing the truth of his statements of imminent judgment (3:7–10). It would mean accepting his proclamation that the coming one effects vindication and judgment (3:11–12). The leaders have refused such recognition (3:7–10). Moreover, Jesus' reference to John's baptism also invokes John's baptism of Jesus in which God declares Jesus to be "my beloved Son," a perspective with which the religious leaders have not agreed (3:17). Given the close connection between John and Jesus (3:2; 4:17) and Jesus' endorsement of John as a prophet from God (11:2–19; 17:9–13), to recognize John's baptism as being "from heaven" would also mean recognizing Jesus as being "from heaven." To recognize the authority of John's actions would mean surrendering their own authority to God's saving purposes manifested in Jesus (cf. 1:21, 23). But the religious leaders name this possibility only to reject it as impossible, thus rejecting a further opportunity to acknowledge God's saving presence in Jesus (21:25b).

The religious leaders move immediately to consider the second option. To take the second option ("of human origin") is also impossible because "we fear the crowd." Like Herod who displayed the ultimate resistance to John by killing him (cf. 14:5), the leaders know that the crowd understands John, rightly, as a prophet (cf. 11:9). To agree with the crowd would mean siding with Jesus' (and thereby God's) perspective, an impossible option. But to dissent from the crowd means a loss of authority over them. Expediently they declare they do not know (21:27a). Intent on exposing the basis for Jesus' actions, their dialogue exposes their own expediency and lack of truthful action.[17]

This consideration of the audience's progression through Matthew 21 prior to the three parables indicates several factors of importance for the audience's interaction with the parables. First, Jesus' conflict has been with

---

[17] Patte, *Matthew*, 294–95.

the religious leaders, not all Israel. While the religious leaders are attacked by, resist, and challenge his actions, others welcome him—the crowds (even though in calling him "prophet" they indicate they do not understand Jesus in God's perspective, 21:11; cf. 3:17; 17:5), the blind and lame (21:14), the children (21:15), and the disciples (21:20 passim). His actions indicate a division between these groups. The parables will confirm this division and will vividly portray the realities contributing to it.

Second, the nature of Jesus' conflict with the religious leaders is clearly identifiable. Their question about Jesus' authority concerns, at root, Jesus' commissioning as his own counter-question makes clear. The audience uses its knowledge of Jesus' God-given authority to save from sins and manifest God's saving presence (1:21, 23) to evaluate the religious leaders' stance toward him. Their resistance is a rejection of God's purposes, a rejection which brings further consequences for the leaders.

The parables' plots will depict this resistance and its consequences. They will also contrast it with a significantly different, positive response exemplified by the community of disciples which, in turn, brings its own responsibilities. These parables thus function as stories embedded in the larger story to reinforce and clarify key developments in the main story. They ensure the audience's understanding, not only of what takes place, but, in relation to the gospel's point of view, its understanding of why and how events happen, and their consequences for both the religious leaders and for the audience's identity and way of life.

2. Matthew 21:28–32:
Parable of a Man Who Had Two Sons

The first parable highlights several elements of the previous conflict for the audience.[18] The vineyard scenario involving the sons and their different

---

[18] Textually I follow the third and fourth revised editions of *The Greek New Testament* (Stuttgart: United Bible Societies, 1983, 1993) which have the first son responding in the negative but then going to the vineyard. For discussion, see Metzger, *Textual Commentary*, 55–56; Scott, *Hear Then the Parable*, 80–81. Lambrecht, *Treasure*, 94, follows the conclusion of J. Schmid, "Das textgeschichtliche Problem der Parabel von der zwei Söhnen Mt 21, 28–32," *Vom Wort des Lebens* (NTAbh 1; FS M. Meinertz; ed. N. Adler; Münster: Aschendorff, 1951) 68–84, who argues for the reverse order, so that the first son says he will go but does not, while the second son says he will not go but does (Metzger's option c).

responses to their father's request that they "go and work in the vineyard today" (21:28–30) emphasizes two important dimensions: the doing of the father's will and the passing of time which enables a first response to be reversed rather than maintained.

The unit is introduced with Jesus' question, "What do you think?" The question invites the engagement of the religious leaders (21:23). To the audience the question suggests, on the basis of its similar use in 18:12, a story to ponder and signals, on the basis of its use by Jesus to Peter in 17:25, important teaching for disciples.[19]

Matt 21:28 briefly sketches a scene centered on working in a vineyard. This setting and action recalls the parable of the householder who pays the workers in the vineyard the same rate though they had worked different hours (20:1–16). The workers oppose the householder's action, because with their evil eye they are unable to see his good action (20:15). These links with 20:1–16 alert the audience to the possibility of further surprising events in this parable.[20]

Several features in the scene lead the audience, at least initially, to expect obedience from the son (21:28). The double use of "son," once in the narrative introduction and once as the father's direct address to him, invokes household relationships in which children honor parents with compliance. The reference to the vineyard and the instruction to work in it invokes standard household economic responsibilities.[21] Matt 21:29a, then, is a major surprise which throws these expectations off-balance. The son says no to working in the vineyard, a response which goes unchallenged by the father. Instead, the verse marks the passing of time (ὕστερον, "afterward"), but then in a surprising reversal, narrates the son's change of mind that leads to his work in the vineyard (21:29b). Matt 21:30 repeats and contrasts this scene with the second son. His positive response seems to restore and affirm the normal expectations for such a situation, but the last two words (οὐκ ἀπῆλθεν) depicting his lack of action undermine them.

Jesus' question in 21:31 poses the central issue, "Which of the two did the will of his father?" The religious leaders answer correctly. The first son, though at first refusing, does what his father wants. The second son, though

[19] In 22:17 the religious leaders will use the same question to address Jesus and he uses it of them in 22:42.

[20] Gundry, *Matthew*, 422–23, notes a number of similarities with 20:1–16. For discussion of 20:1–16, see chapter 6 above.

[21] Carter, *Households and Discipleship*, 19–22, 127–43.

saying he will do it, does not. The audience knows the leaders have answered correctly because their response corresponds with Jesus' previous teaching to disciples about doing God's will (7:24–27; 12:46–50) and with his previous condemnation of hypocrisy (6:2, 5, 16; 7:5; 15:7; cf. 22:18; 23:13, 15, 23, 25, 27, 29).

Jesus' comments in 21:31b–32 indicate, though, that they condemn themselves by their answer. The leaders are among those who have not worked in the vineyard. The parable is constructed, as the audience recognizes, from language and metaphors belonging to the leaders' tradition. The vineyard is a common image for Israel as God's special, though frequently erring, people (Isa 5:1–7; Jer 12:10–11; Ezek 19:10–14; Hos 10:1). The metaphor of "father" and "son" or "children" also images the relationship of God and Israel.[22] Doing the will of God has been a constant requirement throughout the traditions (Exod 20–23; Deut 5) as has been suspicion of those who say one thing but do another (so Jesus' quote from Jer 7:10–11 in 21:13; also Jer 6:10–21; Isa 1:10–20). The leaders have condemned themselves as those who have not worked in the vineyard. By highlighting the correctness of the first son's responsive actions, they betray their own lack of action in response to God.

Jesus names their rejection of John as the crucial test. John came in "the way of righteousness," a phrase which, as the audience recognizes, not only employs a scriptural metaphor for living according to God's purposes (Prov 8:20 [wisdom]; 12:28; 16:31) but which also takes the audience back to the initial presentation of John in Matthew 3. The term "way" (ὁδός) recalls the description of John as the one about whom Isaiah spoke who calls for the preparation of "the way of the Lord" (3:3). John urges preparation by repentance and baptism for God's coming. In the context of Matthew 1–2, the audience understands this coming in relation to Jesus. This "way" is God's saving presence and purposes manifested in Jesus, Emmanuel (cf. 1:21, 23).[23]

The use of "righteousness" points to the same conclusion. The word invokes John's baptism of Jesus "to fulfill all righteousness" (3:15). Given the

---

[22] Deut 8:5; 14:1; 32:6; Ps 68:6; 103:13; Isa 1:1–9; 64:8; Hos 11:1; Sir 23:1; Wis 14:3; 3 Macc 6:3, 8; 7:6. See G. Schrenk and G. Quell, "πατήρ," *TDNT,* 5. 970–82, though Schrenk's comments on the lack of "the spirit of true faith" in early Judaism (pp. 981–82) betray a regrettable anti-Jewish bias and ecclesial triumphalism mandating caution.

[23] Uses of "way" subsequent to Matthew 3 illustrate that the "way of the Lord" requires an ongoing ethical daily living accountable in the judgment (7:13–14) and marked by mission (10:5, 10) and the cross (20:17). The use of the word in 21:8 and 21:19 provides further links with the earlier part of the chapter.

use of "fulfill" in 1:22, 2:15, 17, 23 to indicate the carrying out of God's salvific will in Jesus, "righteousness" in 3:15 suggests a similar enactment of God's previously declared purposes.[24] The audience's knowledge of this term from the Jewish scriptures as indicating human action in accord with and shaped by God's purposes and activity supports this understanding (cf. Jer 22:13–17).

John thus comes in accord with God's salvific purposes, preaching and doing God's will as well as preparing for the coming of Jesus ("way of righteousness"), but the religious leaders have not recognized it (3:7–10). They have not believed his proclamation of God's coming in Jesus and of imminent judgment (3:1–12; cf. 21:25). Their not believing John means not believing Jesus. It parallels the second son in the parable, who does not go to the vineyard (21:30b, 32a). To believe means a way of life in accord with God's purposes marked by active righteousness (cf. 5:20). The absence of that way of life indicates their lack of belief.

But their plight is even worse. Since their initial rejecting response there has been the passing of time. The parable has indicated the passing of time as an opportunity to change one's mind (the first son) or to do what one has said (the second son). But the leaders have not availed themselves of this time nor of its new incentive to believe: that the socially marginal and disenfranchised "tax collectors and the prostitutes believed" John and enter the reign (21:32).[25]

The gospel narrative of John's activity has provided no explicit instances of this belief though the audience could understand that they were included among the generic description of those from Jerusalem and Judea who went out to John to be baptized (3:5–6). Perhaps more important, in the light of this absence, are the scenes of Jesus' merciful and transforming association with the marginalized tax collectors (9:10–11; 10:3; cf. 9:9; 11:19) and sinners (9:10–13; 11:19). That is, "tax collectors and prostitutes" have believed John in that they have repented and are already experiencing God's saving presence manifested in Jesus,[26] for whom John prepared the way and to whom

---

[24] For righteousness as divine activity and human behavior, see Meier, *Law and History,* 76–80; Przybylski, *Righteousness,* 1–12, 91–96.

[25] Levine, *Social and Ethnic Dimensions,* 204–6, emphasizes the social contrast between this group and the powerful and privileged leaders. J. Gibson, "Hoi Telōnai kai hai Pornai," *JTS* 32 (1981) 429–33, argues that this surprising connection has less to do with low moral and ritual standing as with collaboration with the Roman occupying force.

[26] For the way in which the narrative enables the audience to identify the "reign of the heavens" with God's saving presence (1:21, 23; 3:2; 4:17), see chapter 3 above.

John bore witness. But the religious leaders, even when "you saw" these encounters (cf. 9:11; 11:19), do not "afterwards" (ὕστερον, 21:32; cf. 21:29) "repent" (μετεμελήθητε, 21:32; cf. 21:29) and believe. This vocabulary shared between the parable and the explanation clearly contrasts the religious leaders with the first son who used the passing of time to change his mind. The leaders have missed out on and so exclude themselves from encounter with God's saving presence.

In terms of its pragmatic impact the parable presents a double condemnation of the leaders as well as a model and warning for the audience of disciples. The leaders have not done God the Father's will. But neither have they availed themselves of the passing of time and the action of God's saving presence evidenced in the repentance and belief of the tax collectors and prostitutes who changed their rejecting response. The parable evidences the leaders' "hardheartedness" (19:8), their obdurate resistance to and rejection of God's purposes. But, contrary for instance to Drury's and Lambrecht's reading, it does not indicate their final and ultimate rejection.[27] The parable employs but does not sever the father-son image. The parable does not narrate the father disowning the disobedient son or the vineyard. There is still the time and opportunity for the second son to change his mind and go to work in the vineyard. For the audience there is the question of how the son might be persuaded to go and do so. There is also for the audience the challenge and warning to continue to be among those who do the will of God.

3. Matthew 21:33–46: Parable of the Householder, the Vineyard, and the Tenants[28]

The immediate following of the first parable with a second, and Jesus' opening comment, "Hear another parable," create for the audience the expecta-

---

[27] Drury, *Parables in the Gospels*, 96, claims the parable "explains the momentous transfer of divine approval from orthodox Jewry to the unrespectable but responsive gathering of repentant sinners who make up the church." Lambrecht, *Treasure*, 104, notes the parable depicts the Jews' "persistent hardening" upon which "Jesus pronounces their condemnation." My reading is closer to that of Donahue, *Gospel in Parable*, 88–89, who sees the parable holding out to the Judaism of the author's own day the opportunity to do the will of God revealed by Jesus.

[28] For discussion, see n. 1 above, the commentaries (and listed bibliographies), especially Patte, *Matthew*, 297–301; Harrington, *Matthew*, 301–5; Scott, *Hear Then the Parable*, 237–53. See also M. Hubaut, *La parabole des vignerons homicides* (CahRB 16; Paris: Gabalda, 1976) 13–103; K. Snodgrass, *The Parable of the Wicked Tenants* (WUNT 27; Tübingen: Mohr, 1983) 72–110; C. Carlston, *The Parables of the Triple Tradition* (Philadelphia: Fortress, 1975) 40–45.

tion that this second parable will reinforce and develop the insights of the previous parable in several ways. The second parable maintains the general focus on Israel's relationship with God through the image of the vineyard. It repeats the condemnation of the religious leaders by depicting the fateful consequences for the leaders of their persistent rejection of God's purposes. It features a son who says yes to God's purposes and carries them out. But there is also progression in that it identifies another group to take over the role of the displaced leaders as the agents of God's purposes in ensuring the fruitfulness of the vineyard Israel.

As with the previous parable this one employs numerous images from Israel's tradition. The audience knows that "householder" (οἰκοδεσπότης) has been used previously in 10:25 to refer to Jesus, and in 13:27, 20:1, 11 for God. Subsequently in 21:40 he is identified as the vineyard's master (κύριος), a term used in the gospel for God (cf. 21:42).[29] The opening emphasis on the householder's actions of setting up the vineyard by planting, hedging around, digging, and building recalls passages such as Isa 5:1–7 and Jer 2:21, which speak of God "planting" or calling into being Israel.[30] Not mentioned, though, in passages such as Isaiah 5 are the householder/owner's absence in another country and the tenants, who, as agents of the owner, are entrusted with the task of ensuring the fruitfulness of the vineyard. Absent from the parable are any details about the tenants' contract with the owner, the length of time the owner is absent, the growth of the vineyard, or the way in which they are to carry out their responsibilities. In the context of Matthew 21 (cf. 21:23–27), the audience identifies the tenants as religious leaders who have been entrusted by God with responsibility for the vineyard's fruitfulness or faithfulness.

The owner's absence is a crucial element in the development of the parable's plot. It provides not only an element of realism in reflecting a common economic practice, but also the means by which the tenants' accountability to the owner is measured. Accordingly at harvest time ("the season of fruits"), the owner sends "his servants" to collect the fruit but they meet with violent

[29] Matt 1:20, 22, 24; 2:13, 15, 19; 3:3; 4:7, 10; 5:33; 7:21–22; 9:38; 11:25; 21:9.

[30] Verbal parallels between Matt 21:33 and Isa 5:1–2 (LXX) can be noted: ἀμπελών ("vineyard"), ἐφύτευσεν ("planted"), φραγμὸν περιέθηκεν ("made a hedge around"), ὤρυξεν ἐν αὐτῷ ληνὸν ("dug a wine press in it"), ᾠκοδόμησεν πύργον ("built a tower"). Snodgrass' claim, *Wicked Tenants*, 76, that the vineyard represents "the privileges entrusted to the people" is undermined by these connections as well as by the outcome of the story.

resistance and death (21:34–35). The scene is repeated with greater intensity ("more than the first") but the same consequences in 21:36. The tenants dishonor the master's servants and refuse to supply the owner with fruit, stealing it from him by keeping it for themselves. In so doing they refuse to honor his authority as sender of the servants and as owner of the vineyard.

Using its assumed knowledge and that acquired from its progression through the preceding narrative, the audience can identify the servants as prophets sent to Israel on the basis of four observations.[31] 1) The identification of the owner as God, the vineyard as Israel "planted" by God, and the tenants as the religious leaders encourages continuing allegorical reading in terms of Israel's history with God. 2) The audience knows the prophetic tradition in which prophets are frequently identified as God's "servants" (Jer 7:25; Amos 3:7). Though sent by God they experience conflict with and rejection by the people's leaders (cf. Jer 7:25–26; 25:4; 26:5; 29:19; 35:15; 2 Chr 36:15–16; Neh 9:26; Dan 9:6: "we have not listened to your servants the prophets"; *Jub.* 1:12–13). 3) Some identification of particular prophets is possible on the basis of the descriptions of their fate.[32] 4) The audience knows that the gospel has previously identified persecution as a fundamental aspect of the prophetic experience (5:12) and will reinforce this with a lament for Jerusalem's killing and stoning the prophets and those sent to it (cf. 23:37). This context of Israel's history with God encourages the audience to evaluate the actions of the tenants in terms of the foundation covenant requirements of the Decalogue. By dishonoring the owner, stealing his produce, and killing the messengers, the tenants break God's commandments to honor God, not to kill and not to steal.

---

[31] Snodgrass, *Wicked Tenants*, 77–80, esp. n. 26.

[32] Drury, *Parables in the Gospels*, 96–97, suggests particular prophets. Jeremiah is beaten (Jer 20:2), Uriah is killed (Jer 26:20–23; LXX 33:20–23), Azariah/Zechariah is stoned (2 Chr 24:21). The choice of verbs suggests some particular prophets: the *attempt* to kill Uriah but not the actual killing employs the verb ἀποκτεῖναι (Jer 33:21 LXX) used in Matt 21:35; and the verb ἐλιθοβόλησαν ("stoned") appears in both 2 Chr 24:21 and Matt 21:35. See also A. Weiser, *Die Knechtsgleichnisse der synoptischen Evangelien* (SANT 29; Munich: Kösel, 1971) 53–54; Hubaut, *La parabole*, 32–36; idem, "La parabole des vignerons homicides: son authenticité, sa visée première," *RTL* 6 (1975) 51–61. Jeremias, *Parables of Jesus*, 72, J. D. Crossan, "The Parable of the Wicked Husbandmen," *JBL* 90 (1971) 451–65, esp. 453, and Stock, *Matthew*, 332, suggest the two groups represent the pre- and post-exilic prophets. Gundry, *Matthew*, 426, notes the use of stoning for the prophet deemed incorrectly to be false in 2 Chr 24:20–21. He suggests the tenants "treated the servants as false prophets."

After these repeated, unsuccessful efforts the patient owner mercifully tries again. This time he sends his son, expecting the tenants to honor him (21:37). But seized by greed, the tenants agree "among themselves" (ἐν ἑαυτοῖς, 21:38) to resist the master's authority again, just as the religious leaders earlier debated "among themselves" (ἐν ἑαυτοῖς, 21:25) how to avoid recognizing John and Jesus' authority. The tenants kill the son in order to possess his inheritance, the vineyard (21:37–39).[33] Their action challenges the master's authority and expresses their desire to be their own masters. Though some have debated the identification of the son,[34] the audience knows that in the context of the gospel it denotes Jesus. First, the sending of the servants/prophets and the son happens "when the season of fruits drew near" (21:34), a phrase that employs the same verb as is used in 21:1 to denote Jesus' "drawing near" to Jerusalem (ἤγγισαν/ἤγγισεν). Second, Jesus has been identified as God's son previously in the narrative (2:15; 3:17; 4:3, 6; 11:27; 14:33; 16:16; 17:5). Third, the audience knows from the passion predictions (16:21; 17:12, 22; 20:17–19) that Jesus must die at the hands of the religious leaders. The tenants' killing of the son in the parable is consistent with the identification of the tenants as the religious leaders and with the larger plot of the gospel in which the parable is embedded.

The parable ends with a prediction, rather than a description, of the plot's completion. Jesus asks the religious leaders how the owner will respond to the death of his son (21:41). The question provides the religious leaders with

---

[33] Jeremias, *Parables of Jesus,* 74–76, suggests the tenants think that the appearance of the son means the death of the owner. J. D. M. Derrett, "The Parable of the Wicked Vinedressers," *Law in the New Testament* (London: Darton, Longman & Todd, 1970) 296–305, situates their action in viticultural and economic laws and practices.

[34] For example, J. E. Newell and R. R. Newell, "The Parable of the Wicked Tenants," *NovT* 14 (1972) 226–37, argue that in its original form the husbandmen are zealots, Galilean freedom fighters, resisting foreign possession of land; the son belongs to the narrative logic of the parable but does not gain a christological meaning until later in the tradition's development. Both M. Lowe, "From the Parable of the Vineyard to a Pre-Synoptic Source," *NTS* 28 (1982) 257–63, esp. 257–59, and D. Stern, "Jesus' Parables from the Perspective of Rabbinic Literature: The Example of the Wicked Husbandmen," *Parable and Story in Judaism and Christianity* (ed. C. Thoma and M. Wyschogrod; Mahwah: Paulist, 1989) 42–80, esp. 65–68, propose John the Baptist. A. A. Milavec, "A Fresh Analysis of the Parable of the Wicked Husbandmen in the Light of Jewish-Christian Dialogue," *Parable and Story in Judaism and Christianity* (ed. C. Thoma and M. Wyschogrod; Mahwah, NJ: Paulist, 1989) 81–117, esp. 99–104, argues that the son has no "specifiable referent."

the opportunity to complete the story. In doing so, his question and their answer function as in the previous parable (21:31a) to trap the leaders into further self-condemnation. They respond by identifying the tenants as "evilly evil" (κακοὺς κακῶς) thereby unwittingly agreeing with Jesus' previously-given verdict on them as evil (πονηρός, 9:4; 12:34–35, 39; 16:4).[35] They predict that the owner will kill the tenants. The destroyers will be destroyed; those who resisted his authority will be totally subjected to his authority in their death. He will find "other tenants" for the vineyard. Ironically they describe these "other tenants" with a phrase ("will give him fruits in their seasons," v 41) that recalls for the audience the description of the righteous in contrast to the wicked in Ps 1:3.

Jesus does not dispute their response but builds on it by citing Ps 118:22–23. The citation is introduced by the same question he has used in previous disputes with the religious leaders to expose their ignorance of God's purposes previously declared in the scriptures and being manifested in Jesus, "Have you not read . . . ?" (12:3, 5; 19:4; 21:16). As with other citations in the gospel this use of Psalm 118 makes sense only in relation to Jesus. He is rejected by people but vindicated by God. One function of the citation is to show again the leaders' rejection of God's purposes being enacted in Jesus. The leaders do not recognize "the Lord's doing" nor rejoice that "it is marvelous to our eyes" (21:42), the perspective expected of the audience. As with the vineyard parable in 20:1–16, their evil eyes prevent them recognizing God's purposes in Jesus (cf. 20:15). The citation reinforces these purposes. Its building image portrays Jesus as the cornerstone or, more likely, given the son's later place in the sequence of sent messengers (21:34–39), the capstone (of an archway) of the new house of prayer which God is building (21:13–17, 21–22).

Jesus declares that the leaders will lose their role as representatives or agents of and participants in God's reign (21:43). His statement confirms the ending to the parable which they proposed in 21:41 and develops a contrast from the previous parable (21:28–32). There their refusal to "believe John" is contrasted with "the tax collectors and prostitutes" who are already going into the kingdom; here their exclusion is contrasted with those to whom the kingdom will be given. Given the focus throughout on the religious leaders,

---

[35] Louw and Nida, *Lexicon*, 1.754, list κακός and πονηρός in the same subdomain (Subdomain O, 88.106, 88.110) of Domain 88, "Moral and Ethical Qualities and Related Behavior."

and Jesus' specific address to them in 21:40, 42, 43, it is impossible for the audience to understand Jesus' statement as indicating the exclusion of all Israel.[36]

Moreover, Jesus declares God's reign given to a people (ἔθνει) who will produce its "fruits" (καρπούς). The audience has been reminded as recently as the scene of Jesus' cursing of the fig tree (21:18–22) that "fruit" images faithful obedience to and manifestation of God's will and reign (7:16–20). Such fruitfulness involves the reverse of the behavior of the previous "evilly evil" tenants (21:34–39, 41). It means not only acknowledging the owner's claim and authority, not stealing what is his, not rejecting and killing his servants, but also living according to his purposes. Such is the obligation of disciples who have encountered God's saving presence, God's reign, in Jesus' proclamation and actions (4:17–25; 7:16–20).[37] This "people" to whom the reign of God is given (21:43) are the "other tenants" suggested by the religious leaders in 21:41. They will take over the task of enabling the vineyard to produce the fruit which it was established to produce.

The identity of this "people" has been much debated with various suggestions being proposed (Gentiles; the church; leaders of the Jewish Christian church).[38] Given the diverse uses of ἔθνος and given the use here of the singular ἔθνει rather than Matthew's more usual plural, it is not possible for the audience to understand this "people" as an ethnic entity ("Gentiles") who replace Jews as God's people. The emphasis in 21:41, 43 on "bearing fruit" underlines the term's primarily ethical, and not ethnic, nature. Moreover replacement of Israel is not in view in the parable's allegory. The vineyard/Israel is not destroyed; it remains. The owner remains determined to have fruit from it. What changes is the "group of people" or "small sub-

---

[36] With, for example, Harrington, *Matthew,* 304; Gundry, *Matthew,* 430; P. Culbertson, "Reclaiming the Matthean Vineyard Parables," *Encounter* 49 (1988) 257–83, esp. 267; Snodgrass, *Wicked Tenants,* 109; *contra* Crossan, "Wicked Husbandmen," 454; Stock, *Matthew,* 331; Hare, *Matthew,* 248–49; Drury, *Parables in the Gospels,* 97 ("Judaism was condemned and Christianity authorized").

[37] R. J. Dillon, "Towards a Tradition-History of the Parables of the True Israel (Matthew 21,33-22,14)," *Bib* 47 (1966) 1–42, elaborates the emphasis on fruit bearing in relation to the gospel's eschatologically motivated ethics.

[38] In addition to the commentaries, see Snodgrass, *Wicked Tenants,* 90–95; D. R. A. Hare and D. J. Harrington, "'Make Disciples of All the Gentiles' (Matthew 28:19)," *CBQ* 37 (1975) 359–69; J. P. Meier, "Nations or Gentiles in Matthew 28:19?" *CBQ* 39 (1977) 94–102.

group"[39] with the responsibility for ensuring it does produce fruit.[40] The religious leaders have shown their unworthiness for the task that is now being committed to others. The audience knows from throughout the gospel narrative that this other group must be the group of disciples who have been presented as the group constituted by its encounter with the reign of God present in Jesus' words and actions (4:17–23; 5:3, 10; 11:11–12; 12:28; 13:11, 19, 24, 31, 38). It has also been sent in mission to Israel to proclaim and demonstrate the presence of God's reign (10:7–8; cf. 15:24).[41] This people, the ἐκκλησία (16:18) which includes Jews and Gentiles, exists as agents of God's reign seeking fruit from the vineyard for God.[42]

Of significance are the future tenses employed in 21:41 and 21:43. Jesus' question to the religious leaders about how the owner will react to the death of his son assumes no reaction as yet from the owner. Not yet has he killed the tenants; not yet has he given over the vineyard to new tenants. Of course in

---

[39] Saldarini, *Matthew's Christian-Jewish Community*, 59–60, 78–81. Meier, "Nations or Gentiles?," surveys the uses of ἔθνος in Matthew in three categories: 1) seven cases which refer to "Gentiles" (4:15; 6:32; 10:5, 18; 12:18, 21; 20:19); 2) two doubtful cases (20:25–26; 24:9), the latter of which he subsequently moves into the third category; 3) not meaning "Gentiles" but "nation/s" or "people" which includes Jews and Gentiles (21:43, "people;" 24:7, "nation [probably the Jewish nation] against [a gentile] nation"); 24:9, 24:14, 25:32 and 28:19, "nations," including Jews). Also to be noted is that the noun appears in the singular only in 21:43 and 24:9 (2x).

[40] So Harrington, *Matthew*, 303–5; Milavec, "Wicked Husbandmen," 105. Gundry, *Matthew*, 430, sees a democratization of custodianship whereby the vineyard now represents the kingdom (not Israel as in 21:33) and the church replaces not Israel but the religious leaders. See also Hare, *Matthew*, 249. I would prefer to argue (see below) that since the twelve disciples have a representative function throughout the story, the new group to whom the kingdom is entrusted consists of the community of disciples. But while they replace the religious leadership, they do not replace Israel (*contra* Limbrecht, *Treasure*, 123, 196). Their task is a mission one, which includes calling Israel to live faithfully to God's will as revealed by Jesus.

[41] Levine, *Social and Ethnic Dimensions*, 185–204.

[42] Saldarini, *Matthew's Christian-Jewish Community*, 60–61. Perhaps the "people" should be understood as the leadership of the community of disciples. But the twelve disciples seem to function less as leaders of the community of disciples than as representatives of it. Tasks committed to Peter become community tasks (cf. 16:17–19; 18:18). His confession is the community's confession (14:33; 16:16). Discipline is a community role (18:17). There is suspicion of leadership in the community with a more "egalitarian-communal" model being commended (23:8–10). "You who have followed me" participate in "judging" Israel in 19:28. Whatever is envisaged in this scene, the use of a general designation for disciples means that it is not restricted to the twelve.

the fiction of the gospel narrative Jesus' death has not yet taken place, so the future orientation in the discussion of the householder's response is appropriate. But that discussion does not specify when after the son's death he will act. This future orientation thus has a further important effect in introducing not only a note of futurity but also uncertainty about the timing of this punishment and transfer of tenants (cf. 23:2). Such uncertainty is quite consistent with the gospel's presentation of the present-future nature of the kingdom. While it is already present in part in the words and actions of Jesus (cf. 12:28) and some are already entering in (21:31), it is not yet fully present. There is a continuing dimension of ethical living and a future dimension of accountability in the judgment (7:15–27; 10:32–42; 18:21–35). The group taking over the tenancy of the vineyard must continue to live faithfully and fruitfully as it goes about its task, knowing what has happened to the previous tenants and knowing that it must give account in the judgment.[43]

The section ends with the leaders' awareness that Jesus has spoken "concerning them" (21:45).[44] The plural term "parables" enables the audience to draw both parables together (the two sons, 21:28–32; the vineyard and tenants, 21:33–46) as a double condemnation of the leaders. Ironically, while the leaders perceive that *Jesus* spoke about them, there is no indication of their awareness that they had earlier spoken about themselves in 21:41 and 21:31a and that Jesus had simply confirmed their self-condemnation. Nor does their awareness lead to any acceptance of the accuracy of Jesus' depiction of them in the parable as greedy thieves who resist his authority and refuse to give the rightful fruit to the owner. No repentance results in their own living, nor do they reconsider their stance toward or evaluation of Jesus. Their response bears out Jesus' statement about the divisive impact of parables in 13:10–17. The leaders are among those who "see but do not see, hear but do not hear, nor do they understand" (13:13).

Their response is to try and arrest him (21:46). They seek to do to him what the tenants in the parable had done to the son thereby again exposing their evil and condemning themselves. They are prevented from arresting him,

---

[43] Donahue, *Gospel in Parable*, 90–92, argues that the emphasis on fruit bearing indicates the primary recasting of the parable as a warning for the Matthean community against presumption and to emphasize the need for fruitful discipleship.

[44] On the originality of 21:44, see Gundry, *Matthew*, 430 (in support, also Hare, *Matthew*, 250), and Metzger, *Textual Commentary*, 58 (an accretion).

though, by their fear of the crowds' understanding of Jesus (21:46). The leaders continue the same stance as they evidenced with John (cf. 21:26) of seeking to maintain their own authority with the crowds while not recognizing God's. The reference to the crowds' understanding of Jesus as a prophet recalls 21:11. While this confession is inadequate in terms of understanding Jesus as God's Son, it is at least more positive than the leaders' opposition to Jesus. The crowds' inadequate but somewhat positive confession provides a starting point for the fruitful work of the "other tenants," for "the group of people" to whom the oversight of the vineyard has been given.[45]

The leaders thus remain resolute in not perceiving God's saving presence manifested in Jesus. They show themselves to be guilty of not taking advantage of the opportunity to change their response (21:28–32). In the previous parable and scene, Jesus rebukes them for not "believing John" even when they saw tax collectors and prostitutes believing (21:32). As this scene progresses they maintain their unbelief in the face of Jesus' explicit and direct disclosure of his identity as God's Son (21:37) sent from God, commissioned to reveal and carry out God's will. This key perspective, enunciated by the scriptures (2:15), by God (3:17; 17:5), by Jesus (11:27), and by disciples (14:33; 16:16), is not general knowledge but is insight gained from divine revelation in non-public situations (cf. 16:17).[46] The parable functions as their moment of revelation. But just as in the previous scene they do not recognize John's baptism as being "from heaven," here they do not recognize Jesus as being from God. Not to recognize Jesus as God's Son means seeking to arrest him, to put him to death. It means the selection of another people to carry out their role in the vineyard. But this people, hearing the parable, hears the warning that it must remain faithful and fruitful in its task.[47]

In terms of the parable's pragmatic impact, therefore, the audience gains further explanation for the religious leaders' rejection of Jesus. They have failed to honor his identity as God's Son, the one who performs God's saving purposes (1:21, 23). Further, the parable affirms the identity and role of those who do recognize God's purposes. Among this people is found the reign of the heavens, God's saving presence. But such an identity is not internally focussed. This people, blessed by God's saving presence, has the mission task of eliciting faith-

[45] Donahue, *Gospel in Parable,* 92; Carter, "Crowds," 64–67.

[46] Kingsbury, "Wicked Husbandmen," 643–55, esp. 646–52.

[47] So, for example, Carlston, *Parables,* 45.

ful responses from others, including Israel. Such a task requires its own faithful living in the knowledge that it remains accountable to God.

4. Matthew 22:1–14: Parable of the Wedding Feast[48]

Several commentators have noted that along with the basic verisimilitude which the parable creates, there are a significant number of unrealistic aspects:[49]

1) the double invitation (vv 3–4)
2) the universal rejection of the king's invitations (vv 3–5)
3) the shameful treatment and killing of the servants (v 6)
4) the king sending troops to burn the city (v 7)
5) the chronology of proceeding with the wedding immediately after the burning (v 8)
6) the setting for the wedding in the burned city (vv 7–8)
7) the invitation to the unlikely guests (vv 9–10)
8) the inspection of the wedding guests' clothing (v 11)
9) unreasonable expectation and exclusion of a poor guest for not having a wedding garment (vv 11–14).

Scott comments that "the destruction of the verisimilitude forces attention away from the story's story (from what happens) to its discourse (to what it means)."[50]

Several other conventions used by the implied author focus the audience's attention on the parable's meaning: 1) The opening verse, for instance, explicitly names Jesus as the story-teller. The use of his name invokes the opening key event of the gospel narrative in which the angel of the Lord announces to Joseph the naming of Mary's recently conceived baby. The

---

[48] For discussion, see the commentaries (and listed bibliographies), especially Patte, *Matthew*, 301–5; Harrington, *Matthew*, 305–9; Scott, *Hear Then the Parable*, 161–74; see also A. G. van Aarde, "A Historical-Critical Classification of Jesus' Parables and the Metaphoric Narration of the Wedding Feast in Matthew 22:1–14," *God-With-Us: The Dominant Perspective in Matthew's Story* (Hervormde Teologiese Studies Supplementum 5; Pretoria, 1994) 229–47; E. E. Lemcio, "The Parables of the Great Supper and the Wedding Feast: History, Redaction, and Canon," *HBT* 8 (1986) 1–26; E. Wainwright, "God Wills to Invite All to the Banquet: Matthew 22:1–10," *International Review of Mission* 77 (1988) 185–93.

[49] Gundry, *Matthew*, 433; Scott, *Hear Then the Parable*, 162.

[50] Scott, *Hear Then the Parable*, 162.

naming is a commissioning since the baby's names derive from God and denote God's purposes for it:

> . . . and you will call his name Jesus, for he will save his people from their sins (1:21).
> . . . and they will call his name Emmanuel, which means "God with us" (1:23).

The use of the name "Jesus" reminds the audience of Jesus' God-given mission to manifest God's saving presence. The parable is to be read in relation to those purposes.

2) The opening verse employs the phrase "again spoke to them in parables" (22:1). The pronoun "them" (αὐτοῖς) names Jesus' hearers. The audience identifies the religious leaders from the previous chapter (21:15, 23, 45) and in this context expects warning and condemnation. In addition the adverb "again" (πάλιν) and the noun "parables" cause the audience to connect what is to follow with the two preceding parables. From that connection the audience recalls the important themes already articulated and expects further treatment of them: God's repeated efforts to invite people to participate in God's purposes; the frequent rejection; the exclusion of those who do not wish to participate; the inclusion of others. The first parable of the two sons (21:28–32) focussed on John; the second about the vineyard and the tenants focussed on the death of the son (21:33–46). The audience can expect from this progression that this third parable be concerned in some way with "the people" to whom responsibility for the vineyard has been entrusted.

3) The second verse further contributes to the audience's focus on the parable's meaning by naming the reality (the reign of the heavens) being compared by the parable's narrative ("to a man, a king, who made a wedding feast for his son"). The parable lays "the reign of the heavens" beside the action of the story. The interaction between the two redescribes, discloses, creates, envisions God's reign. As we noted earlier, by Matthew 13 the audience "knows" much about God's reign. The fourteen references to the reign after Matthew 13 and prior to Matthew 22 have reinforced and extended that understanding. Gaining prominence has been instruction about the nature and responsibilities of the community of disciples created by the reign's presence (16:19; 18:1, 3, 4, 23; 19:12, 14, 23, 24; 20:1; 21:31, 43). Also important have been the reminders of accountability in the future judgment (16:28; 18:23–35; 20:21–28). The audience can expect either or both dimensions to be addressed in this parable. Its introduction with the passive verb ὡμοιώθη

("is like," "has become like," 13:24; 18:23) rather than the future passive ὁμοιωθήσεται ("will be like") used in some other parables (7:25, 27; 25:1) points at least initially to an emphasis on the experience of the reign in the present as a significant element of the parable.[51] On the basis of its previous experience with parables of the reign (in Matthew 13 for instance), the audience expects this parable to challenge by confirming, to renew by repeating largely familiar material.

4) Moreover, the use of numerous images from the scriptures in the previous parable encouraged the audience to read it as an allegory of God's past and present dealings with God's people and its leaders. The appearance in 22:2–3 of some of these same images (son, servants) and phrases,[52] as well as other well known scriptural images (king, feast), encourages the audience to continue to employ its knowledge of its religious traditions and to read allegorically.

The parable begins by naming its central character, the king. The audience knows that "king" is a common image for God in the scriptures. God the king reigns over the world (Pss 24; 93:1–2) and over the affairs of nations (Ps 47:3) challenging the nations' gods (Isa 41:21). Particularly God reigns over Israel as God's people (1 Sam 8:4–9; Pss 97:1–5; 99:1–5; Isa 44:6) bringing deliverance from exile (Isa 52:7). The day is coming when all nations will acknowledge God as king (Isa 24:23). The audience has also encountered the image previously in the gospel in 5:35 (Jerusalem as God's city) and in a previous parable at 18:23 highlighting the king's forgiving mercy (also introduced by ὡμοιώθη). It is also used for Jesus at 2:2 and 21:5.

A further factor, however, cautions the audience against making an instant identification of the king with God. It knows that "king" has been used negatively for Herod who tries to kill Jesus (2:1, 3, 9), for "kings" who will oppose disciples in their mission (10:18), and for Herod the tetrarch who kills John the Baptist (14:9). In the light of this data, the audience needs to engage the parable further to establish the nature of the image. Does the parable proceed by contrasting the king of the parable with the reign or does it proceed by showing the kingdom's king in action?

---

[51] Carson, "ΟΜΟΙΟΣ Word-Group," 277–82.

[52] Compare "he sent his servants" (ἀπέστειλεν τοὺς δούλους) in 21:34 with 22:3; "again he sent other servants" (πάλιν ἀπέστειλεν ἄλλους δούλους) in 21:36 and 22:4. The killing of the servants in 22:6 repeats one of the verbs used in 21:35 for the servants (ἀπέκτειναν) and in 21:38–39 (2x) for the son.

The king's actions of giving a marriage feast for his son (τῷ υἱῷ αὐτοῦ) points the audience to the latter conclusion. The son, identified as Jesus, was a significant element of the previous parable (cf. 21:37–39, τὸν υἱὸν αὐτοῦ). This identification indicates that this parable's king represents Israel's God. Confirming this conclusion is the marriage feast which the king gives. The audience knows that marriage is used in several prophets as a metaphor for God's covenant relationship with God's people (Hosea 1–3; Jer 2:2–3; 3:1–10; Ezek 16:8–63). It recalls 9:15 which identifies Jesus as the bridegroom present with them. It also knows that feasting and eating invoke multiple dimensions of participation in God's purposes. For example, the Exodus story employs food to present both God's gracious gift and the people's rebellion. God provides food for the grumbling people in the wilderness (Exodus 16; Ps 78:23–25). The Passover festival and meal ensure the continuing celebration of God's relationship with the people (cf. Exodus 12). The return from exile and the making of "an eternal covenant" are celebrated in the invitation to feast on "rich food" (Isaiah 1–3). The prophet envisions God's future triumphant return to Zion where God will make "for all peoples a feast of rich food" (Isa 25:6–10). Wisdom traditions also employ feasting as a symbol of living in God's presence. Lady Wisdom, a manifestation of God's presence and way, symbolizes the offering of life and instruction in God's way (Prov 8:32–36) by inviting people to a feast (Prov 9:1–2; cf. Matt 11:19).

The reference to a wedding feast also invokes associations built up around eating throughout the gospel.[53] The audience knows that food is a gracious gift from God (6:11, 25–31; 14:15–21; 15:32–39) and a symbol of God's goodness (7:9–11; 15:26–27) and transforming presence (13:33).[54] In this context the king's giving of a feast demonstrates the king's goodness (cf. 20:1–16). Jesus' meals with undesirable company such as "tax collectors and sinners" shows the all-inclusive extent of God's goodness which Jesus Emmanuel manifests (9:10–13; 11:18–19). It does not surprise the audience to learn that all sorts of unlikely people are invited to participate in the king's feast. But the audience also knows that meals have been places of division and conflict. Providing food to disciples in mission indicates one's "worthy" acceptance of their proclamation in contrast with those who do not (10:10–15). The reli-

---

[53] Note the suggestive article on Luke-Acts by J. H. Neyrey, "Ceremonies in Luke-Acts: The Case of Meals and Table Fellowship," *The Social World of Luke-Acts: Models for Interpretation* (ed. J. H. Neyrey; Peabody, MA: Hendrickson, 1991) 361–87.

[54] Funk, "Parable of the Leaven," 149–70; Praeder, "Parable of the Leaven," 11–35.

gious leaders have objected to the people Jesus eats with (9:10–13; 11:18–19), to the time and place of eating (12:1–8, the sabbath), and to the disciples' non-observance of the ritual requirements of eating (15:1–20). In turn Jesus has used a food image to warn disciples about the teaching of the religious leaders (16:1–12). In this context the setting of a feast alerts the audience to conflict and division in the parable.[55]

That conflict appears in 22:3b and concerns the non-recognition of the king's authority. The audience knows that the allegory set up with the references to the king, marriage feast, and son plays a crucial role in elaborating the nature of this conflict. The king sends his servants to call those who have been invited to the festivities but they do not wish (ἤθελον) to come. The servants sent by the king denote, as in the previous parable (cf. 21:35–36), the prophets sent by God to the religious leaders.[56] The image of servants who obediently carry out the task for which they are sent emphasizes the authority of the king.[57] So too does the verb "send" in 22:3–4 (ἀπέστειλεν). The audience recalls that the same verb is used for the householder/God sending the servants in 21:34, 36 and the son in 21:37 (cf. 20:2). Previously in the gospel God is designated as "the one who sent" (ἀποστείλαντα) Jesus (10:40; cf. 15:24) and in 11:10 (by means of Mal 3:1) as the one who sent John the prophet. Jesus also has authority to send disciples in mission (10:5, 16) and will send angels in the judgment to cleanse God's reign (13:41).

The verb used to express the servants' task, "to call those who have been called/invited," also underlines the king's authority. The audience knows that the verb "to call" (καλέσαι) has been used previously to express God's authority in commissioning Jesus to save from sins ("you will *call* his name

---

[55] The wedding image has played some role in the gospel. The noun γάμος ("wedding celebration or banquet") appears here for the first time (22:2, 3, 4, 8, 9, 10, 11, 12); the verb γαμέω ("marry") has been used three times, all in negative circumstances (5:32; 19:9, 10), and Jesus has been identified as the bridegroom in 9:15.

[56] Some might argue that the servants, or at least the second group in 22:4 represent disciples or Christian missionaries, so Hendrickx, *Parables of Jesus,* 124; Hare, *Jewish Persecution,* 121–22. Certainly δοῦλος refers to such in the mission discourse of 10:24–25, to disciples in the parables of 13:27–28 and 18:23, 26, 27, 28, 32, and to disciples in 20:27. But given the clear reference to prophets in the salvation-historical allegory of 21:34–36, it seems best to take these references to prophets also. However, given also the continuity between prophets and the Christian community in terms of similar experiences of rejection (5:10–12; 13:10–17), the mission experiences of the authorial audience are not far away.

[57] Compare the centurion who as one under authority (ὑπὸ ἐξουσίαν) commands his servant (δοῦλος) to "do this" and "he does it" (8:9).

Jesus," 1:21) and to manifest God's presence ("and they will *call* his name Emmanuel," 1:23), as well as to express God *calling* Jesus "my Son" from Egypt (2:15). Jesus extends this authority by *calling* disciples (4:21) and by assuring them that in the future completion of God's purposes "they will be *called* God's children" (5:9). Jesus expresses his mission in terms of *calling* not the righteous but sinners (9:13). He uses the same verb in the temple conflict to express God's purposes as indicated by Isa 56:7 ("my house will be *called* a house of prayer," 21:13). The audience knows that the verb "call" has been used throughout to bring into being the divine will and purpose. In being sent by the king "to call the called," the servants bear the king's/God's authority in extending God's call to the recipients.

This emphasis on the authority of the king sets the scene for the leaders' refusal in 22:3b. Though honored by an authoritative invitation from the king, the invited ones "did not wish" to come. They do not reciprocate his honor; they do not value his authority; they publicly shame him.[58] Accordingly the king tries again by sending more servants with descriptions of sumptuous food preparations (22:4). But just as his authority was not recognized, nor is his generous goodness.[59]

Matt 22:5–6 elaborates the recipients' disregard for the king's authority thereby heightening their wrong. First they "disregard" or "neglect" (ἀμελήσαντες) the repeated invitations,[60] a description supported by the absence of any discussion of the king's invitation or the offering of any reasons for not accepting it. The minimal narrative presents the recipients as simply not giving the invitation any consideration. This negative presentation gains intensity by the description of their going about their daily life and its tasks (farm, business) undisturbed by the king's invitation.[61] Moreover in pursuing

---

[58] Neyrey, "Ceremonies in Luke-Acts," 371–74, 381–87; for honor and shame values, see B. J. Malina and J. H. Neyrey, "Honor and Shame in Luke-Acts: Pivotal Values of the Mediterranean World," *The Social World of Luke-Acts: Models for Interpretation* (ed. J. H. Neyrey; Peabody: Hendrickson, 1991) 25–65.

[59] Patte (*Matthew*, 302–3) highlights this two-stage appeal of authority and goodness.

[60] Louw and Nida, *Lexicon*, 1. 356.

[61] For attempts to connect these activities with the Deuteronomic provisions for excusing men from military service, see J. D. M. Derrett, "The Parable of the Great Supper," *Law in the New Testament* (London: Darton, Longman & Todd, 1970) 126–55; P. H. Ballard, "Reasons for Refusing the Great Supper," *JTS* 23 (1972) 341–50; H. Palmer, "Just Married, Cannot Come," *NovT* 18 (1976) 241–57; Scott, *Hear Then the Parable*, 170–71. Such attempts may be more convincing for the Lucan version or for the original Jesus parable than for Matthew's account, which does not contain the important marriage claim.

their daily affairs, they indicate a preference to benefit themselves rather than receive his gift.[62] They show no willingness to recognize the king's authority or to benefit from his goodness. But in a surprising escalation of the conflict, some seize, dishonor, and kill the servants sent with the invitations. The action indicates a complete and violent rejection of the king's authority and goodness.

Their violent and destructive response to the king brings their own destruction. The king, angered by their actions (cf. the master's anger in the parable of 18:34), sends troops to destroy them and their city. Knowledge of both historical events and religious traditions informs the audience's understanding. The audience knows that in 70 C.E. Jerusalem was destroyed by the Romans, an event seen by others also as God's punishment on the city (4 Ezra 3:24–36; 4:22–25; 5:21–30; 2 Bar 1:1–5; 4:1; 6:9; 32:2–3).[63] Given that this parable as with the two preceding ones, is directed to the religious leaders (21:45; 22:1), the audience understands that it is their rejection of God's messengers, particularly God's Son, that accounts for the punishment. The audience also knows the traditions which speak of God bringing judgment on God's people for unfaithfulness to the covenant. The Deuteronomist accounts for the exile in precisely these terms (Deuteronomy 18–30; 1 Kgs 9:1–9). Also to be noted is the description in Isaiah 5 of judgment on Jerusalem. The audience has already observed connections between the previous parable of the vineyard and Isa 5:2 (cf. Matt 21:33). The "burning" of the city coheres with the image of fire and judgment in the prophets (Amos 1:4, 10; Ezek 38:22; 39:6; Mal 4:1), in the preaching of John the Baptist (Matt 3:10, 12), and in Jesus' parables in Matt 13:30, 40, 42, 50.

But this act of punishment does not mean the king is finished with the city.[64] The king declares that those previously invited have shown they were not "worthy" (ἄξιοι) of the honor shown them because they have rejected the invitation. The audience knows from the previous gospel material that the religious leaders' unworthiness consists of their failure to live lives of obedient

[62] Patte, Matthew, 303.

[63] For a dissenting view, see K. H. Rengstorff, "Die Stadt der Mörder (Mt 22,7)," Judentum, Urchristentum, Kirche (BZNW 26; FS J. Jeremias; ed. E. Eltester; Berlin: Töpelmann, 1960) 106–29; Gundry, Matthew, 436–37.

[64] Again I cannot agree with Drury, Parables in the Gospels, 98, who claims the destruction of the city is "the doom of Judaism;" nor with Hendrickx, Parables of Jesus, 121, who sees the whole parable illustrating the judgment of Israel; nor with Lambrecht, Treasure, 119, 123, 133, 137, who also sees the sealing of Israel's fate and its replacement.

actions which reflect their repentance (3:8, ἄξιον τῆς μετανοίας), their failure to "receive" or "listen to" the proclamation of the reign (10:13–14), and their failure to "take [their] cross and follow" Jesus (10:37–38). Now the king issues a more general invitation sending his servants to call (καλέσατε, cf. 22:3–4) "as many as you find" to the wedding feast (22:9). This sending indicates the church's mission as tenants of the vineyard (cf. 21:43). The king's invitation, expressed by the same verb καλέω, is the same as that sent to the first invited guests. This time it is effective. God's gracious invitation fills the feasting room with those who this time respond positively, not negatively, to it.[65]

While the inviting of "all whom they found" may include Gentiles,[66] the parable emphasizes not nationality or gender or primarily socio-economic level[67] but the inclusiveness of all ethical types, "the bad and the good" (πονηρούς τε καὶ ἀγαθούς, 22:10). This is a familiar emphasis and pairing for the audience. In the parables of Matthew 13, for instance, the mission and community of disciples incorporates the wheat and weeds (13:24–30), the "doers of lawlessness" and the righteous (13:40–43), the good and the bad, the evil and the righteous (13:48–49), reflecting God's merciful actions which extend to all including the "bad and the good" (πονηρούς καὶ ἀγαθούς), "the just and the unjust" (δικαίους καὶ ἀδίκους, 5:45). The audience has also learned in the parables of Matthew 13 that now is not the time to separate the good from the bad and that the task for doing so belongs not to the community of disciples but to God at the judgment.

This knowledge provides the audience with the necessary orientation for the last part of the parable. While the guests recline at the feast, the king comes in to look at them (22:11). He sees a guest without a wedding garment

---

[65] D. O. Via, "The Relationship of Form and Content in the Parables: The Wedding Feast," *Int* 25 (1971) 171–84, esp. 182.

[66] Scott, *Hear Then the Parable*, 163, Hendrickx, *Parables of Jesus*, 126. Gundry, *Matthew*, 436–37, protests the identification of 22:7 with the fall of Jerusalem in 70 because the universal mission begins after the resurrection not after 70. Yet if Luz, *Matthew 1–7*, 76, 84–87, is right that the gentile mission is a recent post-70 commitment of the Matthean community and is being sustained by the gospel story, the understanding of the third sending after the burning of the city (22:8–10) may well reflect the history of Matthew's audience. However, on the basis of my reading of 21:33–45, and on the lack of ethnic emphasis in 22:8-10, I would disagree with Luz, *Matthew 1–7*, 88, that the "mission in Israel has come to an end."

[67] Levine, *Social and Ethnic Dimensions*, 211–15, emphasizes that the privileged and elite refuse the invitation while, as in 21:28–32, those lacking status and authority accept. There is no denying this contrast but I would argue that without enforcing a false divide emphasis falls on ethical inclusivity.

and inquires as to its absence. The guest, being unable to answer the challenge (cf. 22:34), is thrown out. The absence of the wedding garment is clearly a serious offense (whatever the practicalities of the recent invitation).

The audience is left with the task of making sense of the scene.[68] In the context of the previous parables in Matthew 21, the absence of the wedding garment suggests failure to discern and honor the authority and goodness of the king. It also suggests a failure to behave or live in a manner appropriate to the status of being one invited by the king. These conclusions are strengthened by the audience's knowledge of the previous judgment scenes in the gospel invoked by the language in 22:13 of "bind" (13:30), "outer darkness" (cf. 8:12; also 25:30) and "weep and gnash their teeth" (8:12; 13:42, 50; also 24:51; 25:30). These scenes also indicate failure to accept or believe Jesus and his proclamation as an important element (cf. 8:10–12; 13:3–9, 18–23, 36–38). This guest, though inside the wedding feast, is guilty of the same sorts of offenses as those who did not honor the invitation, and suffers the same fate.[69]

In pragmatic terms, this final scene functions as a warning and encouragement for the audience.[70] The audience, like the man, has heard and responded to the call by coming to the wedding. But his lack of honor for the king and his lack of appropriate behavior once inside the feast lead to his exclusion. The audience is warned that responding to the call is not the end but the beginning of God's purposes. To be called *and* chosen means to continue the honoring of God (22:37–39) and the ongoing doing of God's will (7:24–27; 12:46–50) until the final judgment.[71] To live in this manner is the means of demonstrating chosenness. For the audience to heed the warning of the parable is to be encouraged with the experience of continuing participation in God's purposes.

[68] Derrett, "Parable of the Great Supper," 142, emphasizes that inappropriate clothing is an insult; Dillon, "Towards a Tradition-History," 37–41, thinks the image recalls baptismal instruction.

[69] This reformulates the argument of D. C. Sim, "The Man Without the Wedding Garment," *HeyJ* 31 (1990) 165–78.

[70] For example, A. Ogawa, "Paraboles de l'Israel véritable?: Reconsidération critique de Mt. xxi 28–xxii 14," *NovT* 21 (1979) 121–49, esp. 149.

[71] B. F. Meyer, "Many (=All) Are Called, but Few (=Not All) Are Chosen," *NTS* 36 (1990) 89–97, esp. 94–96; Donahue, *Gospel in Parable*, 95–96.

CHAPTER 8

Final Parables in the Eschatological Discourse in Matthew 24–25

(by Heil)

A progression of comparisons and parables concludes the fifth and final major Matthean discourse, the eschatological discourse in Matthew 24–25:[1]

1. Matt 24:23–28: Comparison of lightning with the coming of the Son of Man

2. Matt 24:29–35: Knowing summer is near compared with knowing the Son of Man is near

3. Matt 24:36–41: The coming of the Flood compared with the coming of the Son of Man

4. Matt 24:42–44: Readiness for a thief compared to readiness for the Son of Man

[1] On the Matthean eschatological discourse, see, in addition to the commentaries: J. Lambrecht, "The Parousia Discourse: Composition and Content in Mt., XXIV–XXV," *L'Évangile selon Matthieu: Rédaction et théologie* (BETL 29; ed. M. Didier; Gembloux: Duculot, 1971) 309–42; S. Brown, "The Matthean Apocalypse," *JSNT* 4 (1979) 2–27; F. W. Burnett, *The Testament of Jesus-Sophia: A Redaction-Critical Study of the Eschatological Discourse in Matthew* (Lanham, MD: University Press of America, 1981); idem, "Prolegomenon to Reading Matthew's Eschatological Discourse: Redundancy and the Education of the Reader in Matthew," *Reader Response Approaches to Biblical and Secular Texts* (Semeia 31; ed. R. Detweiler; Decatur: Scholars, 1985) 91–109; V. K. Agbanou, *Le discours eschatologique de Matthieu 24–25: Tradition et rédaction* (Ebib 2; Paris: Gabalda, 1983); W. S. Vorster, "A Reader-Response Approach to Matthew 24:3–28," *Hervormde Teologiese Studies* 47 (1991) 1099–1108; I. Broer, "Redaktionsgeschichtliche Aspekte von Mt. 24:1–28," *NovT* 35 (1993) 209–33; K. Weber, *The Events of the End of the Age in Matthew* (Ph.D. Diss.; Washington: Catholic University of America, 1994) 93–100.

5. Matt 24:45–51: Parable comparing a servant who is faithful and wise or wicked
6. Matt 25:1–13: Parable of the reign the of heavens comparing wise and foolish maidens
7. Matt 25:14–30: Parable comparing servants who are given talents by their lord
8. Matt 25:31–46: Parable of judgment comparing the righteous and the unrighteous

The question that the disciples privately put to Jesus after he predicted to them the future destruction of the temple (24:1–2; cf. 23:38) introduces the theme of the eschatological discourse: "Tell us, when (πότε) will these things be and what will be the sign of your coming (cf. 23:39) and the end (συν-τελείας) of the age?" (v 3). Jesus begins to address the question of "when" by assuring them that although many will come in his name and mislead many by claiming to be the Christ (vv 4–5), and although they will hear of wars and reports of wars, "this is not yet (οὔπω) the end (τέλος)" (v 6). Nation will arise against nation and kingdom against kingdom and there will be famines and earthquakes, but all these things are only the beginning of the "birth-pangs" (vv 7–8). "Then" (τότε) the disciples will be betrayed, killed, and hated by all nations (v 9). And "then" (τότε) many will be scandalized and betray and hate one another (v 10). Many false prophets will arise and mislead many (v 11). Because of the increase of lawlessness the love of many will grow cold (v 12). But the one who perseveres to the end (τέλος) will be saved (v 13). The gospel of the reign will be preached throughout the whole world as testimony to all the nations, and only "then will come the end (τότε ἥξει τὸ τέλος)" (v 14).

Further addressing the question of "when" (πότε) will be the end (v 3), Jesus tells the disciples that "when" (ὅταν) they see "the abomination of deso-lation" standing in the holy place (v 15), "then" (τότε, v 16) is the time for flee-ing (vv 16–20). For "then" (τότε) will be the final and definitive great affliction of all time (v 21). But "those days" (ἡμέραι ἐκεῖναι, v 22[2x]; cf. v 19) of great affliction before the end will be shortened for the sake of the elect (v 22).

The first comparison of the eschatological discourse, the comparison of lightning with the coming of the Son of Man (v 27), occurs in the next unit (24:23–28), which begins by continuing to address the question of "when" (πότε, v 3): "Then (τότε, v 23; cf. vv 9, 10, 14, 16, 21) if someone says to you . . ." (v 23). A literary inclusion involving a theme of place establishes the integrity of this unit. The unit begins with an announcement of place, "the

Christ is here (ὧδε) or here (ὧδε)" (v 23), moves to an announcement that the Christ is in the "desert" or in the "inner rooms" (v 26), and concludes with a statement that "where" (ὅπου) the corpse is, "there" (ἐκεῖ) the vultures will gather (v 28). That this unit (24:23–28) follows the unit (24:14–22) that concludes with a reference to the great affliction (θλῖψις, v 21) that will take place in "those days" (ἡμέραι ἐκεῖναι, v 22 [2x]; cf. v 19) and precedes the unit (24:29–35) that begins with a reference to the time after the affliction (θλῖψιν) of "those days" (ἡμερῶν ἐκείνων) (v 29) confirms its integrity.[2]

References to "heaven" and "earth" form an inclusion that enables the audience to establish the integrity of the next unit (24:29–35), which contains the second comparison, the comparison between knowing when summer is near and knowing when the Son of Man is near (vv 32–33). It begins by describing the dissolution of the cosmos, including the stars falling from heaven (οὐρανοῦ) and the powers of the heavens (οὐρανῶν) being shaken (v 29). Then the sign of the Son of Man will appear in heaven (οὐρανοῦ) and all the tribes of the earth (γῆς) will mourn (v 30). It concludes by referring again to the dissolution of the universe: Heaven (οὐρανὸς) and earth (γῆ) will pass away (v 35).[3]

A theme of "not knowing" unifies the third unit (24:36–41) with its comparison between the coming of the Flood during Noah's time and the coming of the Son of Man (vv 37–39). No one knows (οὐδεὶς οἶδεν) the day (ἡμέρας) or the hour (ὥρας) of the coming of the Son of Man except the Father (v 36). Just as they did not know (οὐκ ἔγνωσαν) until the Flood came and took them all away, thus will be the coming of the Son of Man (v 39). People will not know what is happening. One of two men in a field will be taken and the other left; one of two women at a mill will be taken and the other left (vv 40–41).[4]

---

[2] The following treat 24:23–28 as a distinct unit in the eschatological discourse: Agbanou, *Le discours eschatologique*, 41, 93–102; Meier, *Matthew*, 284–86; Sand, *Matthäus*, 486–88; Patte, *Matthew*, 339–40; Blomberg, *Matthew*, 360–61; Stock, *Matthew*, 367–69.

[3] Matt 24:29–35 is usually treated as two separate units, 24:29–31 and 24:32–35. Although Agbanou, *Le discours eschatologique*, 41, treats 24:29–36 as a unit, he admits that v 36 has no structural link with the preceding verses, but constitutes a unity in itself that serves as a transition between the first and second part of the discourse.

[4] Agbanou, *Le discours eschatologique*, 42: "Les vv. 40–41 sont construits parallèlement avec les mêmes verbes. Ils sont une application de la comparaison, tandis que le v. 42 constitue la pointe qui introduit directement à la parabole suivante."

A theme of being "awake" and "ready" as a result of "not knowing" when the Son of Man will come unifies the fourth unit (24:42–44) with its comparison between being ready for a thief and being ready for the Son of Man (vv 43–44). After the third-person address of the third unit (24:36–41) the shift to second person address indicates the beginning of a new unit that applies the consequences of the third unit directly to the audience: "Stay awake, therefore (γρηγορεῖτε οὖν), for you do not know (οὐκ οἴδατε, cf. v 36) on what day (cf. v 36) your Lord is coming (ἔρχεται)" (v 42). This opening verse forms an inclusion with the second-person address of the final verse: "Therefore (διὰ τοῦτο) you also must be ready (γίνεσθε ἕτοιμοι), for at an hour (cf. v 36) you do not expect (οὐ δοκεῖτε) the Son of Man is coming (ἔρχεται)" (v 44). This inclusion, along with the notice that the householder would have "stayed awake" (ἐγρηγόρησεν, v 43), establishes the integrity of the fourth unit.[5]

A return to third-person address after the second-person address of the fourth unit as well as references to "servant" (δοῦλος, vv 45, 46, 48; αὐτόν in v 47 referring to δοῦλος in v 46; δούλου, v 50; αὐτὸν in v 51 referring to δούλου, in v 50) and to "lord" (κύριος, vv 45, 46, 48, 50; αὐτοῦ in v 47 referring to κύριος in v 46) unify the fifth unit (24:45–51), the parable comparing a faithful and a wicked servant.[6]

References to bridal "maidens" (vv 1, 7, 11) both "wise" (vv 2, 4, 8, 9) and "foolish" (vv 2, 3, 8) and to the "bridegroom" (vv 1, 5, 6, 10) as well as the theme of "staying awake" because of "not knowing" enable the audience to establish the integrity of the sixth unit (25:1–13), a parable of the reign of the heavens comparing wise and foolish bridal maidens. The answer of the bridegroom to the foolish maidens, who pleaded for the lord to open the door (v 11), introduces the theme of "not knowing": "Amen I say to you, I do not know (οὐκ οἶδα) you" (v 12). With an antithetical complement to the maidens becoming drowsy and falling asleep (v 5) and a continuation of the theme of "not knowing" the unit concludes by applying the parable to the audience: "Stay awake, therefore (γρηγορεῖτε οὖν, cf. 24:42), for you know neither (οὐκ οἴδατε, cf. 24:36, 42) the day (ἡμέραν, cf. 24:36, 42) nor the hour (ὥραν, cf. 24:36, 44)" (v 13).[7]

---

[5] Although 24:36–41 and 24:42–44 are closely related and many combine them into one unit, the second person address distinguishes 24:42–44 as a unit in itself, distinct from the preceding (24:36–41) and following (24:45–51) units.

[6] On the structural unity of 24:45–51, see also Agbanou, *Le discours eschatologique,* 42.

[7] On the structural unity of 25:1–13, see also Agbanou, *Le discours eschatologique,* 42. We

References to "servant(s)" (δούλους, v 14; δούλων, v 19; vv 21, 23, 26; δοῦλον, v 30), "lord" (κυρίου, vv 18, 21, 23; κύριος, vv 19, 21, 23, 26; κύριε, vv 20, 22, 24), and "talent(s)" (τάλαντα, vv 15, 16, 20 [4x], 22 [3x], 28; τάλαντον, vv 25, 28) unify the seventh unit (25:14–30), a parable comparing servants who are given talents by their lord.[8]

A theme of separation and judgment based on what was done to "the least ones" (vv 34–40, 41–45) unifies the eighth and final unit (25:31–46) of the eschatological discourse, a parable of judgment by the Son of Man comparing the righteous and the unrighteous. The unit begins with a climactic reference to the coming of the Son of Man (25:31; cf. 24:3, 27, 30, 37, 39, 44) followed by a separation for judgment of all nations like sheep are separated from goats (vv 32–33). It concludes with a separation of the unrighteous who go to eternal punishment from the righteous who go to eternal life (v 46).[9]

1. Matthew 24:23–28: Comparison of Lightning with the Coming of the Son of Man

After the disciples asked Jesus, "Tell us, when will these things be and what will be the sign of your coming and the end of the age?" (v 3), he warned them about being misled. As he then began his warning, "Beware lest anyone (τις) mislead you (ὑμᾶς)" (v 4), so now he continues, "Then if anyone (τις) says to you (ὑμῖν)" (v 23). Whereas he first warned that many will come in his name claiming, "I am the Christ (ὁ Χριστός)," and will mislead many (v 5), he now warns against believing anyone who would mislead them by pointing out the whereabouts of the Christ: "Behold the Christ (ὁ Χριστός) is here," or, "He is here" (v 23).

Jesus' warning that "many false prophets (ψευδοπροφῆται) will arise (ἐγερθήσονται, cf. v 7)" (v 11) now progresses to "false christs (ψευδόχριστοι) and false prophets (ψευδοπροφῆται) will arise (ἐγερθήσονται)" (v 24). His warning against anyone who would mislead (πλανήσῃ, v 4), the many false christs who will mislead (πλανήσουσιν) many (v 5), and the many

---

cannot agree with his comment that v 13 does not fit well with the content of the text because vigilance does not play an important role in the parable. He ignores or underestimates the "falling asleep" in the parable (v 5), which complements the command to "stay awake" in v 13.

[8] On the structural unity of 25:14–30, see also Agbanou, *Le discours eschatologique*, 43.

[9] On the structural unity of 25:31–46, see also Agbanou, *Le discours eschatologique*, 43, who notes: "Le dernier verset offre une conclusion adaptée à la péricope et accentue à nouveau la séparation faite au début."

false prophets who will mislead (πλανήσουσιν) many (v 11), now progresses to the warning against the false christs and false prophets who will give great signs and wonders in order to mislead (πλανῆσαι), if possible, even the elect (v 24). That God will shorten "those days" (vv 19, 22) of the great eschatological affliction (v 21) for the sake of the elect (ἐκλεκτοὺς, v 22) encourages the disciples and the Matthean audience, who are called to see themselves among the elect (ἐκλεκτοὺς, v 24), not to be misled about where the Christ will appear during his coming (v 3) after his resurrection.[10] Jesus' own authoritative prophecy uttered in the perfect tense to emphasize its continuing validity, "Behold I have told you beforehand (προείρηκα)" (v 25), stands in contrast to the misleading assertions of the false christs and false prophets.[11] It not only warns but prepares the disciples and the audience not to be misled.

The singular, "if (ἐάν) anyone says (εἴπῃ) to you (ὑμῖν)" (v 23), progresses to the plural, "if (ἐὰν) then they (the false christs and false prophets, v 24) say (εἴπωσιν) to you (ὑμῖν)" (v 26). The assertions, "Behold (ἰδοὺ) the Christ is here," or, "He is here" (v 23) become more specific: "Behold (ἰδοὺ) he is in the desert," or, "Behold (ἰδοὺ) he is in the inner rooms" (v 26). To see the Christ the disciples are not to go out to the desert, a distant and open place, nor are they to believe that the Christ is in the inner rooms, a near and hidden place (v 26).[12] Commands that the disciples not believe (μὴ πιστεύσητε) the Christ is here (v 23) and that they not believe (μὴ πιστεύσητε) he is in the inner rooms (v 26) form an inclusion that envelopes Jesus' warning that the disciples not be misled about where the Christ will appear.

A comparison explains why the disciples and the audience should not be misled about the coming of the Christ. For just as (ὥσπερ) lightning comes out of the east and appears as far as the west, so (οὕτως) will be the coming of the Son of Man (v 27). That the coming (παρουσία) of Jesus as the messianic Son of Man will be like the sudden and universal appearance of lightning begins to answer more directly the question the disciples put to Jesus at the

[10] The reference to the "elect" (ἐκλεκτοὺς, v 24) follows and precedes references to "you" (ὑμῖν, vv 23, 25), the disciples Jesus is addressing. The parable of the marriage feast (22:1–14) encouraged the audience to distinguish themselves as the few "chosen" or "elect" (ἐκλεκτοί) from the many who are called (22:14).

[11] McKay, "On the Perfect," 316–17.

[12] Agbanou, *Le discours eschatologique,* 96; on the background of "desert" and "inner rooms" here, see p. 101.

beginning of the discourse about his coming, "What will be the sign of your coming (παρουσίας) and the end of the age?" (v 3). The coming of the Son of Man will be as sudden and as universally visible to those on earth as lightning (ἀστραπή)—from one end of the sky to the other—so that there will be neither the time nor the necessity to point out its location.[13] Indeed, the Son of Man's coming will be as easy for everyone to locate as a carcass can be located by seeing vultures circling over it in the sky: "Where (ὅπου) the carcass is, there (ἐκεῖ) the vultures will gather" (v 28).[14]

The comparison of this unit (24:23–28) of the eschatological discourse has the following pragmatic effect: That the coming of Jesus as the Son of Man after his resurrection will be like the sudden and universally visible appearance of lightning enables the Matthean audience not to be misled by those who, according to Jesus' authoritative prophecy that warns and prepares the audience, will attempt to point out the location of his coming before it happens.

2. Matthew 24:29–35: Knowing Summer Is Near Compared with Knowing the Son of Man Is Near

Jesus continues the discourse by declaring that immediately after the affliction of those days (v 29), that is, the great affliction that has not been from the beginning of the world until now, nor ever will be (v 21), the great affliction during those days that will be shortened for the sake of the elect (v 22), the world will dissolve. The sun will be darkened, and the moon will not give its light, and the stars will fall from the sky (LXX Isa 13:10; 34:4),[15] for the powers of the heavens will be shaken (v 29).[16]

In further answer to the disciples' question, "when (πότε) will these things be and what will be the sign (σημεῖον) of your coming and the end of the age?" (v 3), Jesus declares that "then" (τότε) the sign (σημεῖον) of the Son of

---

[13] J. Zmijewski, "ἀστραπή," *EDNT* 1. 175. J. A. Oñate Ojeda, "Nota exegética: Pues, así como el relámpago," *Burgense* 32 (1991) 569–72, maintains that ἀστραπή here should not be translated as "lightning" but as the "brilliance" or "splendor" of the sun that goes from east to west.

[14] On the possible OT background to 24:28 in Job 39:30, see Gundry, *Use*, 88–89. For the translation of ἀετοί here as "vultures," which were grouped with "eagles" in antiquity, see BAGD, 19.

[15] For the OT background, see Gundry, *Use*, 51–52.

[16] On the explicative sense of the last καὶ in v 29, translated "for," see Agbanou, *Le discours eschatologique*, 105.

Man will appear in heaven (v 30). In correspondence to the previous comparison that the coming of Jesus as the Son of Man will be like lightning that comes out of the east and appears (φαίνεται) as far as the west—from one end of the sky to the other (v 27), the sign of the Son of Man will appear (φανήσεται) in the sky. And "then" (τότε), as a complement to the sign that will appear in "heaven" (οὐρανῷ), all the tribes of people on the "earth" (γῆς) will mourn (Zech 12:10, 14),[17] as they see the Son of Man coming upon the clouds of "heaven" (οὐρανοῦ) (Dan 7:13–14)[18] with power and great glory (v 30).[19] After the powers (δυνάμεις) of the heavens have been shaken to end the world and the heavenly lights have been extinguished (v 29), Jesus will come as the Son of Man with his power (δυνάμεως) and the brightness of his great glory (v 30).[20]

When he comes as Son of Man, Jesus will send out his angels with a great trumpet blast (Isa 27:13),[21] and they will gather his elect from the four winds, from one end of the heavens to the other (Deut 30:4) (v 31). This continues the eschatological discourse's concern for the final salvation of the "elect," whom the disciples and Matthean audience are to see as themselves. After describing the beginning (v 8) of eschatological tribulations (vv 4–12), Jesus exhorted, "But the one who perseveres to the end, this one will be saved (σωθήσεται)" (v 13; cf. 10:22). He continued by stating that unless those days of the final and definitive affliction (v 21) are shortened, no one will be saved (ἐσώθη), but for the sake of the elect (ἐκλεκτοὺς) those days will be short-

---

[17] Gundry, *Matthew*, 488–89: "The context in Matthew favors a mourning of despair; the context in Zechariah favors a mourning of regret, perhaps of repentance. But the point of Matthew's allusion lies in the wide extent of the mourning—over against private manifestations in deserts and backrooms—not in the reason for mourning."

[18] On the OT background in Zechariah and Daniel here, see Gundry, *Matthew*, 488–89; idem, *Use*, 52–54.

[19] Lambrecht, "Parousia Discourse," 324: "The Son of man Himself is the sign (epexegetical genitive), namely what Jesus will be with glory and power at his parousia." Gundry, *Matthew*, 488: "All in all, the echoes of vv 3 and 27 and the anticipations of later phrases show that the sign of the Son of man is his own appearance when he comes, not some kind of standard or ensign waved ahead of him."

[20] Agbanou, *Le discours eschatologique*, 105: "Il y a sans doute un contraste voulu entre les δυνάμεως qui seront ébranlées et le Fils de l'Homme qui vient μετὰ δυνάμεως, puis entre le Fils de l'Homme qui vient avec δοξῆς alors que les astres s'éteignent."

[21] Gundry, *Matthew*, 489: "Thus Christ's return will be plainly audible as well as unmistakably visible." On the trumpet (σάλπιγγος) here as an eschatological instrument for signaling, see H. Lichtenberger, "σάλπιγξ," *EDNT*, 3. 225.

ened (v 22). The false christs and false prophets will try to mislead even the elect (ἐκλεκτούς) (v 24). But at the end the angels will gather for salvation the elect (ἐκλεκτοὺς) (v 31), those who have persevered to the end (v 13) and not been misled (v 24). Although the powers of the heavens (οὐρανῶν) will be shaken (v 29), the elect, scattered throughout the whole world in preaching the gospel of the reign to all peoples (v 14), will be gathered from the four winds, from one end of the heavens (οὐρανῶν) to the other (v 31). The universal gathering of the elect from one end of the heavens to the other corresponds to the Son of Man's universal appearance from the east to the west (v 27).[22]

Returning to the direct second-person address of his audience (cf. vv 23–26) after the third-person descriptions of the coming of the Son of Man and of the end of the world (vv 27–31), Jesus introduces the comparison (vv 32–33) of this unit: "From the fig tree learn the comparison" (v 32).[23] When (ὅταν) already the branch of the fig tree becomes tender and sprouts leaves, "you know that (γινώσκετε ὅτι) summer is near (ἐγγύς)" (v 32).[24] With an emphatic application to his audience, "So (οὕτως, cf. v 27) also you (καὶ ὑμεῖς)," Jesus draws out the comparison: "When (ὅταν) you see all these things, you know that (γινώσκετε ὅτι) he (the Son of Man)[25] is near (ἐγγύς), at the gates" (v 33).[26] "When you see (ὅταν ἴδητε) all these things (πάντα ταῦτα)" (v 33) includes "when you see" (ὅταν ἴδητε) the abomination of des-

---

[22] The "elect" correspond to the "righteous" (δίκαιοι) who will shine like the sun in the reign of their Father after "the Son of Man will send out his angels" (cf. 24:31), and they collect from his reign all causes of scandal and those who do lawlessness, and they throw them into the furnace of fire, where there will be the weeping and gnashing of teeth (13:41–43; cf. 16:27).

[23] On the comparison of the budding fig tree, see J. Dupont, "La parabole du figuier qui bourgeonne (Mc, XIII,28–29 et par.)," *RB* 75 (1968) 526–48; Klauck, *Allegorie und Allegorese*, 316–25; Donahue, *Gospel in Parable*, 58; Scott, *Hear Then the Parable*, 338–42.

[24] Gundry, *Matthew*, 490: "Most Palestinian trees, being evergreen, keep their leaves throughout the winter. The almond tree loses its leaves in the wintertime and sprouts early in the spring. The fig tree, however, loses its leaves in wintertime but does not sprout till late in the spring. Therefore its budding signifies the approach of summer."

[25] The subject of ἐγγύς (near) is not expressed, but the preceding context referring to the coming of the Son of Man (vv 27, 30) indicates that he or his coming is the subject. See Agbanou, *Le discours eschatologique*, 106.

[26] On the imagery of standing at the gates or doors (θύραις), R. Kratz, "θύρα," *EDNT*, 2. 160, remarks: "The spatial image of standing at the *door* is used of direct temporal proximity (Acts 5:9), most often with an eschatological aspect (Mark 13:29 par. Matt 24:33; Jas 5:9)." See also Rev 3:20.

olation (v 15), recalls "all these things" (πάντα ταῦτα) that are the beginning of the eschatological birth-pangs (v 8), and embraces all of the tribulations of the great affliction of the final days (vv 4–26).[27] The spatial comparison that where the coming of the Son of Man appears will be as obvious and universally visible as lightning (v 27) progresses to a temporal comparison that when the great eschatological tribulations occur the Son of Man will be as near as summer is near when a fig tree sprouts its leaves (vv 32–33).

With a solemn and authoritative "Amen I say to you" (cf. 23:36), Jesus announces that "this generation," that is, all of the evil, perverse, unrepenting, and unbelieving kind of people who have rejected and opposed Jesus and God's other agents in the past (cf. 11:16; 12:39–42, 45; 16:4; 17:17; 23:36),[28] and who will oppose and try to mislead the disciples before the end of the world, will not pass away until all these things (πάντα ταῦτα, cf. v 33) have taken place (v 34). In other words, "all these things," the tribulations of the great affliction of the final days (vv 4-26), the climactic perpetrations of "this generation," are certain to occur. Although heaven and earth will pass away (v 35a) after the affliction of the final days when the universe comes to an end (v 29), Jesus insists that "my words" (λόγοι μου), the words not only of this eschatological discourse but all of the words of Jesus' teaching in the gospel,[29] will not pass away (v 35b). The authoritative "words" of Jesus provide his audience with a firm and permanent foundation for surviving the onslaught of the final tribulations (cf. 7:24–27) and being numbered among the "elect" who will be gathered for salvation in the reign of the heavens (vv 22, 24, 31).

[27] Agbanou, Le discours eschatologique, 106: "L'antécédent de πάντα ταῦτα est alors tout ce qui est rapporté depuis le début jusqu'au v. 26."

[28] Gundry, Matthew, 491: ". . . he [Matthew] may intend 'this generation' to be understood as meaning 'this kind.' The emphasis would then fall on the perversity of the scribes, Pharisees, and Sadducees (see the contexts of 12:39; 16:4), and the chronological extent of the generation would remain open. After all, in 23:35-36 'this generation' included not only Jesus' contemporaries, but also those who had killed Zechariah the OT prophet several hundred years ealier. . . . Presumably 'this generation' included such murderers all the way back to Abel."

[29] "These words of mine" (μου τοὺς λόγους τούτους) in 7:24, 26 refer to the preceding words of the first discourse, the sermon on the mount (Matthew 5–7). "These words" (τοὺς λόγους τούτους) in 7:28 and 19:1 refer to Jesus' words in the sermon on the mount and community discourse (17:22–18:35), respectively. The announcement that Jesus finished "all these words" (πάντας τοὺς λόγους τούτους) in 26:1 climactically concludes not only the eschatological discourse (24–25) but all of the words of Jesus' previous teaching in the gospel. See J. P. Heil, The Death and Resurrection of Jesus: A Narrative-Critical Reading of Matthew 26–28 (Minneapolis: Fortress, 1991) 23.

With regard to pragmatics, the comparison of this unit (24:29–35) assures the audience that just as they know that when the fig tree produces its leaves summer is near, so they will know that when they experience the great affliction of the final days the coming of Jesus as the Son of Man is near. They are invited to make the words of Jesus, especially the promise that when he comes as Son of Man he will gather them for final salvation, the firm and lasting foundation of their lives, a foundation that will outlast the passing away of heaven and earth.

3. Matthew 24:36–41: The Coming of the Flood Compared with the Coming of the Son of Man

Continuing to answer the disciples' question of when will be his coming (παρουσίας) as the Son of Man and the end of the age (v 3), Jesus announces: "Concerning that day and hour no one knows, neither the angels of heaven nor the Son,[30] but only the Father alone" (v 36).[31] The focus now narrows from "those days" (ἡμέραι ἐκεῖναι) of the greatest affliction (vv 19, 22, 29) to "that day" (ἡμέρας ἐκείνης) and hour of the coming of Jesus as the Son of Man at the end of the world. The introduction of this unit's comparison, "for just as (ὥσπερ) the days of Noah, so (οὕτως) will be the coming of the Son of Man (ἔσται ἡ παρουσία τοῦ υἱοῦ τοῦ ἀνθρώπου)" (v 37), advances the previous comparison regarding the coming of Jesus as the Son of Man: "For just as (ὥσπερ) lightning comes out of the east and appears as far as the west, so (οὕτως) will be the coming of the Son of Man (ἔσται ἡ παρουσία τοῦ υἱοῦ τοῦ ἀνθρώπου)" (v 27).

This unit's comparison then further develops. "Just as (ὥσπερ) the days (ἡμέραι) of Noah" (v 37) progresses to "as" (ὡς) in those days (ἡμέραις ἐκείναις)[32] before the flood people were conducting their lives as usual, eating and drinking, marrying and being given in marriage, until the day (ἡμέρας) Noah entered into the ark (v 38), and they did not know until the flood came and took them all away (Gen 6:13–7:24), "so (οὕτως) will be the coming of the Son of Man (ἔσται ἡ παρουσία τοῦ υἱοῦ τοῦ ἀνθρώπου)" (v 39). That in "those days" before the flood they did not know (οὐκ ἔγνωσαν) "the day" the

---

[30] For including the variant reading "nor the Son," see Metzger, *Textual Commentary,* 62; Gundry, *Matthew,* 492.

[31] Gundry, *Matthew,* 492: "The addition of 'alone' accentuates the ignorance of all but the Father concerning the exact time of the Son's coming."

[32] "Those" (ἐκείναις) is omitted is some manuscripts; see *UBSGNT,* 4th ed., 95.

flood came (vv 38–39) exemplifies how no one will know (οὐδεὶς οἶδεν) "the day" nor the hour of the coming of the Son of Man (v 36) in "those days" of the greatest affliction (vv 19, 22, 29).

The emphatically repeated comparison, "so will be the coming of the Son of Man" (vv 37, 39; cf. v 27), is then completed. "Then" (τότε), that is, when the Son of Man comes, two men will be in the field going about their ordinary business, similar to the people before the coming of the flood (v 38). Without knowing the day or the hour of the Son of Man's coming, one will be taken along (παραλαμβάνεται), that is, gathered along with the elect for salvation in the reign of the heavens (v 31),[33] as those who were taken along in the ark with Noah were saved from the flood, and one will be left (v 40). Complementing the two men, two women will be going about their work of grinding at the mill. Without knowing the day or the hour of the Son of Man's coming, one will be likewise taken along (παραλαμβάνεται) for salvation and one will be left (v 41).[34]

The comparison of this unit (24:36–41) warns the audience that, although they will know in general when the Son of Man is near (24:29–35), they will not know the exact day or hour of his coming. Just as in the days of Noah people were in the midst of their ordinary activity, unaware of the coming of the great flood, so people will be going about their normal tasks, unaware of the day or hour when Jesus will come as the Son of Man.

4. Matthew 24:42–44: Readiness for a Thief Compared to Readiness for the Son of Man

After the comparison of the coming of the Son of Man with the days of Noah (vv 36–41), narrated as third-person discourse, Jesus returns to the direct second-person address of his audience (cf. vv 32–34) as he draws out the consequence of the comparison: "Watch, therefore, for you do not know on what day your Lord is coming" (v 42). Jesus applies his previous general state-

---

[33] For this meaning of "being taken along," see Meier, *Matthew,* 291; Sand *Matthäus,* 499; Gnilka, *Matthäusevangelium,* 2. 338; Harrington, *Matthew,* 342–43; Morris, *Matthew,* 614.

[34] That one man and one woman will be left or forsaken (ἀφίεται, vv 40–41) after the others have been taken along with the elect whom the angels of the Son of Man will gather (ἐπισυνάξουσιν, v 31) for salvation parallels how the temple of Jerusalem will be left or forsaken (ἀφίεται, 23:38) after Jesus wanted to gather (ἐπισυναγαγεῖν; ἐπισυνάγει, 23:37) the children of Jerusalem to himself for salvific refuge. See also Brown, "Matthean Apocalypse," 16.

ment that no one knows (οὐδεὶς οἶδεν) about that day or hour (v 36) specifically to his audience: "You do not know (οὐκ οἴδατε) what day" (v 42). The previous references to not knowing when will be "the coming of the Son of Man" (vv 37, 39) progress to a more personal application of not knowing when "your Lord is coming" (v 42). The disciples and Matthean audience do not know precisely when Jesus will come again as the Son of Man and their personal Lord.

As the command to "watch" (v 42) progresses to the command to "know this" (v 43), the comparison of this unit begins. Whereas the audience is to watch (γρηγορεῖτε) because they do not know (οὐκ οἴδατε) on what day (ποίᾳ ἡμέρᾳ) their Lord is coming (ἔρχεται) (v 42), if the householder had known (ᾔδει) on what watch of the night (ποίᾳ φυλακῇ)[35] the thief was coming (ἔρχεται), he would have watched (ἐγρηγόρησεν) and not have allowed his house to be broken into (v 43). In the comparison "what day" narrows to "what watch" of the night, the audience becomes the householder, and the coming of "your Lord" becomes the coming of the thief. The implication is that the audience, like the householder, is to be on the watch, because their Lord will come, like the thief, at an unexpected time.

Jesus concludes this unit by applying the comparison explicitly and emphatically to the audience: "Therefore (διὰ τοῦτο)[36] you also (καὶ ὑμεῖς) must be ready, because at an hour you do not expect the Son of Man is coming" (v 44). The command to watch (γρηγορεῖτε), because you do not know (οὐκ οἴδατε) on what day your Lord is coming (ἔρχεται) (v 42) now becomes the command to be ready (ἕτοιμοι), because at an hour you do not expect (οὐ δοκεῖτε) the Son of Man is coming (ἔρχεται). The temporal focus has narrowed from "day" (v 42) to "watch" of the night (v 43) to "hour" (v 44). The disciples are to watch (v 42) and be ready (v 44) like the householder who would have watched (v 43), because their Lord (v 42) will come as the Son of Man (v 44) like a thief (v 43) not only on a day they do not know (v 42) but at an hour they do not expect (v 44). Indeed, no one knows the day or the hour of the coming of Jesus as the Son of Man except the Father (v 36).

---

[35] BAGD, 868; R. Kratz, "φυλακή," *EDNT*, 3. 441.

[36] After surveying the occurrences of διὰ τοῦτο (therefore) in Matthew, Orton, *Understanding Scribe*, 141, concludes: ". . . the phrase διὰ τοῦτο in Matthew is used most frequently *in a position of climax*, when, with some intensification of emphasis, Jesus makes a portentous statement . . ."

Pragmatically, the comparison of this unit (24:42–44) calls for the audience, like the householder, who would have watched if he knew when the thief was coming, to be watchful and ready for the coming of Jesus as their Lord and the Son of Man on a day they do not know and at an hour they do not expect.[37]

5. Matthew 24:45–51: Parable Comparing a Servant Who is Faithful and Wise or Wicked

Jesus initiates the parable of this unit with the question: "Who then is the faithful and wise servant whom the lord appointed over his household servants to give them their food at the proper time?" (v 45).[38] By beginning with a question Jesus already engages the audience to apply the parable to themselves.[39] "The lord" (ὁ κύριος) of the parable represents Jesus, just referred to as "your Lord" (ὁ κύριος ὑμῶν, v 42). The disciples are to see themselves as the faithful and wise servant (δοῦλος) of the lord. The audience knows that Jesus already related himself to his disciples as lord (κύριος) to servant (δοῦλος) (10:24–25) and called for the disciples to be a servant (δοῦλος) of their fellow disciples (20:27), represented in the parable by the "household servants" (οἰκετείας)[40] over whom the lord has appointed the servant with the responsibility "to give them their food at the proper time" (v 45).[41]

That the disciples are to be "wise" like the wise (φρόνιμος) servant of the parable (v 45) recalls Jesus' appeal in the parable that concluded the sermon on the mount. Everyone who hears the words of Jesus in the sermon and does

---

[37] Blomberg, *Interpreting the Parables,* 277–78, sees two main points to the comparison of the householder and the thief. But his two points are reducible to the one we are proposing.

[38] On the parable in 24:45–51, see, in addition to the commentaries: Agbanou, *Le discours eschatologique,* 133–42; Donahue, *Gospel in Parable,* 98–101; Scott, *Hear Then the Parable,* 208–12; Blomberg, *Interpreting the Parables,* 190–93; D. J. Harrington, "Polemical Parables in Matthew 24–25," *USQR* 44 (1991) 293–94; Charette, *Recompense,* 151–53; Lambrecht, *Treasure,* 189–98.

[39] Donahue, *Gospel in Parable,* 98: "[The question] sets the tone for the following parables and summons the readers or hearers to answer this question in their lives. In the parable it is evident who is the wise and faithful servant; the question to the hearers is: 'Will you be such also?'"

[40] BAGD, 556–57; Gundry, *Matthew,* 496.

[41] On the OT reference to Ps 104:27 for "to give them their food at the proper time," see Gundry, *Matthew,* 496; idem, *Use,* 89.

them is like a wise (φρονίμῳ) man who built his house on a foundation of rock (7:24). In another comparison in the missionary discourse Jesus exhorted his disciples who are to share in his ministry to be wise (φρόνιμοι) as serpents (10:16). Now this parable's faithful and wise servant who gives his fellow servants their food at the proper time (v 45) calls for the disciples to be wise servants by faithfully fulfilling the responsibility their Lord Jesus has given them to provide for the needs of their fellow disciples (20:26–27) during the "proper time," the time when they are watching and ready for their Lord to come as the Son of Man (vv 42–44).

Blessed (μακάριος) with divine approval and the promise of eschatological reward in the reign of the heavens (cf. 5:3–11; 11:6; 13:16; 16:17)[42] is that faithful and wise servant whom his lord will find doing what he has appointed him to do when he comes (v 46). "When his lord comes (ἐλθὼν)" (v 46) refers to the unknown day Jesus is coming (ἔρχεται) as "your Lord" (v 42), the unexpected hour Jesus is coming (ἔρχεται) as the Son of Man (v 44). With a solemn, direct second-person address of his audience, "Amen I say to you," Jesus confirms the servant's divine blessing with the eschatological promise that his Lord, who appointed (κατέστησεν) him over his household servants (v 45), now will appoint (καταστήσει) him over all his possessions (v 47), an expression of his eschatological blessing in the reign of the heavens.[43]

In contrast to that (ἐκεῖνος, v 46) faithful and wise servant who is blessed, that (ἐκεῖνος, v 48) same servant proves to be wicked if he says in his heart, "My lord is delayed" (v 48).[44] Rather than taking care of his fellow household servants over whom the lord appointed him (v 45), he begins to beat his fellow servants (v 49). Rather than giving them their food at the proper time (v 45), he himself eats and drinks with drunkards (v 49). The wicked servant's mistreatment of his fellow servants (συνδούλους) by beating them and with-

---

[42] Donahue, *Gospel in Parable*, 98: "Such a servant is 'blessed,' a term in Matthew that suggests divine approval rather than simple human happiness." See also G. Strecker, "μακάριος," *EDNT*, 2. 376–79.

[43] Gnilka, *Matthäusevangelium*, 2. 343: "Nur die Seligpreisung könnte von Ferne andeuten, dass mehr auf dem Spiel steht als eine irdische Stellung."

[44] Lambrecht, *Treasure*, 189: "In Matt 24:48 the sentence begins as follows: 'But if *that* wicked servant . . .'; we may paraphrase: 'But if that (same) servant is wicked . . .'" Charette, *Recompense*, 151: "It is clear that the parable is not describing two servants, but rather two possible, though completely disparate, responses open to the one servant." See also Agbanou, *Le discours eschatologique*, 136.

holding their food recalls the forgiven servant's mistreatment of one of his fellow servants (συνδούλων, 18:28; cf. 18:29, 31, 33) by withholding forgiveness in the parable of the unforgiving servant (18:21–35) in the community discourse.

The lord of that servant who thought "my lord" is delayed (v 48) will come on a day he does not expect and at an hour he does not know (v 50). That the lord of the servant will come (ἥξει, v 50) advances the theme of Jesus coming (ἐλθών, v 46; ἔρχεται, v 42) as the Lord of his disciples, represented by the servant. That the lord will come on a day the servant does not expect and at an hour he does not know (v 50) reinforces Jesus' command for his disciples to watch, because they do not know on what day their Lord is coming (v 42), and to be ready, because the Son of Man is coming at an hour they do not expect (v 44). Rather than being blessed with an eschatological reward in the reign of the heavens (vv 46–47), the wicked servant will receive eschatological punishment. The lord will cut him in two (cf. Dan 13:55, 59) and put him, who ate and drank with (μετά) drunkards (v 49), with (μετά) the hypocrites,[45] "where there will be the weeping and gnashing of teeth" (v 51; cf. 8:12; 13:42, 50; 22:13).[46]

This unit's comparison of a servant who is either faithful and wise or wicked (24:45–51) persuades the audience to take care of the needs of those entrusted to them in order to be like the faithful and wise servant who, by giving his fellow servants their food at the proper time, demonstrates what it means to be watching and ready for the unexpected time of Jesus' final coming as Lord and Son of Man. By so doing they will experience blessedness in the reign of the heavens rather than the eternal punishment of the wicked servant who, thinking that his Lord would be delayed, mistreated his fellow servants and therefore was not watching and ready for the coming of his Lord.

---

[45] This is the final, climactic use of the term "hypocrites" (ὑποκριταί) in Matthew, which refers to godless people and is often applied to Jesus' adversaries (6:2, 5, 16; 7:5; 15:7; 22:18; 23:13, 14, 15). See also H. Giesen, "ὑποκριτής," EDNT, 3. 403–4.

[46] Gundry, Matthew, 497: ". . . the bad slave continues to exist only in a punitive afterlife. The cutting in two of his present body simply represents an extremely severe punishment that appropriately launches him into that kind of afterlife."

6. Matthew 25:1–13: Parable of the Reign of the Heavens Comparing Wise and Foolish Maidens

"Then" (τότε), that is, when Jesus comes as the Son of Man at the end of the age (24:3, 27, 30, 37, 39, 42, 44, 50), the reign of the heavens will be like the case of ten maidens who took their lamps and went out to meet the bridegroom (25:1).[47] The meeting of the bridegroom (νυμφίου) depicts the return of Jesus, the "bridegroom" (νυμφίος), after he is taken away from his disciples by his death (9:15). The comparison of the ten maidens to what the reign of the heavens will be like (ὁμοιωθήσεται) include five who are foolish (μωραὶ) and five who are wise (φρόνιμοι) (v 2). This recalls for the audience the parable that concluded the sermon on the mount. Everyone who hears the words of Jesus and does them will be like (ὁμοιωθήσεται) a wise (φρονίμῳ) man (7:24), but everyone who hears the words and does not do them will be like (ὁμοιωθήσεται) a foolish (μωρῷ) man (7:26).[48] The wise (φρόνιμοι) and foolish maidens who go out to meet the bridegroom when he comes also echo the previous parable's servant who is either faithful and wise (φρόνιμος) or wicked when his lord comes (24:45–51).

As the foolish man built his house on sand (7:26) and as the wicked servant beat his fellow servants and ate and drank with drunkards (24:49), so the foolish maidens did not take with them oil for their lamps (v 3). But as the wise man built his house on rock (7:24) and as the faithful and wise servant gave his fellow servants their food at the proper time (24:45), so the wise maidens took flasks of oil with their lamps (v 4). Whereas the wicked servant thought his lord would be delayed (χρονίζει) (24:48) but he was not (24:50), the bridegroom is actually delayed (χρονίζοντος) so that all the maidens became drowsy and slept (v 5).

---

[47] On the parable in 25:1–13, see, in addition to the commentaries: K. P. Donfried, "The Allegory of the Ten Virgins (Matt 25:1–13) as a Summary of Matthean Theology," *JBL* 93 (1974) 415–28; W. Schenk, "Auferweckung der Toten oder Gericht nach den Werken: Tradition und Redaktion in Mattäus xxv 1–13," *NovT* 20 (1978) 278–99; H. Weder, *Gleichnisse Jesu*, 239–49; A. Puig i Tàrrech, *La parabole des dix vierges (Mt 25,1–13)* (AnBib 102; Rome: Biblical Institute, 1983); Agbanou, *Le discours eschatologique*, 143–53; Donahue, *Gospel in Parable*, 101–5; Blomberg, *Interpreting the Parables*, 193–97; Harrington, "Polemical Parables," 294–96; Lambrecht, *Treasure*, 199–215.

[48] The parables of the wise and foolish maidens (25:1–13) and of the wise and foolish men (7:24–27) are the only two parables in Matthew introduced by the future tense verb of comparison, ὁμοιωθήσεται. According to Carson, "ΟΜΟΙΟΣ Word-Group," 279: ". . . the verb in the future passive is used exclusively in connection with the kingdom at its consummation."

When at midnight came the cry to go out and meet the bridegroom (v 6), all the maidens arose and trimmed their lamps (v 7).[49] The faithful and wise servant was appointed to give (δοῦναι) his fellow servants their food at the proper time (24:45). But when the foolish maidens, at the time that their lamps are going out, ask their wise fellow maidens to give (δότε) them some of their oil (v 8), the wise maidens wisely recognize that there is not enough oil for all and direct their foolish fellow maidens to go rather to those who sell oil and buy some for themselves (v 9). The foolish maidens foolishly expect their wise fellow maidens to compensate for their own lack of preparation.

While the foolish maidens went away to buy oil the bridegroom came (v 10). The previous references to the future coming of Jesus as the Son of Man (24:27, 30, 37, 39, 42, 44) and to what will happen when the lord of the wicked servant will come (ἥξει) (24:50) now progress to what happens when the bridegroom came (ἦλθεν). Those maidens who were ready (ἕτοιμοι), who thus fulfilled Jesus' command to the disciples to be ready (ἕτοιμοι) for the unknowable time of his coming (24:44), entered with the bridegroom into the wedding feast and the door was closed (v 10). In contrast to the wicked servant, who ate and drank with (μετὰ) drunkards (24:49) and so was placed with (μετὰ) the hypocrites (24:51) when his lord came, the wise and prepared maidens entered the wedding feast "with him" (μετ' αὐτοῦ), Jesus, the bridegroom.

By hearing and doing the words of Jesus, the wise man built his house on a foundation of rock so that it survived the storm of final age tribulations and ruin in the last judgment (7:24–25).[50] But now by being prepared with oil for their lamps, the wise maidens actually enter into the wedding feast (v 10), representative of entering the reign of the heavens (v 1; 22:1–14). Not only must the righteousness of the disciples surpass that of the scribes and Pharisees if they are to enter (εἰσέλθητε) the reign of the heavens (5:20), not only must they do the will of God if they will enter (εἰσελεύσεται) the reign of the heavens (7:21), and not only must they turn and become like children if they are to enter (εἰσέλθητε) the reign of the heavens (18:3), but they must be prepared for the delay of Jesus' coming, like the wise and prepared maidens, who entered (εἰσῆλθον) the wedding feast of the reign (v 10). The disciples will be

---

[49] Against the idea that the maidens' sleeping and rising symbolize death and resurrection, see the perceptive comments of Gundry, *Matthew*, 500.

[50] Gnilka, *Matthäusevangelium*, 1. 282; Gundry, *Matthew*, 135; Hagner, *Matthew 1–13*, 191.

as prepared as the wise maidens who took oil for their lamps, if each, like the wise man, hears and does (ποιεῖ) the words of Jesus (7:24), which reveal the will of his Father each is to do (ποιῶν) in order to enter the reign of the heavens (7:21).

Later the foolish maidens came also saying, "Lord, Lord, open for us!" (v 11). But the lord, the bridegroom, solemnly replied, "I do not know you" (οὐκ οἶδα ὑμᾶς) (v 12). This echoes Jesus' reply, "I never knew you (οὐδέποτε ἔγνων ὑμᾶς), depart from me you doers of lawlessness" (7:23), to those who will cry on the day of his coming, "Lord, Lord," and point to their prophesying, exorcizing, and working wonders in his name (7:22). But not everyone who says "Lord, Lord" will enter the reign of the heavens, only the one who does the will of Jesus' Father in heaven (7:21), in order to become a member of the family known to Jesus (12:50). As the bridegroom, Jesus does not know the foolish maidens, because they are not members of his family who do the will of his Father.

By hearing but not doing the words of Jesus, the foolish man built his house on sand, so that it did not survive the storm of final age tribulations but suffered great destruction in the last judgment (7:26–27). Now by not being prepared with oil for their lamps, and thus not doing the words of Jesus, the foolish maidens did not enter into the wedding feast of the reign of the heavens (vv 10–12). Whereas the man who entered the wedding feast of the reign of the heavens that the king gave for his son (22:2) was thrown out because he did not have a wedding garment (22:11–13), the foolish maidens are not even allowed to enter into the wedding feast of the reign because they were not prepared for the delayed, unknown time of Jesus' final coming as the bridegroom.

Since no one knows (οἶδεν) the day or the hour of his coming as the Son of Man (24:36), Jesus already exhorted his disciples, "Watch, therefore, for you do not know (γρηγορεῖτε οὖν, ὅτι οὐκ οἴδατε) on what day your Lord is coming" (24:42). Since he could come like a thief at any time (24:43), Jesus further urged, "Therefore you also must be ready, for at an hour you do not expect (δοκεῖτε) the Son of Man is coming" (24:44). Although the wicked servant thought his Lord would be delayed (24:48), Jesus warned that his Lord will come on a day he does not expect (προσδοκᾷ) and at an hour he does not know (γινώσκει) (24:50). Now, applying the parable in which the Lord of the maidens is actually delayed (v 5) directly to his disciples, Jesus further warns: "Watch, therefore, for you do not know (γρηγορεῖτε οὖν, ὅτι οὐκ οἴδατε) the day or the hour" (v 13). The disciples (and audience) must be constantly ready and prepared whether Jesus' coming as Son of Man is delayed (25:1–13) or not (24:45–51).

With regard to pragmatics, the parable comparing the reign of the heavens with the story of the wise and foolish maidens (25:1–13) warns the audience to reckon with a possible delay of unknown duration for Jesus' final coming as Son of Man. Like the wise maidens they must be prepared to enter the wedding feast of the reign of the heavens whenever Jesus comes as the bridegroom. They will be ready and enter with Jesus if he knows them as members of his family, as those who hear and do the words of Jesus that reveal the will of his heavenly Father. Unlike the foolish maidens who did not reckon with delay, were unprepared, and so could not enter the reign because Jesus did not know them, the audience must not foolishly expect their fellow Christians to be able to help them, if they themselves are not personally prepared and ready for the unknown day and hour of Jesus' final coming.

7. Matthew 25:14–30: Parable Comparing Servants Who Are Given Talents by Their Lord

In close connection with the preceding parable, the disciples must watch for the unknown day and hour of Jesus' coming (v 13), "for" (γὰρ) it, that is, the reign of the heavens (v 1),[51] will be like (ὥσπερ) the case of a man who, going on a journey, called his own servants and entrusted to them his possessions (v 14).[52] To one he gave five talents,[53] to another two, and to another one, each according to his own ability, and went on a journey (v 15). The man represents Jesus, his journey represents the absence of Jesus after his resurrection and before his final coming (cf. 24:3), and his servants represent the disciples. That the servant who received the five talents aggressively and energetically

---

[51] Meier, *Matthew*, 298–99; Gnilka, *Matthäusevangelium*, 2. 358–59; Morris, *Matthew*, 626–27.

[52] On the parable in 25:14–30, see, in addition to the commentaries: Weder, *Gleichnisse Jesu*, 193–210; Agbanou, *Le discours eschatologique*, 155–69; Donahue, *Gospel in Parable*, 105–9; C. Dietzfelbinger, "Das Gleichnis von den anvertrauten Geldern," *BTZ* 6 (1989) 222–33; Scott, *Hear Then the Parable*, 217–35; Blomberg, *Interpreting the Parables*, 214–17; Harrington, "Polemical Parables," 296–97; F. Manns, "La parable des talents: Wirkungsgeschichte et racines juives," *RSR* 65 (1991) 343–62; Charette, *Recompense*, 153–55; Lambrecht, *Treasure*, 217–44; Weber, *Events*, 135–36; Herzog, *Parables as Subversive Speech*, 150–68.

[53] Originally a measure of weight, "talent" (τάλαντον) came to refer to a unit of coinage of very high value; see BAGD, 803.

"worked" (ἠργάσατο) with them (v 16) recalls for the audience the theme of the disciples as "workers" (ἐργάται, 9:37; cf. 9:38; 10:10; 20:1–2, 8), who are to gather the "harvest" of people (9:37; cf. 4:19) into the reign of the heavens with the healing and preaching authority Jesus gave them (10:1, 7–8).[54] That the servant who received five talents and the one who received two talents gained another five talents and another two talents respectively (vv 16–17) resonates with how the disciples, as "sowers" who are to "sow" the word of the gospel, can expect to yield a remarkably abundant harvest of people for the reign of the heavens (13:8, 23).[55]

The servant who received one talent went away and dug a hole in the ground and hid the money "of his lord" (v 18). The emphasis on the man as the "lord" of the servant underlines that the money still belongs to the lord and has only been entrusted to the servant to be a steward of it. The previous wicked servant's thinking that "my lord is delayed (χρονίζει)" (24:48) and the bridegroom's actual "delaying" (χρονίζοντος) (25:5) now progress to the lord of those servants coming after a "long time" (πολὺν χρόνον) to settle accounts with them (v 19). That the lord of those servants comes (ἔρχεται) after a long time represents how Jesus comes (ἔρχεται) as Lord and Son of Man at an unknown day and unexpected hour (24:42, 44; cf. 24:3, 27, 30, 37, 39, 50; 25:6).

After the servant who received the five talents presented his lord with another five that he gained (v 20), his lord rewarded him: "Well done, good and faithful servant, you were faithful over little, I will appoint you over much; enter into the joy of your lord" (v 21). That the servant addressed as good and faithful (πιστέ) was faithful (πιστός) over little, so that his lord will appoint (καταστήσω) him over much likens him to the faithful (πιστός) and wise servant (24:45) whose lord will appoint (καταστήσει) him over all his possessions (24:47). Despite their very high value the talents are designated as "little" in comparison with the "much" (v 21), the heavenly reward for the

54 Weaver, *Missionary Discourse*, 78–81. The disciples never actually exercise in the narrative the authority and ministry Jesus entrusted to them; they are to do so in the time after Jesus' resurrection and before his final coming, the time represented by the absence of the man on a journey in the parable (v 14).

55 The "talents" in the parable seem to be a rather general and open-ended symbol of all that Jesus has entrusted to his disciples for promoting the reign of the heavens during the time between his resurrection and final coming. The monetary talents of the parable, then, can even symbolically embrace what is currently understood by the word "talent," namely, native, God-given abilities.

faithful stewardship of earthly gifts. As the wise and prepared maidens entered (εἰσῆλθον) with the bridegroom into the wedding feast of the reign of the heavens (25:10), so the good and faithful servant is invited to enter (εἴσελθε) into the heavenly joy of his lord (v 21). The servant who received two talents and gained another two is rewarded with entrance into the reign of the heavens (vv 22–23) just like the servant entrusted with five talents. Important is not the amount with which one is entrusted but whether one is a productive steward in accord with one's ability (v 15) of whatever amount has been entrusted.

In contrast to the two previous servants who took the risk of doing business with the talents entrusted to them, the servant who received the one talent is still holding (εἰληφώς, v 24) it.[56] Although he knows that his lord is a demanding person who "reaps where you do not sow and gathers where you do not scatter" (v 24), paralyzed by fear he hid his lord's talent in the ground and presents him with only his one talent (v 25). That he hid "your" (σου) talent in the ground and declared to his lord, "Behold you have what is yours (σόν)" (v 25), indicates that he safely preserved and did not lose what belongs to his lord. But it also underscores his failure to be a faithful, risk-taking, and productive steward of the talent entrusted to him by his lord.

In further contrast to the good and faithful servants (vv 21, 23), who took the risk of working with the talents entrusted to them and as a result doubled them, the lord addresses this servant as wicked and lazy (v 26). Precisely because he knows that his lord "reaps where I do not sow and gathers where I do not scatter" (v 26), he should have at least taken the minimum risk of depositing his lord's money with the bankers, so that he would have received back what was his with interest (v 27).

The servant's acknowledgement and the lord's acceptance that he "reaps where he does not sow and gathers where he does not scatter" (vv 24, 26) subtly expresses how the talents symbolically embrace the preaching and healing ministry the Lord Jesus entrusted to his disciples as stewards to risk a productive increase of people entering the reign of the heavens. The Lord Jesus "reaps" (θερίζων) a harvest where he does not "sow" (ἔσπειρας) the

---

[56] The use of the perfect participle, εἰληφώς, for "receive" most likely emphasizes that the servant is still holding the talent he received rather than doing business and working with it like the other servants; Zerwick and Grosvenor, *Grammatical Analysis*, 1. 83. McKay, "On the Perfect," 311 n. 46: "In Mt xxv 24 ὁ τὸ ἓν τάλαντον εἰληφώς focuses attention on this man in a way that λαβών did not do in verse 18 (or 16 or 20). Part of this effect may be in suggesting *who had received and was still holding*, but I do not think that this is necessarily so."

seed and "gathers" (συνάγων, cf. 3:12; 13:30) a harvest where he does not "scatter" (διεσκόρπισας) the seed,[57] because he has entrusted his disciples with his ministry of "scattering" and "sowing" (ὁ σπείρων τοῦ σπείρειν, 13:3) the seed, the word of the gospel, that will produce an abundant harvest of people for the reign of the heavens (13:3–8, 18–23). They are his workers who are to gather for him the "harvest" (θερισμὸν) of people (9:37–38) into the reign of the heavens with the healing and preaching authority he gave them (10:1, 7–8).

Although the servant safely preserved and did not lose his lord's one talent, the lord shockingly commands that the talent be taken away from him and given to the one who has the ten talents (v 28). As the audience recalls, Jesus previously explained that the disciples, but not the crowds, have been given by God to know the mysteries of the reign of the heavens as they are expressed in the parables discourse (13:11). He then promised that whoever has this knowledge, "it will be given to him and he will abound" (δοθήσεται αὐτῷ καὶ περισσευθήσεται), but whoever does not have it, "even what he has will be taken from him" (καὶ ὃ ἔχει ἀρθήσεται ἀπ' αὐτοῦ) (13:12). This promise is now confirmed and developed. The one talent has been taken away from the servant because he did not risk working productively with it to know and experience the mystery of the reign of the heavens (cf. 25:1). "For" (γὰρ) to the servant who has "all" (παντὶ), that is, the servant who has experienced the mystery of the reign of the heavens by taking the risk to double his talents, "it will be given and he will abound" (δοθήσεται καὶ περισσευθήσε-ται), but the one servant who does not have, "even what he has will be taken from him" (καὶ ὃ ἔχει ἀρθήσεται ἀπ' αὐτοῦ) (v 29).[58]

The foolish maidens, who were unprepared for the delay of the bride-groom, were not allowed to enter into the wedding feast of the reign of the heavens (25:10–12). This served as a warning for the disciples to be watchful for the unknown day and hour of Jesus' final coming (25:13). The wicked ser-vant, who thought his lord would be delayed so that he mistreated his fellow servants, was likewise excluded from the reign (24:48–51). His eschatological

---

[57] We are taking "reaping where one does not sow and gathering where one does not scat-ter" as a synonymous parallelism, so that "scattering" refers to scattering seed; see U. Busse, "διασκορπίζω," *EDNT*, I. 311. If one understands the "scattering" as winnowing, separating the wheat from the chaff, then we have a progressive parallelism, progressing from reaping a harvest of seed that was sown to gathering the harvest after it has been winnowed.

[58] Edwards, "*Gar* in Matthew," 650: "This is a wisdom-like statement which, at the same time, purports to explain what principles will be operative in the future."

punishment of being cut in two and placed with the hypocrites, "where there will be the weeping and gnashing of teeth" (24:51) likewise serves as a warning for the unexpected day and unknown hour of Lord Jesus' coming (24:50). Now, the useless servant, who fearfully failed to take the risk to be a productive steward with what was entrusted to him to experience the reign of the heavens, is commanded to be thrown into the outer darkness of eschatological exclusion from the reign, "where there will be the weeping and gnashing of teeth" (v 30).[59] His punishment serves as a dramatic warning for the disciples to be watchful for the unknown day and hour of Jesus' final coming (25:13) by taking the risk to be productive stewards with whatever talents they have been entrusted.

Pragmatically, the parable comparing the reign of the heavens with the story of servants who are given various amounts of talents by their lord (25:14–30) warns the audience to be like those servants who took the risk of being productive stewards by aggressively and energetically working with whatever amount of talents were entrusted to them for promoting and thus experiencing the reign of the heavens. It is not enough for them to cautiously conserve the talents entrusted to them like the lazy and useless servant paralyzed by fear. Otherwise they will not be prepared and qualified to enter into the final joy of the reign of the heavens at the unknown day and hour of Jesus' final coming.

8. Matthew 25:31–46: Parable of Judgment Comparing the Righteous and the Unrighteous

"When the Son of Man finally comes in his glory and all the angels with him, then he will sit on the throne of his glory" (v 31).[60] This climaxes the previous

[59] This is the final, climactic occurrence in Matthew of the refrain, "where there will be the weeping and gnashing of teeth" (cf. 8:12; 13:42, 50; 22:13; 24:51) to express the extreme anguish of final exclusion from the reign of the heavens.

[60] On 25:31–46 see, in addition to the commentaries, O. L. Cope, "Matthew XXV: 31–46: 'The Sheep and the Goats' Reinterpreted," *NovT* 11 (1969) 32–44; J.-C. Ingelaere, "La 'parabole' du jugement dernier (Matthieu 25/31–46)," *RHPR* 50 (1970) 23–60; D. R. Catchpole, "The Poor on Earth and the Son of Man in Heaven: A Re-appraisal of Matthew XXV. 31–46," *BJRL* 61 (1979) 355–97; E. Brandenburger, *Das Recht des Weltenrichters: Untersuchung zu Matthäus 25,31–46* (SBS 99; Stuttgart: Katholisches Bibelwerk, 1980); A. Feuillet, "Le caractère universel du jugement et la charité sans frontières en Mt 25,31–46," *NRT* 102 (1980) 179–96; Agbanou, *Le discours eschatologique*, 173–98; J. M. Court, "Right and Left: The Implications for Matthew 25.31–46," *NTS* 31 (1985) 223–33; J. R. Donahue, "The 'Parable' of

references to Jesus' "coming" as the Son of Man and Lord at an unknown day and unexpected hour (cf. 24:3, 27, 30, 37, 39, 42, 44, 50; 25:6, 19) in "glory" (16:27) and with "much glory" (24:30). The previous references to the "angels" that will accompany and assist him in the final judgment (13:41, 49; 16:27; 24:31) now become "all" the angels with him (v 31), contributing to the universality of the scene. Jesus promised his disciples that when the Son of Man sits "on the throne of his glory," they too will sit on twelve thrones judging the twelve tribes of Israel (19:28). That the Son of Man will now sit "on the throne of his glory" thus places him in the position for judging (v 31).

"All the peoples" (πάντα τὰ ἔθνη) will be gathered before the Son of Man (v 32). This includes "all the peoples" (πάντων τῶν ἐθνῶν) who will hate the disciples because of the name of Jesus (24:9) and "all the peoples" (πᾶσιν τοῖς ἔθνεσιν) to whom the gospel of the reign will be preached throughout the whole world as testimony to them before the coming of the end (24:14). Since the Son of Man, when he comes at the end of the world in the glory of his Father with his angels, will repay "each one" (ἑκάστῳ) according to one's conduct (16:27), "all the peoples" (v 32) include everyone without exception and thus indicate a scene of universal and final judgment.[61]

That Jesus as the Son of Man will separate all the people from one another as (ὥσπερ) a shepherd separates the sheep from the goats (v 32) begins the comparison.[62] He will place the sheep on his right, the side of favor, for the comparison with the goats on the left (v 33).[63] Jesus, the new-born king

---

the Sheep and Goats: A Challenge to Christian Ethics," *TS* 47 (1986) 3–31; idem, *Gospel in Parable*, 109–25; D. O. Via, "Ethical Responsibility and Human Wholeness in Matthew 25:31–46," *HTR* 80 (1987) 79–100; S. W. Gray, *The Least of My Brothers: Matthew 25:31–46: A History of Interpretation* (SBLDS 114; Atlanta: Scholars, 1989); E. Farahian, "Relire Matthieu 25,31–46," *Greg* 72 (1991) 437–57; Charette, *Recompense*, 155–59; Lambrecht, *Treasure*, 260–84; L. Panier, "Le Fils de l'Homme et les nations: Lecture de Mt 25,31–46," *Sémiotique et Bible* 69 (1993) 39–52; Weber, *Events*, 130–37

[61] Although τὰ ἔθνη refers to the Gentiles in Matthew (4:15; 6:32; 10:5, 18; 12:18, 21; 20:19, 25), πάντα τὰ ἔθνη (24:9, 14; 25:32; 28:19) refers to "all" the nations or peoples including the Jews and excluding no one. See Farahian, "Relire," 440; Charette, *Recompense*, 156; Lambrecht, *Treasure*, 275.

[62] For the OT background (Ezek 34:17) and Matthean use of the shepherd metaphor here, see Heil, "Ezekiel 34," 705.

[63] Gundry, *Matthew*, 512: "Palestinian shepherds commonly herded mixed flocks of sheep and goats, but separated the sheep and goats in the evening because sheep prefer the open air at night and goats need the warmth of shelter. The greater value of sheep and their white color suit them to stand for the saved. Because most people are right-handed, the right hand often symbolizes favor."

(βασιλεὺς) of the Jews (2:2), who, as the audience recalls, entered Jerusalem as her king (βασιλεύς) (21:5), now represents the king (βασιλεὺς), the Son of Man acting as the shepherd, who will address the sheep on his right: "Come, those blessed of my Father, inherit the reign (βασιλείαν) prepared for you from the foundation of the world" (v 34). Whereas in previous parables the king (βασιλεῖ) of the reign (βασιλεία) of the heavens (18:23; 22:2) referred to God the Father, in this climactic scene of universal judgment Jesus himself functions as the king of the reign of his Father.[64]

The audience remembers that in the sermon on the mount Jesus declared blessed (μακάριοι) those among his disciples and the crowds (5:1–2) who are meek, for they will inherit (κληρονομήσουσιν) "the land" (5:5; cf. Ps 37:11), a symbolic reference to the reign (cf. 5:3).[65] He promised that every disciple who leaves home, family, and fields for the sake of his name will inherit (κληρονομήσει) eternal life (19:29), a synonym for the reign.[66] These promises are confirmed as Jesus directs the blessed (εὐλογημένοι) sheep to inherit (κληρονομήσατε) the reign (v 34). As sheep the disciples, who, in distinction from the crowds, were given to know the mysteries of the reign of the heavens (13:11), the things hidden "from the foundation of the world" (ἀπὸ καταβολῆς κόσμου) (13:35)[67] in the parables discourse, now inherit the eschatological reign itself, prepared for them "from the foundation of the world" (ἀπὸ καταβολῆς κόσμου) (v 34).

The reason (γὰρ, v 35)[68] the sheep are blessed with the reign is that they served Jesus himself in accord with the way that Jesus not only served those in need but taught and empowered his disciples to serve those in need:

1) That "I was hungry and you gave (ἐδώκατέ) me to eat (φαγεῖν)" (v 35) means the sheep have done for Jesus what Jesus himself commanded his disciples to do for the hungry crowds when he commanded them, "You give

---

[64] R. L. Mowery, "The Matthean References to the Kingdom: Different Terms for Different Audiences," *ETL* 70 (1994) 401: ". . . Jesus declared that 'the king' will direct 'the ones blessed of my Father' to inherit 'the kingdom' prepared for them (25,34). Though the latter reference to the kingdom does not have a genitive qualifier, the presence of the words 'my Father' earlier in this verse suggests that this kingdom is the Father's kingdom."

[65] Meier, *Matthew*, 40; Gundry, *Matthew*, 69; Sand, *Matthäus*, 101; Morris, *Matthew*, 98.

[66] Schottroff, "ζῶ," *EDNT*, 2. 106. The sheep who inherit "the reign" in v 34 are the righteous who enter "eternal life" in v 46.

[67] For including the word "world" (κόσμου) here, see Metzger, *Textual Commentary*, 33–34; Gundry, *Matthew*, 271.

[68] Edwards, "*Gar* in Matthew," 647.

(δότε) them to eat (φαγεῖν)" (14:16). After he miraculously increased an insufficient amount of food twice (14:17; 15:34), he empowered his disciples to feed those who were hungry as he gave (ἔδωκεν in 14:19; ἐδίδου in 15:36) the food to his disciples who in turn gave it to the crowds.

2) That the sheep received the reward of the reign because "I was thirsty and you gave me drink (ἐποτίσατέ)" (v 35) accords with Jesus' teaching the disciples that "whoever receives you receives me" (10:40) and whoever gives a drink (ποτίσῃ) of cold water to one of these little ones simply because he is a disciple will surely not lose his reward (10:42), the eschatological reward of the reign.[69]

3) That "I was a stranger and you welcomed me" (v 35) means the sheep have imitated Jesus, who welcomed strangers with mercy (9:13) when he shared the hospitality of table fellowship with estranged public sinners (9:9 13; 11:19) and when he healed foreigners (8:5–13; 15:21–28). Jesus' teaching of love of enemies (5:43–48) embraces the hospitable welcoming of strangers.

4) That "I was naked (γυμνὸς) and you clothed (περιεβάλετέ) me" (v 36) means the sheep have served Jesus by emulating his compassion (9:36; 14:14; 15:32; 20:34) in accord with his teaching to love one's neighbor as oneself (22:39; Lev 19:18), especially as it is expressed in Isa 58:7 (LXX): "Share your bread with one who is hungry and bring the unsheltered poor into your home; if you see someone naked (γυμνὸν), clothe (περίβαλε) him, and do not disdain your blood relatives."[70]

5) That "I was sick (ἠσθένησα) and you took care of me" (v 36) means the sheep have ministered to Jesus in accord with his authoritative command and empowerment for the disciples to heal the sick (ἀσθενοῦντας) (10:8). They thus share in and extend the compassionate healing ministry of Jesus himself, who "took on our sicknesses (ἀσθενείας) and bore our diseases" (8:17; Isa 53:4).[71]

6) That "I was in prison (φυλακῇ) and you came to me" (v 36) means the sheep assisted Jesus not only as one in critical need but in the way that, as the audience knows from the previous narrative, disciples should assist their master. The disciples of John the Baptist assisted him after he was handed over (4:12) and put in prison (φυλακῇ) (14:3, 10). They served as intermedi-

---

69 Weaver, *Missionary Discourse,* 122.

70 Gundry, *Use,* 142–43.

71 Heil, "Healing Miracles," 274–87.

aries between John and Jesus (9:14; 11:2) and after John was beheaded in prison (14:10), they took away his body and buried it (14:12).

In the explanation of the parable of the weeds (13:36–43) the disciples and the implied audience were invited to see themselves as the righteous (δίκαιοι) who will shine like the sun in the reign of their Father (13:43) in contrast to those disciples who do lawlessness (13:41) and are excluded from the reign (13:42). The righteous are those who do the righteousness (δικαιο-σύνην) (5:20; 6:1, 33), the will of Jesus' Father, that enables them to enter the reign of the heavens (5:20; 7:21). According to the parable of the fish net (13:47–50) the angels will separate the evil ones, the rotten fish/people (13:48) that Jesus and his disciples will collect as "fishers" of people, from the midst of the righteous (δικαίων) (13:49), the disciples themselves as well as the righteous people, the good "fish" (13:48), they will gather in their ministry (4:19). Now the disciples and the audience are invited to see themselves as the sheep, the righteous (δίκαιοι), who have served the Jesus they now address as "Lord" (Κύριε) (v 37), just as they were to identify themselves in the pre-ceding parables as the faithful and wise servant of their absent Lord (κύριος, 24:45, 46, 48, 50), as the wise maidens of the bridegroom addressed as "Lord, Lord" (Κύριε κύριε, 25:11), and as the servants who doubled the tal-ents of the one they address as "Lord" (Κύριε, 25:20, 22).

But the righteous sheep are surprised that it was Jesus himself whom they had served. Their three questions addressed to the "Lord," each introduced with the same words of incredulous astonishment that it was "you," repeat the compassionate conduct that gained them the reign: "When did we see *you* (πότε σε εἴδομεν) hungry and feed you, or thirsty and give you drink? And when did we see *you* (πότε δέ σε εἴδομεν) a stranger and welcomed you, or naked and clothed you? And when did we see *you* (πότε δέ σε εἴδομεν) sick or in prison and come to you?" (vv 37–39).

Jesus as the king adds to the surprise not only by identifying himself with the needy whom the righteous have helped but by designating the needy as members of his new family: "Amen I say to you, inasmuch as you did it for one of these least brothers of mine, you did it for me" (v 40). Not only are the dis-ciples who do the will of the Father in heaven the mother and sisters and brothers (ἀδελφοί) of Jesus (12:49–50), but now even the lowliest among the needy belong to the family of Jesus' brothers (ἀδελφῶν) (v 40). Not only is each disciple, "one of these little ones" (ἕνα τῶν μικρῶν τούτων, 10:42; 18:6, 10, 14), who humbles himself like a child and believes in Jesus a member of Jesus' family, but now each "one of these least brothers of mine" (ἑνὶ τούτων τῶν ἀδελφῶν μου τῶν ἐλαχίστων, v 40), each needy one, is likewise a member of Jesus' family. Jesus has thus expanded his family to embrace not only the "little ones" (μικρῶν) but even the "least ones" (ἐλαχίστων).

This surprising designation of the needy "least ones" as members of Jesus' family opens the comparison to an additional level of meaning. Now the disciples and implied audience are to see themselves not only in the righteous sheep who take care of the needy but also in the needy "least ones" themselves, since both the disciples as "little ones" and the needy as "least ones" are part of Jesus' family. Just as Jesus identified himself with "these least brothers of mine" so that whatever is done to them is done to him (v 40), so Jesus identified himself with his disciples when he sent them out on their mission with the words, "whoever receives you receives me" (10:40).

As disciples commissioned by Jesus to extend his ministry of announcing and bringing about the reign, the audience may find themselves in need of care and hospitality like the needy "least ones." Since they are to take no money on their mission (10:9), disciples may find themselves in need of food or drink (10:42) like the "least ones" (vv 35, 37). They must rely upon the care and hospitality of others, since "the worker deserves his food" (10:10). Like the "least ones" (vv 35, 38) they will be strangers seeking to be hospitably welcomed into the homes of others (10:11–13) and persecuted refugees fleeing from city to city (10:23). Like the naked "least ones" (vv 36, 38) they may be in need of clothing, since they are not to take a traveling bag, second tunic, or sandals with them (10:10). Like the "least ones" (vv 36, 39) they may find themselves sick or imprisoned because of the expected hardship and persecution of their mission (10:16–23). But as needy "least ones" the disciples can be encouraged that those who take care of them will be rewarded with the reign (v 34).[72]

In contrast to those on the right whom Jesus the king will command, "Come, those blessed of my Father, inherit the reign prepared (ἡτοιμασ

---

[72] Usually just one of these two levels of meaning (disciples as sheep or disciples as least ones) is chosen. But attention to the narrative progression and reading process indicates how both meanings are operative. Based on the progression of the preceding parables, in which the audience is to identify with the faithful and wise rather than wicked servant (24:45–51), with the wise rather than foolish maidens (25:1–13), and with those doubling their talents rather than with the one who preserved his one talent (25:14–30), the audience first naturally identifies with the righteous sheep rather than with the goats (vv 32–33). But once Jesus surprisingly identifies the least ones as his brothers, then the audience can see themselves not only in the righteous sheep but also in the needy least ones.

μένην) for you from the foundation of the world" (v 34), to those on the left he will command, "Depart from me those accursed into the eternal fire prepared (ἡτοιμασμένον) for the devil and his angels" (v 41). That the reign was prepared by God (divine passive) for the blessed, righteous sheep from the beginning, but the eternal fire was originally prepared not for the accursed goats but only for the devil and his angels underlines the tragedy of their fate. The reason (γὰρ, v 42) the goats are cursed for the eternal fire is that their behavior toward Jesus was precisely the opposite of that of the sheep. For the third time the audience experiences the criteria of judgment, but this time negatively: "For I was hungry and you did *not* give me to eat, I was thirsty and you did *not* give me drink, I was a stranger and you did *not* welcome me, naked and you did *not* clothe me, sick and in prison and you did *not* take care of me" (vv 42–43).[73]

Like the righteous sheep the goats are surprised that it was Jesus himself whom they had failed to serve. Their single question addressed to the "Lord" begins with the same words of incredulous astonishment uttered thrice by the righteous, "When did we see *you* (πότε σε εἴδομεν, cf. vv 37–39) hungry or thirsty or a stranger or naked or sick or in prison and not serve you?" (v 44). Their query quickly and powerfully brings the audience once again through the list of criteria for judgment climaxed by their self-condemning failure: "And we did *not* serve *you*." The goats failed to serve (διηκονήσαμέν, v 44) the Jesus who called each of his disciples to be a servant (διάκονος) of one another in order to be great (20:26), just as Jesus himself, as the Son of Man, did not come to be served (διακονηθῆναι) but to serve (διακονῆσαι) (20:28).

Once again the audience experiences the shock of Jesus identifying himself with the "least ones." His answer to the goats, "Amen I say to you, inasmuch as you did *not* do it to one of these least ones, you did *not* do it to me" (v 45), affirms their failure in contrast to the sheep (v 40). But Jesus' omission this time of the words "brothers of mine" (cf. v 40) indicates how the goats should have cared for the "least ones" simply because they are the neediest, without knowing they are also brothers of Jesus.

The comparison that began with the separation of all people into sheep

---

[73] Note the complementary combination of being sick and in prison evident in the progression from "I was sick and you *took care of me*, I was in prison and you *came to me*" (v 36) to "when did we see you sick or in prison and *come to you?*" (v 39) to "I was sick and in prison and you did not *take care of me*" (v 43).

and goats (v 32) reaches its climactic contrast as the goats, like the unfaithful servant (24:51), the foolish maidens (25:11–12), and the useless servant (25:30), went away to eternal punishment, but the righteous sheep, like the faithful and wise servant (24:47), the wise maidens (25:10), and the productive servants (25:21, 23), to eternal life (v 46). After the negative experience of the goats the comparison returns to and concludes with the positive experience of the sheep.

But the negative experience adds an important dimension to both levels of meaning. Without it the fate of the righteous could be interpreted as simply their good fortune for choosing to help the least ones. But the judgment of the goats (vv 41–46) indicates that helping the least ones is a necessary requirement not just an option. The disciples and the audience are warned that they *must* be the righteous who take care of the needy least ones to enter the eternal life (v 46) of the reign (v 34), otherwise they are the goats who go to their eternal punishment (v 46) in the eternal fire (v 41). Likewise, the disciples and the audience, insofar as they become like the needy least ones in their mission of bringing about the reign, are encouraged that they must and will be assisted by the righteous.

Jesus' shocking identification of himself with the needy least ones, whom he calls his own brothers (v 40), adds a new twist to the theme of being prepared for the unknown time of Jesus' final coming as developed in the previous comparisons of the eschatological discourse (24:23–25:30). There is a sense in which Jesus is not really absent at all. The audience is to prepare for the final coming of Jesus at the end of the age (24:3) by serving the Jesus who is still present in the needy least ones they help and who is present with the audience themselves when they become his least brothers. This special presence of Jesus contributes to the Matthean theme of Jesus' abiding presence with the audience. As Emmanuel he represents "God with us" (1:23). Wherever two or three disciples are gathered in his name to restore a brother to the community, Jesus is in their midst (18:20). Indeed, as the risen Lord he is with us always until the end of the age (28:20).

The comparison of the judgment of the righteous sheep with the unrighteous goats (25:31–46) has a double pragmatic effect: 1) It urges the audience to be the righteous sheep who must take care of the neediest, the "least ones," in the world as a way of serving Jesus himself until his final coming. By doing so they will be blessed at the last judgment by inheriting the eternal life of the reign God has prepared for them. 2) It encourages the audience to become needy least ones in their mission of bringing the reign to the world. As least ones they can be assured of Jesus' presence with them as members of his own family. They can take the risk of becoming needy least ones because the righteous must and will take care of them.[74]

Conclusion

The conclusion of the fifth and final discourse in Matthew, the eschatological discourse (24–25), involves the audience in a progressive series of comparisons and parables that indicate how they are to prepare themselves for the final coming of Jesus as the Son of Man at the end of the age (24:3).

1) That the coming of Jesus as the Son of Man after his resurrection will be like the sudden and universally visible appearance of lightning enables the audience not to be misled by those who will attempt to point out the location of his coming before it happens (24:23–28).

2) Just as the audience knows that when the fig tree produces its leaves summer is near, so they will know that when they experience the great affliction of the final days the coming of Jesus as the Son of Man is near. They are invited to make the prophetic and authoritative words of Jesus the firm and lasting foundation of their lives, a foundation that will outlast the passing away of heaven and earth (24:29–35).

3) Although the audience will know in general when the Son of Man is near, they will not know the exact day or hour of his coming. Just as in the days of Noah people were in the midst of their ordinary activity, unaware of the coming of the great flood, so people will be going about their normal tasks, unaware of the day or hour when Jesus will come as the Son of Man (24:36–41).

4) Like the householder who would have watched if he knew when the

---

[74] We have treated the scene of last judgment in 25:31–46 as a parabolic comparison or "parable" in the more general sense. There are good reasons for also considering it to be a "parable" in the strict sense: 1) The metaphorical comparison of the sheep and goats is not limited to vv 32–33 but introduces the comparison of the righteous and unrighteous that is sustained throughout the entire scene. It is a *comparison* from beginning to end, constituting a complete narrative that can stand on its own as a parable in the strict sense. 2) It stands in the line of and climaxes the previous parables of separation and comparison that are oriented to the final judgment (7:24–27; 13:24–30, 36–43, 47–50; 24:45–51; 25:1–13, 14–30). 3) Like previous parables it gives its audience a surprising experience of the reign of the heavens by calling them to help the neediest with whom Jesus identifies himself. By doing so they are already experiencing the reign present with Jesus as they are assured of entering the eternal life of the eschatological reign.

thief was coming, the audience is to be watchful and ready for the coming of Jesus as their Lord and the Son of Man on a day they do not know and at an hour they do not expect (24:42–44).

5) The audience is to take care of the needs of those entrusted to them in order to be like the faithful and wise servant who, by giving his fellow servants their food at the proper time, demonstrates what it means to be watching and ready for the unexpected time of Jesus' final coming as Lord and Son of Man. By so doing they will experience blessedness in the reign of the heavens rather than the eternal punishment of the wicked servant who, thinking that his Lord would be delayed, mistreated his fellow servants and therefore was not watching and ready for the coming of his Lord (24:45–51).

6) The audience is to reckon with a possible delay of unknown duration for Jesus' final coming. Like the wise maidens they must be prepared to enter the wedding feast of the reign whenever Jesus comes as the bridegroom. They will be ready and enter with Jesus if he knows them as members of his family, as those who hear and do the words of Jesus that reveal the will of his Father. Unlike the foolish maidens who did not reckon with delay, were unprepared, and so could not enter the reign because Jesus did not know them, the audience must not foolishly expect their fellow Christians to be able to help them, if they themselves are not prepared and ready for the unknown day and hour of Jesus' final coming (25:1–13).

7) The audience is to be like those servants who took the risk of being productive stewards by aggressively and energetically working with whatever amount of talents were entrusted to them for promoting and experiencing the reign. It is not enough for them to merely conserve the talents entrusted to them like the lazy and useless servant paralyzed by fear. Otherwise they will not be prepared and qualified to enter into the final joy of the reign at the unknown day and hour of Jesus' final coming (25:14–30).

8) Rather than the unrighteous goats the audience is to be the righteous sheep who must take care of the neediest, the "least ones," in the world as a way of serving Jesus himself until his final coming. By doing so they will be blessed at the last judgment by inheriting the eternal life of the reign God has prepared for them. They are also encouraged to become needy least ones themselves in their mission of bringing the reign to the world. As least ones they can be assured of Jesus' presence with them. They can take the risk of becoming needy least ones because the righteous must and will take care of them (25:31–46).

CHAPTER 9

Conclusion
(by Carter)

This experiment with hearing the parables in Matthew's gospel has focussed on the interaction between the authorial audience and Matthew's parables in their final form and context within the gospel. Such an approach, known as audience-oriented criticism, a subcategory of narrative or literary criticism, has not been the usual way of studying parables. More recent work has either sought to relocate the parables in the ministry of the historical Jesus or to focus on the changes which the redactor Matthew makes to them.

Our approach has concentrated on four areas: 1) We have worked with the final or current textual form of the parables. We have not attempted to reconstruct an earlier version but have focussed on the form as we find it in the gospel. 2) We have been attentive to the placement of the parable in its current literary context embedded within the gospel. We have not sought, for example, a different setting in the life of the historical Jesus. 3) We have noticed intratextual connections between the parable and other parts of the gospel. We have located the parables within the plot of the gospel. We have made explicit the contribution of the knowledge that the audience has gained from earlier in the gospel and that it continues to employ as it interacts with the parables. 4) Rather than focussing on the intent of Jesus the parable teller, or of Matthew their redactor, we have been concerned with what happens as the authorial audience interacts with the parables.

In order to pursue this concern with the interaction between the parables and the audience, we have adopted several strategies. We have adopted from

P. J. Rabinowitz the notion of the authorial audience.[1] This audience, as much as we can reconstruct it, is the audience the gospel writer has "in mind" in writing the gospel. It is the author's impression or understanding of a late first century community of followers of Jesus, perhaps located in the large city of Antioch in Syria where it has experienced recent and bitter conflict with a synagogue community. Moreover we have employed "reader-response" or, more accurately, "hearer-response" criticism to explore the audience's interaction with the parables. We have argued throughout that the audience plays an active role in making meaning as it engages the parables. It connects words, sentences, sections. It uses knowledge gained from earlier in the gospel or assumed from other texts or from its socio-cultural experience to supply "blanks" or "gaps" in the text. It creates characters from their actions and words. It orders and unifies the plot in terms of sequences, hierarchy, causes, and effects. We have utilized the notion of narrative progression to emphasize the audience's progress through the gospel as a whole and through its subsections. We have noted, for example, the impact of sequences of comparisons prior to a parable (7:13–23; 24:23–44). We have also been attentive to the audience's progression through sequences of parables (13:1 52; 21:28–22:14; 24:45–25:46).

A further key aspect of this interaction has been expressed by the term *pragmatics*. This dynamic is informed by speech act theory which emphasizes not only the informative but the performative dimensions of language. This term denotes what happens for the audience in the acts of hearing and having heard the parables. It embraces the audience's thoughts and feelings, its attitudes and perspectives, the actions and lifestyle it is urged to live as it engages the parables. We have underlined that interaction with the parables does not only mean for the audience renewed or confirmed understandings and insight (though these are important). Insights from their interaction means a way of life of discipleship.

This pragmatic dimension is evident in the verbs that we have employed in describing the interaction between the audience and the parables. In this interaction the audience is warned, urged, challenged, encouraged, strengthened, and renewed. It is instructed to do the will of God, exhorted to appreciate its privileged identity, urged to persevere and to be patient, to forgive, to understand. These actions are expressions and consequences of their

---

[1] Rabinowitz, "Whirl Without End."

encounter with the reign of the heavens, God's saving presence, manifested in Jesus' actions and words. The parables depict what happens when that reign comes among human beings. Sometimes its presence seems invisible and inconsequential; in other parables it is visible and transformative. The reign upsets "normal" expectations and patterns of living. It envisions new possibilities of reality. It creates different ways of living and relating. The parables confirm, repeat and extend what the audience "knows" about the reign of the heavens from its previous discipleship and from its interaction with earlier parts of the narrative. In such repetition is the renewal of the audience's commitment and active discipleship.

The authorial audience is to live this life of discipleship in several social contexts, all of which are marked by difficult, even hostile, circumstances:

1) The presence of the reign of the heavens creates a community of disciples (4:17–22; chaps. 5–7). Here in the context of internal community relationships the will of God, revealed in Jesus' teaching, is to be done in the knowledge that disciples will have to give account in the judgment (7:24–27). That will is marked by mercy and forgiveness as foundational aspects of it (18:23–35).

2) Discipleship is lived in the context of a society which more often than not rejects the "word of the reign," the good news that God's reign is among human beings in Jesus. The parable of the sower and its explanation, for example, discloses to the audience the work of "the evil one," of "trouble and persecution," and "the cares of the world and the lure of wealth" in preventing the proclamation being received positively. The parable warns the audience not to succumb to such forces and affirms their positive reception of the word (13:3–9, 18–23). Their life of faithful discipleship, as the parable of the wheat and weeds reveals, continues in the context of negative responses until the final sorting by God in the yet future judgment (13:24–30). The community of disciples as a minority and marginal entity must patiently and faithfully persevere in this context.

3) This life of discipleship is also located in the parables in relation to God's previous history with Israel and its leaders. This history has probably been experienced by the authorial audience in terms of a bitter dispute with a synagogue community. In the parables the history has been largely, though not exclusively, marked by the leaders' rejection of God's purposes and messengers (21:34–39; 22:3–6). God continues to provide these leaders with chances to repent (21:28–32). Yet their role of enabling Israel to be faithful to

and fruitful in God's purposes is shown to have passed to "another group of people" (21:43). This group is entrusted with the same responsibility of producing fruit (21:43) and is warned through the narrative progression that it too awaits judgment for its faithfulness to the task, and condemnation awaits those who fail to live in a way appropriate to this task (22:11–14).

We have sought to hear the parables in this gospel in the context of the authorial audience's interaction with them (as much as that is possible). That is, we have sought to reconstruct the interaction in terms of an audience that actualizes the text in a positive and active way as a consenting audience. But as J. Fetterly has demonstrated, *actual audiences* do not always consent to the roles and response that comprise a positive and open interaction with a text.[2] That is, actual audiences can and do resist taking up the role of the authorial audience.

Actual audiences know, for instance, that in a piece of writing or speech they are supposed to admire certain values or perspectives or actions. Yet while being able to identify those expected responses from its interaction with the communication, an audience may, because of their gender or social position or national origin or ethnicity or life experience or ideological or religious commitments, withhold that admiration. Actual audiences know, for instance, that in a piece of propaganda they are supposed to "buy" the argument and claims. Yet while recognizing the position being commended, audiences can and do refuse to assent to it, refuse to feel the pride or hate, refuse to take the commended actions. With some forms of communication an audience may consent to follow a line of argument in order to understand it, without thereby indicating agreement with it. Or in thinking along with a communication they may agree with some aspects and disagree with others. But in order to disagree or to refuse to play the role of the authorial audience, an actual audience first becomes aware of or identifies this role as it interacts with the communication. In becoming aware it evaluates whether it will consent (wholly or partially) or resist (wholly or partially).

To focus, therefore, as we have done on the authorial audience's interaction with the parables is not to suggest a privileged hearing of this material from Matthew's gospel. It is, rather, to open up a dialogue. It is to invite consideration of such perspectives and lifestyle by contemporary audiences, especially (but not exclusively) Christian audiences. Such dialogical consider-

---

[2] Fetterly, *Resisting Reader.*

ation is necessary because actual (contemporary) audiences exist in very different social locations, with diverse religious commitments, gender experiences, and ideological perspectives. It is necessary for the task of hearing these ancient stories in different moments and places in the church's history. And such dialogue, arising in the interactions between readers and these parables, ensures that audiences and readers continue their age-old role of being active participants in the act of making meaning.

Bibliography

Achtemeier, P. J. "*Omne verbum sonat:* The New Testament and the Oral Environment of Late Western Antiquity." *JBL* 109 (1990) 3–27.

Agbanou, V. K. *Le discours eschatologique de Matthieu 24–25: Tradition et rédaction.* Ebib 2. Paris: Gabalda, 1983.

Allison, D. C. "The Structure of the Sermon on the Mount." *JBL* 106 (1987) 423–45.

Anderson, J. C. *Matthew's Narrative Web: Over, and Over, and Over Again.* JSNTSup 91. Sheffield: JSOT, 1994.

——. "Matthew: Gender and Reading." *The Bible and Feminist Hermeneutics.* Semeia 28. Ed. M. A. Tolbert. Chico, CA: Scholars, 1983, 3–27.

Aristotle, *The Poetics.* LCL. Cambridge: Harvard University, 1939.

Armstrong, G. C. *Aristotle: The Metaphysics.* LCL. Vol. XVIII. Cambridge, MA: Harvard University, 1935.

Austin, J. L. *How To Do Things with Words.* Oxford: Oxford University, 1962.

Bailey, J. L., and Vander Brock, L. D. *Literary Forms in the New Testament.* Louisville: Westminster/John Knox, 1992.

Bal, M. "Notes on Narrative Embedding." *Poetics Today* 2 (1981) 41–59.

Balch, D. "Household Ethical Codes in Peripatetic Neopythagorean and Early Christian Moralists." SBLASP 16 (1977) 397–404.

——. *Let Wives Be Submissive: The Domestic Code of 1 Peter.* SBLMS 26. Chico, CA: Scholars Press, 1981.

——. "Household Codes." *Greco-Roman Literature and the New Testament.* Ed D. Aune. Atlanta: Scholars, 1988, 25–50.

——. "Neopyhthagorean Moralists and the New Testament Household Codes." *ANRW* II.26.1 (1992) 380–411.

Ballard, P. H. "Reasons for Refusing the Great Supper." *JTS* 23 (1972) 341–50.

Balz, H. "οὐαί." *EDNT,* 2. 540.

Barr, D. L. "Speaking of Parables: A Survey of Recent Research." *TSF Bulletin* 6 (May–June 1983) 8–10.

Barth, G. "Matthew's Understanding of the Law." *Tradition and Interpretation in Matthew.* Ed. G. Bornkamm, G. Barth, and H. J. Held. London: SCM, 1963, 105–12.

Barth, J. "Tales within Tales within Tales." *Antaeus* 43 (1981) 45–63.

Barton, S. C. *Discipleship and Family Ties in Mark and Matthew.* SNTSMS 80. Cambridge: Cambridge University, 1994.

Bauckham, R. "The Coin in the Fish's Mouth." *Gospel Perspectives: Volume 6: The Miracles of Jesus.* Eds. D. Wenham and C. Blomberg. Sheffield: JSOT, 1986, 219–52.

Beare, F. W. *The Gospel According to Matthew.* San Francisco: Harper & Row, 1982.

Berendsen, M. "Formal Criteria of Narrative Embedding." *Journal of Literary Semantics* 10 (1981) 79–94.

Berger, K. "πρόσωπον." *EDNT,* 3. 180–81.

Berkey, R. "ΕΓΓΙΖΕΙΝ, ΦΘΑΝΕΙΝ, and Realized Eschatology." *JBL* 82 (1963) 177–87.

Biers, R. "Purification of the Temple: Preparation for the Kingdom of God." *JBL* 90 (1971) 82–90.

Blomberg, C. L. "The Parables of Jesus: Current Trends and Needs in Research." *Studying the Historical Jesus: Evaluations of the State of Current Research.* Ed. B. Chilton and C. Evans. Leiden: Brill, 1994, 231–54.

———. "Interpreting the Parables of Jesus: Where Are We and Where Do We Go from Here?" *CBQ* 53 (1991) 50–78.

———. *Interpreting the Parables.* Downers Grove, IL: InterVarsity, 1990.

———. *Matthew.* NAC 22. Nashville: Broadman, 1992.

Böcher, O. "γέεννα." *EDNT,* 1. 239–40.

Bonnard, P. *L'évangile selon saint Matthieu.* CNT. Neuchâtel: Delachaux & Niestlé, 1963, 1970.

Boring, M. E. "The Kingdom of God in Mark." *The Kingdom of God in 20th-Century Interpretation.* Ed. W. Willis. Peabody: Hendrickson, 1987, 131–45.

Bornkamm, G. "Der Aufbau der Bergpredigt." *NTS* 24 (1977–78) 419–32.

———. "End-Expectation and Church in Matthew." *Tradition and Interpretation in Matthew.* G. Bornkamm, G. Barth, and H. J. Held. Philadelphia: Westminster, 1963, 15–51.

Botha, J. E. *Jesus and the Samaritan Woman: A Speech Act Reading of John 4:1–42.* NovTSup 65. Leiden: Brill, 1991.

Brandenburger, E. *Das Recht des Weltenrichters: Untersuchung zu Matthäus 25,31–46.* SBS 99. Stuttgart: Katholisches Bibelwerk, 1980.

Breech, J. *The Silence of Jesus: The Authentic Voice of the Historical Man.* Philadelphia: Fortress, 1983.

Brodie, T. L. "Fish, Temple Tithe, and Remission: God-based Generosity of Deuteronomy 14–15 as One Component of Matt 17:22–18:35." *RB* 99 (1992) 697–718.

Broer, I. "ἄγγελος.." *EDNT,* 1. 13–16.

——. "Redaktionsgeschichtliche Aspekte von Mt. 24:1–28." *NovT* 35 (1993) 209–33.

Brooks, J. A. "The Unity and Structure of the Sermon on the Mount." *Criswell Theological Review* 6 (1992) 15–28.

Brown, E. K. *Rhythm in the Novel.* Toronto: University of Toronto, 1950.

Brown, R. E. *The Birth of the Messiah.* New York: Doubleday, 1977, 1993.

——. "The Pater Noster as an Eschatological Prayer." *New Testament Essays.* New York: Paulist, 1965, 1982, 217–53.

Brown, S. "The Matthean Apocalypse." *JSNT* 4 (1979) 2–27.

Burchard, C. "Senfkorn, Sauerteig, Schatz und Perle in Matthäus 13." SNTSU 13 (1988) 5–35.

Burkett, W. "Hellenistische Pseudopythagorica." *Philologus* 105 (1961) 16–43, 226–46.

Burnett, F. W. "Characterization and Reader Construction of Characters in the Gospels." *Characterization in Biblical Literature. Semeia* 63. Ed. E. S. Malbon and A. Berlin. Atlanta: Scholars Press, 1993, 3–28.

——. *The Testament of Jesus-Sophia: A Redaction-Critical Study of the Eschatological Discourse in Matthew.* Lanham, MD: University Press of America, 1981.

——. "Prolegomenon to Reading Matthew's Eschatological Discourse: Redundancy and the Education of the Reader in Matthew." *Reader Response Approaches to Biblical and Secular Texts. Semeia* 31. Ed. R. Detweiler. Decatur: Scholars, 1985, 91–109.

Busse, U. "διασκορπίζω." *EDNT,* 1. 311.

Cameron, R. "Parable and Interpretation in the Gospel of Thomas." *Forum* 2 (1986) 3–39.

Caplan, H. *[Cicero] Ad C. Herennium De Ratione Dicendi (Rhetorica ad Herennium).* Cambridge, MA: Harvard University, 1954.

Caragounis, C. C. *The Son of Man: Vision and Interpretation.* WUNT 38. Tübingen: Mohr-Siebeck, 1986.

Carlston, C. "Parable and Allegory Revisited: An Interpretive Review." *CBQ* 43 (1981) 228–42.

——. *The Parables of the Triple Tradition.* Philadelphia: Fortress, 1975.

Carson, D. A. "The ΟΜΟΙΟΣ Word-Group as Introduction to Some Matthean Parables." *NTS* 31 (1985) 277–82.

Carter, W. *Households and Discipleship: A Study of Matthew 19–20.* JSNTSup 103. Sheffield: JSOT, 1994.

———. *What Are They Saying About Matthew's Sermon on the Mount?* Mahwah, NJ: Paulist, 1994.

———. "Challenging by Confirming, Renewing by Repenting: The Parables of the 'Reign of the Heavens' in Matthew 13 as Embedded Narratives." *Society of Biblical Literature 1995 Seminar Papers.* Ed. E. H. Lovering, Jr. SBLSP 34. Atlanta: Scholars, 1995, 399–424.

———. "Kernels and Narrative Blocks: The Structure of Matthew's Gospel." *CBQ* 54 (1992) 187–204.

———. *Matthew: Storyteller, Interpreter, Evangelist.* Peabody, MA: Hendrickson, 1996.

———. "Recalling the Lord's Prayer: The Authorial Audience and Matthew's Prayer as Familiar Liturgical Experience." *CBQ* 57 (1995) 514–30.

———. "Matthew 4:18–22 and Matthean Discipleship: An Audience-Oriented Perspective." *CBQ* 59 (1997) 58–75.

———. "The Crowds in Matthew's Gospel." *CBQ* 55 (1993) 54–68.

———. "'Solomon in All His Glory': Intertextuality and Matthew 6.29." *JSNT* 65 (1997) 3–25.

Cassidy, R. J. "Matthew 17:24–27—A Word on Civil Taxes." *CBQ* 41 (1979) 571–80.

Catchpole, D. R. "The Poor on Earth and the Son of Man in Heaven: A Re-appraisal of Matthew XXV. 31–46." *BJRL* 61 (1979) 355–97.

Charette, B. *The Theme of Recompense in Matthew's Gospel.* JSNTSup 79. Sheffield: JSOT, 1992.

Chatman, S. *Story and Discourse: Narrative Structure in Fiction and Film.* Ithaca: Cornell University, 1978.

Cherry, C. *On Human Communication.* Cambridge, MA: MIT, 1957.

Childs, B. "Excursus II: Interpretation of the Parables within a Canonical Context." *The New Testament as Canon: An Introduction.* Philadelphia: Fortress, 1985, 531–40.

Chilton, B. "REGNUM DEI DEUS EST." *SJT* 31 (1978) 261–70.

Collins, J. J. "The Kingdom of God in the Apocrypha and Pseudepigrapha." *The Kingdom of God in 20th-Century Interpretation.* Ed. W. Willis. Peabody, MA: Hendrickson, 1987, 81–95.

Cope, O. L. *Matthew: A Scribe Trained for the Kingdom of Heaven.* CBQMS 5. Washington: The Catholic Biblical Association, 1976.

———. "Matthew XXV: 31–46: `The Sheep and the Goats' Reinterpreted." *NovT* 11 (1969) 32–44.

Corrington, G. P. "Redaction Criticism." *To Each Its Own Meaning: An Introduction to Biblical Criticisms and Their Application.* Ed. S. McKenzie and S. Haynes. Louisville: Westminster/John Knox, 1993.

Court, J. M. "Right and Left: The Implications for Matthew 25.31–46." *NTS* 31 (1985) 223–33.

Crosby, M. *House of Disciples: Church, Economics, and Justice in Matthew.* Mary-knoll, NY: Orbis, 1988.

Crossan, J. D. *In Parables: The Challenge of the Historical Jesus.* New York: Harper & Row, 1973.

———. *The Dark Interval: Towards a Theology of Story.* Niles, IL: Argus, 1975.

———. "The Parable of the Wicked Husbandmen." *JBL* 90 (1971) 451–65.

Crouch, J. *The Origin and Intention of the Colossian Haustafel.* FRLANT 109. Göttingen: Vandenhoeck & Ruprecht, 1972.

Culbertson, P. "Reclaiming the Matthean Vineyard Parables." *Encounter* 49 (1988) 257–83.

Culpepper, R. A. *Anatomy of the Fourth Gospel: A Study in Literary Design.* Philadelphia: Fortress, 1983.

Cuvillier, E. *Le concept de παραβολή dans le second Évangile.* EBib 19. Paris: Gabalda, 1993.

Danker, F. *Benefactor: Epigraphic Study of a Graeco-Roman and New Testament Semantic Field.* St. Louis: Clayton, 1982.

Darr, J. A. "Narrator as Character: Mapping a Reader-Oriented Approach to Narration in Luke-Acts." *Characterization in Biblical Literature.* Semeia 63. Ed. E. S. Malbon and A. Berlin. Atlanta: Scholars, 1993, 43–60.

Davies, W. D., and Allison, D. C. *The Gospel According to Saint Matthew: Volume I: Introduction and Commentary on Matthew I–VII.* ICC. Edinburgh: T. & T. Clark, 1988.

———. *The Gospel According to Saint Matthew: Volume II: Commentary on Matthew VIII–XVIII.* ICC. Edinburgh: Clark, 1991.

de Boer, M. C. "Ten Thousand Talents? Matthew's Interpretation and Redaction of the Parable of the Unforgiving Servant (Matt 18:23–35)." *CBQ* 50 (1988) 214–32.

de Goedt, M. "L'explication de la parabole de l'ivraie (Mt. XIII, 36–43)." *RB* 66 (1959) 32–54.

Deidun, T. "The Parable of the Unmerciful Servant (Mt 18:23–35)." *BTB* 6 (1976) 203–24.

Derrett, J. D. M. "῞Ησαν γὰρ ἁλιεῖς (Mk I 16). Jesus's Fishermen and the Parable of the Net." *NovT* 22 (1980) 125–31.

———. "Peter's Penny." *Law in the New Testament.* London: Darton, Longman & Todd, 1970, 247–65.

———. "The Parable of the Unmerciful Servant." *Law in the New Testament.* London: Darton, Longman & Todd, 1970, 32–47.

———. "Workers in the Vineyard: A Parable of Jesus." *JJS* 25 (1974) 64–91.

———. "The Parable of the Wicked Vinedressers." *Law in the New Testament.* London: Darton, Longman & Todd, 1970, 296–305.

———. "The Parable of the Great Supper." *Law in the New Testament.* London: Darton, Longman & Todd, 1970, 126–55.

de Ru, G. "The Conception of Reward in the Teaching of Jesus." *NovT* 8 (1966) 202–22.

Dibelius, M. *An die Kolosser, an die Epheser, an Philemon.* HNT. Tübingen: Mohr, 1913.

Dietzfelbinger, C. "Das Gleichnis von den anvertrauten Geldern." *BTZ* 6 (1989) 222–33.

Dillon, R. J. "Ravens, Lilies, and the Kingdom of God (Matthew 6:25–33/Luke 12:22–31)." *CBQ* 53 (1991) 605–27.

———. "Towards a Tradition-History of the Parables of the True Israel (Matthew 21,33–22,14)." *Bib* 47 (1966) 1–42.

Dirlmeier, F. "Die Zeit der 'Grossen Ethik'." *Rheinisches Museum für Philologie* 88 (1939) 214–43.

Dodd, C. H. *The Parables of the Kingdom.* London: Collins, 1961.

Donahue, J. R. *The Gospel in Parable: Metaphor, Narrative, and Theology in the Synoptic Gospels.* Philadelphia: Fortress, 1988.

———. "The 'Parable' of the Sheep and Goats: A Challenge to Christian Ethics." *TS* 47 (1986) 3–31.

Donfried, K. P. "The Allegory of the Ten Virgins (Matt 25:1–13) as a Summary of Matthean Theology." *JBL* 93 (1974) 415–28.

Drury, J. *The Parables in the Gospels: History and Allegory.* New York: Crossroad, 1985.

Dschulnigg, P. "Positionen des Gleichnisverständnisses im 20. Jahrhundert: Kurze Darstellung von fünf wichtigen Positionen der Gleichnistheorie (Jülicher, Jeremias, Weder, Arens, Harnisch)." *TZ* 45 (1989) 335–51.

Duling, D. "Matthew and Marginality." SBLASP 32 (1993) 642–71.

———. "Norman Perrin and the Kingdom of God: Review and Response." *JR* 64 (1984) 468–83.

du Plessis, J. G. "Pragmatic Meaning in Matthew 13:1–23." *Neot* 21 (1987) 33–56.

Dupont, J. "Le point de vue de Matthieu dans le chapitre des paraboles." *L'Evangile selon Matthieu: Rédaction et théologie.* BETL 29. Ed. M. Didier. Gembloux: Duculot, 1972, 221–59.

———. "Les implications christologiques de la parabole de la brebis perdue." *Jésus aux origines de la christologie.* BETL 40. Ed. J. Dupont. Gembloux: Duculot, 1975, 331–50.

———. "Les Ouvriers de la Vigne." *NRT* 79 (1957) 785–97.

———. "La parabole du figuier qui bourgeonne (Mc, XIII,28–29 et par.)." *RB* 75 (1968) 526–48.

Eagleton, T. *Literary Theory: An Introduction.* Minneapolis: University of Minnesota, 1983.

Eco, U. *The Role of the Reader.* Bloomington: Indiana University, 1979.

Edwards, R. A. "Narrative Implications of *Gar* in Matthew." *CBQ* 52 (1990) 636–55.

------. "The Use of ΠΡΟΣΕΡΧΕΣΘΑΙ in the Gospel of Matthew." *JBL* 106 (1987) 65–74.

Egan, K. "What Is a Plot?" *New Literary History* 9 (1978) 455–73.

Egger, W. "παιδίον." *EDNT*, 3. 4–5.

Einstadt, S. and Roniger, L. "Patron-Client Relations as a Model of Structuring Social Exchange." *Comparative Studies in Society and History* 22 (1980) 42–77.

Elliott, J. H. "Matthew 20:1–15: A Parable of Invidious Comparison and Evil Eye Accusation." *BTB* 22 (1992) 52–65.

Evans, C. A. "On the Isaianic Background of the Sower Parable." *CBQ* 47 (1985) 464–68.

------. *To See and Not Perceive: Isaiah 6. 9–10 in Early Jewish and Christian Interpretation.* JSOTSup 64. Sheffield: JSOT, 1989.

Everett, W. J. *God's Federal Republic: Reconstructing our Governing Symbol.* New York: Paulist, 1988.

------. "Sunday Monarchists and Monday Citizens." *Christian Century* 106 (1989) 503–5.

Farahian, E. "Relire Matthieu 25,31–46." *Greg* 72 (1991) 437–57.

Farmer, R. "The Kingdom of God in the Gospel of Matthew." *The Kingdom of God in 20th-Century Interpretation.* Ed. W. Willis. Peabody, MA: Hendrickson, 1987, 119–30.

Fenton, J. C. *Saint Matthew.* Harmondsworth: Penguin, 1963.

Fetterly, J. *The Resisting Reader.* Bloomington: Indiana University, 1978.

Feuillet, A. "Le caractère universel du jugement et la charité sans frontières en Mt 25,31–46." *NRT* 102 (1980) 179–96.

Fowler, R. M. "Who Is 'the Reader' in Reader Response Criticism?" *Reader Response Approaches to Biblical and Secular Texts. Semeia* 31. Ed. R. Detweiler. Decatur: Scholars, 1985, 5–23.

Frankemölle, H. "Kommunikatives Handeln in Gleichnissen Jesu: Historisch-kritische und pragmatische Exegese: Eine kritische Sichtung." *NTS* 28 (1982) 61–90.

------. *Jahwe-Bund und Kirche Christi: Studien zur Form und Traditionsgeschichte des "Evangeliums" nach Matthäus.* NTAbh 10, 2d ed. Münster: Aschendorff, 1974.

Funk, R. W. "The Parable as Metaphor." *Language, Hermeneutic, and Word of God: The Problem of Language in the New Testament and Contemporary Theology.* New York: Harper & Row, 1966, 133–62.

------. "Beyond Criticism in Quest of Literacy: The Parable of the Leaven." *Int* 25 (1971) 149–70.

------. "The Looking-Glass Tree Is for the Birds." *Int* 27 (1973) 3–9.

Funk, R. W., Scott, B. B., and Butts, J. R., *The Parables of Jesus: Red Letter Edition, A Report of the Jesus Seminar.* Sonoma, CA: Polebridge, 1988.

Garland, D. E. *Reading Matthew.* New York: Crossroad, 1993.

——. "Matthew's Understanding of the Temple Tax (Matt 17:24–27)." SBLASP 26 (1987) 190–209.

Garnsey, P. and Saller, R. *The Roman Empire*. Berkeley: University of California, 1987.

Genuyt, F. "Matthieu 13: L'enseignement en paraboles." *Sémiotique et Bible* 73 (1994) 30–44.

Gerhardsson, B. "If We Do Not Cut the Parables Out of Their Frames." *NTS* 37 (1991) 321–35.

——. "The Seven Parables in Matthew XIII." *NTS* 19 (1972–73) 16–37.

Gibson, J. "Hoi Telōnai kai hai Pornai." *JTS* 32 (1981) 429–33.

Giesen, H. "ταπεινόω." *EDNT*, 3. 334–35.

——. "ταπεινός." *EDNT*, 3. 333.

——. "ὑποκριτής." *EDNT*, 3. 403–4.

Glover, F. C. "Workers for the Vineyard." *ExpTim* 86 (1975) 310–11.

Gnilka, J. *Das Matthäusevangelium: Kommentar zu Kap. 1, 1–13, 58*. HTKNT 1/1. Freiburg: Herder, 1986.

——. *Das Matthäusevangelium: Kommentar zu Kap. 14, 1–28, 20 und Einleitungsfragen*. HTKNT 1/2. Freiburg: Herder, 1988.

Gray, S. W. *The Least of My Brothers: Matthew 25:31–46: A History of Interpretation*. SBLDS 114. Atlanta: Scholars, 1989.

Grilli, M. *Comunità e Missione: Le direttive di Matteo: Indagine esegetica su Mt 9, 35–11, 1*. Frankfurt: Lang, 1992.

Gryglewicz, F. "The Gospel of the Overworked Workers." *CBQ* 19 (1957) 190–98.

Guelich, R. *The Sermon on the Mount*. Dallas: Word, 1982.

——. "The Matthean Beatitudes: 'Entrance-Requirements' or Eschatological Blessings?" *JBL* 95 (1976) 415–34.

Gundry, R. H. *Matthew: A Commentary on His Literary and Theological Art*. Grand Rapids, MI: Eerdmans, 1982.

——. *The Use of the Old Testament in St. Matthew's Gospel*. NovTSup 18. Leiden: Brill, 1967.

Guthrie, K. and Fideler, D. R. *The Pythagorean Sourcebook and Library*. Grand Rapids, MI: Phanes, 1987.

Hagner, D. A. *Matthew 1–13*. WBC 33A. Dallas: Word, 1993.

——. "Matthew's Eschatology," *To Tell the Mystery: Essays on New Testament Eschatology in Honor of Robert H. Gundry*. JSNTSup 100. Ed. T. E. Schmidt and M. Silva. Sheffield: JSOT, 1994, 49–71.

Hahn, F. "υἱός." *EDNT*, 3. 381–92.

Hare, D. R. A. *Matthew*. Louisville: John Knox, 1993.

——. *The Theme of Jewish Persecution of Christians in the Gospel According to Matthew*. SNTSMS 6. Cambridge: Cambridge University, 1967.

Hare, D. R. A. and Harrington, D. J. "'Make Disciples of All the Gentiles' (Matthew 28:19)." *CBQ* 37 (1975) 359–69.

Harnisch, W. "The Metaphorical Process in Matthew 20:1–15." SBLASP 16 (1977) 231–50.

Harrington, D. J. "The Mixed Reception of the Gospel: Interpreting the Parables in Matt 13:1–52." *Of Scribes and Scrolls: Studies on the Hebrew Bible, Intertestamental Judaism, and Christian Origins*. College Theological Society Resources in Religion 5. Ed. H. W. Attridge, J. J. Collins, and T. H. Tobin. Lanham, MD: University Press of America, 1990, 195–201.

———. "Polemical Parables in Matthew 24–25." *USQR* 44 (1991) 293–94.

———. *The Gospel of Matthew*. SP 1. Collegeville: Liturgical Press, 1991.

Hartman, L. "Some Unorthodox Thoughts on the 'Household-Code Form'." *The Social World of Formative Christianity and Judaism*. Ed. J. Neusner et al. Philadelphia: Fortress, 1988, 219–32.

Hasler, V. "βρυγμός." *EDNT*, 1. 227–28.

Haufe, G. "παραβολή." *EDNT*, 3. 15.

Havener, I. *Q: The Sayings of Jesus*. GNS 19. Wilmington: Glazier, 1987.

Hedrick, C. W. *Parables as Poetic Fictions: The Creative Voice of Jesus*. Peabody, MA: Hendrickson, 1994.

Heichelheim, F. "Syria." *An Economic Survey of Ancient Rome*. Ed. T. Frank. Baltimore: Johns Hopkins University, 1938, 4. 121–258.

Heil, J. P. "The Narrative Roles of the Women in Matthew's Genealogy." *Bib* 72 (1991) 538–45.

———. "Significant Aspects of the Healing Miracles in Matthew." *CBQ* 41 (1979) 274–87.

———. "Reader-Response and the Narrative Context of the Parables about Growing Seed in Mark 4:1–34." *CBQ* 54 (1992) 271–86.

———. "Ezekiel 34 and the Narrative Strategy of the Shepherd and Sheep Metaphor in Matthew." *CBQ* 55 (1993) 698–708.

———. *The Gospel of Mark as a Model for Action: A Reader-Response Commentary*. New York: Paulist, 1992.

———. *Jesus Walking on the Sea: Meaning and Gospel Functions of Matt 14:22–33, Mark 6:45–52 and John 6:15b–21*. AnBib 87. Rome: Biblical Institute, 1981.

———. *The Death and Resurrection of Jesus: A Narrative-Critical Reading of Matthew 26–28*. Minneapolis: Fortress, 1991.

Heinemann, H. "The Conception of Reward." *JJS* 1 (1948) 85–89.

Hendrickx, H. *The Parables of Jesus*. London: Chapman, 1986.

Herzog, W. R. *Parables as Subversive Speech: Jesus as Pedagogue of the Oppressed*. Louisville: Westminster/Knox, 1994.

Hill, D. *The Gospel of Matthew*. NCB. Grand Rapids, MI: Eerdmans, 1972.

——. "The Figure of Jesus in Matthew's Story: A Response to Professor Kingsbury's Literary-Critical Probe." *JSNT* 21 (1984) 37–52.

Hofius, O. "βλασφημία." *EDNT*, 1. 219–21.

Horbury, W. "The Temple Tax." *Jesus and the Politics of His Day*. Ed. E. Bammel and C. F. D. Moule. Cambridge: CUP, 1984, 265–86.

Howell, D. B. *Matthew's Inclusive Story: A Study of the Narraitve Rhetoric of the First Gospel*. JSNTSup 42. Sheffield: JSOT, 1990.

Hubaut, M. *La parabole des vignerons homicides*. CahRB 16. Paris: Gabalda, 1976, 13–103.

——. "La parabole des vignerons homicides: son authenticité, sa visée première." *RTL* 6 (1975) 51–61.

Hummel, R. *Die Auseinandersetzung zwischen Kirche und Judentum im Matthäusevangelium*. BEvT 33. Munich: Kaiser, 1963, 1966.

Hunzinger, C.-H. "σίναπι." *TDNT* 7. 287–91.

Ingelaere, J.-C. "La 'parabole' du jugement dernier (Matthieu 25/31–46)." *RHPR* 50 (1970) 23–60.

Isasi-Díaz, A. M. "Solidarity: Love of Neighbor in the 1980's." *Lift Every Voice: Constructing Christian Theologies from the Underside*. Ed. S. B. Thistlethwaite and M. P. Engels. New York: Harper & Row, 1990, 31–40, 303–5.

Iser, W. *The Act of Reading*. Baltimore: Johns Hopkins University, 1978.

——. *Prospecting*. Baltimore: Johns Hopkins University, 1989.

——. "The Reading Process: A Phenomenological Approach." *Reader-Response Criticism: From Formalism to Post-Structuralism*. Ed. J. P. Tompkins. Baltimore: Johns Hopkins University, 1980, 65–68.

Jensen, C. *Philodemi Peri Oikonomias*. Leipzig: Teubner, 1906.

Jeremias, J. *The Parables of Jesus*. New York: Scribner's, 1963.

Jülicher, A. *Die Gleichnisreden Jesu*. 2 vols. Tübingen: Mohr, 1888, 1899.

Kee, H. C. "The Transformation of the Synagogue after 70 C.E.: Its Import for Early Christianity." *NTS* 36 (1990) 1–24.

——. *Medicine, Miracles and Magic in New Testament Times*. SNTSMS 55. Cambridge: Cambridge University, 1986.

——. *Miracle in the Early Christian World: A Study in Sociohistorical Method*. New Haven: Yale University, 1983.

Kelber, W. H. *The Oral and the Written Gospel: The Hermeneutics of Speaking and Writing in the Synoptic Tradtion, Mark, Paul, and Q*. Philadelphia: Fortress, 1983.

Kertelge, K. "λύω." *EDNT*, 2. 368–69.

Kiilunen, J. "Der nachfolgewillige Schriftgelehrte: Matthäus 8.19–20 im Verständnis des Evangelisten." *NTS* 37 (1991) 268–79.

Kilpatrick, G. D. *The Origins of the Gospel According to St. Matthew.* Oxford: Clarendon, 1946.

Kingsbury, J. D. *The Parables of Jesus in Matthew 13.* Richmond: John Knox, 1969.

———. *Matthew as Story.* 2d ed. Philadelphia: Fortress, 1988.

———. "Reflections on 'the Reader' of Matthew's Gospel." *NTS* 34 (1988) 442–60.

———. "The Plot of Matthew's Story." *Int* 46 (1992) 347–56.

———. "The Figure of Jesus in Matthew's Story: A Literary-Critical Probe." *JSNT* 21 (1984) 3–36.

———. "The Parable of the Wicked Husbandmen and the Secret of Jesus' Divine Sonship in Matthew." *JBL* 105 (1986) 643–55.

———. *Matthew: Structure, Christology, Kingdom.* Philadelphia: Fortress, 1975.

———. "The Place, Structure, and Meaning of the Sermon on the Mount Within Matthew." *Int* 41 (1987) 131–43.

———. "The Developing Conflict between Jesus and the Jewish Leaders in Matthew's Gospel: A Literary-Critical Study." *CBQ* 49 (1987) 57–73.

———. "The Verb AKOLOUTHEIN ("To Follow") as an Index of Matthew's View of his Community." *JBL* 97 (1978) 56–73.

Kissinger, W. S. *The Parables of Jesus: A History of Interpretation and Bibliography.* ATLA Bibliography Series 4. Metuchen, NJ: Scarecrow, 1979.

Klauck, H.-J. *Allegorie und Allegorese in synoptischen Gleichnistexten.* NTAbh 13. Münster: Aschendorff, 1978.

Knox, B. "Silent Reading in Antiquity." *Greek Roman and Byzantine Studies* 9 (1968) 421–35.

Kratz, R. "θύρα." *EDNT,* 2. 160–61.

———. "φυλακή." *EDNT,* 3. 441.

Kretzer, A. "ἀπόλλυμι." *EDNT,* 1. 135–36.

———. *Die Herrschaft der Himmel und die Söhne des Reiches.* SBM 10. Stuttgart: Katholisches Bibelwerk, 1971.

Lattke, M. "On the Jewish Background of the Synoptic Concept, 'The Kingdom of God'." *The Kingdom of God. Issues in Religion and Theology 5.* Ed. B. Chilton. London: Fortress/SPCK, 1984, 72–91.

Lambrecht, J. *Out of the Treasure: The Parables in the Gospel of Matthew.* Louvain Theological and Pastoral Monographs 10. Louvain: Peeters/Eerdmans, 1992.

———. "Parables in Mt 13." *TvT* 17 (1977) 25–47.

———. "The Parousia Discourse: Composition and Content in Mt., XXIV–XXV." *L'Evangile selon Matthieu: Rédaction et théologie.* BETL 29. Ed. M. Didier. Gembloux: Duculot, 1972, 309–42.

Légasse, S. "Jésus et l'impôt du Temple (Matthieu 17,24–27)." *ScEs* 24 (1972) 361–77.

Lemcio, E. E. "The Parables of the Great Supper and the Wedding Feast: History, Redaction, and Canon." *HBT* 8 (1986) 1–26.

Lerner, G. *The Creation of Patriarchy*. New York: Oxford University, 1986.

Levine, A. J. *The Social and Ethnic Dimensions of Matthean Social History*. Lewiston: Mellen, 1988.

Lichtenberger, H. "πῦρ." *EDNT,* 3. 197–200.

———. "σάλπιγξ." *EDNT,* 3. 225–26.

Linnemann, E. *Jesus of the Parables: Introduction and Exposition*. New York: Harper & Row, 1966.

Lohfink, G. "Das Gleichnis vom Sämann (Mk 4,3–9)." *BZ* 30 (1986) 36–69.

Lotman, J. M. "Point of View in a Text." *New Literary History* 6 (1975) 339–52.

Louw J. and Nida, E. *Greek-English Lexicon of the New Testament*. New York: United Bible Societies, 1988, 1989.

Love, S. "The Household: A Major Social Component for Gender Analysis in the Gospel of Matthew." *BTB* 23 (1993) 21–31.

Lowe, M. "From the Parable of the Vineyard to a Pre-Synoptic Source." *NTS* 28 (1982) 257–63.

Lührmann, D. "Wo man nicht mehr Sklave oder Freier ist: Überlegungen zur Struktur frühchristlicher Gemeinden." *WD* 13 (1975) 53–83.

———. "Neutestamentliche Haustafeln und Antike Ökonomie." *NTS* 27 (1980–81) 83–97.

Luz, U. *Matthew 1–7: A Commentary*. Minneapolis: Augsburg, 1989.

———. *Matthew in History: Interpretation, Influence and Effects*. Minneapolis: Fortress, 1994.

———. *Das Evangelium nach Matthäus*. EKKNT 1/2. Zürich: Benziger, 1990.

Mack, B. *The Lost Gospel*. San Francisco: Harper, 1993.

Malherbe, A. *Moral Exhortation: A Greco-Roman Sourcebook*. Philadelphia: Westminster, 1986.

Malina, B. J. and Neyrey, J. H. "Honor and Shame in Luke-Acts: Pivotal Values of the Mediterranean World." *The Social World of Luke-Acts: Models for Interpretation*. Ed. J. H. Neyrey. Peabody, MA: Hendrickson, 1991, 25–65.

Malina B. J. and Rohrbaugh, R. *Social-Science Commentary on the Synoptic Gospels*. Minneapolis: Fortress, 1992.

Manek, J. "Fishers of Men." *NovT* 2 (1958) 138–41.

Manns, F. "La parable des talents: Wirkungsgeschichte et racines juives." *RSR* 65 (1991) 343–62.

Manson, T. *The Sayings of Jesus*. London: SCM, 1949.

Marguerat, D. "L'Eglise et le monde en Matthieu 13,36–43." *RTP* 110 (1978) 111–29.

Marin, L. "Essai d'analyse structurale d'un récit-parabole: Matthieu 13,1–23." *ETR* 46 1971) 35–74.

Martin, F. "Parler: Matthieu 13." *Sémiotique et Bible* 52 (1988) 17–33.

Matera, F. J. "The Plot of Matthew's Gospel." *CBQ* 49 (1987) 233–53.

McCall, M. H. *Ancient Rhetorical Theories of Simile and Comparison.* Cambridge, MA: Harvard University, 1969.

McCane, B. R. "'Let the Dead Bury Their Own Dead': Secondary Burial and Matt 8:21–22." *HTR* 83 (1990) 31–43.

McEleney, N. J. "The Unity and Theme of Matthew 7:1–12." *CBQ* 56 (1994) 490–500.

———. "Mt 17:24–27—Who Paid the Temple Tax? A Lesson in Avoidance of Scandal." *CBQ* 38 (1976) 178–92.

McIver, R. K. "One Hundred-Fold Yield—Miraculous or Mundane? Matthew 13.8, 23; Mark 4.8, 20; Luke 8.8." *NTS* 40 (1994) 606–8.

McKay, K. L. "On the Perfect and Other Aspects in New Testament Greek." *NovT* 23 (1981) 289–329.

———. "Time and Aspect in New Testament Greek." *NovT* 34 (1992) 209–28.

———. *A New Syntax of the Verb in New Testament Greek: An Aspectual Approach.* Studies in Biblical Greek 5. New York: Lang, 1994.

Meier, J. P. *A Marginal Jew: Rethinking the Historical Jesus: Volume Two: Mentor, Message, and Miracles.* Anchor Bible Reference Library. New York: Doubleday, 1994.

———. *Law and History in Matthew's Gospel.* AnBib 71. Rome: Biblical Institute, 1976.

———. *The Vision of Matthew: Christ, Church and Morality in the First Gospel.* New York: Paulist, 1979.

———. *Matthew.* NTM 3. Wilmington: Glazier, 1980.

———. "Nations or Gentiles in Matthew 28:19?" *CBQ* 39 (1977) 94–102.

Metzger, B. M. *A Textual Commentary on the Greek New Testament.* London: United Bible Societies, 1971.

Meyer, B. F. "Many (=All) Are Called, but Few (=Not All) Are Chosen." *NTS* 36 (1990) 89–97.

Meyer, P. W. "Context as a Bearer of Meaning in Matthew." *USQR* 42 (1988) 69–72.

Michaels, J. R. "The Kingdom of God and the Historical Jesus." *The Kingdom of God in 20th-Century Interpretation.* Ed. W. Willis. Peabody, MA: Hendrickson, 1987, 109–18.

Milavec, A. A. "A Fresh Analysis of the Parable of the Wicked Husbandmen in the Light of Jewish-Christian Dialogue." *Parable and Story in Judaism and Christianity.* Ed C. Thoma and M. Wyschogrod. Mahwah, NJ: Paulist, 1989, 81–117.

Mitton, C. L. "Expounding the Parables VII: The Workers in the Vineyard (Matthew 20:1–16)." *ExpTim* 77 (1966) 301–11.

Moore, S. *Literary Criticism and the Gospels: The Theoretical Challenge.* New Haven: Yale University, 1989.

Morris, L. *The Gospel According to Matthew.* Grand Rapids: Eerdmans, 1992.

Mowery, R. L. "The Matthean References to the Kingdom: Different Terms for Different Audiences." *ETL* 70 (1994) 398–405.

Neufeld, D. *Reconceiving Texts as Speech Acts: An Analysis of 1 John.* Biblical Interpretation Series 7. Leiden: Brill, 1994.

Newell, J. E. and Newell, R. R. "The Parable of the Wicked Tenants." *NovT* 14 (1972) 226–37.

Neyrey, J. H. "Ceremonies in Luke-Acts: The Case of Meals and Table Fellowship." *The Social World of Luke-Acts: Models for Interpretation.* Ed. J. H. Neyrey. Peabody, MA: Hendrickson, 1991, 361–87.

Nützel, J. M. "δένδρον." *EDNT,* 1. 285.

Ogawa, A. "Paraboles de l'Israel véritable? Reconsidération critique de Mt. xxi 28–xxii 14." *NovT* 21 (1979) 121–49.

Oñate Ojeda, J. A. "Nota exegética: Pues, así como el relámpago." *Burgense* 32 (1991) 569–72.

Orton, D. E. *The Understanding Scribe: Matthew and the Apocalyptic Ideal.* JSNTSup 25. Sheffield: JSOT, 1989.

Palmer, H. "Just Married, Cannot Come." *NovT* 18 (1976) 241–57.

Pamment, M. "The Kingdom of Heaven According to the First Gospel." *NTS* 27 (1981) 211–32.

Panier, L. "Le Fils de l'Homme et les nations: Lecture de Mt 25,31–46." *Sémiotique et Bible* 69 (1993) 39–52.

Patrick, D. "The Kingdom of God in the Old Testament." *The Kingdom of God in 20th-Century Interpretation.* Ed. W. Willis. Peabody, MA: Hendrickson, 1987, 67–79.

Patte, D. *The Gospel According to Matthew: A Structural Commentary on Matthew's Faith.* Philadelphia: Fortress, 1987.

——. "Bringing Out of the Gospel-Treasure What Is New and What Is Old: Two Parables in Matthew 18–23." *Quarterly Review* 10 (1990) 79–108.

Perrin, N. *Jesus and the Language of the Kingdom.* Philadelphia: Fortress, 1976.

Perry, M. "Literary Dynamics: How the Order of a Text Creates Its Meanings." *Poetics Today* 1 (1979–80) 35–64, 311–61.

Pesch, W. "δραχμή, δίδραχμον." *EDNT,* 1. 353–54.

Petersen, N. R. "'Point of View' in Mark's Narrative." *The Poetics of Faith: Essays Offered to Amos Niven Wilder: Part 1: Rhetoric, Eschatology, and Ethics in the New Testament. Semeia* 12. Ed. W. A. Beardslee. Missoula, MT: Scholars, 1978, 97–121.

——. *Literary Criticism for New Testament Critics.* Philadelphia: Fortress, 1978.

Phillips, G. A. "History and Text: The Reader in Context in Matthew's Parables Discourse." *Reader Response Approaches to Biblical and Secular Texts. Semeia* 31. Ed. R. Detweiler. Decatur, IL: Scholars, 1985, 111–38.

Porter, S. E. *Verbal Aspect in the Greek of the New Testament, with Reference to Tense and Mood.* Studies in Biblical Greek 1. New York: Lang, 1989.

Powell, M. A. *What Is Narrative Criticism?* Minneapolis: Fortress, 1990.

——. "Expected and Unexpected Readings in Matthew: What the Reader Knows." *Asbury Theological Journal* 48 (1993) 31–51.

——. "The Plot and Subplots of Matthew's Gospel." *NTS* 38 (1992) 187–204.

——. "Matthew's Beatitudes: Reversals and Rewards of the Kingdom." *CBQ* 58 (1996) 460–79.

——. "A Typology of Worship in the Gospel of Matthew." *JSNT* 57 (1995) 3–17.

Praechter, K. "Metapos, Theages und Archytas bei Stobaeus." *Philologus* 50 (1891) 29–57.

Praeder, S. "The Parable of the Leaven." *The Word in Women's Worlds.* Wilmington: Glazier, 1988, 11–35.

Przybylski, B. *Righteousness in Matthew and His World of Thought.* SNTMS 41. Cambridge: Cambridge University, 1980.

Puig i Tàrrech, A. *La parabole des dix vierges (Mt 25,1–13).* AnBib 102. Rome: Biblical Institute, 1983.

Rabinowitz, P. J. "Whirl Without End: Audience-Oriented Criticism." *Contemporary Literary Theory.* Ed. G. D. Atkins and L. Morrow. Amherst: University of Massachusetts, 1989, 81–100.

——. *Before Reading: Narrative Conventions and the Politics of Interpretation.* Ithaca: Cornell University, 1987.

——. "Truth in Fiction: A Reexamination of Audiences." *Critical Inquiry* 4 (1977) 121–42.

Radl, W. "αἰτέω." *EDNT,* 1. 43.

Ramaroson, L. "'Parole-semence' ou 'Peuple-semence' dans la parabole du Semeur?" *ScEs* 40 (1988) 91–101.

Rengstorff, K. H. *Mann und Frau im Urchristentum.* Cologne: Westdeutscher, 1954.

——. "Die Stadt der Mörder (Mt 22,7)." *Judentum, Urchristentum, Kirche.* BZNW 26. FS J. Jeremias. Ed. E. Eltester. Berlin: Töpelmann, 1960, 106–29.

Riches, J. "Parables and the Search for a New Community." *The Social World of Formative Christianity and Judaism.* Ed. J. Neusner et al. Philadelphia: Fortress, 1988, 235–63.

Ricoeur, P. *Paul Ricoeur on Biblical Hermeneutics.* Semeia 4. Ed. J. D. Crossan. Missoula, MT: Scholars, 1975.

——. "Appropriation." *Hermeneutics and the Human Sciences.* Ed. J. B. Thompson. Cambridge: Cambridge University, 1981, 182–93.

Rimmon-Kenan, S. *Narrative Fiction.* New York: Methuen, 1983.

Russell, L. M. *Household of Freedom: Authority in Feminist Theology.* Philadelphia: Westminster, 1987.

Sabourin, L. "The Parables of the Kingdom." *BTB* 6 (1976) 137–60.

Saldarini, A. J. *Matthew's Christian-Jewish Community.* Chicago: University of Chicago, 1994.

Sand, A. *Das Evangelium nach Matthäus.* RNT. Regensburg: Pustet, 1986.

——. "καρδία." *EDNT,* 2. 249–51.

Sanders, E. P. *Jesus and Judaism.* Philadelphia: Fortress, 1985.

Schenk, W. "στρέφω." *EDNT,* 3. 280–81.

——. "Auferweckung der Toten oder Gericht nach den Werken: Tradition und Redaktion in Matthäus xxv 1–13." *NovT* 20 (1978) 278–99.

Schenke, L. "Die Interpretation der Parabel von den 'Arbeitern im Weinberg' (Mt 20:1–15) durch Matthäus." *Studien zum Matthäusevangelium: Festschrift für Wilhelm Pesch.* Ed. L. Schenke. Stuttgart: Katholisches Bibelwerk, 1989, 245–68.

Schlosser, J. *Le Règne de Dieu dans les dits de Jésus.* Ebib. 2 vols. Paris: Gabalda, 1980.

Schmid, J. "Das textgeschichtliche Problem der Parabel von der zwei Söhnen Mt 21, 28–32." *Vom Wort des Lebens.* NTAbh 1. FS M. Meinertz. Ed. N. Adler. Münster: Aschendorff, 1951, 68–84.

Schnider, F. "Von der Gerechtigkeit Gottes: Beobachtungen zum Gleichnis von den Arbeitern im Weinberg (Mt 20, 1–16)." *Kairos* 23 (1981) 88–95.

Schottroff, L. "ζῶ." *EDNT,* 2.105–9.

——. "Human Solidarity and the Goodness of God: The Parable of the Workers in the Vineyard." *God of the Lowly.* Ed. W. Schottroff and W. Stegemann. New York: Orbis, 1984, 129–47.

Schrenk, G. "δίκαιος." *TDNT,* 3. 182–91.

Schrenk, G. and Quell, G. "πατήρ." *TDNT* 5. 970–82.

Schroeder, D. *Die Haustafeln des neuen Testaments.* Diss. Hamburg, 1959.

Schüssler Fiorenza, E. *In Memory of Her: A Feminist Theological Reconstruction of Christian Origins.* New York: Crossroad, 1989.

——. "Discipleship and Patriarchy: Early Christian Ethos and Christian Ethics in a Feminist Perspective." *The Annual of the Society of Christian Ethics.* (1982) 131–72.

——. "The Ethics of Interpretation: De-Centering Biblical Scholarship." *JBL* 107 (1988) 3–17.

Schwank, B. "Dort wird Heulen und Zähneknirschen sein." *BZ* 16 (1972) 121–22.

——. "τάλαντον." *EDNT,* 3. 332.

——. "δηνάριον." *EDNT,* 1. 296.

Schweizer, E. *The Good News According to Matthew.* Atlanta: John Knox, 1975.

Scott, B. B. *Hear Then the Parable: A Commentary on the Parables of Jesus.* Minneapolis: Fortress, 1989.

——. "The Birth of the Reader in Matthew." *Faith and History: Essays in Honor of*

Paul W. Meyer. Ed. J. T. Carroll, C. H. Cosgrove, and E. E. Johnson. Atlanta: Scholars, 1990, 35–54.

——. "The Birth of the Reader." *How Gospels Begin. Semeia* 52. Ed. D. E. Smith. Atlanta: Scholars, 1991, 83–102.

——. "The King's Accounting: Matthew 18:23–34." *JBL* 104 (1985) 429–42.

Searle, J. R. *Speech Acts: An Essay in the Philosophy of Language.* Cambridge: Cambridge University, 1969.

——. *Expression and Meaning: Studies in the Theory of Speech Acts.* Cambridge: Cambridge University, 1979.

Segal, A. "Matthew's Jewish Voice." *Social History of the Matthean Community: Cross-Disciplinary Approaches.* Ed. D. Balch. Minneapolis: Fortress, 1991.

Segalla, G. "Perdono 'cristiano' e correzione fraterna nella comunità di 'Matteo' (Mt 18,15–17.21–35)." *Studia Patavina* 38 (1991) 499–518.

Senior, D. *What Are They Saying About Matthew?* New York: Paulist, 1983.

Shepherd, W. *The Narrative Function of the Holy Spirit as a Character in Luke-Acts.* SBLDS 147. Atlanta: Scholars, 1994.

Shryock, R. *Tales of Storytelling: Embedded Narrative in Modern French Fiction.* American University Studies 2/206. New York: Lang, 1993.

Sider, J. W. "The Meaning of *Parabole* in the Usage of the Synoptic Evangelists." *Bib* 62 (1981) 453–70.

——. "Rediscovering the Parables: The Logic of the Jeremias Tradition." *JBL* 102 (1983) 61–83.

Sim, D. C "The Gospel of Matthew and the Gentiles." *JSNT* 57 (1995) 19–48.

——. "The Man Without the Wedding Garment." *HeyJ* 31 (1990) 165–78.

Smith, B. H. "Narrative Versions, Narrative Theories." *Critical Inquiry* 7 (1980) 213–36.

Smith, C. "Fishers of Men." *HTR* 52 (1959) 187–203.

Snodgrass, K. *The Parable of the Wicked Tenants.* WUNT 27. Tübingen: Mohr, 1983.

Sranron, G. A *Gospel for a New Peoples Studies in Matthew.* Edinburgh. T. & T. Clark, 1992

Stark, R. "Antioch as the Social Situation for Matthew's Gospel." *Social History of the Matthean Community: Cross-Disciplinary Approaches.* Ed. D. Balch. Minneapolis: Fortress, 1991, 189–210.

Staudinger, F. "δέω." *EDNT* 1. 292–94.

Stenger, W. "βασανίζω." *EDNT,* 1. 200–201.

Stern, D. "Jesus' Parables from the Perspective of Rabbinic Literature: The Example of the Wicked Husbandmen." *Parable and Story in Judaism and Christianity.* Ed. C. Thoma and M. Wyschogrod. Mahwah, NJ: Paulist, 1989, 42–80.

Stock, A. *The Method and Message of Matthew.* Collegeville: Liturgical Press, 1994.

Strecker, G. *The Sermon on the Mount.* Abingdon: Nashville, 1988.

———. "μακάριος." *EDNT,* 2. 376–79.

Strobel, A. "ἀνάγκη." *EDNT,* 1. 77–79.

Suleiman, S. R. "Introduction: Varieties of Audience-Oriented Criticism." *The Reader in the Text: Essays on Audience and Interpretation.* Ed. S. R. Suleiman and I. Crosman. Princeton: Princeton University, 1980, 3–45.

———. "Redundancy and the 'Readable' Text." *Poetics Today* 1 (1980) 119–42.

Tellan, S. "La Chiesa di Matteo e la correzione fraterna: Analisi di Mt 18,15–17." *Laurentianum* 35 (1994) 91–137.

Tevel, J. M. "The Labourers in the Vineyard: The Exegesis of Matthew 20:1–17 in the Early Church." *VC* 46 (1992) 356–80.

Thesleff, H. *An Introduction to the Pythagorean Writings of the Hellenistic Period.* Abo: Abo Akademi, 1961.

Thiselton, A. C. "Reader-Response Hermeneutics, Action Models, and the Parables of Jesus." *The Responsibility of Hermeneutics.* Ed. R. Lundin, A. C. Thiselton, and C. Walhout. Grand Rapids: Eerdmans, 1985) 79–113.

Thomas, J. C. "The Kingdom of God in the Gospel According to Matthew." *NTS* 39 (1993) 136–46.

Thompson, W. G. *Matthew's Advice to a Divided Community: Mt. 17,22–18,35.* AnBib 44. Rome: Biblical Institute, 1970.

Thraede, K. "Ärger mit der Freiheit: Die Bedeutung von Frauen in Theorie und Praxis der alten kirche." *"Freunde in Christus werden . . .": Die Beziehung von Mann und Frau als Frage an Theologie und Kirche.* Ed. G. Scharffenorth and K. Thraede. Berlin: Burckhandthaus, 1977, 35–182.

———. "Zum historischen Hintergrund der 'Haustafeln' des NT." *Pietas: Festschrift für Bernhard Kötting.* Ed. E. Dassman and K. S. Frank. Münster: Aschendorff, 1980.

Tolbert, M. A. *Perspectives on the Parables: An Approach to Multiple Interpretations.* Philadelphia: Fortress, 1979.

Tompkins, J. P. "An Introduction to Reader-Response Criticism." *Reader-Response Criticism: From Formalism to Post-Structuralism.* Ed. J. P. Tompkins. Baltimore: Johns Hopkins University, 1980.

Trilling, W. *Das Wahre Israel: Studien zur Theologie des Matthäus-Evangeliums.* SANT 10. 3d ed. Munich: Kösel, 1964.

Uspensky, B. *A Poetics of Composition.* Berkeley: University of California, 1973.

Vaage, L. *Galilean Upstarts: Jesus' First Followers According to Q.* Valley Forge: Trinity, 1994.

van Aarde, A. G. "Resonance and Reception: Interpreting Mt 17:24–27 in Context." *Scriptura* 29 (1989) 1–12.

———. "A Silver Coin in the Mouth of a Fish (Matthew 17:24–27)–A Miracle of Nature, Ecology, Economy and the Politics of Holiness." *Neot* 27 (1993) 1–25.

———. "A Historical-Critical Classification of Jesus' Parables and the Metaphoric Narration of the Wedding Feast in Matthew 22:1–14." *God-With-Us: The Dominant Perspective in Matthew's Story.* Hervormde Teologiese Studies Supplementum 5. Pretoria, 1994, 229–47.

Van Segbroeck, F. "Le scandale de l'incroyance: La signification de Mt. XIII, 35." *ETL* 41 (1965) 360–65.

van Tilborg, S. *The Jewish Leaders in Matthew.* Leiden: Brill, 1972.

Verner, D. *The Household of God.* SBLDS 71. Chico, CA: Scholars, 1983.

Verseput, D. J. *The Rejection of the Humble Messianic King: A Study of the Composition of Matthew 11–12.* Frankfurt: Lang, 1986.

Via, D. O. *The Parables: Their Literary and Existential Dimensions.* Philadelphia: Fortress, 1967.

———. "The Relationship of Form and Content in the Parables: The Wedding Feast." *Int* 25 (1971) 171–84.

———. "Ethical Responsibility and Human Wholeness in Matthew 25:31–46." *HTR* 80 (1987) 79–100.

Viviano, B. "The Kingdom of God in the Qumran Literature." *The Kingdom of God in 20th-Century Interpretation.* Ed. W. Willis. Peabody: Hendrickson, 1987, 97–107.

Vorster, W. S. "The Structure of Matthew 13." *Neot* 11 (1977) 130–38.

———. "A Reader-Response Approach to Matthew 24:3–28." *Hervormde Teologiese Studies* 47 (1991) 1099–108.

Wainwright, E. *Towards a Feminist Reading of the Gospel According to Matthew.* BZNW 60. Berlin: de Gruyter, 1991.

———. "God Wills to Invite All to the Banquet: Matthew 22:1–10." *International Review of Mission* 77 (1988) 185–93.

Walker, R. *Die Heilsgeschichte im ersten Evangelium.* FRLANT 91. Göttingen: Vandenhoeck & Ruprecht, 1967.

Watty, W. "Jesus and the Temple—Cleansing or Cursing?" *ExpTim* 93 (1982) 235–39.

Weaver, D. J. *Matthew's Missionary Discourse: A Literary Critical Analysis.* JSNTSup 38. Sheffield: JSOT, 1990.

Weber, B. "Alltagswelt und Gottesreich: Überlegungen zum Verstehenshintergrund des Gleichnisses vom 'Schalksknecht' (Matthäus 18,23–34)." *BZ* 37 (1993) 161–82.

———. "Vergeltung oder Vergebung!? Matthäus 18,21–35 auf dem Hintergrund des 'Erlassjahres'." *TZ* 50 (1994) 124–51.

———. "Schulden erstatten—Schulden erlassen: Zum matthäischen Gebrauch einiger juristischer und monetärer Begriffe." *ZNW* 83 (1992) 253–56.

Weber, K. *The Events of the End of the Age in Matthew.* Diss. Washington: Catholic University of America, 1994.

Weder, H. *Die Gleichnisse Jesu als Metaphern: Traditions- und redaktions-*

geschichtliche Analysen und Interpretationen. FRLANT 120. 2d ed. Göttingen: Vandenhoeck & Ruprecht, 1980.

Weidinger, K. *Die Haustafeln, ein Stück urchristlicher Paranese.* UNT 14. Leipzig: Heinrich, 1928.

Weiser, A. *Die Knechtsgleichnisse der synoptischen Evangelien.* SANT 29. Munich: Kösel, 1971.

Wenham, D. "The Structure of Matthew XIII." *NTS* 25 (1978–79) 516–22.

White, H. C. "Introduction: Speech Act Theory and Literary Criticism." *Speech Act Theory and Biblical Criticism. Semeia* 41. Ed. H. C. White. Decatur: Scholars,1988, 1–24.

Wilder, A. *The Language of the Gospel: Early Christian Rhetoric.* New York: Harper & Row, 1964.

———. *Jesus' Parables and the War of Myths.* Philadelphia: Fortress, 1982.

Wilkins, M. J. *The Concept of Disciple in Matthew's Gospel.* NovTSup 59. Leiden: Brill, 1988.

Willhelm, F. "Die Oeconomic der Neupythagoreer Bryson, Kallikratidas, Periktione, Phintys." *Rheinisches Museum für Philologie* 70 (1915) 161–223.

Wire, A. C. "Gender Roles in a Scribal Community." *Social History of the Matthean Community: Cross-Disciplinary Approaches.* Ed. D. Balch. Minneapolis: Fortress, 1991, 87–121.

Wischmeyer, O. "Matthäus 6,25–34 par: Die Spruchreihe vom Sorgen." *ZNW* 85 (1994) 1–22.

Wittig, S. "Formulaic Style and the Problem of Redundancy." *Centrum* 1 (1973) 123–36.

Wrege, H.-T. "καρπός." *EDNT,* 2. 251–52.

Wuellner, W. *The Meaning of "Fishers of Men."* Philadelphia: Westminster, 1967.

Zeller, E. *Die Philosophie der Griechen in ihrer geschichtlichen Entwicklung dargestellt.* Leipzig: Niestlé, 1919, 1923.

Zerwick, M. *Biblical Greek.* Rome: Biblical Institute, 1963.

Zerwick, M. and Grosvenor, M. *A Grammatical Analysis of the Greek New Testament.* 2 vols. Rome: Biblical Institute, 1974, 1979.

Zmijewski, J. "ἀστραπή." *EDNT,* 1. 174–75.

Index of Ancient Sources

Index of Names

The Catholic Biblical Quarterly
Monograph Series (CBQMS)

1. Patrick W. Skehan, *Studies in Israelite Poetry and Wisdom* (CBQMS 1) $9.00 ($7.20 for CBA members) ISBN 0-915170-00-0 (LC 77-153511)

2. Aloysius M. Ambrozic, *The Hidden Kingdom: A Redactional-Critical Study of the References to the Kingdom of God in Mark's Gospel* (CBQMS 2) $9.00 ($7.20 for CBA members) ISBN 0-915170-01-9 (LC 72-89100)

3. Joseph Jensen, O.S.B., *The Use of tôrâ by Isaiah: His Debate with the Wisdom Tradition* (CBQMS 3) $3.00 ($2.40 for CBA members) ISBN 0-915170-02-7 (LC 73-83134)

4. George W. Coats, *From Canaan to Egypt: Structural and Theological Context for the Joseph Story* (CBQMS 4) $4.00 ($3.20 for CBA members) ISBN 0-915170-03-5 (LC 75-11382)

5. O. Lamar Cope, *Matthew: A Scribe Trained for the Kingdom of Heaven* (CBQMS 5) $4.50 ($3.60 for CBA members) ISBN 0-915170-04-3 (LC 75-36778)

6. Madeleine Boucher, *The Mysterious Parable: A Literary Study* (CBQMS 6) $2.50 ($2.00 for CBA members) ISBN 0-915170-05-1 (LC 76-51260)

7. Jay Braverman, Jerome's Commentary on Daniel: A Study of Comparative Jewish and Christian Interpretations of the Hebrew Bible (CBQMS 7) $4.00 ($3.20 for CBA members) ISBN 0-915170-06-X (LC 78-55726)

8. Maurya P. Horgan, *Pesharim: Qumran Interpretations of Biblical Books* (CBQMS 8) $6.00 ($4.80 for CBA members) ISBN 0-915170-07-8 (LC 78-12910)

9. Harold W. Attridge and Robert A. Oden, Jr., *Philo of Byblos,* The Phoenician History (CBQMS 9) $3.50 ($2.80 for CBA members) ISBN 0-915170-08-6 (LC 80-25781)

10. Paul J. Kobelski, *Melchizedek and Melchireša^c* (CBQMS 10) $4.50 ($3.60 for CBA members) ISBN 0-915170-09-4 (LC 80-28379)

11. Homer Heater, *A Septuagint Translation Technique in the Book of Job* (CBQMS 11) $4.00 ($3.20 for CBA members) ISBN 0-915170-10-8 (LC 81-10083)

12. Robert Doran, *Temple Propaganda: The Purpose and Character of 2 Maccabees* (CBQMS 12) $4.50 ($3.60 for CBA members) ISBN 0-915170-11-6 (LC 81-10084)

13. James Thompson, *The Beginnings of Christian Philosophy: The Epistle to the Hebrews* (CBQMS 13) $5.50 ($4.50 for CBA members) ISBN 0-915170-12-4 (LC 81-12295)

14. Thomas H. Tobin, S.J., *The Creation of Man: Philo and the History of Interpretation* (CBQMS 14) $6.00 ($4.80 for CBA members) ISBN 0-915170-13-2 (LC 82-19891)

15. Carolyn Osiek, *Rich and Poor in the Shepherd of Hermes* (CBQMS 15) $6.00 ($4.80 for CBA members) ISBN 0-915170-14-0 (LC 83-7385)

16. James C. VanderKam, *Enoch and the Growth of an Apocalyptic Tradition* (CBQMS 16) $6.50 ($5.20 for CBA members) ISBN 0-915170-15-9 (LC 83-10134)

17. Antony F. Campbell, S.J., *Of Prophets and Kings: A Late Ninth-Century Document (1 Samuel 1-2 Kings 10)* (CBQMS 17) $7.50 ($6.00 for CBA members) ISBN 0-915170-16-7 (LC 85-12791)

18. John C. Endres, S.J., *Biblical Interpretation in the Book of Jubilees* (CBQMS 18) $8.50 ($6.80 for CBA members) ISBN 0-915170-17-5 (LC 86-6845)

19. Sharon Pace Jeansonne, *The Old Greek Translation of Daniel 7-12* (CBQMS 19) $5.00 ($4.00 for CBA members) ISBN 0-915170-18-3 (LC 87-15865)

20. Lloyd M. Barré, *The Rhetoric of Political Persuasion: The Narrative Artistry and Political Intentions of 2 Kings 9-11* (CBQMS 20) $5.00 ($4.00 for CBA members) ISBN 0-915170-19-1 (LC 87-15878)

21. John J. Clabeaux, *A Lost Edition of the Letters of Paul: A Reassessment of the Text of the Pauline Corpus Attested by Marcion* (CBQMS 21) $8.50 ($6.80 for CBA members) ISBN 0-915170-20-5 (LC 88-28511)

22. Craig Koester, *The Dwelling of God: The Tabernacle in the Old Testament, Intertestamental Jewish Literature, and the New Testament* (CBQMS 22) $9.00 ($7.20 for CBA members) ISBN 0-915170-21-3 (LC 89-9853)

23. William Michael Soll, *Psalm 119: Matrix, Form, and Setting* (CBQMS 23) $9.00 ($7.20 for CBA members) ISBN 0-915170-22-1 (LC 90-27610)

24. Richard J. Clifford and John J. Collins (eds.), *Creation in the Biblical Traditions* (CBQMS 24) $7.00 ($5.60 for CBA members) ISBN 0-915170-23-X (LC 92-20268)

25. John E. Course, *Speech and Response: A Rhetorical Analysis of the Introductions to the Speeches of the Book of Job, Chaps. 4-24* (CBQMS 25) $8.50 ($6.80 for CBA members) ISBN 0-915170-24-8 (LC 94-26566)

26. Richard J. Clifford, *Creation Accounts in the Ancient Near East and in the Bible* (CBQMS 26) $9.00 ($7.20 for CBA members) ISBN 0-915170-25-6 (LC 94-26565)

27. John Paul Heil, *Blood and Water: The Death and Resurrection of Jesus in John 18-21* (CBQMS 27) $9.00 ($7.20 for CBA members) ISBN 0-915170-26-4 (LC 95-10479)

28. John Kaltner, *The Use of Arabic in Biblical Hebrew Lexicography* (CBQMS 28) $7.50 ($6.00 for CBA members) ISBN 0-915170-27-2 (LC 95-45182)

29. Michael L. Barré, S.S., *Wisdom, You Are My Sister: Studies in Honor of Roland E. Murphy, O.Carm., on the Occasion of His Eightieth Birthday* (CBQMS 29) $13.00 ($10.40 for CBA members) ISBN 0-915170-28-0 (LC 97-16060)

30. Warren Carter and John Paul Heil, *Matthew's Parables: Audience-Oriented Perspectives* (CBQMS 30) $10.00 ($8.00 for CBA members) ISBN 0-915170-29-9 (LC 97-44677)

Order from:

The Catholic Biblical Association of America
The Catholic University of America
Washington, D.C. 20064